The
Complete Works
of
Yu Wujin

俞 吾 金 全 集

第 16 卷

外文文集

俞吾金 著

北京师范大学出版集团
BEIJING NORMAL UNIVERSITY PUBLISHING GROUP
北京师范大学出版社

俞吾金教授简介

俞吾金教授是我国著名哲学家，1948年6月21日出生于浙江萧山，2014年10月31日因病去世。生前任复旦大学文科资深教授、哲学学院教授，兼任复旦大学学术委员会副主任暨人文学术委员会主任、复旦大学学位委员会副主席暨人文社科学部主席、复旦大学国外马克思主义与国外思潮研究中心（985国家级基地）主任、复旦大学当代国外马克思主义研究中心（教育部重点研究基地）主任、复旦大学现代哲学研究所所长；担任教育部社会科学委员会委员、教育部哲学教学指导委员会副主任、国务院哲学学科评议组成员、全国外国哲学史学会常务理事、全国现代外国哲学学会副理事长等职；曾任德国法兰克福大学和美国哈佛大学访问教授、美国 Fulbright 高级讲座教授。俞吾金教授是全国哲学界首位长江学者特聘教授、全国优秀教师和国家级教学名师。俞吾金教授是我国八十年代以来在哲学领域最具影响力的学者之一，生前和身后出版了包括《意识形态论》《从康德到马克思》《重新理解马克思》《问题域的转换》《实践与自由》《被遮蔽的马克思》等在内的30部著作（包括合著），发表了400余篇学术论文，在哲学基础理论、马克思主义哲学、外国哲学、国外马克思主义、当代中国哲学文化和美学等诸多领域都有精深研究，取得了令人瞩目的成就，为深入推进当代中国哲学研究做出了杰出和重要的贡献。

《俞吾金全集》主编

汪行福　吴　猛

《俞吾金全集》编委会（按姓名拼音排序）

本卷编校组

张双利　徐英瑾

序　言

　　俞吾金教授是我国哲学界的著名学者，是我们这一代学人中的出类拔萃者。对我来说，他既是同学和同事，又是朋友和兄长。我们是恢复高考后首届考入复旦大学哲学系的，我们住同一个宿舍。在所有的同学中，俞吾金是一个好学深思的榜样，或者毋宁说，他在班上总是处在学与思的"先锋"位置上。他要求自己每天读150页的书，睡前一定要完成。一开始他还专注于向往已久的文学，一来是"文艺青年"的夙愿，一来是因为终于有机会沉浸到先前只是在梦中才能邂逅的书海中去了。每当他从图书馆背着书包最后回到宿舍时，大抵便是熄灯的前后，于是那摸黑夜谈的时光就几乎被文学占领了。先是莎士比亚和歌德，后来大多是巴尔扎克和狄更斯，最后便是托尔斯泰和陀斯妥耶夫斯基了。好在一屋子的室友都保留着不少的文学情怀，这情怀有了一个共鸣之地，以至于我们后来每天都很期待去分享这美好的时刻了。

　　但是不久以后，俞吾金便开始从文学转到哲学。我们的班主任老师，很欣赏俞吾金的才华，便找他谈了一次话，希望他在哲学上一展才华。不出所料，这个转向很快到来了。我们似乎突然

发现他的言谈口吻开始颇有些智者派的风格了——这一步转得很合适也很顺畅，正如黑格尔所说，智者们就是教人熟悉思维，以代替"诗篇的知识"。还是在本科三年级，俞吾金就在《国内哲学动态》上发表了他的哲学论文《"蜡块说"小考》，这在班里乃至于系里都引起了不小的震动。不久以后，他便在同学中得了个"苏老师"（苏格拉底）的雅号。看来并非偶然，他在后来的研究中曾对智者派（特别是普罗泰戈拉）专门下过功夫，而且他的哲学作品中也长久地保持着敏锐的辩才与文学的冲动；同样并非偶然，后来复旦大学将"狮城舌战"（在新加坡举行的首届国际华语大专辩论赛）的总教练和领队的重任托付给他，结果是整个团队所向披靡并夺得了冠军奖杯。

本科毕业后我们一起考上了研究生，1984年底又一起留校任教，成了同事。过了两年，又一起考上了在职博士生，师从胡曲园先生，于是成为同学兼同事，后来又坐同一架飞机去哈佛访学。总之，自1978年进入复旦大学哲学系以来，我们是过从甚密的，这不仅是因为相处日久，更多的是由于志趣相投。这种相投并不是说在哲学上或文学上的意见完全一致，而是意味着时常有着共同的问题域，并能使有差别的观点在其中形成积极的和有意义的探索性对话。总的说来，他在学术思想上始终是一个生气勃勃地冲在前面的追问者和探索者；他又是一个犀利而有幽默感的人，所以同他的对话常能紧张而又愉悦地进行。

作为哲学学者，俞吾金主要在三个方面展开他长达30多年的研究工作，而他的学术贡献也集中地体现在这三个方面，即当代国外马克思主义、马克思哲学、西方哲学史。对他来说，这三个方面并不是彼此分离的三个领域，毋宁说倒是本质相关地联系起来的一个整体，并且共同服务于思想理论上的持续探索和不断深化。在我们刚进复旦时，还不知"西方马克思主义"为何物；而当我们攻读博士学位时，卢卡奇的《历史与阶级意识》已经是我们必须面对并有待消化的关键文本了。如果说，这部开端性的文本及其理论后承在很大程度上构成了与"梅林—普列汉诺夫正统"的对立，那么，系统地研究和探讨国外马克思主义的立场、

观点和方法，就成为哲学研究(特别是马克思主义哲学研究)的一项重大任务了。俞吾金在这方面是走在前列的，他不仅系统地研究了卢卡奇、科尔施、葛兰西等人的重要哲学文献，而且很快又进入到法兰克福学派、存在主义的马克思主义、弗洛伊德主义的马克思主义、结构主义的马克思主义，等等。不久，哲学系组建了以俞吾金为首的当代国外马克思主义教研室，他和陈学明教授又共同主编了在国内哲学界影响深远的教材和文献系列，并有大量的论文、论著和译著问世，从而使复旦大学在这方面成为国内研究的重镇并处于领先地位。2000 年，教育部在复旦建立国内唯一的"当代国外马克思主义研究中心"(人文社会科学重点研究基地)，俞吾金自此一直担任该基地的主任，直到 2014 年去世。他组织并领导了内容广泛的理论引进、不断深入的学术研究，以及愈益扩大和加深的国内外交流。如果说，40 年前人们对当代国外马克思主义还几乎一无所知，而今天中国的学术界已经能够非常切近地追踪到其前沿了，那么，这固然取决于学术界同仁的共同努力，但俞吾金却当之无愧地属于其中的居功至伟者之一。

当俞吾金负责组建当代国外马克思主义学科时，他曾很热情地邀请我加入团队，我也非常愿意进入到这个当时颇受震撼而又所知不多的新领域。但我所在的马克思主义哲学史教研室却执意不让我离开。于是他便对我说：这样也好，"副本"和"原本"都需要研究，你我各在一处，时常可以探讨，岂不相得益彰？看来他对于"原本"——马克思哲学本身——是情有独钟的。他完全不能满足于仅仅对当代国外马克思主义的各种文本、观点和内容的引进介绍，而是试图在哲学理论的根基上去深入地理解它们，并对之开展出卓有成效的批判性发挥和对话。为了使这样的发挥和对话成为可能，他需要在马克思哲学基础理论的研究方面获得持续不断的推进与深化。因此，俞吾金对当代国外马克思主义的探索总是伴随着他对马克思哲学本身的研究，前者在广度上的拓展与后者在深度上的推进是步调一致、相辅相成的。

在马克思哲学基础理论的研究领域，俞吾金的研究成果突出地体现

在以下几个方面。第一，他明确主张马克思哲学的本质特征必须从其本体论的基础上去加以深入的把握。以往的理解方案往往是从近代认识论的角度提出问题，而真正的关键恰恰在于从本体论的层面去理解、阐述和重建马克思哲学的理论体系。我是很赞同他的这一基本观点的。因为马克思对近代哲学立足点的批判，乃是对"意识"之存在特性的批判，因而是一种真正的本体论批判："意识在任何时候都只能是被意识到了的存在，而人们的存在就是他们的现实生活过程。"这非常确切地意味着马克思哲学立足于"存在"——人们的现实生活过程——的基础之上，而把意识、认识等等理解为这一存在过程在观念形态上的表现。

因此，第二，就这样一种本体论立场来说，马克思哲学乃是一种"广义的历史唯物主义"。俞吾金认为，在这样的意义上，马克思哲学的本体论基础应当被把握为"实践—社会关系本体论"。它不仅批判地超越了以往的本体论(包括旧唯物主义的本体论)立场，而且恰恰构成马克思全部学说的决定性根基。因此，只有将马克思哲学理解为广义的历史唯物主义，才能真正把握马克思哲学变革的实质。

第三，马克思"实践"概念的意义不可能局限在认识论的范围内得到充分的把握，毋宁说，它在广义的历史唯物主义中首先是作为本体论原则来起作用的。在俞吾金看来，将实践理解为马克思认识论的基础与核心，相对于近代西方认识论无疑是一大进步；但如果将实践概念限制在认识论层面，就会忽视其根本而首要的本体论意义。对于马克思来说，至为关键的是，只有在实践的本体论层面上，人们的现实生活才会作为决定性的存在进入到哲学的把握中，从而，人们的劳动和交往，乃至于人们的全部社会生活和整个历史性行程，才会从根本上进入到哲学理论的视域中。

因此，第四，如果说广义的历史唯物主义构成马克思哲学的实质，那么这一哲学同时就意味着"意识形态批判"。因为在一般意识形态把思想、意识、观念等等看作是决定性原则的地方，唯物史观恰恰相反，要求将思想、意识、观念等等的本质性导回到人们的现实生活过程之中。

在此意义上，俞吾金把意识形态批判称为"元批判"，并因而将立足于实践的历史唯物主义叫做"实践诠释学"。所谓"元批判"，就是对规约人们的思考方式和范围的意识形态本身进行前提批判，而作为"实践诠释学"的历史唯物主义，则是在"元批判"的导向下去除意识形态之蔽，从而揭示真正的现实生活过程。我认为，上述这些重要观点不仅在当时是先进的和极具启发性的，而且直到今天，对于马克思哲学之实质的理解来说，依然是关乎根本的和意义深远的。

俞吾金的博士论文以《意识形态论》为题，我则提交了《历史唯物主义的主体概念》和他一起参加答辩。答辩主席是华东师范大学的冯契先生。冯先生不仅高度肯定了俞吾金对马克思意识形态批判理论的出色研究，而且用"长袖善舞"一词来评价这篇论文的特点。学术上要做到长袖善舞，是非常不易的：不仅要求涉猎广泛，而且要能握其枢机。俞吾金之所以能够臻此境地，是得益于他对哲学史的潜心研究；而在哲学史方面的长期探索，不仅极大地支持并深化了他的马克思哲学研究，而且使他成为著名的西方哲学史研究专家。

就与马哲相关的西哲研究而言，他专注于德国古典哲学，特别是康德、黑格尔哲学的研究。他很明确地主张：对马克思哲学的深入理解，一刻也离不开对德国观念论传统的积极把握；要完整地说明马克思的哲学革命及其重大意义，不仅要先行领会康德的"哥白尼式革命"，而且要深入把握由此而来并在黑格尔那里得到充分发展的历史性辩证法。他认为，作为康德哲学核心问题的因果性与自由的关系问题，在"按照自然律的因果性"和"由自由而来的因果性"的分析中，得到了积极的推进。黑格尔关于自由的理论可被视为对康德自由因果性概念的一种回应：为了使自由和自由因果性概念获得现实性，黑格尔试图引入辩证法以使自由因果性和自然因果性统一起来。在俞吾金看来，这里的关键在于"历史因果性"维度的引入——历史因果性是必然性的一个方面，也是必然性与自由相统一的关节点。因此，正是通过对黑格尔的精神现象学、法哲学和历史哲学等思想内容的批判性借鉴，马克思将目光转向人类社会

发展中的历史因果性；但马克思又否定了黑格尔仅仅停留于单纯精神层面谈论自然因果性和历史因果性的哲学立场，要求将这两种因果性结合进现实的历史运动中，尤其是使之进入到对市民社会的解剖中。这个例子可以表明，对马克思哲学之不断深化的理解，需要在多大程度上深入到哲学史的领域之中。正如列宁曾经说过的那样：不读黑格尔的《逻辑学》，便无法真正理解马克思的《资本论》。

就西方哲学的整体研究而言，俞吾金的探讨可谓"细大不捐"，涉猎之广在当代中国学者中是罕见的。他不仅研究过古希腊哲学（特别是柏拉图和亚里士多德哲学），而且专题研究过智者派哲学、斯宾诺莎哲学和叔本华哲学等。除开非常集中地钻研德国古典哲学之外，他还更为宏观地考察了西方哲学在当代实现的"范式转换"。他将这一转换概括为"从传统知识论到实践生存论"的发展，并将其理解为西方哲学发展中的一条根本线索。为此他对海德格尔的哲学下了很大的功夫，不仅精详地考察了海德格尔的"存在论差异"和"世界"概念，而且深入地探讨了海德格尔的现代性批判及其意义。如果说，马克思的哲学变革乃是西方哲学范式转换中划时代的里程碑，那么，海德格尔的基础存在论便为说明这一转换提供了重要的思想材料。在这里，西方哲学史的研究再度与马克思哲学的研究贯通起来：俞吾金不仅以哲学的当代转向为基本视野考察整个西方哲学史，并在这一思想转向的框架中理解马克思的哲学变革，而且站在这一变革的立场上重新审视西方哲学，特别是德国古典哲学和当代西方哲学。就此而言，俞吾金在马哲和西哲的研究上可以说是齐头并进的，并且因此在这两个学术圈子中同时享有极高的声誉和地位。这样的一种研究方式固然可以看作是他本人的学术取向，但这种取向无疑深深地浸染着并且也成就着复旦大学哲学学术的独特氛围。在这样的氛围中，当代国外马克思主义的研究要立足于对马克思哲学本身的深入理解之上，而对马克思哲学理解的深化又有必要进入到哲学史研究的广大区域之中。

今年 10 月 31 日，是俞吾金离开我们 10 周年的纪念日。十年前我

曾撰写的一则挽联是："哲人其萎乎，梁木倾颓；桃李方盛也，枝叶滋荣。"我们既痛惜一位学术大家的离去，更瞩望新一代学术星丛的冉冉升起。十年之后，《俞吾金全集》由北京师范大学出版社出版了——这是哲学学术界的一件大事，许多同仁和朋友付出了积极的努力和辛勤的劳动，我们对此怀着深深的感激之情。这样的感激之情不仅是因为这部全集的告竣，而且因为它还记录了我们这一代学者共同经历的学术探索道路。一代人有一代人的使命，俞吾金勤勉而又卓越地完成了他的使命：他将自己从事哲学的探索方式和研究风格贡献给了复旦哲学的学术共同体，使之成为这个共同体悠长传统的组成部分；他更将自己取得的学术成果作为思想、观点和理论播洒到广阔的研究领域，并因而成为进一步推进我国哲学学术的重要支点和不可能匆匆越过的必要环节。如果我们的读者不仅能够从中掌握理论观点和方法，而且能够在哲学与时代的关联中学到思想探索的勇气和路径，那么，这部全集的意义就更其深远了。

吴晓明

2024 年 6 月

主编的话

一

2014 年 7 月 16 日，俞吾金教授结束了一个学期的繁忙教学工作，暂时放下手头的著述，携夫人赴加拿大温哥华参加在弗雷泽大学举办的"法兰克福学派对资本主义的批判"的国际学术讨论会，并计划会议结束后自费在加拿大作短期旅游，放松心情。但在会议期间俞吾金教授突感不适，虽然他带病作完大会报告，但不幸的是，到医院检查后被告知脑部患了恶性肿瘤。于是，他不得不匆忙地结束行程，回国接受治疗。接下来三个月，虽然复旦大学华山医院组织了最强医疗团队精心救治，但病魔无情，回天无力。2014 年 10 月 31 日，在那个风雨交加的夜晚，俞吾金教授永远地离开了我们。

俞吾金教授的去世是复旦大学的巨大损失，也是中国哲学界的巨大损失。十年过去了，俞吾金教授从未被淡忘，他的著作和文章仍然被广泛阅读，他的谦谦君子之风、与人为善之举被亲朋好友广为谈论。但是，在今天这个急剧变化和危机重重的世界中，我们还是能够感到他的去世留

下的思想空场。有时，面对社会的种种不合理现象和纷纭复杂的现实时，我们还是不禁会想：如果俞老师在世，他会做如何感想，又会做出什么样的批判和分析！

俞吾金教授的生命是短暂的，也是精彩的。与期颐天年的名家硕儒相比，他的学术生涯只有三十多年。但是，在这短短的三十多年中，他通过自己的勤奋和努力取得了耀眼的成就。

1983 年 6 月，俞吾金与复旦大学哲学系的六个硕士、博士生同学一起参加在广西桂林举行的"现代科学技术和认识论"全国学术讨论会，他们在会上所做的"关于认识论的几点意见"（后简称"十条提纲"）的报告，勇敢地对苏联哲学教科书体系做了反思和批判，为乍暖还寒的思想解放和新莺初啼的马克思主义哲学新的探索做出了贡献。1993 年，俞吾金教授作为教练和领队，带领复旦大学辩论队参加在新加坡举办的首届国际大专辩论赛并一举夺冠，在华人世界第一次展现了新时代中国大学生的风采。辩论赛的电视转播和他与王沪宁主编的《狮城舌战》《狮城舌战启示录》大大地推动了全国高校的辩论热，也让万千学子对复旦大学翘首以盼。1997 年，俞吾金教授又受复旦大学校长之托，带领复旦大学学生参加在瑞士圣加仑举办的第 27 届国际经济管理研讨会，在该次会议中，复旦大学的学生也有优异的表现。会后，俞吾金又主编了《跨越边界》一书，嘉惠以后参加的学子。

俞吾金教授 1995 年开始担任复旦大学哲学系主任，当时是国内最年轻的哲学系主任，其间，复旦大学哲学系大胆地进行教学和课程体系改革，取得了重要的成果，荣获第五届全国高等学校优秀教学成果一等奖，由他领衔的"西方哲学史"课程被评为全国精品课程。在复旦大学，俞吾金教授是最受欢迎的老师之一，他的课一座难求。他多次被评为最受欢迎的老师和研究生导师。由于教书育人的杰出贡献，2009 年他被评为上海市教学名师和全国优秀教师，2011 年被评为全国教学名师。

俞吾金教授一生最为突出的贡献无疑是其学术研究成果及其影响。他在研究生毕业后不久就出版的《思考与超越——哲学对话录》已显示了

卓越的才华。在该书中，他旁征博引，运用文学故事或名言警句，以对话体的形式生动活泼地阐发思想。该书妙趣横生，清新脱俗，甫一面世就广受欢迎，成为沪上第一理论畅销书，并在当年的全国图书评比中获"金钥匙奖"。俞吾金教授的博士论文《意识形态论》一脱当时国内博士论文的谨小慎微的匠气，气度恢宏，新见迭出，展现了长袖善舞、擅长宏大主题的才华。论文出版后，先后获得上海市哲学社会科学优秀成果一等奖和国家教委首届人文社会科学优秀成果一等奖，成为青年学子做博士论文的楷模。

俞吾金教授天生具有领军才能，在他的领导下，复旦大学当代国外马克思主义研究中心 2000 年被评为教育部人文社会科学重点研究基地，他本人也长期担任基地主任，主编《当代国外马克思主义评论》《国外马克思主义研究报告》《国外马克思主义与国外思潮译丛》等，为马克思主义的国际交流建立了重要的平台。他长期担任复旦大学哲学学院的外国哲学学科学术带头人，参与主编《西方哲学通史》和《杜威全集》等重大项目，为复旦大学成为外国哲学研究重镇做出了突出贡献。

俞吾金教授的学术研究不囿一隅，他把西方哲学和马克思哲学结合起来，提出了许多重要的概念和命题，如"马克思是我们同时代人""马克思哲学是广义的历史唯物主义""马克思哲学的认识论是意识形态批判""从康德到马克思""西方哲学史的三次转向""实践诠释学""被遮蔽的马克思""问题域的转换"等，出版了一系列有影响的著作和文集。由于俞吾金教授在学术上的杰出贡献和影响力，他获得各种奖励和荣誉称号，他是全国哲学界首位"长江学者奖励计划"特聘教授，在钱伟长主编的"20 世纪中国知名科学家"哲学卷中，他是改革开放以来培养的哲学家中的唯一入选者。俞吾金教授在学界还留下许多传奇，其中之一是，虽然他去世已经十年了，但至今仍保持着《中国社会科学》发文最多的记录。

显然，俞吾金教授是改革开放后新一代学人中最有才华、成果最为丰硕、影响最大的学者之一。他之所以取得令人瞩目的成就，不仅得益

于他的卓越才华和几十年如一日的勤奋努力，更重要的是缘于他的独立思考的批判精神和"为天地立心、为生民立命"的济世情怀。塞涅卡说："我们不应该像羊一样跟随我们前面的羊群——不是去我们应该去的地方，而是去它去的地方。"俞吾金教授就是本着这样的精神从事学术的。在他的第一本著作即《思考与超越》的开篇中，他就把帕斯卡的名言作为题记："人显然是为了思想而生的；这就是他全部的尊严和他全部的优异；并且他全部的义务就是要像他所应该的那样去思想。"俞吾金教授的学术思考无愧于此。俞吾金教授以高度的社会责任感从事学术研究。复旦大学的一位教授在哀悼他去世的博文中曾写道："曾有几次较深之谈话，感到他是一位勤奋的读书人，温和的学者，善于思考社会与人生，关注现在，更虑及未来。记得 15 年前曾听他说，在大变动的社会，理论要为长远建立秩序，有些论著要立即发表，有些则可以暂存书箧，留给未来。"这段话很好地刻画了俞吾金教授的人文和道德情怀。

正是出于这一强烈担当的济世情怀，俞吾金教授出版和发表了许多有时代穿透力的针砭时弊的文章，对改革开放以来的思想解放和文化启蒙起到了推动作用，为新时期中国哲学的发展做出了重要贡献。但是，也正因为如此，他的生命中也留下了很多遗憾。去世前两年，俞吾金教授在"耳顺之年话人生"一文中说："从我踏进哲学殿堂至今，30 多个年头已经过去了。虽然我尽自己的努力做了一些力所能及的事情，但人生匆匆，转眼已过耳顺之年，还有许多筹划中的事情没有完成。比如对康德提出的许多哲学问题的系统研究，对贝克莱、叔本华在外国哲学史上的地位的重新反思，对中国哲学的中道精神的重新阐释和对新启蒙的张扬，对马克思哲学体系的重构等。此外，我还有一系列的教案有待整理和出版。"想不到这些未完成的计划两年后尽成了永远的遗憾！

二

俞吾金教授去世后，学界同行在不同场合都表达了希望我们编辑和出版他的全集的殷切希望。其实，俞吾金教授去世后，应出版社之邀，我们再版了他的一些著作和出版了他的一些遗著。2016年北京师范大学出版社出版了他的《哲学遐思录》《哲学随感录》《哲学随想录》三部随笔集，2017年北京师范大学出版社出版了《从康德到马克思——千年之交的哲学沉思》新版，2018年商务印书馆出版了他的遗作《新十批判书》未完成稿。但相对俞吾金教授发表和未发表的文献，这些只是挂一漏万，远不能满足人们的期望。我们之所以在俞吾金教授去世十年才出版他的全集，主要有两个方面的原因。一是俞吾金教授从没有完全离开我们，学界仍然像他健在时一样阅读他的文章和著作，吸收和借鉴他的观点，思考他提出的问题，因而无须赶着出版他的全集让他重新回到我们中间；二是想找个有纪念意义的时间出版他的全集。俞吾金教授去世后，我们一直在为出版他的全集做准备。我们一边收集资料，一边考虑体例框架。时间到了2020年，是时候正式开启这项工作了。我们于2020年10月成立了《俞吾金全集》编委会，组织了由他的学生组成的编辑和校对团队。经过数年努力，现已完成了《俞吾金全集》二十卷的编纂，即将在俞吾金教授逝世十周年之际出版。

俞吾金教授一生辛勤耕耘，留下650余万字的中文作品和十余万字的外文作品。《俞吾金全集》将俞吾金教授的全部作品分为三个部分：(1)生前出版的著作；(2)生前发表的中文文章；(3)外文文章和遗作。

俞吾金教授生前和身后出版的著作(包含合著)共三十部，大部分为文集。《俞吾金全集》保留了这些著作中体系较为完整的7本，包括《思考与超越——哲学对话录》《问题域外的问题——现代西方哲学方法论探要》《生存的困惑——西方哲学文化精神探要》《意识形态论》《毛泽东智

慧》《邓小平：在历史的天平上》《问题域的转换——对马克思和黑格尔关系的当代解读》。其余著作则基于材料的属性全部还原为单篇文章，收入《俞吾金全集》的《马克思主义哲学研究文集（上、下）》《外国哲学研究文集（上、下）》以及《国外马克思主义研究文集（上、下）》等各卷中。这样的处理方式难免会留下许多遗憾，特别是俞吾金教授的一些被视为当代学术名著的文集（如《重新理解马克思》《从康德到马克思》《被遮蔽的马克思》《实践诠释学》《实践与自由》等）未能按原书形式收入到《俞吾金全集》之中。为了解决全集编纂上的逻辑自洽性以及避免不同卷次的文献交叠问题（这些交叠往往是由于原作根据的不同主题选择和组织材料而导致的），我们不得不忍痛割爱，将这些著作打散处理。

俞吾金教授生前发表了各类学术文章 400 余篇，我们根据主题将这些文章分别收入《马克思主义哲学研究文集（上、下）》《国外马克思主义哲学研究文集》《外国哲学研究文集（上、下）》《马克思主义中国化研究文集》《中国思想与文化研究》《哲学观与哲学教育论集》《散论集》（包括《读书治学》《社会时评》和《生活哲思》三卷）。在这些卷次的编纂过程中，我们除了使用知网、俞吾金教授生前结集出版的作品和在他的电脑中保存的材料外，还利用了图书馆和网络等渠道，查找那些散见于他人著作中的序言、论文集、刊物、报纸以及网页中的文章，尽量做到应收尽收。对于收集到的文献，如果内容基本重合，收入最早发表的文本；如主要内容和表达形式略有差异，则收入内容和形式上最完备者。在文集和散论集中，对发表的论文和文章，我们则按照时间顺序进行编排，以便更好地了解俞吾金教授的思想发展和心路历程。

除了已发表的中文著作和论文之外，俞吾金教授还留下了多篇已发表或未发表的外文文章，以及一系列未发表的讲课稿（有完整的目录，已完成的部分很成熟，完全是为未来出版准备的，可惜没有写完）。我们将这些外文论文收集在《外文文集》卷中，把未发表的讲稿收集在《遗作集》卷中。

三

《俞吾金全集》的编纂和出版受到了多方面的支持。俞吾金教授去世后不久，北京师范大学出版社就表达了想出版《俞吾金全集》的愿望，饶涛副总编辑专门来上海洽谈此事，承诺以最优惠的条件和最强的编辑团队完成这一工作，这一慷慨之举和拳拳之心让人感佩。为了高质量地完成全集的出版，出版社与我们多次沟通，付出了很多努力。对北京师范大学出版社饶涛副总编辑、祁传华主任和诸分卷的责编为《俞吾金全集》的辛勤付出，我们深表谢意。《俞吾金全集》的顺利出版，我们也要感谢俞吾金教授的学生赵青云，他多年前曾捐赠了一笔经费，用于支持俞吾金教授所在机构的学术活动。经同意，俞吾金教授去世后，这笔经费被转用于全集的材料收集和日常办公支出。《俞吾金全集》的出版也受到复旦大学和哲学学院的支持。俞吾金教授的同学和同事吴晓明教授一直关心全集的出版，并为全集写了充满感情和睿智的序言。复旦大学哲学学院原院长孙向晨也为全集的出版提供了支持。在此我们表示深深的感谢。

《俞吾金全集》的具体编辑工作是由俞吾金教授的许多学生承担的。编辑团队的成员都是在不同时期受教于俞吾金教授的学者，他们分散于全国各地高校，其中许多已是所在单位的教学和科研骨干，有自己的繁重任务要完成。但他们都自告奋勇地参与这项工作，把它视为自己的责任和荣誉，不计得失，任劳任怨，为这项工作的顺利完成付出自己的心血。

作为《俞吾金全集》的主编，我们深感责任重大，因而始终抱着敬畏之心和感恩之情来做这项工作。但限于水平和能力，《俞吾金全集》一定有许多不完善之处，在此敬请学界同仁批评指正。

汪行福　吴　猛

2024 年 6 月

CONTENTS

Section Four　Short Essays

Interpretations of Marxist Philosophy

1.1 On Two Different Conceptions of Historical Materialism[①]

It is a well known fact that historical materialism is one of Marx's two great discoveries. Its relationship with Marx's philosophy is an important theoretical matter. Currently, there are two popular opinions in academia: first, Marx's philosophy is the combination of dialectical materialism and historical materialism, and historical materialism is the result of extending the principles of dialectical materialism to the field of social history; second, historical materialism is the "basis and core" of Marx's philosophy. Except for some minor differences, the second opinion also takes historical materialism as the doctrine that is applied only to the field of social history. Moreover, it doesn't explain what's the "non-basic and non-core" part of the Marx's philosophy. As long as the "non-basic and non-core" part has not been clarified, the so-called "basis and core" was no

---

① Editor's note: This paper was originally published in *Social Sciences in China*, 2008, vol. 29, no. 3, translated from *Zhongguo Shehui Kexue* (《中国社会科学》), no. 6, 1995, pp. 96-107.

more than a casual wording. By comparison, the first opinion is closer to grasping the essence of Marx's philosophy. However, in the final analysis, both of these opinions have narrowed the theoretical scope of historical materialism and, to some extent, obscured Marx's epochal contribution to his philosophy.

Therefore, we propose the third opinion: historical materialism is where Marx's epoch-making philosophical creation lies. The Mature Marx did not put forward any philosophical theory other than historical materialism. In other words, historical materialism is exactly the other name for Marx's philosophy. In this way, the conception of historical materialism that we will be discussing in the following gets a new connotation. To explain the difference between the above-mentioned two opinions and ours, and demonstrate the most important these opinions and demonstrate the most important contribution of historical materialism, we might as well call the well-known two opinions of historical materialism "the narrow conception of historical materialism" and the historical materialism we advocate "the broad conception of historical materialism". We shall focus on this topic with the following discussion.

The Narrow Conception of Historical Materialism

What actually is "the narrow conception of historical materialism?" We define this as the historical materialism that is applied only to the field of social history. Here the field of social history involved is also in its narrow sense, which corresponds to the "society" part of the philosophical concept of "world" that has never been seriously reflected upon (which consists of three major parts: nature, society, and thinking). Narrated together with the "extension theory", which was familiarized and has been accepted by many for a long time, this conception still has a dominant influence in the academic circles through traditional philosophical textbooks.

The so-called "extension theory" treats historical materialism as the result of extending general materialism or dialectical materialism into the field of social history. There is a process of its formation and development. When talking about Marx's transformation of Hegelian philosophy, Engels writes in his work Ludwig Feuerbach and the Outlet of Germany's Classical Philosophy that "the separation from Hegelian philosophy was here also the result of a return to the materialist standpoint… But here the materialistic world outlook was taken really seriously for the first time and was carried through consistently (at least in its basic features) in all domains of knowledge concerned."[①] This argument contains two meanings: the first is a reinstatement that materialism is the foudation of Marx's philosophy; the second meaning is that the materialistic world framework must be "applied" to all fields of knowledge (including the field of social history). Therefore, Engels has already proposed such an opinion that historical materialism is the materialism that is applied in the field of social history. Of course, the "materialism" that Engels used refers to modern materialism, which, according to his version of *Anti-Duhring*, is essentially dialectical. Hence, though Engels' "materialist dialectics" doesn't involve the concept of "dialectical materialism", he has already laid the ideological foundation for this conception. The tendency of understanding the structure of Marx's philosophy as two levels is thus revealed here: on the basic level, moden materialism is in accordance with the "nature" part in the conception of

---

① Frederick Engels, *Ludwig Feuerbach and the End of Classical German Philosophy* (Moscow: Progress Publisher, 1946), from Marx Engels Internet Archive 1994. See http://www. marxists. org/archive/marx/works/1886/ludwig-feuerbach/ch04. htm.

"world"; on the other level, which is the application or "extension" level, is historical materialism in accordance with the "society" part in the conception of "world". This can be seen clearly from the structure of other works such as *the Outlet* and *Anti-Dühring*. When talking about philosophical questions, Engels always discusses nature-related philosophical questions at first and then incorporates that into the field of social history.

As an active disseminator of Marxist theory, Plekhanov accepts and expounds further Engels' understanding pattern of Marx's philosophy. He says that "we use the terminology 'dialectical materialism', which is the only one can be used to explain Marx's philosophy correctly." ① When explaining the relationship between dialectical materialism and historical materialism, he adds that "… Because dialectical materialism involves history, Engels sometimes called it historical. This adjective is not to describe the characteristics of materialism, but only to indicate one of the fields it was applied to explain." ② In Plekhanov's view, the basic level of Marx's philosophy is dialectical materialism, while the application level level is historical materialism. Plekhanov doesn't put the relationship between dialectical materialism and historical materialism as the core issue of Marx's philosophy. It is Lenin who realizes the importance of this issue and discusses it. In the book *Materialism and Empirio-Criticism*, Lenin explicitly points out that "Marx and Engels scores of times termed their philosophical views dialectical materialism." ③ After affirming that the basic level of Marx's philosophy is dialectical materialism, Lenin writes that: "It is

---

① Plekhanov, *The Development of the Monist View of History*, trans. Bo Gu (Shanghai: SDX Joint Publishing Company, 1961), p. 198.

② Plekhanov, *Collected Pilosophical Work*, vol. 2 (Shanghai: SDX Joint Publishing Company, 1961), p. 311.

③ Lenin, *Lenin's Collected Works*, vol. 14 (Moscow: Progress Publishers), 1972. See http://www.marxists.org/archive/lenin/works/1908/mec/pref01.htm#v14pp72h-019.

therefore quite natural that they should have devoted their attention not to a repetition of old ideas but to a serious theoretical *development* of materialism, its application to history, in other words, to the *completion* of the edifice of materialist philosophy *up to its summit*."① Lenin's opinion is very clear. He draws an analogy between Marx's philosophy and an edifice, positing dialectical materialism as its foundation and historical materialism as its summit. Lenin's book *Materialism and Empirio-Criticism* also talks about dialectical materialism first (taking nature as the object), and then historical materialism (taking history as the object). It should be noted that it is not a viewpoint occasionally expressed but a consistent thought for Lenin to understand historical materialism as the "extension" and "application" of dialectical materialism in the field of social history. In the article *The Three Sources and Three Component Parts of Marxism* (1913), Lenin points out that: "Marx deepened and developed philosophical materialism to the full, and extended the cognition of nature to include the cognition of *human society*. His *historical materialism* was a great achievement in scientific thinking."② In the article *Karl Marx*, Lenin also educes that: "The discovery of the materialist conception of history, or more correctly, the consistent continuation and extension of materialism into the domain of social phenomena."③ In this way, the prototype of "extension theory" was already formed at Lenin's time.

Lenin's above-mentioned opinion is stated more explicitly by Stalin.

<hr>

① Lenin, *Lenin's Collected Works*, vol. 14 (Moscow: Progress Publishers, 1972); Lenin, *Collected Works*, vol. 2 (Beijing: People's Publishing House, 1995), p. 179.
See http://www. marxists. org/archive/lenin/works/1908/mec/four7. htm # v14pp72h-238.
② Lenin, *Lenin's Collected Works*, vol. 19 (Moscow: Progress Publishers, 1977).
See http://www. marxists. org/archive/lenin/works/1913/mar/x01. htm.
③ Lenin, *Lenin's Collected Works*, vol. 21 (Moscow: Progress Publishers, 1974).
See http://www. marxists. org/archive/lenin/works/1914/granat/ch02. htm.

Stalin writes like this: "Historical materialism is the extension of the principles of dialectical materialism to the study of social life, an application of the principles of dialectical materialism to the phenomena of the life of society, to the study of society and of its history."[①] From then on, "extension theory" becomes the fixed mode to understand Marx's philosophy. This mode exerts a significant influence not only on the orthodox philosophical researchers of Marx's philosophy in Soviet Union, East Europe, and China. Moreover, it influences researchers beyond this disciplinary boundary. For instance, as early as 1927, when Kautsky published his book The Materialist Conception of History, he points out that: "Historical materialism is the materialism applied in history."[②] Even for the "Western Marxists" whom were renowned for their originality, this theory was also influential. For example, works that reflects the author's approval of the above mentioned understanding mode include but are not limited to Wilhelm Reich's work *Dialektischer Materialismus und Psychoanalyse* (1929) and Alfred Schmidt's treatise *On the Relationship of History and Nature in Dialectical Materialism* (1965). To sum up, in the view of "extension theory", historical materialism is just the "extension" or "application" of dialectical materialism in the field of social history. In other words, the conception of historical materialism here is just the "narrow conception of historical materialism" that accords with the "society" part of the traditional conception of the "world".

---

① Stalin, *Dialectical and Historical Materialism* (Manika Barua: Mass Publications, 1938). See http://www. marxists. org/reference/archive/stalin/works/1938/09. htm.

② Karl Kautsky, *The Materialist Conception of History*, 1927.

Predicament of the Narrow Conception of
Historical Materialism

Now let us investigate further the theoretical difficulties posed by the "narrow conception of historical materialism", and whether it can, as claimed by writers of the traditional philosophical textbooks, fully elucidate the substantive content of Marx's philosophy.

First, let us discuss this: from the perspective of general materialism or dialectical materialism, can we get the same insights into social history that we gain from the historical materialism? Our answer is no. The so-called "general materialism", in Lenin's words, holds that, "The existence of matter does not depend on sensation. Matter is primary. Sensation, thought, and consciousness are the supreme product of matter organized in a particular way. These thoughts are typical for Marx and Engels."[①] In Lenin's view, Feuerbach also adheres to the viewpoint of general materialism. Indeed, Feuerbach is a pure materialist when examining the nature; however, once entering the field of social history, he he becomes a historical idealist by attributing the change of social history to religion. Just as Marx criticizes: "As far as Feuerbach is a materialist he does not deal with history, and as far as he considers history he is not a materialist. With him materialism and history diverge completely ... "[②] This tells us

---

① *Lenin Collected Works*, vol. 14 (Moscow: Progress Publishers, 1972); Lenin, *Collected Works*, vol. 2 (Beijing: People's Publishing House, 1995), p. 51.
See http://www. marxists. org/archive/lenin/works/1908/mec/one2. htm.
② *Marx-Engels Collected Works*, vol. 5 (Moscow: Progress Publishers, 1975).
See http://www. marxists. org/archive/marx/works/1845/german-ideology/ch01b. htm.

that from the standpoint of general materialism, the historical materialism can not be brought out. Moreover, since the standpoint general materialism insisted on is abstract, diverging from social history, it will inevitably fall into the position of historical idealism when examining social history. Then, as a conclusion, could the application of dialectical materialism in the field of social history lead to historical materialism? We believe that it is impossible either. As mentioned above, dialectical materialism takes "nature" as its object, while within the hierarchical order of the world, nature precedes society. Moreover, human beings and their activities can only be socially displayed, which means that the nature examined here is abstract in the sense that it is detached from human beings and their activities. Consequently, in the domain of dialectical materialism, the so-called "being" refers to the material that is abstract and detached from human beings and their activities. However, in the field of social history, everything changes. The "social being" in this field contains human beings, their purposes, and their activities. We cannot get the conclusion of historical materialism by converting general materialism into dialectical materialism (whose object of study is still detached from human). The reason is that the extension starts from an abstract premise, and concrete conclusion can not be deduced from abstract premise (note: this is completely different from the research method "from abstract to concrete".) Instead of an abstratc nature that is detached from any specific human, what aligns with the fundamental stance of historical materialism is the "humanized nature" or the "historical nature"; similarly, instead of an abstract nature that is detached from human, it is the concrete modalities of material that present themselves as elements of human's production activities. (such as raw material, tools, and products). In brief, although dialectical materialism has made the materialism to be dialectical, its application can not lead to the conclusion of historical materialism, because the material world or nature as the carrier of dialectics is still expressed in an abstract and pre-society way.

Second, within the "narrow conception of historical materialism", historical materialism is understood as the "summit" of the edifice of Marx's philosophy, which indicate it as the "highest" or "final" result. In other words, the fundamental theory of historical materialism is not the basis but the extension of Marx's philosophy; it is not Marx's starting point to investigate all issues, but only the partial conclusion extended from his research in the field of social history. As a result, the revolutionary role of historical materialism in the history of philosophy is narrowed, weakened, marginalized, even masked. This is because we still understand it as a secondary or "extended" result. We still prioritize general materialism, which has existed thorughout the history of philosophy, or dialectical materialism, as the foundational principles that precedes historical materialism. To understand Marx's philosophy in such a way is bound to miss its essence.

Finally, through the "narrow conception of historical materialism", Marx's philosophy is turned into positivism, of which only the application value is opened up, and such value is applied only to the field of social history in the narrow sense. In the book *The German Ideology*, Marx writes that: "Where speculation ends—in real life—there real, positive science (Positive Wissenschaft) begins: the representation of the practical activity, of the practical process of development of men… When reality is depicted, philosophy as an independent branch of knowledge (Die Selbstaendige Philosophie) loses its medium of existence. At the best its place can only be taken by a summing-up (Zusammenfassung) of the most general results, abstractions which arise from the observation of the historical development of men."[①] In this paragraph, Marx emphasizes that "history" as the "positive science" would would replace the "speculative" philosophy; and "a summing-up of the most general results, abstractions which arise from the observation of the historical development of men" (hereinafter referred to as "summing-up") would replace "philosophy as an independent branch of knowledge". This paragraph of Marx is often understood as the following: in the field of social history, philosophy ends and gives place to the "positive science", which is history. This turns Marx's conception of history (namely, historical materialism) into positivism. In fact, what Marx rejects here is not the whole philosophy, but mainly Hegel's philosophy of history. The "speculation" and "philosophy as an independent branch of knowledge" mentioned above is precisely this kind of philosophy of history. Then, after the end of the philosophy of history, is there only the history as "positive science" left alone? Marx's answer is obviously negative. The summation articulated by Marx above is just the conception of history upon which the positive empirical hstory is predicated. This conception of history is just Marx's historical materialism. Historical materialism is a new philosophical theory, and it is the premise of our research in all the fields (not only the field of social history in its traditional narrow sense). The "narrow conception of historical materialism" restricts the theory of historical materialism to the narrow field of social history, and emphasizes that it is the result of applying general materialism. This will inevitably turn it into positive science, and make it lose its profound philosophical connotation and its role as the theoretical premise.

---

① *Marx-Engels Collected Works*, vol. 5 (Moscow: Progress Publishers, 1975). See http://www. marxists. org/archive/marx/works/1845/german-ideology/ch01a. htm#a2.

Influenced by the Western Marxism thoughts, the understanding and criticism of the "extension theory" in Soviet, Eastern European, and Chinese academia are becoming clear. Since the 1980s, the Chinese academics have formed an influential new opinion. This opinion, which is a reversal of "extension theory", emphasizes that historical materialism is the "basis and core" of Marx's philosophy. All the epistemology, methodology, and category theory discussed in dialectical materialism should be newly discussed based on historical materialism. On the way of reinterpreting Marx's philosophy, this reversal of the "extension theory" is indeed an extremely important theoretical progress. However, this "basis and core" theory does not finally surpass the "narrow conception of historical materialism". Why is it? Firstly, though this theory opposes regarding historical materialism as the application of dialectical materialism in the field of social history, it still insists that historical materialism corresponds to the field of social history in its traditional sense. That is to say, historical materialism still corresponds to the "society" in the traditional conception of "world". (nature, society, thinking). Secondly, if we call historical materialism the "basis and core" of Marx's philosophy, then what is the "non-basic and non-core" part of Marx's philosophy? Could we call the aforementioned epistemology, methodology, and category theory the "non-basic and non-core" part? If so, how could it be different from the "extension theory" narrowing the content of historical materialism? Thirdly, the theory is not thorough because it retains the original conception of dialectical materialism. Thus, on the one hand, the theoretical fault can not be fundamentally cleaned up; on the other hand, people's theoretical vision still remains in the "narrow conception of historical materialism". This is the reason why they can neither understand the essence of Marx's philosophy nor grasp the true meaning of the epoch-making philosophical revolution launched by Marx.

The Broad Conception of Historical Materialism

The above discussion shows that as long as people stay in "the narrow conception of historical materialism", it would be impossible for them to understand the real essence and great significance of Marx's epoch-making philosophical revolution. In our opinion, Marx's philosophy should be understood as "the broad conception of historical materialism", which is defined as the following: first, the "society" studied by historical materialism is neither a partial conception nor another applied field, but a whole conception by itself second, historical materialism is not just the "basis and core" of Marx's philosophy, it is the entirety of Marx's philosophy. The Mature Marx's philosophy is just historical materialism; in fact, the Mature Marx did not put forward any philosophical theory other than historical materialism. Historical materialism contains its own view of nature, epistemology, methodology, and category theory, and it doesn't need to set a "dialectical materialism" to study these issues. In this way, Marx's philosophy could avoid the result of "duality" (dialectical materialism studies nature, while historical materialism studies society). Of course, to enter into "the broad conception of historical materialism", we should begin by clarifying the following questions.

The first question is: what is actually the overall prospect of the "world" of historical materialism? As mentioned above, the "extension theory" believes that the world consists of three parts, namely, nature, society, and thinking; the "basis and core" theory does not oppose this division of three parts, but only adjusts the order and rewrites the structure as society, nature, and thinking. It can not be denied that this rewriting is of great theoretical significance. The former the former proceeds from the abstract nature, which is detached from human purposeful activities, to explore everything; the latter proceeds from the field of social history to explore everything. However, the overall prospect of the "world" is already destroyed by those who insist on either the "extension theory" or the "basis and core" theory, for they separate society from nature and thinking. In other words, the concept of "society" we talk about here is still a narrow conception of society. However, for Marx, such concept should be a broad one, containing nature, human beings, and human thinking activities. In *Economic and Philosophic Manuscript of 1844*, Marx writes that "Thus *society* is the complete unity of man with nature—the true resurrection fo nature—the true resurrection of nature-the consistent naturalism of man and the consistent humanism of nature."[1] This exposition tells us that society is not something independent of human thinking and nature, but the unity of human being (of course including human thinking) and nature. Marx also says that "the *entire so-called history of the world* is nothing but the creation of man through human labour, nothing but the emergence of nature for man".[2] Therefore, Marx's broad conception of society shows a complete world picture, and what "the broad conception of historical materialism" will show is just this world picture. Once this complete world picture is shown by Marx's concept of "society" or "social life", the narrow "society" concept and the "narrow conception of historical materialism" will be dethroned theoretically.

---

[1] Karl Marx, *Economic and Philosophic Manuscripts of 1844*, trans. Martin Mulligan (Moscow: Progress Publishers, 1959).
See http://www. marxists. org/archive/marx/works/1844/manuscripts/comm. htm.
[2] Karl Marx, *Economic and Philosophic Manuscripts of 1844*, trans. Martin Mulligan (Moscow: Progress Publishers, 1959).
See http://www. marxists. org/archive/marx/works/1844/manuscripts/comm. htm.

The second question is: what kind of historicity is emphasized by the historical materialism? The so-called "historicity" is the social-historical characteristics, or the horizon in which human beings, human thinking, human activities, and the perceptual world that is faced by human beings are demonstrated. For the "narrow conception of historical materialism", historicity is valid only in the traditional field of social history. As a result of the ignorance of the historicity of nature, when people examine the nature with "narrow conception of historical materialism", they are bound to have an abstract materialist attitude. Just as Marx criticizes, "The weak points in the abstract materialism of natural science, a materialism that excludes history and its process, are at once evident from the abstract and ideological conceptions of its spokesmen, whenever they venture beyond the bounds of their own speciality."[1] This restriction, and even dispelling, of the role of historicty is also evident in the fields of epistemology, methodology, and category theory. On one hand, people put these three theories together with the view of nature, discussing them within the realm of dialectical materialism, and these discussions are developed in the way of "pre-historical materialism"; on the other hand, when exploring these three theories, people take out historicity when examining nature, thus making these three theories abstract. In particular, the exploration of methodology is distorted to be abstract sophistry due to the negligence of the social-historical connotation of the carrier of dialectics; the exploration of category theory is distorted to be a game of concepts due to the negligence of the real social relations that the categories are drawn from the exploration of epistemology is distorted to be abstract epistemology due to

---

① Karl Marx, "Chapter XV: Machinery and Modern Industry, Section 1: the development of machinery, Footnote 4," in *Capital*, vol. 1 (Moscow: Progress Publishers, 1977). See http://www.marxists.org/archive/marx/works/1867-c1/ch15.htm#S1.

the negligence of the social-historical characteristics of cognitive subject. In the book *Materialism and Empirio-Criticism*, Lenin always discusses cognitive subject's feeling and thinking of the outside world while leaving aside the social historicity of the subject. This is criticized by Korsch: "Lenin always deals with these relations from an abstract epistemological standpoint. He never analyses knowledge on the same plane as other socio-historic forms *of* consciousness, and he never examines it as a historical phenomenon, as the ideological 'superstructure' of the economic structure of society at any given time."[1] It is different from this that, for "the broad conception of historical materialism", historicity is not solely applicable to the field of social history in its conventional understanding but extends to all fields of inquiry.

When we examine the nature starting from "the broad conception of historical materialism", historicity is already put into the nature, which is not something abstract and detached from human. Thus, it becomes the "humanized nature", "historical nature". So Marx said: "The nature which develops in human history—the genesis of human society—is man's *real* nature; hence nature as it develops through industry, even though in an *estranged* form, is true *anthropological* nature."[2] Similarly, natural science will lose its abstract materialistic, or rather idealistic, orientation and people will historically examine how it increasingly enters into human life, changes human life, and prepares for the liberation of human beings

---

[1] Karl Korsch, "The Present State of the Problem of 'Marxism and Philosophy'- An Anti-Critique, Footnote 30," in *Marxism and Philosophy*, trans. Fred Halliday (New York: Monthly Review Press, 1970).
See http://www. marxists. org/archive/korsch/19xx/notes. htm#n30.

[2] Karl Marx, "Private Property and Communism," in *Economic and Philosophic Manuscripts of 1844*, trans. Martin Mulligan (Moscow: Progress Publishers, *1959*).
See http://www. marxists. org/archive/marx/works/*1844*/manuscripts/comm. htm.

in practice through industry. In brief, natural science and human science will merge into one science. Thus, we shall not examine the movement of the so-called "nature itself" independent of human practical activities. Rather, we shall examine, through the media of practical activities, how the relationship between human beings and nature develops; we will not discuss the subjects and results of researches in natural science by putting aside all the historical conditions, but try to research the realistic historical relationship between natural science and human beings. Similarly, with the prior incorporation of historicity, the three aforementioned theories will no longer be abstract.

In terms of epistemology, it no longer views a cognitive subject as an abstract container of cognition, which constantly questions on the origin of cognition at the beginning of history. The basic task is to clarify in advance the social history attribute of cognitive subject and object before the development of cognitive process. In other words, the whole cognitive process is based on social-practical activities of human beings. For example, Marx insists that the ideas of the ruling class are in every epoch the ruling ideas. "For instance, in an age and in a country where royal power, aristocracy, and bourgeoisie are contending for mastery and where, therefore, mastery is shared, the doctrine of the separation of powers proves to be the dominant idea and is expressed as an 'eternal law'."[1] If people put aside concrete historical background and discuss the "separation of powers" only from abstract epistemology, they will be entalged with some empty concepts and therefore unable to grasp the essence of this discourse. Thus it can be seen that only by clarifying in advance the social-historical

---

[1]   Karl Marx, "Part I: Feuerbach, B. The Illusion of the Epoch, The German Ideology," in *Marx-Engels Collected Works*, vol. 5 (Moscow: Progress Publishers, 1975).
See http://www.marxists.org/archive/marx/works/1845/german-ideology/ch01b.htm#b3.

connotation of any cognitive activities, one may correctly examine these cognitive activities.

In terms of methodology, people no longer solely extract and discuss the dialectics or put it together with its abstract undertaker, the material or nature detached from human beings' purposeful activities. Instead, they put it together with its real carrier, the existential human practical activities. Thus, our methodology will not be satisfied with the abstract way of discussing scholastic problems such as the identity and struggle of opposites, but take the alienated labor and the dethronement of alienated labor as central issues of discussion.

In terms of category theory, what we will not discuss are the relationships between categories that are abstract and detached from all the social-historical content. These relationships include those between cause and effect, content and form, phenomenon and essence, contingency and necessity, possibility and reality. What we will discuss is the internal connection between categories and real social relations. "He fails to see that *economic categories* are but *abstractions* of those real relations, that they are truths only in so far as those relations continue to exist."①All in all, once people enter the view of "the broad conception of historical materialism", clarifying the historicity in advance will become their fundamental premise and starting point of all research activities.

The third question is: in the view of "the broad conception of historical materialism", how should one perceive the concept of dialectical materialism? It is without doubt that we can't take the abstract nature, which

---

① Karl Marx, "Letter from Marx to Pavel Vasilyevich Annenkov," in *Letters of Marx and Engels 1846*; See *Marx-Engels Collected Works*, vol. 4 (Beijing: People's Publishing House, 1995), p. 536.
See http://www. marxists. org/archive/marx/works/1846/letters/46_12_28. htm.

is detached from human beings, as our study object. Otherwise, it will efface the essential differences between Marx's philosophy and all of the old materialist philosophy. As we have pointed out, Marx would never combine abstract dialectis with abstract materialism. So if we want to keep this old concept, we have to change its meaning. Dialectical materialism should be seen as a synonym for historical materialism(the broad), which manifests the dialectical characteristic of the historical materialism. Marx himself has a lot of important discussions on dialectics, in which the following words have special significance: "The outstanding achievement of Hegel's *Phänomenologie* and of its final outcome, the dialectic of negativity as the moving and generating principle, is thus first that Hegel conceives the self-creation of man as a process, conceives objectification as loss of the object, as alienation and as transcendence of this alienation; that he thus grasps the essence of *labour* and comprehends objective mantrue, because real man-as the outcome of man's *own labour*."① In this paragraph, Marx tells us the following: firstly, the "dialect" he emphasizes not that whose undertaker is abstract material world or abstract nature, but that whose undertaker and subject are labor — the existential practical activities of human beings — and human history is opened up on the basis of this labor dialectic; secondly, the dialectic he emphasizes is "the dialectic of negativity". Marx reveals the substantive characteristics of dialectic as "negativity" because he wishes to indicate that his theory is essentially different from the positivist thought beginning with Comte. The core concept of positivism *positive* can be explained both as "proven" and "affirmative", so the positivist study of the outside world implies at

① Karl Marx, "Critique of Hegel's Philosophy in General," in *Economic and Philosophic Manuscripts of 1844*, trans. Martin Mulligan (Moscow: Progress Publishers, 1959).
See http://www. marxists. org/archive/marx/works/1844/manuscripts/hegel. htm.

the same time the affirmation and identification of the outside world. Contrarily, on the other hand, as the core concept of dialectic, the meaning of *negative* is also very clear: it is "negative". In other words, the dialectic in essence is critical and revolutionary; it neither worships any existing thing in the outside world, nor describes the outside world with a simple affirmative. Rather, it examines everything critically, even traditional beliefs that have long been accepted through education. Therefore, when it comes to the "dialectic in its rational form" as Marx advocates, he points out that "it includes in its comprehension and affirmative recognition of the existing state of things, at the same time also, the recognition of the negation of that state, of its inevitable breaking up."[①] From the above discussion we can see that it is necessary to retain the concept of dialectical materialism as the synonym for "the broad conception of historical materialism", for it manifests the critical and revolutionary nature of Marx's philosphy. It also reveals a fundamental resistance to the various attempts to take Marx's philosophy as positivism. Moreover, the term "historical" in "the broad conception of historical materialism" is essentially consistent with the term "dialectical" in its synonym "dialectical materialism".

The fourth question is: how to look upon the relationship between "the broad conception of historical materialism" and the conception of practical materialism? We believe that the "practical" manifested by practical materialism, the "historical" manifested by historical materialism, as well as the "dialectical" manifested by its synonym dialectical materialism, are equally original. Moreover, they are inseparable in the sense that one cannot be reduced to the other two. There merely indicate different aspects

---

① Karl Marx, "Afterword to the Second German Edition," in *Capital*, vol. 1 (Moscow: Progress Publishers, 1977).
See http://www.marxists.org/archive/marx/works/1867-c1/p3.htm.

of Marx's philosophy. It is also significant to retain the conception of practical materialism as the synonym for "the broad conception of historical materialism". New paragraph as mentioned before, the unified world picture of "the broad conception of historical materialism" is constructed and opened up by practical activities. Marx says that "All social life is essentially practical. All mysteries which lead theory to mysticism find their rational solution in human practice and in the comprehension of this practice."[①] Here, Marx does not say that "all social life" is based on practical activities (some people misunderstand Marx in this way and therefore interpret practical materialism as the basis of historical materialism. However, in this way, the practical principle contained by historical materialism itself is extracted, and thus fragmented), What he actually wants to say is this: practical activities are included in "all social life". In other words, the unified world picture of "all social life" is just constructed and opened up by practical activities. This is precisely the important point that distinguishes Marx's philosophy from traditional philosophy. If the doctrines of old materialism unify the world picture by abstract material, diverse idealist doctrines do it by abstract idea, such as spirit or will. Marx is different from them since he advocates for the construction and exploration of the entire world picture through practical activities. In fact, it is in the view of practical activities that two things are accomplished: first, the abstract and parallel relationship of nature, society (in its narrow sense), and thinking, is dethroned; second, the unity and integrity of "society" or "all social life" as "world" picture are confirmed. New paragraph, it is through the concept of "praxis" that Marx reveals the intentionality of all

①　Karl Marx, *Theses On Feuerbach*, trans. Cyril Smith, 2002.
See http://www. marxists. org/archive/marx/works/1845/theses/index. htm.

consciousness, notion, and text. That is to say, all of the consciousness, notion, and text, are connected with human practical activities, and no matter how mystic, how inconceivable they represent, people can reveal their substantive connotation by tracing back to the practical activities they intend. new paragraph. The third point is more important. The fundamental purpose of Marx's philosophy to transform the existing world is also demonstrated by practical activities. The basic difference between Marx's philosophy and all of the old philosophy is that the latter goes no further than interpreting the world, while Marx believes that to change the world is the fundamental task new philosophy faced with. It should be noted that though "the broad conception of historical materialism" actually proceeds from historical existential-practical activities and therefore penetrate everything, when the concept itself is considered, the "practical" can not be displayed directly as practical materialism. For all these reasons, it is necessary to retain the concept of practical materialism. We definitely could regard "practical materialism" as the synonym for "the broad conception of historical materialism", and they manifest respectively the essence of Marx's philosophy from different points of view.

To sum up, only by delving into the perspective of "the broad conception of historical mateirlaism" can one truely grasp Marx's philosophical stance, conprehensively understand the internal connection of a series of philosophical concepts associated with it, and throrougly clarify any ideological confusion or misconceptions about the essence of Marx's philosophy prevalent prevalent in previous theoretical research.

Enlightenment of the Broad Conception of Historical Materialism

After a deep investigation of the difference between "the narrow conception of historical materialism" and "the broad conception of historical materialism", we are now in a position to explain the theoretical significance of putting forward "the broad conception of historical materialism".

First of all, highlighting "the broad conception of historical materialism" allows us to break through the framework of traditional textbook system and move forward in philosophical research. In recent years, there are a number of discussions on the system of Marx's philosophy. New progress has been achieved on many important issues including ontology, the relationship between truth and value, the relationship between cognition and evaluation, and the relationship between alienation, and humanitarianism. However, our understanding of the system of Marx's philosophy has not yet fundamentally broken through the framework of the popular "extension theory". Yet the introduction of "the broad conception of historical materialism" still help us to jump out of the traditional mode of thinking and obtain a new understanding of the relationship between historical materialism and Marx's philosophy.

Secondly, calling attention to "the broad conception of historical materialism" will enable us to gain a new understanding of the epochal revolution brought about by historical materialism in the human intellectual history. Proponents of the "extension theory" still takes the basic part of Marx's philosophy as general materialism or dialectical materialism, and historical materialism is only the positive result of applying this basic part in the field of social history. In this way, the significance of Marx's epoch-making philosophical revolution is neglected, and the essential differences between Marx's philosophy and traditional philosophy are effaced. This is because people still stand on the basis of traditional philosophy and use the concepts left by traditional philosophy in an uncritical way. These concepts include world, nature, material, thinking, being, subject, object, materialism, idealism, etc. Even if people understand dialectical materialism (in its traditional sense) as Marx's new creation in philosophy, they still understand Marx' philosophy in the old framework of traditional philosophy, for they always put aside the social-historical characteristics (such as fetishism) of the concrete mode of material (such as commodity), and this leads them to discuss the materiality of world in an abstract way. The "basis and core" theory, though it is a progress compared with "extension theory", still underestimates the epochal significance of Marx's philosophical revolution, for it neither gets rid of the influence of "the narrow conception of historical materialism", nor reflects systematically and newly the above-mentioned basic concepts. Proceeding from "the broad conception of historical materialism", we can find out that historical materialism not only clarifies the premise for all philosophical research, but also provides the key to our understanding of all the past and contemporary philosophical theories. In short, historical materialism is a radical revolution in the field of philosophy, and it has fundamentally changed people's way of thinking.

Finally, focusing on "the broad conception of historical materialism" shows us a brand new problem domain of philosophical research. Under the promise of clarifying in advance the historicity, we will newly reflect all of the traditional philosophical issues we have been accustomed to for a long time. These include the world outlook, the view of nature, material view, ontology, epistemology, dialectics, category theory and other basic philosophical issues. As reflection deepens, the genuine theoretical essence of Marx's philosophy will gradually reveal itself before us.

1.2　異なる二つの史的唯物論概念[①]

　　広く知られているように、史的唯物論はマルクスの二つの偉大な発見の一つである。そして、その史的唯物論とマルクス哲学との関係は、重要な理論上の問題として議論されている。この問題は以前、広範な論争を引き起こしましたが、現在でも実質的な進展が見られていない。

　　現在の学術界では、一般的に次の二つの見解が主流である。一つ目は、マルクス哲学には弁証法的唯物論と史的唯物論という二つの側面があり、史的唯物論は弁証法的唯物論の原理を社会や歴史の領域に応用したものだというものである。二つ目は、史的唯物論がマルクス哲学の基礎であり核心であるとするものである。この二つの見解にはかなりの違いがありますが、共通する問題も抱えている。第二の見解は、史的唯物論を社会歴史の領域に限定された学説と捉え、マルクス哲学の基礎であり核心である史的唯物論とその他の部分との関係をまだ十分に明らかにしていない点で第一の見解と共通している。そして、第二の見解は、史的唯物論とマル

①　Editor's note: This paper, which is the Japanese abridged edition of the previous article, was published in『唯物論研究』,第 16 巻,第 50 號,1997 年冬.

クス哲学の本質的な関係を理解しようとする点で、第一の見解に近づいている。結局のところ、これら二つの見解はともに、史的唯物論の理論的内容の幅を狭める傾向があり、そのためにマルクス哲学の画期的な貢献が十分に認識されていないという状況になってしまう。

　本論文では、第三の見解として次のような主張を提案したいのである。史的唯物論はマルクスの画期的な哲学の源泉であり、彼の哲学は史的唯物論そのものである（拙稿「唯物史観とその歴史命運の思考」、『学術月刊』一九九四年第七号）。言い換えれば、史的唯物論がマルクス哲学の核心であるということである。このため、本論文で使用する史的唯物論の概念は、従来のものとは異なる新しい内容を含んでいる。本論文の見解とこれまでの二つの見解との根本的な違いを明らかにするため、また、史的唯物論がマルクス哲学における最も重要な貢献であることを示すために、本論文では史的唯物論に関する二つの異なる概念を提案する。すなわち、これまでの見解が提唱する史的唯物論を「狭義の史的唯物論概念」とし、本論文で提唱する史的唯物論を「広義の史的唯物論概念」と呼ぶことである。これから、この主題について具体的に論じていこう。

1

　「狭義の史的唯物論概念」とは何であろうか。これは、社会歴史の領域にのみ適用される史的唯物論の考え方を意味している。この概念は伝統的な哲学教科書に取り上げられてきたことで、今でも学術界に大きな影響を与えている。その原因は、この概念が推広論と一緒に述べられているからである。

　「推広論」とは、一般的唯物論や弁証法的唯物論を社会歴史の領域に適用した結果が史的唯物論だとする理解を指している。この形成と

発展は過程的なものである。エンゲルスは「フォイエルバッハ論」の中で、マルクスがヘーゲル哲学をどのように改造したかについて次のように述べています。ヘーゲル哲学との分離は、そこにおいてもまた唯物論の観点へ回帰することによっておこなわれた。……ここにおいてはじめて唯物論的な世界観が良に良剣に取り扱われ、この世界観が、問題になっているあらゆる知識領域（少なくとも主要な側面において）徹底的に貫徹されたのである」。この論述は二つの意味が見られる。第一に、マルクス哲学の基礎的部分が唯物論であるということ。第二に、唯物論的世界観の適用は必ずあらゆる知識領域（社会歴史領域を含む）に及ぶべきであるということ。つまり、エンゲルスは、史的唯物論は唯物論を社会歴史の領域に応用したものだという見解を提起しているのである。エンゲルスにとって、「唯物論」は現代唯物論を指しており、また彼の『反デューリング論』によれば、現代唯物論も本質的に弁証法的なものだ。だから、エンゲルスは「唯物弁証法」という用語を使いつつも、「弁証法的唯物論」という概念を使用しなかったが、この概念の思想的基礎をすでに築いていた。ここで、マルクス哲学の構造を二つの層に分ける傾向が明らかになる。すなわち、基礎部分は現代唯物論、応用部分は史的唯物論とする理解である。この点は『フォイエルバッハ論』や『反デューリング論』などの著作の構造にも見られる。エンゲルスは、いつも自然界を対象とした一般哲学問題を先に論じ、その後で社会歴史領域の哲学問題を論じている。

　　プレハーノフは、マルクス主義学説の積極的な伝播者として、エンゲルスのマルクス主義哲学を引き継ぎ、より明確に進展させた。

　　…

　　ブレハノフによれば、マルクス主義哲学の基礎は弁証法的唯物論であり、その応用は史的唯物論である。ブレハノフが弁証法的唯物論と史的唯物論の関係をマルクス主義哲学の重要な問題として論じていなかったとしたら、レーニンがこの問題の重要性を十分に明らかにす

ることができたであろうか。

　　　…

　レーニンはマルクス哲学を一つの「建物」に例え、その基礎を弁証法的唯物論、上部構造を史的唯物論とした。彼の著書『唯物論と経験批判論』でも、弁証法的唯物論（自然界を対象にする）を先に取り上げ、その後で史的唯物論（社会歴史領域を対象にする）を論じている。史的唯物論は弁証法的唯物論を社会歴史領域に「押し広げ」〔「推広」〕、あるいは「運用」したものであるという理解は、レーニンが一貫して持っていた思想である。

　　　…

　このように、「推広論」の雛形がすでにレーニンの時代に形成されていたのである。レーニンの見解は、スターリンによってさらに明確に述べられている。スターリンは「史的唯物論は、弁証法的唯物論の諸命題を、社会生活の研究に押し広げたものであり、弁証法的唯物論の諸命題を、社会生活の現象に、社会の研究に、社会史の研究に応用したものである」と書いている（『ソ連共産党小史』、人民出版社、一九七五年版、一一五―一一六頁）。

　ここから、「推広論」という概念が人々のマルクス主義哲学における固定観念を形成するきっかけとなった。このアイデアは、ソ連、東欧、中国だけでなく、その他の地域の研究者にも広く影響を与えたのである。

2

　次に、さらに検討を深めて、「狭義の史的唯物論概念」の問題点はどこにあるのか、また伝統的な教科書の編集者たちが主張したように、この概念でマルクス主義哲学の最も本質的な内容を十分に示すことがで

きたかどうかを見てみよう。

　まず、一般的唯物論あるいは弁証法的唯物論から出発し、社会歴史の領域において史的唯物論の見解に到達できるかどうかという問題を検討してみよう。この問題に対する回答は、残念ながら否定的である。なぜなら、フォイエルバッハは自然を考察する際には典型的な唯物論者であったが、社会歴史の領域に踏み込むと宗教の変化から歴史の変遷を解釈する史的観念論者になってしまったからである。マルクスは次のように批判している。「フォイエルバッハは唯物論者であるときは歴史は彼の視野の外にあり、彼が歴史を論じるときには唯物論者ではない。彼においては唯物論と歴史は完全に両岸に離れている」（邦訳全集三一五一）。それらの言葉は、以下のことを示している。

　一般的な唯物論から史的唯物論に発展させることはできないだけでなく、一般的唯物論は抽象的で歴史から切り離されているため、社会や歴史を考えると必然的に史的観念論に陥ってしまう。そのため、弁証法的唯物論を使って社会や歴史に応用し、史的唯物論を導き出すことも難しいと考えられる。なぜなら、弁証法的唯物論は自然界を研究の対象としており、その世界観は自然、社会、思考の順序に基づいて展開されるからである。

　われわれの世界の図式において、自然が社会の前に置かれている限り、人間および人間の活動は社会の様式によって展開される。したがって、われわれが考察する自然は、人間およびその活動から切り離された抽象的な自然だと言える。弁証法的唯物論の対象は、このような抽象的自然に他ならない。そのため、弁証法的唯物論の領域で論じる「存在」もまた、人間の活動から分離された抽象的物質を指すことになる。しかし、社会歴史の領域では、状況はまったく異なる。この領域で語られる「社会的存在」には、人間およびその目的と活動が含まれている。社会歴史の考察において、ただ人間の目的と動機の次元にとどまるならば、史的観念論の立場に陥りやすい。したがって、自然界につい

ての人間から切り離された唯物論を、弁証法的に展開する方法、つまり一般的な唯物論を弁証法的唯物論に変え、そしてその過程で人間と切り離したまま、それを人間の目的や動機に満ちた社会歴史の領域に導入するという方法では、史的唯物論を導き出すことはできない。なぜなら、この「導く」という行為自体が抽象的であり、抽象的な前提から具体的な結論を導き出すことはできないからである（これは「抽象から具体へ」の研究方法とは違うという点に注意してほしい）。これに対して、史的唯物論の基本的な立場に適するのは、人間から分離された抽象的な自然ではなく、「人間化された自然」や「歴史的な自然」であり、人間から分離された抽象的な物質ではなく、人間の生産的活動の一要素として現れる具体的な物質の形態である。要するに、弁証法的唯物論が唯物論を弁証法的に展開したとしても、弁証法の対象である物質的世界や自然界が依然として抽象的な社会以前の姿で現れているため、弁証法を歴史の領域に応用しても、史的唯物論を導き出すことは不可能だということである。

　次に、「狭義の史的唯物論概念」では、史的唯物論をマルクス哲学の「上部構造」あるいは「最終的な成果」として理解します。つまり、史的唯物論はマルクス哲学の基礎部分ではなく、押し広げされた部分であり、マルクスがすべてを考察する出発点ではなく、彼が歴史の領域を研究した際に導き出した局部的な結論だとされる。このようにして、哲学史における史的唯物論の画期的な変革作用は狭められ、極端な場合には隠されてしまう。ななぜなら、われわれは依然として史的唯物論を第二義的なもの、「押し広げられた」ものと理解し、哲学史上古くからある一般的唯物論、あるいはせいぜい弁証法化した唯物論を基礎として史的唯物論の前に置くからである。このように理解されたマルクス哲学は、必然的にその本質が失われるのである。

　最後に、「狭義の史的唯物論概念」は、マルクス哲学を実証化し、その応用価値を強調する一方で、ある原理を社会歴史の領域でのみ用い

られるものとして捉えるようになった。ここでマルクスの重要な論述に触れておく。

…

　『ドイツ・イデオロギー』の一節で、マルクスは、歴史学としての「実証科学」によって「思弁哲学」を代替すること、そして、「人類歴史の観察から抽象された最も一般的な結果の総合」（以下「総合」と略称）によって「独立した哲学」に取って代えることを強調している。通常、このマルクスの一節は次のように理解される。社会歴史領域において哲学はすでに終わり、その代わりとなるのが実証科学としての歴史学である。これがマルクスの歴史観（史的唯物論）の実証主義化だとされる。しかし、ここでマルクスが排斥したのは全ての哲学ではなく、主にヘーゲルを代表とする歴史哲学であり、彼が「思弁」や「独立した哲学」と述べているのは、この歴史哲学を指している。では、歴史哲学の終焉の後に残るのは実証科学としての歴史学だけなのだろうか。マルクスはそれを否定している。マルクスが述べている「総合」とは、まさに実証的、経験的な歴史学に基づいた歴史観であり、この種の歴史観こそ史的唯物論である。言うまでもなく、史的唯物論は一種の新しい哲学説であり、それは伝統的な意味での幻想的な連関を現実の連関に代わる歴史哲学ではなく、現実的、経験的な観察から抽象されたものである。そしてこれは、あらゆる領域を研究するための（伝統的な意味における社会歴史領域に限らず）理論的な前提とすべきものである。したがって、「狭義の史的唯物論概念」は、史的唯物論学説を社会歴史領域に限定し、それを一般唯物論の応用に過ぎないと強調することで、必然的にそれを実証科学化し、深い哲学的内容を失わせる結果となってしまう。

　ルカーチをはじめとした「西洋マルクス主義」の影響のもとに、ソ連、東欧、中国の哲学界で「拡張論」に対する批判が次第に明らかになる。1980年代以来、中国の学術界では影響力のある新しい見解が形成される。この見解は「拡張論」の方向を逆転させ、史的唯物論がマルク

ス哲学の基礎と核心であることを強調することになる。もともと弁証法的唯物論の部分で議論されていた認識論、方法論、範疇論などはすべて史的唯物論の基礎の上で議論されるべきものとしてになった。これはマルクス哲学の再理解における重要な進展とも言える。しかし、この新しい「基礎・核心論」は、最終的には「狭義の史的唯物論概念」を超克することはできなかった。

　その理由は、三つ挙げられる。第一に、この理論は史的唯物論を弁証法的唯物論の社会歴史領域への適用と見ることに反対しているが、史的唯物論を社会歴史領域に対応したものと見なしている。第二に、たとえ史的唯物論がマルクス哲学の基礎・核心だと称していても、マルクス哲学の基礎・核心ではない部分は何であろうかということがまた明らかにしていない。特に、認識論や方法論、範疇論などが基礎や核心の一部であるのかどうかが明示されていない。もしこれらの内容が核心の全部であるとすれば、史的唯物論の内容が狭められる恐れがある。第三に、この理論的主張は本来の意味における弁証法的唯物論の概念にとどまっている。このように、一方では「拡張論」の理論的失策を十分に明らかにできず、他方では人々の視野が依然として「狭義の史的唯物論概念」にとどまっているため、「基礎・核心論」はマルクスの哲学の本質を深く理解するには不十分であると言えるのである。

3

　以上述べたことから明らかなように、「狭義の史的唯物論」の概念に留まる限り、マルクスの革新的な哲学の真の実質と意義を理解することはできない。マルクス哲学は「広義の史的唯物論概念」で捉えなければならない。ここて、「広義の史的唯物論概念」という言葉は、次のような意味を持っている。

第一に、史的唯物論は、伝統的意味での社会歴史領域だけでなく、人間のあらゆる研究領域にも適用されるべきである。第二に、史的唯物論は、マルクス哲学の「基礎・核心」であるだけでなく、マルクス哲学の全体であるということである。つまり、マルクス哲学とは史的唯物論そのものであり、マルクスは史的唯物論以外の哲学理論を創設していないとも言える。したがって、基礎・核心論者が主張するように、史的唯物論の基礎の上に認識論、方法論、範疇論を研究することはできない。なぜなら、それは実際には「狭義の史的唯物論の概念」にとどまってしまうからである。すでに述べたように、「広義の史的唯物論概念」には、認識論、方法論、範疇論が含まれている。この「広義の史的唯物論概念」に取り組むには、まず以下の問題を明確にしなければならない。

　第一の問題は、史的唯物論の世界の全体構造は何かということである。「推広論」者は、世界は自然、社会、思考の三つの部分から成り立っているとしている。「基礎・核心論」者もこの三分法に反対せず、ただ順序を社会、自然、思考に変えることを求めている。前者が抽象的な自然から考察を始めるのに対し、後者は社会歴史領域から出発するので、その順序の変更には重要な理論的意義があることは否定できない。しかし、どのように出発しようとも、世界の全体構造は既に破壊されている。それは、社会と自然、思考を分けてしまっているからである。ここで論じている「社会」の概念が狭義のものであり、それと違って、マルクスにおける「社会」の概念は、広義の自然、人間、思考活動を含むものである。『経済学・哲学草稿』において、マルクスは次のように書いている。「社会は、人間と自然界との本質的な一体性の成就、自然界の真の復活、人間によって実現された自然主義または自然界によって実現された人間主義である」（全集邦訳四〇一四五八）。マルクスにとって、社会は人間と自然の外にあるものではなく、それ自体が人間と自然の統一である。また、彼はこうも言っている。「いわゆる世界史の全体は、人間労働による人間の産出、自然の人間にとっての生成」（同上、邦訳四

六一七）。したがって、マルクスの広義の社会が提示している社会概念は、全体としての世界図式であり、「広義の史的唯物論概念」が提示すべきものもこのような世界図式である。この完全な世界図式がマルクスの「社会」あるいは「社会生活」の概念を通して提示されたので、「狭義の社会」概念と「狭義の史的唯物論概念」もまた理論上超克されたのである。

　　第二の問題は、史的唯物論が強調する歴史性がどのようなものかということである。いわゆる「歴史性」とは、社会歴史の特性であり、それは人間の思考と活動、人間が直面する感性的な世界に提示される境域である。「狭義の史的唯物論の概念」では、歴史性は伝統的な社会歴史領域で初めて有効となる。したがって、「狭義の史的唯物論の概念」を用いて自然を考察するとき、自然の歴史性を無視することで、必然的に一種の抽象的な唯物論に陥る。マルクスも次のように指摘している。「歴史過程を排除する抽象的自然科学的唯物論の欠陥は、その唱導者たちが自分の専門の外にでしゃばるときに示す抽象的で観念論的な見解によってもわかる」（『資本論』第一巻邦訳、二三a一四八七）。このような歴史性の制限や解消は、認識論、方法論、範疇論の研究にも表れている。人々はこれらを自然観と並列にして検討し、弁証法的唯物論の一部として考えたが、それらの考察は史的唯物論の方式で展開されたものではない。また、これらの三論を考察する際には、自然を考察するときと同様に歴史性が抜き去られ、抽象化されている。方法論の考察は、弁証法の担い手としての社会歴史の内容を軽視することで抽象的な論弁に変わり、範疇論の考察も、範疇が引き出される現実の社会関係を軽視することで概念遊びに変わる。それに対して「広義の史的唯物論概念」では、歴史性は伝統的な意味における社会歴史領域だけでなく、あらゆる領域に適用される。マルクスの社会概念は広義であり、その社会の歴史性、つまり歴史性は、研究者が考察するすべての領域の前提であり、研究者の活動もすべてその中で展開される。

「広義の史的唯物論概念」から自然を考察するとき、歴史性は自然の中に入り込み、自然は決して人間と分離した抽象物ではなく、「人間化した自然」や「歴史的自然」になる。マルクスは次のように言っている。「人類の歴史において、すなわち、人間社会が生み出される過程において形成された自然界は、人間の現実的な自然界である。したがって、産業（たとえ疎外された形式でもってであれ）を形成された自然界は、真の人間学的自然界である」（全集邦訳第四〇－四六四）。このように、「広義の史的唯物論概念」は「自然界自身」がどのように運動するかを抽象的に考察するのではなく、実践活動の媒介を通して人間と自然の関係がどのように発展するかを考察する。同様に、「広義の史的唯物論概念」から出発して上記の三論を考察する際には、歴史性があらかじめ組み込まれるので、それらが決して抽象的なものにはならない。

　　…

　第三の問題は、「広義の史的唯物論概念」において、弁証法的唯物論という概念をどう扱うかということだ。この問題に対して、「広義の史的唯物論概念」に基づく二つの選択肢がある。もしそれが本来の意味を保持し、人間と分離した抽象的な自然界を研究対象とするならば、継続する必要はない。もしこの概念が継続するなら、その意味を変えなければならない。つまり、それは史的唯物論（広義の）と同じ意味にならなければならない。でも、両者が同じ意味を持つなら、弁証法的唯物論の概念を保持する意味があるのだろうか。本稿は、その意味があると主張したい。なぜなら、この概念を通して史的唯物論（広義の）の弁証法的性質を明らかにすることができるからである。

　第四の問題は、「広義の史的唯物論概念」と実践的唯物論概念との関係をどう扱うかということである。この問題は複雑だが、簡単に言えば、史的唯物論（広義の）が明らかにする歴史性や、実践的唯物論が明らかにする実践性、弁証法的唯物論（広義の史的唯物論と同じ意味）が明らかにする弁証法性は、すべて同じ始原性を持ち、それら相互の間は

分離できない。それらは一つの概念であり、ある概念が他の二つの概念の基礎だとは言えない。すべてがマルクス哲学であり、異なる側面から呼称されているに過ぎない。以上のように、「広義の史的唯物論概念」の視点に立つことで、既存の理論研究における思想的混乱を整理し、史的唯物論と他の関連概念に対する適切な理解を明確にすることができる。

4

「狭義の史的唯物論の概念」と「広義の史的唯物論概念」の違いを深く考察したことで、理論的な意義を説明する条件が整っている。

まず、「広義の史的唯物論概念」の提起は、伝統的な教科書体系の枠組みを打破し、哲学研究を本当に前進させる可能性を示すことができる。近年、マルクス哲学体系の改革に関する多くの議論がなされ、多くの著作が発表されている。その中で、存在論、真理と価値の関係、認識と評価の関係、疎外とヒューマニズムなどの問題について新しい見解が提起されている。しかし、今までのマルクス哲学体系に対する認識は、根本的には「推広論」の枠組みを突破できていない。多くの論者は「推広論」に対して激しい批判を行っているが、その構造や基本概念の使用を見ると、議論の中心以外の部分で「推広論」の体系を無批判に借用していることが多い。

…

次に、「広義の史的唯物論概念」の提起は、唯物史観が人類思想の発展史において実現した時代を画する変革に対する新たな理解をもたらすことができる。「推広論」の視点では、マルクス哲学の基礎部分は依然として一般的唯物論や弁証法的唯物論であり、史的唯物論はその基礎部分が社会歴史領域に応用された成果に過ぎない。このように、マ

ルクスの革新的な哲学創造の意義が埋没され、マルクス哲学と伝統的な哲学の根本的な違いが拭い去られてしまう。なぜなら、依然として伝統的哲学の基礎に立ち、無批判に伝統的哲学の概念（世界、自然、物質、思考、存在、主体、客体、唯物論、観念論など）を使用しているからである。たとえ弁証法的唯物論（元来の意味における）をマルクス哲学の新たな創造だと理解しても、唯物論に対する理解が伝統的な哲学の視野に留まっているため、物質の具体的形態（例えば商品）の社会的歴史的特殊性（例えば物神崇拝）を無視して、抽象的に世界の物質性を論じることになる。そのため、依然として伝統的な哲学の枠組みの中でマルクス哲学を理解していることになる。名前は新しくとも、概念は依然として古いままである。「基礎・核心論」は「推広論」に対して一歩進んでいるが、「狭義の史的唯物論の概念」の影響から抜け出せておらず、これまでに提起された基本概念に対する系統的な新たな反省に至っておらず、そのため、マルクス哲学の革新の意義を依然として低く評価する結果になっている。

　「広義の史的唯物論概念」から出発するとき、史的唯物論は、あらゆる哲学研究の前提であるだけでなく、これまでの、また現代のすべての哲学学説を理解する鍵を提供するということが分かる。旧哲学の基礎の上でマルクス哲学を理解すべきではなく、マルクス哲学の基礎の上で旧哲学を理解すべきである。言い換えれば、史的唯物論は哲学領域における根本的な革命であり、それは基礎から人々の思考様式を変えたのである。

　最後に、「広義の史的唯物論概念」の提起は、新たな哲学研究の問題領域を示す。歴史性を前提とすることで、世界観や自然観、存在論、認識論、弁証法、範疇論など、すべての伝統的な哲学問題を再考する余地が生まれます。これらの考察が深まるにつれて、マルクス哲学の真の理論的な形と姿がより明確に浮かび上がってくることを期待できるだろう。

1.3　From Moral Evaluation to Historical Evaluation^①

—A Transfer of Perspective in the Development of Marx's Notion of Alienation

1

There are many mutually incompatible interpretations of Marx's theory of alienation. My own
approach is the following:

Firstly, Marx uses the concept of alienation
throughout his life. The development of this concept may be divided into three stages. The first
stage ranges from 1840 to August 1844 as wit-
nessed by works such as the "Doctoral Dissertation" (latter half of 1840 to March 1841), "Contribution to a Critique of Hegel's Philosophy of
Law" (summer of 1843), "On the Jewish Question" (autumn of 1843), "Contribution to a

---

①　Editor's note: This paper was originally published in *Social Sciences in China*,
no. 3, 2003, pp. 45-52, translated by Luo Jun from *Zhongguo Shehui Kexue* (《中国社会科
学》), no. 2, 2003, pp. 95-105, revised by David Kelly.

Critique of Hegel's Philosophy of Right. Introduction" (the end of 1843 to January 1844), "Comments on James Mill, *Éléments d'économie politique*" (the first half of 1844) and "Economic and Philosophic Manuscripts of 1844" (April to August 1844). The second stage ranges from September 1844 to the beginning of 1848 as attested by such works as *The Holy Family* (September to November 1844), "Theses on Feuerbach" (written in the spring of 1845), *The German Ideology* (1845–1846), "Circular against Kriege" (May 1846), *The Poverty of Philosophy* (the first half of 1847), "Moralizing Criticism and Critical Morality" (late October 1847) and *Manifesto of the Communist Party* (December 1847 to January 1848). The third stage is marked by works such as *Economic Manuscripts* 1857–1858, *Economic Manuscripts* 1861-1863, *Theories of Surplus-Value* (1861–1863) and *Capital* (1867).

Next, throughout the evolution of Marx's concept of alienation we find a fundamental "transformation of perspective." This takes place in the second stage. In our opinion, young Marx views alienation from the perspective of "moral evaluation first"[1], while in his mature years, he sees it in terms of "historical evaluation first." There are fundamental differences between these two perspectives. On the one hand, alienation is a negative phenomenon that shall be morally condemned. On the other hand, it is also a historically objective ad inevitable phenomenon whose positive

---

[1] American scholar B. Ollman opined that he was inclined to think Marx did not have a theory of ethics. See Bertrand Ollman, *Alienation—Marx's Conception of Man in Capitalist Society* (second edition), Cambridge University Press, 1976, p. 44. Of course, Even if Marx had not advanced an independent theory of ethics it did not by any means prevent him from thinking and making evaluations in ethical terms. In fact, it is just because B. Ollman did not differentiate two different perspectives of Marx's conception of alienation that his work *Alienation—Marx's Conception of Man in Capitalist Society* did not produce any new substantive ideas.

significance should receive full—fledged affirmation in historical terms. In terms of the overall train of thought, the former falls within the domain of communism or humanism in an ethical sense based on abstract human nature, while the latter falls within that of historical materialism based on the objective inevitability of historical evolution.

Thirdly, the role played by the concept of alienation in Marx's theory of historical materialism is not merely symbolic or marginal, but fundamental and substantial. If fetishism, which is a special expression of alienation that tears away the mythical veil of traditional abstract materialism, clears away the intellectual obstacles for people to accept historical materialism, then the general expressions of alienation reveal the objective trend of human social development and ensure the possibility of establishing the theory of the "three social formations" to be the capstone of historical materialism.

2

Let's now turn to the first stage in the development of Marx's concept of alienation, that is, the theory of the young Marx. [①] if In his "Doctoral Dissertation", Marx's usage of the concept of alienation mainly aligns with those found in Hegel's works. Yet, in "Contribution to the Critique of Hegel's Philosophy of Right", "On the Jewish Question" and "Contribution to the Critique of Hegel's Philosophy of Law. Introduction," Marx already has the tendency to use the concept in the sense found in Feuerbach

---

① David McAllen, *The Young Hegelians and Marx* (London and Basingstoke: MacMillan and Co. Ltd., 1969).

and Powell. Notably, as a result of studies of the national economy in "Comments on James Mill, *Éléments d'économie politique*" and *Economic and Philosophic Manuscripts of 1844*, Marx's concept of alienation displays its own characteristics: He develops a new concept of "alienated labor" and analyzes its meaning in a four-fold manner.

Indeed, the study of national economy plays an extremely important role in shaping and evolving the young Marx's concept of alienation. The inclusion of this dimension allows Marx to extend his sights beyond the field of vision of Hegel, Feuerbach, Powell and Hess, thereby raising the study of alienation to a completely new plane. Meanwhile, we must be soberly aware that the young Marx is largely confined within the theoretical framework of "communism" or "humanism" in an ethical sense based on abstract human nature. This train of thought thus conditions his unique perspective on alienation—the perspective of "moral evaluation first."

For example, Marx points out in "Comments on James Mill, *Éléments d'économie politique*" that, in the credit system of capitalist society, it seems as though the dominance of alien, material forces is broken, lthe relationship of self — estrangement is abolished, and man has once more human relations to man. "But this abolition of estrangement, this *return* of man to himself and therefore to other men is only an *appearance*; the self-estrangement, the dehumanization, is all the more *infamous* and *extreme* because its element is no longer commodity, metal, paper, but man's *moral* existence, man's *social* existence, the *inmost depths* of his heart, and because under the appearance of man's trust in man it is the height of distrust and complete estrangement."[1] In Marx's view, in credit

---

① Karl Marx and Frederick Engels, *Selected Works* (Moscow: Progress Publishers, 1983), vol. 3, p. 214.

"By a 'good' man, the one who bestows his trust, understands, like Shylock, a man who is 'able to pay.'" In credit, man does not acquire his own dignity; on the contrary, he is reduced to something that can be mortgaged as commodity, money, capital, or interest. Similarly, the death of a debtor (usually the poor) is understood as the death of a creditor's capital together with the interest. Therefore, Marx hit the nail on the head when he says that "Credit is the *economic* judgment on the *morality* of the man."[1] It is from the perspective of "the moral evaluation first" that Marx probed into the alienation common in the relations among the people in the capitalist countries.

Here is another example: again, Marx exposes the prevalent alination within capitalist societies from the perspective of "moral valuation first" in the *Economic and Philosophic Manuscripts of 1844*. He writes scathingly, "It is true that labor produces wonderful things for the rich—but for the worker it produces privation. It produces palaces—but for the worker, hovels. It produces beauty—but for the worker, deformity."[2] Meanwhile, Marx also condemns the concealment of alienation by political economy. "...Political economy," he states, "—despite its worldly and voluptuous appearance—is a true moral science, the most moral of all the sciences. Self-renunciation, of life and of all human needs, is its principal thesis. The less you eat, drink and buy books; the less you go to the theatre, the dance hall, the public house; the less you think, love, theorize, sing, paint, fence, etc., the more you save—the greater becomes your treasure which neither moths nor rust devour—your capital. The less you

---

[1]   Karl Marx and Frederick Engels, *Selected Works* (Moscow: Progress Publishers, 1983), vol. 3, p. 215.

[2]   Karl Marx and Frederick Engels, *Selected Works* (Moscow: Progress Publishers, 1983), vol. 3, p. 273.

are, the less you express your own life, the more you have, i. e., the greater is your alienated life, the greater is the store of your estranged being. "① Specifically, in the population theory of political economy, workers who are sparing in procreation will be "ethical." Wielding the weapon of moral critique, the young Marx strongly denounces the alienation in capitalist societies and the veiling of this phenomenon by political economy.

What was his starting point in doing this? The following words shall throw light on this question: "*Communism* as the positive transcendence of *private property* as *human self-estrangement*, and therefore as the real *appropriation* of the *human* by and for man; communism therefore as the complete return of man to himself as a *social*(i. e., human) being—a return accomplished consciously and embracing the entire wealth of previous development. This communism, as fully developed naturalism, equals humanism, and as fully developed humanism equals naturalism ... "② Here, "communism," "humanism", and "naturalism", are all similar terms. If we say the concept of "communism" embodies young Marx's links in theoretical origin with the French doctrines of utopian communism, then "humanism" and "naturalism" (identity of man with nature) reveals his intellectual links in Feuerbach's homocentric theory. Clearly, the essence of both doctrines consists of ethical ideas based on the abstract conception of human nature. The angle from which he observes alienation and other social issues is still "moral evaluation first." If he makes any historical evaluation of the phenomenon of alienation, it is only of marginal and subordinate significance.

---

① Karl Marx and Frederick Engels, *Selected Works* (Moscow: Progress Publishers, 1983), vol. 3, p. 309.

② Karl Marx and Frederick Engels, *Selected Works* (Moscow: Progress Publishers, 1983), vol. 3, p. 296.

3

Now let's turn to the second stage in the development of Marx's concept of alienation, which is the stage of transformation of perspective. In this stage, Marx creates the doctrine of historical materialism through in—depth studies in human history at the same time, he gradually shifts his perspective from "moral evaluation first" to "historical evaluation first" in his investigating of alienation.

In *The Holy Family*, Marx no longer agrees with the young Hegelians in seeing alienation as merely an idea, especially a moral one. Instead, he proposes to interpret it by investigating real historical activities. The change in perspective is displayed specifically in the following important exposition: "The propertied class and the class of the proletariat present the same human self-estrangement. But the former class feels at ease and strengthened, it recognizes estrangement as *its own power* and has in it the *semblance* of a human existence. The latter feels annihilated in estrangement; it sees in it its powerlessness and the reality of an inhuman existence."[①] Here, Marx begins to evaluate alienation objectively and from a historical perspective. His primary concern is not with the moral responsibilities of the propertied class for the wretched proletariat in estrangement, but with the fact that the former, too, is an objective and historical product of estrangement.

In *The German Ideology*, Marx states, "The proletariat can thus

---

① Karl Marx and Frederick Engels, *Selected Works* (New York: International Publishers, 1976), vol. 4, p. 36.

only exist *world-historically*, just as communism, its activity, can only have a 'world-historical' existence. World-historical existence of individuals, i. e. , existence of individuals which is directly linked up with world history."① This brilliant *aperçu* signifies that the young Marx's general assumption of communism and humanism on the basis of an abstract human essence has been transcended. He strips off the moral outfit of Feuerbach's humanistic theory and begins switching over to the stance of historical materialism. This implies that Marx begins to reject the approach of "moral evaluation first", which is detached from real history, as he observes and studies all social phenomena, including alienation. He writes, "The communists do not preach morality at all, as Stirner does so extensively."② In Marx's view, alienation is first and foremos a historical phenomenon instead of a purely psychological or moral one, therefore, any observation of alienation must take the correct understanding of real history as the starting point.

In his works such as "Circular Against Kriege," *The Poverty of Philosophy* and "Moralizing Criticism and Critical Morality," Marx further liquidates the abstract moral preaching of the "romantic school," the "humanist school," the "fraternal school", and the school of "true socialism", thereby clarifying their speculative basis and inadequacy. His perspective of "historical evaluation first" is expressed in the most concentrated way in this sentence from *Manifesto of the Communist Party*: "The bourgeoisie, historically, has played a most revolutionary part."③ Here Marx affirms

---

① Karl Marx and Frederick Engels, *Selected Works* (Moscow: Progress Publishers, 1983), vol. 5, p. 49.

② Karl Marx and Frederick Engels, *Selected Works* (Moscow: Progress Publishers, 1983), vol. 5, p. 247.

③ Karl Marx and Frederick Engels, *Selected Works* (Moscow: Progress Publishers, 1983), vol. 6, p. 486.

the objective historical role of the bourgeoisie as well as the objective historical significance of general alienation in capitalist societies. This clearly shows that Marx has extricated himself from the sentimentalism in which his youthful "moral evaluation first" is steeped, and that he now replaces this with the perspective of "historical evaluation first" as his starting point in treating social and historical phenomena (including alienation) in their entirety.

4

Finally, let's examine the third stage in the development of Marx's concept of alienation. Interestingly enough, this stage, which bears the richest and the most profound implications, has received the least scholarly attention. Here we focus on Marx's theory of alienation as is enunciated in the *Economic Manuscripts 1857–1858* and *Capital*.

Marx advances the well-known theory of "three social formations" in *Economic Manuscripts 1857–1858*. This theory has three layers of meaning. First, alienation and materialization came into being only after human history has progressed to the second social formation. Alienation and materialization, as certain form of historical phenomena, do have their objective niches in the real history. Second, alienation and materialization have positive historical significance, for they enable the formation of a "system of universal social material exchange, full relations, multiple demand and full-fledged ability." Third, based on material dependence, alienation at this stage provides objectively the material foundation for the third social formation—the communist society. It is out of this consideration that Marx writes in connection with the "universally developed individuals" that "the degree and universality of wealth where *this* individuality becomes possible supposes production on the basis of exchange values as a prior condition, whose universality produces not only the alienation of the individual from himself and others, but also the universality and the comprehensiveness of his relations and capacities."[1] In other words, universal alienation and the full development of individual abilities as two aspects of the course of human history must coincide. We shall not see alienation in capitalist society in terms of "moral evaluation first." Instead, we should prioritize "historical evaluation first" and see the positive significance of alienation in history. In fact, without the real and universal alienation serving as a medium, communism and fully-developed individuals would remain forever mythological. According to Marx, any attempt to talk about the full development of the individual without delving into universal alienation is nothing but a mere "romantic".

In *Capital*, Marx unfolded his concept of alienation in two directions: on the one hand, with the introduction of the new concept of "natural historical process", the principle of "historical evaluation first" is enunciated with greater clarity. In the preface to the first German edition of *Capital*, Marx writes, "I paint the capitalist and the landlord in no sense *couleur de rose*. But here individuals are dealt with only in so far as they are the personifications of economic categories, embodiments of particular class-relations and class-interests. My standpoint, from which the evolution of the economic formation of society is viewed as a process of natural history, can less than any other make the individual responsible for the relations whose creature he socially remains, however much he may subjectively raise him-

---

[1] Karl Marx and Frederick Engels, *Selected Works* (Moscow: Progress Publishers, 1983), vol. 28, Chapter II, Section 3.

self above them."[1] Here, Marx stresses that when we observe various social phenomena, including alienation in economic life, we should not prioritize individuals' subjective motives and moral responsibility in terms of abstract human nature or essence. Instead, we should take objective laws as the point of departure to explain how these phenomena (including alienation) were made possible at a specific stage in the course of historical development. In short, the focus of attention is objective historical movements and evaluations rather than subjective moral notions and abstract moral evaluation. In Marx's view, the reason vulgar economy loses its ability to criticize "the estranged outward appearances of economic relations"[2] lay just in its lack of the perspective of "historical evaluation first."

On the other hand, Marx devotes his efforts to exposing the most important form of alienation in the capitalist society—the fetishism of commodities, thus clearing away the last obstacle for the people to accept the theory of historical materialism. It is well known that philosophers always rest content with talking about "abstract matter," while Marx tells us that, in the historical formation of capitalism, the concrete form of abstract matter is the mountains of commodities. Moreover, "A commodity is therefore a mysterious thing, simply because in it the social character of men's labor appears to them as an objective character stamped upon the product of that labor; because the relation of the producers to the sum total of their own labor is presented to them as a social relationship, not

---

[1] Karl Marx, *Capital* (Moscow: Foreign Languages Publishing House, 1959), vol. 1, p. 10.

[2] Karl Marx, *Capital* (Moscow: Foreign Languages Publishing House, 1959), vol. 3, p. 817.

between themselves, but between the products of their labor. "① The core idea behind commodity fetishism, seen as a prime manifestation of alienation, is that product relationships obscure the genuine human relations, while the essence of historical materialism isn't to boast about "the world being unified in matter". Rather, it should expose the genuine relations between men beneath commodities, which are the concrete form of matter, and thereby bringing about a revolutionary transformation of capitalist society. In other words, even a huge number of textbooks about the philosophy of Marx can get published in this era of mechanical copying, people cannot go beyond the level of traditional materialism as embodied in d'Holbach nor step into the field of vision of historical materialism, and this is because they merely abandon themselves to abstract discourse on the materiality of the world. Going beyond traditional materialism and stepping into historical materialism are made possible only by delving into Marx's criticism of alienation, especially the fetishism of commodities. In a word, Marx's historical materialism never forsakes the concept of alienation (including fetishism); on the contrary, only through this concept does it fully achieves its theoretical integrity and displays its critical nature.

To sum up, the perspective of the Mature Marx completely shifts to "historical evaluation first" when observing the issue of alienation. Does this mean that Marx completely gave up the moral evaluation portion? No, he did not. In fact, moral evaluation and historical evaluation are unified by Marx at his mature age, but with priority given to historical evaluation.

---

① Karl Marx, *Capital* (Moscow: Foreign Languages Publishing House, 1959), vol. 2, p. 72.

5

The above discussions may lead us to the following three conclusions:

Firstly, the concept of alienation ran through Marx's theorizing all his life and carved an important niche in the theory of historical materialism. [1] Such being the case, then why in some of his works does he use the term alienation frequently, in others rarely, and in the rest never at all? An answer is not long coming. In fact, the phenomenon can be reasonably explained if we see it from another angle. Although he never ceases to use the concept of alienation, Marx knew clearly that it was an obscure philosophical jargon, difficult for lay people to grasp. So he distinguished texts of two different types when deciding whether to use the term or not. One is "texts for internal research," such as *Economic and Philosophic Manuscripts of 1844* and *Economic Manuscripts 1857-1858*, written for his own use. In both works, Marx uses the term "alienation" frequently. The other is "texts for publication and polemics." In these works, Marx seldom uses the concept of alienation. The reasons are simple. To enable lay readers, who do not know much about philosophy to grasp his ideas, Marx has to use the least possible highly technical jargon like "alienation." For the other, German writers at that time were especially wont to abuse the concept of alienation. In polemics with these people, in order to clearly

---

[1] Just as the former Soviet scholar Narkiss pointed out in his writing "On the Evolution of the Concept of 'Alienation' in the History of Philosophy," "We do not think it right for the category of alienation to be used outside the domain of social life. It is a category of historical materialism," Ref. Lu Meilin et al. , eds. , *Yihua Wenti* (*The Problem of Alienation*, Shanghai: Shanghai Literature and Art Publishing House, 1986), vol. 1, p. 214.

differentiate his outlook from his adversaries, Marx wisely avoided using the word "alienation." This difference in narration should by no means be mistaken as proof that Marx in his mature years forsake the concept of alienation. On the contrary, this skill of Marx as a great scholar to differentiate between methods of research and narration compels admiration from us. In fact, although the concept of alienation is seldom used by Marx in the second category of texts, its implications are strewn everywhere, which reminds us that what matters is essence and not forms.

Secondly, in investigating alienation and other social phenomena, historical materialism adheres to the principle of "historical evaluation first" while at the same time giving due consideration to moral evaluation. As two theoretical perspectives "historical evaluation first" and "moral evaluation first" are opposed to each other, but as two dimensions of evaluation they may be linked together. Neither can be substituted for the other. We have noticed that in the first stage of the evolution of Marx's concept of alienation, moral evaluation not only takes precedence, but is also in an absolutely dominant position, so it might be called a "strong factor of evaluation." Although historical evaluation was sometimes resorted to by the young Marx, it was in a marginal and weak position, so it might be called a "weak factor of evaluation." In the second stage of the evolution of Marx's concept of alienation, i. e., in the period of "change of perspectives," with change appearing in Marx's general train of thought, moral evaluation gradually loses the upper hand and degenerates into a "weak factor of evaluation." On the other hand, historical evaluation is on a steady rise and, as soon as the theoretical perspective of "historical evaluation first" is established, ascends into a "strong factor of evaluation." In the third evolutionary stage, historical evaluation takes full and undisputed precedence, but Marx does not give up moral evaluation. He furnished it enough leeway on a platform in conformity with objective demands of historical evaluation, thus eliminating the sentimentalism and romanticism common to past moral evaluations and giving it true realism.

Thirdly, in understanding Marx's concept of alienation, only when readers themselves have switched from the perspective of "moral" to that of "historical evaluation first", will the "perspective shift" underlying the evolution of Marx's concept of alienation become apparent. For a long time, in the studies of Marx's concept of alienation, the "moral evaluation first" perspective has always occupied a dominant position and people have habitually poured out their noble moral indignation and condemnation against the universal alienation in the capitalist society exposed by Marx. At the same time, however, due to the absence or marginalization of the dimension of historical evaluation, they have never seen the objective certainty of alienation as a historical phenomenon and the positive significance it contains. In fact, without universal alienation and materialization based on dependence on things, there would be no full-fledged development of individuals, to say nothing of a communist society based on such free personality. Of course, communism will sublate alienation through the abolition of private ownership, but it cannot do so before it comes into being. What really matters, therefore, is to observe and understand the objective historical phenomenon from the perspective of "historical evaluation first" and abstract and noble moral indignation is of no avail.

Popular grasp of Marx's concept of alienation has remained at the level of young Marx's understanding of the same concept, unaware of the development of Marx's concept of alienation itself and the fundamental "change of perspective" accomplished in the course of this development. History and practice show over and again that only when we have a good command of the theory of historical materialism, conscientiously study the works of the mature Marx, and shift our perspective to "historical evaluation first," will the true meaning of Marx's concept of alienation present itself to us.

1.4 Thing, Value, Time, and Freedom[①]

—A Consideration of Some Key Concepts in Marx's Philosophical System

Introduction

Based on the prior grasp of the three basic dimensions of Marx's philosophy, i. e., practice, e-conomy-philosophy, and ontology, the author has primarily found a new path to reconstruct Marx's philosophical system. Limited by theme and length, this paper will mainly discuss the important points following four key concepts and their interrelations in the reconstruction of Marx's philosophy—thing, value, time, and freedom.

From Abstract Matter to Concrete Things

The view of matter told by recent Chinese

---

① Editor's note: This paper was originally published in *Frontiers of Philosophy in China*, vol. 1, no. 1, 2006, pp. 114-123, translated by Tang Jie from *Zhexue Yanjiu* (《哲学研究》), no. 11, 2004, pp. 3-10.

textbooks on Marxist philosophy is a view of "abstract matter" that was criticized by Marx long ago.

In *Economic and Philosophic Manuscripts of 1844*, Marx wrote:

Industry is the real historical relationship of nature, and therefore of natural science, to man. If then it is conceived of as the open revelation of human faculties, then the human essence of nature or the natural essence of man will also be understood. Natural science will then lose its one-sidedly materialist [abstrakt materille], or rather idealistic, orientation and become the basis of human science as it has already, though in an alienated form, become the basis of actual human life. ①

It is notable here that Marx created the very important concept of "industry," and comprehended it as the necessary medium to enable scientific research to leave the "abstract material" orientation. In fact, real nature is the nature mediated by industry, whereas real matter is the matter mediated by human productive labor. Rather than something else, industry is an open book concerning the essential force of humanity, and it is just the concrete exhibition of human practice, especially of human productive labor.

In *Capital*, Marx further pointed out: "The weakness of the abstract materialism of natural science, a materialism which excludes the historical process, are immediately evident from the abstract and ideological conceptions expressed by its spokesmen whenever they venture beyond the

---

① Marx, "Economic and philosophical manuscripts of 1844," in McLellan D. (ed.), *Karl Marx: Selected Writings* (Oxford: Oxford University Press, 2000), p. 102.

bounds of their own specialty".① This indicates that the essential difference of Marx's view of matter from all the former philosophers, whether materialists or idealists, consists in this: Marx never abstractly talked about matter beyond human activities, i. e., never talked about the materiality of the world as recent Chinese textbooks on Marxist philosophy did. Marx always took the most basic practice, i. e., the productive labor, as his starting point, and he historically explored the concrete configuration of matter, i. e., *concrete* thing, and thereby carried out a critical examination on the prevailing phenomena of "reification" and "fetishism" that arose from the capitalist economical relations.

We should see that some contemporary Western scholars have observantly noticed and disclosed the practical and revolutionary tendency of Marx's view of matter. From the point of view of Lukacs, the keystone of Marx's view of matter is not to talk loudly in a classroom about "world being unified in matter," a dogma also held by the old materialists, but rather through disclosing the reification phenomenon and reification consciousness to arouse the class consciousness of the proletariat, and thereby to impel them to recast the capitalist society in the way of practice. When talking about Marx, Gramsci pointed out:

Clearly, for the philosophy of praxis, "matter" should be understood neither in the meaning that it has acquired in natural science nor in any of the meanings that one finds in the various materialistic metaphysics. The various physical (chemical, mechanical etc.) properties of matter which together constitute matter itself should be considered, but only to the extent that they become a productive "economical

---

① Marx, *Capital*, vol. 1 (New York: Vintage Books, 1977), p. 494, footnote.

element". Matter as such therefore is not our subject but how it is
socially and historically organized for production, and natural sci-
ence should be seen correspondingly as essentially a historical catego-
ry, a human relation. ①

Heidegger, when talking about how to deal with Marx's materialism,
made a very important point: to engage Marx's system, one needs to get
rid of such naive ideas about materialism and such simple denials of it. The
nature of such materialism consists not in the assertion that everything is
material (Stoff) but in a metaphysical prescription according to which all
beings appear as materials (Material) of labor. ② Schmidt, in his representative work, *Marx's Concept of Nature*, continually expressed the
same notion:

> *It is not just because the working Subjects mediate the material of nature*
> *through themselves that it is impossible to speak of matter as a supreme*
> *principle of being. Men are not concerned in their production with matter*
> *"as such," but always with its concrete, quantitatively and qualitatively*
> *determined forms of existence.* ③

All these opinions indicate that the essential difference between Marx
and old materialists consists in the fact that Marx did not talk about abstract matter from a static epistemological point of view; instead, he

---

① Gramsci, *Selections from the Prison Notebooks* (New York: International Publishers, 1971), pp. 465-466.

② See Heidegger, *Ueber Den Humanismus* (Frankfurt A. M.: Suhrkamp Verlag,
1975), p. 27.

③ Schmidt, *Marx's Concept of Nature* (London: New Left Books, 1971), p. 34.

talked about modes of concrete matter as factors of production, i. e. , concrete things, from a dynamical view of practice. In fact, Marx never indulged himself in tracing a material world that existed before the emergence of human beings, just as what the old materialists and later editors of textbooks on Marxist philosophy did. For Marx, there is no significance for men to trace a material world independent of them. Thus, Marx pointed out: "I can in practice only relate myself humanly to an object if the object relates itself humanly to man."① On all accounts, things are not objects of man's static observation but are factors of human practice, especially of productive labor.

Then, what does Marx mean by concrete things? Owing to the fact that his starting point is not human society in general but the special social system of capitalism, Marx thinks that, in capitalist economic relations, the concrete things appear as a huge accumulation of commodities. He wrote: "the commodity (die Ware) is, first of all, an external object, a thing (ein Ding) which through its qualities satisfies human needs of whatever kind."② As soon as commodities as things are produced in a great mass, the phenomenon of "reification" or "fetishism" spreads out. Through his research, Marx profoundly reveals the essence of these phenomena:

The form of wood, for instance, is altered if a table is made out of it. Nevertheless the table continues to be wood, an ordinary, sensuous thing. But as soon as it emerges as a commodity, it changes into a thing which transcends sensuousness. It not only stands with its feet

---

① Marx, "Economic and philosophical manuscripts of 1844," in McLellan D. (ed.), *Karl Marx: Selected Writings* (Oxford: Oxford University Press, 2000), p. 100.

② Marx, *Capital*, vol. 1 (New York: Vintage Books, 1977), p. 125.

on the ground, but, in relation to all other commodities, it stands on
its head, and evolves out of its wooden brain grotesque ideas, far
more wonderful than if it were to begin dancing of its own free
will. ①

Thus, it can be seen that the practical and revolutionary orientation of
Marx's view of matter just consists in the critique of the widely spreading
phenomena of "reification" or "fetishism" in capitalist society and in the
disclosure of the real relations between people from the relations between
things. The editors of recent Chinese textbooks on Marxist philosophy satisfy themselves with abstractly talking about "world being unified in matter," a view already held by old materialists; this will hinder our grasp of
that essential orientation of Marx's view of matter. What is more important is that Marx elicited the concept of value not through abstract matter
but concrete things.

From Use Value to Exchange Value

As stated above, in capitalist economic relations, concrete things appear as a huge accumulation of commodities. Then, how did Marx eco-
nomically-philosophically look into the commodity, the cell of capitalist society? He thinks that the thing as commodity has two basic properties:
firstly, "the usefulness of a thing makes it a use-value (Gebrauch-
swert)."② That is to say, the thing as commodity always meets certain

---

① Marx, *Capital*, vol. 1 (New York: Vintage Books, 1977), pp. 163-164.
② Marx, *Capital*, vol. 1 (New York: Vintage Books, 1977), p. 126.

human needs, whereas its "use value" is just realized in the process of men's consuming or using it. "Riches" (Reichtums) in the normal sense indeed means a pile of things as commodities. In this sense, for Marx, use value always constitutes the material content of riches, no matter what social form riches take. Secondly, "'exchange-value' (Tauschwert) appears first of all as the quantitative relation, the proportion, in which use-values of one kind exchange for use-values of another kind. This relation changes constantly with time and place."[①] The thing as commodity has exchange value just because the commodity itself is produced for exchange. For Marx, there are two essential differences between use value and exchange value: first, use value is commodity's natural property or natural being, whereas exchange value is commodity's social property or social being; second, as use value, different commodities are different from each other in quality, whereas as exchange value, different commodities are different from each other only in quantity. It is very important to recognize these two points.

We must point out that there have been always misunderstandings of Marx's theory of value in philosophical circles. This could be seen from Marx's *Marginal notes on Adolf Wagner's Textbook of political economy*, which he wrote in his later years. An essential error of Wagner is that he mistakes Marx's "use value" for "value." When recounting this wrong understanding of Wagner, Marx recapitulated: " the general concept 'value' arises from the behavior of men towards the things found in the external world which satisfy their needs … "[②] Obviously, this sentence is Marx's generalization of Wagner's wrong view, but people mistake it for

---

① Marx, *Capital*, vol. 1 (New York: Vintage Books, 1977), p. 126.

② Marx, " 'Notes' on Adolph Wagner," in *Marx: Later Political Writings* (Cambridge: Cambridge University Press, 1996), p. 236.

Marx's own view of value. ① As a matter of fact, so long as we have read this paper in earnest, we would find that Marx very sharply criticized Wagner's theory of value, accusing that Wagner was keen on talking about a general theory of value and always intended to show his brightness by using the word "value". In addition, this "enables him to stick with the traditional German academic confusion of 'use-value', and 'value', since both have the word 'value' in common." ②

From the point of view of Marx, use value "does not play the role of its opposite number, of 'value', which has nothing in common with it, other than that [the word] 'value' appears in the term 'use-value'." ③ Marx here tells us explicitly that we should not assert that "use value" is just "value" simply on the basis that the name of "use value" contains the word "value." There is an essential difference between "use value" and "exchange value," which Marx usually called "value" for short.

Indeed, when Wagner tried to understand and talk about Marx's theory of value from the relation between people's needs and external things, he confused these two concepts. Marx revealed ruthlessly the language game played by Wagner:

> He achieves this by re-christening what in political economy is commonly called "use-value" as "value" pure and simple, "according to German usage." And as soon as "value" pure and simple has been found, it serves in turn for deriving "use value" again from "value pure

---

① Li Lianke, *Introduction to Philosophy of Value* (Beijing: The Commercial Press, Ltd., 1999), p. 63.

② Marx, "'Notes' on Adolph Wagner," in *Marx: Later Political Writings* (Cambridge: Cambridge University Press, 1996), p. 231.

③ Marx, "'Notes' on Adolph Wagner," in *Marx: Later Political Writings* (Cambridge: Cambridge University Press, 1996), p. 242.

and simple. " For that, one has only to replace the fragment "use, " which has been dropped, in front of "value" pure and simple. ①

To thoroughly disclose the possible confusions that arose from Wagner's *Textbook of political economy*, Marx points out:

The one thing that is clearly at the basis of this German idiocy is that linguistically the words "value" or "worth" were employed at first for useful things themselves, which existed for a long time just as "labor-products, " before they came to be commodities. But that has nothing to do with the scientific definition of commodity-"value. " ②

People may ask, why did Marx elucidate again and again the difference between "use value" and "value" (i. e., "exchange value")? Here, his point is that the "use value" only refers to the natural properties or natural being of the thing as commodity, whereas value or exchange value refers to the social properties or social being of the thing as a commodity. It indicates two different orientations in the discussions of the theory of value in Marx's philosophy.

For traditional Chinese textbooks on Marxist philosophy, the problem of value is ignored. Since the 1980s, people have begun to explore value theory contained in Marx's philosophy. However, Wagner's misunderstanding, which identifies "use value" with "value, " has always dominated

---

① Marx, "'Notes' on Adolph Wagner, " in *Marx: Later Political Writings* (Cambridge: Cambridge University Press, 1996), p. 237.

② Marx, "'Notes' on Adolph Wagner, " in *Marx: Later Political Writings* (Cambridge: Cambridge University Press, 1996), p. 245.

people's minds. So long as this kind of misunderstanding is not eliminated, what people are concerned with will always be the "use value" as the natural property of things, and this will result in people's indifference to "value" as the social property of things. Nevertheless, in a certain sense, all the secrets of Marx's philosophy of economy are concealed in its theory of "value." Why would we say this?

If "use value" is only concerned with the relation between men and the natural properties of things, in short, the relation between men and things, then "value" (i. e., exchange value) is concerned with the relation between men and the social properties of things, in short, the relation between people. In the economic domain, just as Marx pointed out: "exchange-values" (*exchange-value* does not exist unless [there are] at least two of them) represent something *common to them* [commodities] which is wholly independent 'of their use-values' (i. e. here, of their natural form), namely value."① That is to say, in the economic domain, the concrete expression of value is the exchange value, which is concerned with interpersonal economic relations. Beyond the economic domain, value is concerned with a series of important notions representing interpersonal relations, such as human rights, life, feelings, convictions, goodness, equality, democracy, freedom, justice, and so on. In fact, for Marx, the essence of the value problem never consists in the relation between people and things but in the relation between people.

For a long time, Chinese philosophers understood Marx's theory of value only by appealing to the "use value," i. e., the relation between people's needs and available things. This limitation has resulted in the fact

---

① Marx, "'Notes' on Adolph Wagner," in *Marx: Later Political Writings* (Cambridge: Cambridge University Press, 1996), p. 230.

that our research on the "exchange value" in the economic domain was neglected, and the fact that our research on the series of value forms concerning the relations between people outside the economic domain was neglected. Indifference to these two aspects not only made it hard for people to gain a real understanding of Marx's theory of value but also made the reconstruction of Marx's philosophical system along his own line of thought impossible. Actually, without encountering the problem of value, especially without encountering the problem of "exchange value" in the economic domain, we will not be able to understand Marx's view of time, which is my next topic.

From Natural Time to Social Time

Concerning the problem of time, all recent Chinese textbooks on Marxist philosophy focused on natural time. The so-called "natural time" means time understood and illustrated according to the mode of matter's motion taking place in nature. This natural time, separated from human activities, cannot historically show the connotational difference of the concepts of time in various societies, and it cannot profoundly demonstrate the special social and historical meaning of the theory of time in capitalist societies and its intrinsic relation to the important theoretical problems of value and freedom. This concept of time did not make a thorough critique and clarification of the theoretical assumptions of the old materialistic concept of time; that is to say, it only methodologically tried to overcome the mechanical characteristic of the traditional concept of time, but it did not make any fundamental transformations of the abstract carrier of the traditional concept of time (i. e., abstract matter separated from human activities of practice). In this way, Marx's originative theory of time was put on the basis of traditional materialism, and thus, its epoch-making significance was concealed.

Marx's view of time is not a view of natural time held by traditional philosophy and the textbooks of Marxist philosophy but a view of "social time." In other words, Marx's view of time did not take the static observation of human beings on motions of matter in nature as its starting point but took human practice of production as its starting point.

According to Marx, we should not illustrate human productive labor on the basis of abstract matter and the view of natural time; instead, we should understand and illustrate the problem of matter and time on the basis of productive labor. It is in the process of productive labor that abstract matter separated from human beings transforms into the basic factors of production (e.g., factory buildings and equipments of production, raw materials of production, instruments of production, products, castoffs of the process of production, etc.) immediately and consequently appears as human-related existence. In the capitalist mode of production, the general form of matter is commodity, and commodity is created by labor. Hence, Marx said, "labor is the living, form-giving fire; it is the transience of things, their temporality, as the process of their formation by living time."① Noticeably, Marx mentions "living time" here. This living time is in accordance with productive labor as "living, form-giving fire" and it endows matter with "form." From this important passage, we can draw the following three conclusions:

First of all, social time originates in human productive labor. As

---

① Karl Marx and Frederick Engels, *Collected Works*, vol. 28 (Moscow: Progress Publishers, 1986), p. 286.

pointed out by C. C. Gould, "for Marx, labor is the origin of time—both of human time-consciousness and of the objective measure of time."① In other words, it is labor that created time and brought it into the world. Gould thinks that Marx's view of time and that of Kant's have something in common; that is, they both start from human activities. However, Kant sets off from human activities of consciousness, whereas Marx sets off from human productive labor. As for Heidegger, although he discussed time on the basis of the existent activities of "Dasein itself," he "comprehended the temporal activities of Dasein not as the objectifying activities and not as social activities which change the nature."② This is the fundamental difference between his theory of time and that of Marx's.

Secondly, social time is different from uniformly flowing natural time; it has different essential characteristics in different phases of history. Gould noticed: "Marx further suggests that the use of time as a measure varies historically. Thus it might be said that for him time is itself qualitatively different at different stages of social development".③ In the precapitalist phase, labor was measured not by time but by the different use values of goods. Only when society developed into, as Marx mentioned, the second phase, that is to say, the phase of capitalism, "the possibility of time as a measure for labor arises."④ In addition, in the third phase of social development, i. e., the communist society depicted by Marx, what constitutes a kind of measurement of abundance is precisely "free time or time for the free development of individualities. In this society,

---

① C. C. Gould, *Marx's Social Ontology* (Boston: The MIT Press, 1978), p. 41.
② Heidegger, *Ueber Den Humanismus* (Frankfurt A. M.: Suhrkamp Verlag, 1975), p. 62.
③ C. C. Gould, *Marx's Social Ontology* (Boston: The MIT Press, 1978), p. 64.
④ C. C. Gould, *Marx's Social Ontology* (Boston: The MIT Press, 1978), p. 64.

labor becomes the creative activity of self-realization, which according to Marx is 'real freedom'."①

Thirdly, the essential mode of social time in the domain of economy is "socially necessary labor-time [Gesellschaftlich notwendige Arbeitszeit]." As is known, the goal of capitalist production is exchange value, but the quantity of value of the commodity as the ground of the exchange value is measured by "socially necessary labor-time." Marx says, "socially necessary labor-time is the labor-time required to produce any use-value under the conditions of production normal for a given society and with the average degree of skill and intensity of labor prevalent in that society."②

For Marx, socially necessary labor-time is objective, for it is determined not by any individual producer of commodity with his own subjective desire but is demonstrated in certain historical conditions. This time is like a special kind of ether, determining the proportion of all the "social things" (gesellschaftliche Dinge, i.e., commodity) in the lifeworld: "what exclusively determines the magnitude of the value of any article is therefore the amount of labor socially necessary, or the labor-time socially necessary for its production."③ From this statement, we can also see that Marx's "social time" is always related to "exchange value" of the commodity as social being. Both the denial of the problem of value made by the writers of recent Chinese textbooks on Marxist philosophy and the misunderstanding made by contemporary scholars of axiology, who mistook value for "use value," are obstacles for a precise understanding of Marxist philosophy.

We can see from what we have discussed above that Marx never speaks of the problem of time metaphysically beyond all the historical

---

① C. C. Gould, *Marx's Social Ontology* (Boston: The MIT Press, 1978), p. 68.
② Marx, *Capital*, vol. 1 (New York: Vintage Books, 1977), p. 129.
③ Marx, *Capital*, vol. 1 (New York: Vintage Books, 1977), p. 129.

conditions but always considers this problem under the special social and historical conditions of the capitalist society. The epoch-breaking significance of Marx's view of "social time" consists in that he offered the new concept of "socially necessary labor-time" and revealed the secret of the value of commodity, and with this new concept, he divided worker's productive process into "necessary labor time" and "surplus labor time," and thus revealed the secret of "surplus value." The importance of Marx's view of "social time" consists also in that the problem of freedom, which we will discuss below, is precisely developed on this kind of special horizon of time, and since recent Chinese textbooks on Marxist philosophy did not understand Marx's view of time correctly, Marx's view of freedom and his discussion of the relation between freedom and time are all outside their field of vision.

From epistemological freedom to ontological freedom

The concept of freedom is very important in Marx's philosophy, but it has been misunderstood for a long time. As we all know, former Soviet philosophers М. Розеиталя and П. Юдина defined freedom in their *A Small Dictionary of Philosophy* as such:

> *Freedom consists not in the escape from natural laws in imagine, but in the knowledge of them and in the ability to apply them to practice … the necessity and regularity of nature are primary, whereas the human will and consciousness are secondary. People act blindly and unwarily before they know the necessity. But they will learn how to control the necessity and to use it to serve the society once they get to know it.*

Therefore, free activity is possible only on the basis of knowledge about necessity. Freedom is nothing but the necessity which is recognized. ①

This is a typical understanding, and almost every textbook on Marxist philosophy expounds the concept of freedom in the same way. We can infer three conclusions from these sentences: first, Marx's concept of freedom belongs to epistemology, and the ontological implication of freedom has hardly been appreciated. Secondly, freedom is connected with necessity, i.e., the natural regularity. Thirdly, freedom is not the escape from the necessity of nature in imagination but the correct knowledge of necessity.

At first sight, it is worthy of no rebuke to understand the concept of freedom epistemologically, because the more deeply we know the necessity of nature, the more freely we act and know. Actually, such a view is completely specious. For if it were true, we would infer from it that the scientists are the freest, since they are most acquainted with the necessity of nature. Furthermore, it would be nonsense for people to strive for freedom and liberty through social movement and revolution, and what is required for them to do would just be to study sciences. Thus, the concept of freedom, though it is so important to human existence, degenerates into a mere epistemological concept. Led by such a concept, even ethics could not be set up, for the free will of human beings is the basis of ethics, and if freedom is nothing but the knowledge of necessity, nobody needs to be morally responsible for his own behavior.

It is well known that epistemology is concerned with the relation

---

① М. Розенталя and П. Юдина, *A Small Dictionary of Philosophy* (Beijing: SDX Joint Publishing Company, 1973), pp. 171-172.

between human-beings and nature, while ontology deals with the relationship among individual human-beings. Kant expressly said: "independence from the determining causes of the world of sense (an independence which reason must always ascribe to itself) is freedom."[1] Actually, Sartre, a contemporary philosopher, explained more definitely: "there is no determinism—man is free, man is freedom."[2] That is to say, people's freedom has nothing to do with people's knowledge of the sensuous world but is related only to the ontological domain, to the free will of man. In Kant's opinion, if someone persists in speaking of freedom on the basis of natural necessity, such freedom "is just like a revolving brochette, it can revolve automatically by itself once someone winds it."[3]

Marx accepted Kant's conception, and his idea of freedom should above all be ontologically elucidated, i. e., people live in the world first of all as agents with free will, and then they come to know things according to his own intention for living. Marx wrote: "as pure ideas, equality and freedom are merely idealized expressions of this exchange; developed in juridical, political and social relations, they are merely this basis at a higher level."[4] This important passage shows that Marx regarded the philosophy of economy as an entrance to reveal the ontological meaning of the concept of freedom and that from the beginning, he linked the concept of freedom closely with that of time, interpreted time as the horizon on which freedom

---

[1] Kant, *Foundations of the Metaphysics of Morals* (New York: The Macmillan Publishing Company, 1989), p. 71.

[2] Sartre, *Existentialism and Humanism* (London: Eyre Methuen Ltd., 1978), p. 34.

[3] Kant, *Kritik der praktischen Vernunft* (Frankfurt A. M.: Suhrkamp Verlag, 1989), p. 222.

[4] Karl Marx and Frederick Engels, *Collected Works*, vol. 28 (Moscow: Progress Publishers, 1986), p. 176.

can be actually unfolded.

Marx wrote: "time is in fact the active existence of the human being. It is not only the measure of human life. It is the space for its development."[1] This is to say that time is ontologically the necessary condition under which human beings achieve freedom. If men spend all their time (except for time used on their necessary sleep) on earning their living, it is impossible for them to have any freedom. As a result, human freedom or "human positive existence" is just based on the time, which could actually be freely disposed by humans. Marx further maintained: "in relation to the whole of society, the production of *disposable time* [can] also [be considered] as the creation of time for the production of science, art, etc."[2] For Marx, the development of science, art, and other public activities of humans are all realized in the free time of society, and "the free time of society is based on the absorption of the worker's time by compulsory labor; thus he loses room for intellectual development, for that is time."[3]

Then, how does such a condition of time come into being? Marx's answer is: "wage labor, in general, makes its appearance only when the productive power has already been developed to such an extent that a significant amount of time has been set free. This setting-free is already a historical product here."[4] Actually, it is the capitalistic mode of production that "can dissociate considerable amount of time," and this creates the

---

① Karl Marx and Frederick Engels, *Collected Works*, vol. 33 (Moscow: Progress Publishers, 1991), p. 493.

② Karl Marx and Frederick Engels, *Collected Works*, vol. 28 (Moscow: Progress Publishers, 1986), p. 328.

③ Karl Marx and Frederick Engels, *Collected Works*, vol. 30 (Moscow: Progress Publishers, 1988), p. 301.

④ Karl Marx and Frederick Engels, *Collected Works*, vol. 29 (Moscow: Progress Publishers, 1987), p. 29.

conditions for some people to possess other people's time, in other words, for some people to deprive others of their freedom. Just in this sense, Marx said, "the theft of alien labor time, which is the basis of present wealth."[1] On the one hand, the capitalists amass their own capital and wealth through the value produced by the workers' surplus labor time; on the other hand, they also deprive workers of freedom through usurping surplus labor time of the workers.

It is doubtless that Marx's philosophy, as a revolutionary philosophy, primarily strives for the workers' time and freedom. Thus, Marx wrote in his *Capital*: "a realm of necessity, beyond it begins that development of human energy which is an end in itself, the true realm of freedom, which, however, can blossom forth with this realm of necessity as its basis. The shortening of the working-day is its basic prerequisite."[2] Here, "the shortening of the working-day" means the shortening of the workers' labor time. For Marx, this is the "basic prerequisite" for workers to have access to freedom, because "the saving of labor time is equivalent to the increase of free time, i. e. time for the full development of the individual."[3] We can see from the above analysis that, in Marx's philosophy, freedom and time are inseparably related to each other.

Marcuse had a profound understanding of Marx's theory of time and freedom. He divided modern people's ordinary living time into two parts: one is "working time" (Arbeitzeit), i. e., the time people have to spend to earn a living, the other is "free time" (Freizeit), i. e., the leisure time that

---

① Karl Marx and Frederick Engels, *Collected Works*, vol. 29 (Moscow: Progress Publishers, 1987), p. 91.

② Marx, *Capital*, vol. 3, in Mclellan D. (ed.), *Karl Marx: Selected Writings* (Oxford: Oxford University Press, 2000), p. 535.

③ Karl Marx and Frederick Engels, *Collected Works*, vol. 29 (Moscow: Progress Publishers, 1987), p. 97.

people can freely dispose after work. He wrote: "The first precondition of freedom is to decrease the working-time so as to make the amount of mere working-time no longer block the human development."[1] These words show that Marcuse understood not only the philosophical meaning of Marx's theory of time developed in his theory of economy but also the interrelationship between Marx's doctrine of freedom and that of time. Through an analysis of the increasingly stronger phenomenon of automatization in the modern capitalistic society, he pointed out that the automatization would be likely to reverse the relation between free time and working time, which is the foundation of the existing civilization; that is, it is possible to minimize the working time and to make the free time be the dominant time. That reversal would lead to the radical revaluation of various values. He wrote thus: "after being free from the requirements of ruling, the quantitative decrease of working-time and working-energy will lead to a qualitative change of human existence: what determines the existent contents of human will be the free time, rather than the working time."[2] As a matter of fact, what Marcuse expounded here is the idea expressed by Marx. When he talked about the future society, Marx said, "then wealth is no longer measured by labor time but by disposable time."[3]

Although he harshly criticized various phenomena of alienation in modern civilization (which are even embodied in the control of men's free time), Marcuse still maintained that both the development of technology

---

[1]   Marcuse, *Triebstrukur und Gesellschaft* (Frankfurt A. M.: Suhrkamp Verlag, 1970), p. 152.

[2]   Marcuse, *Triebstrukur und Gesellschaft* (Frankfurt A. M.: Suhrkamp Verlag, 1970), p. 218.

[3]   Karl Marx and Frederick Engels, *Collected Works*, vol. 29 (Moscow: Progress Publishers, 1987), p. 94.

and the decrease of working time prepare the objective conditions for modern people to enjoy more freedom. From the above considerations, we can conclude that the essence of Marx's idea of freedom can only be brought to light from an ontological point of view.

In a word, by means of the four key concepts, "thing", "value", "time", and "freedom", we have sketched the new path to the reconstruction of Marx's system of philosophy. Of course, this reconstruction process is very complicated, and many theoretical problems are still open to exploration. We look forward to scholars' comments.

1.5 Inspirations from Marx's Diagnosis of Modernity[①]

As is well known, Marx left a tremendously rich intellectual heritage. Even though J. F. Lyotard, one of the world's leading post-modernists, regarded Marxism in its legitimate form as "meta-narrative" that must be rejected, he nonetheless admitted that Marxism could also develop into a critical form of knowledge.[②] In fact, a lot of contemporary researchers believe that Marx was a true forerunner of critical reflection on modernity. For example, Best and Kellner point out in *The Postmodern Turn*(1997) that Karl Marx was the first social theorist to develop the concepts of modernity and pre-modernity and evolve full theoretical viewpoints on modernity.[③] Although Marx never directly used the term "modernity", his profound insight into the modern society characterized

---

① Editor's note: This paper was originally published in *Social Sciences in China*, no. 2, 2005, pp. 3-11, translated by Feng Yihan from *Zhongguo Shehui Kexue* (《中国社会科学》), no. 1, 2005, pp. 4-10, revised by Sally Borthwick.

② J. F. Lyotard, *The Postmodern Condition: A Report on Knowledge* (Minnesota: University of Minnesota Press, 1984).

③ S. Best and D. Kellner, *The Postmodern Turn* (New York: Guilford, 1997).

by capitalism contained a comprehensive indirect diagnosis of modernity.

It must be pointed out that Marx's diagnosis of modernity was undertaken from a special perspective, the perspective of economic philosophy, which determines the particularity of the concepts used by Marx. However, it is this special perspective that enabled Marx to have a firm grasp of the essence of modernity and put a full picture of it clearly before the eyes of his readers. Even today it still possesses an undying appeal and offers profoundly stimulating insights.

Deification of Commodities:
The Starting Point of the Diagnosis of Modernity

Marx's diagnosis of modernity began with the most common thing in everyday life in modern society—the commodity. In the first volume of his great work *Capital*, he pointed out at the very beginning, "The wealth of those societies in which the capitalist mode of production prevails, presents itself as 'an immense accumulation of commodities,' its unit being a single commodity. Our investigation must therefore begin with the analysis of a commodity."[1] In the view of Marx, a commodity as an object outside us, is a thing that by its properties satisfies human wants of some sort or another. A commodity has two fundamental properties: use-value, i.e., its utility, which is its natural existence, and exchange-value, i.e., its capacity for being exchanged, which is its social existence.

In the opinion of Marx, a commodity appears, at first sight, a very

---

[1] Karl Marx, *Capital*, vol. 1 (Moscow, Foreign Languages Publishing House, 1959), p. 35.

trivial thing, and easily understood. Analysis shows that it is, in reality, a very queer thing, abounding in metaphysical subtleties and theological strangeness. "The form of wood, for instance, is altered, by making a table out of it. Yet, for all that, the table continues to be that common, everyday thing, wood. But so soon as it steps forth as a commodity, it is changed into something transcendent. It not only stands with its feet on the ground, but, in relation to all other commodities, it stands on its head, and evolves out of its wooden brain grotesque ideas, far more wonderful than 'table-turning' ever was."[1] In the eyes of Marx, the mystical character of commodities, the appearance of the fetishism of commodities, does not originate in their use-value, but in an illusion: "A commodity … in it the social character of men's labor appears to them as an objective character stamped upon the product of that labor; because the relation of the producers to the sum total of their own labor is presented to them as a social relation, existing not between themselves, but between the products of their labor."[2]

As a result of this widespread false impression, the fetishism of commodities constitutes the everyday consciousness of modern society and a basic notion of modernity. In the view of Marx, modern society is positioned chiefly for the production of exchange value. As a particular commodity, money, the universal equivalent in exchange activities, brings about tremendous changes to the life of modern era, and along with these changes its enigmatic character becomes more conspicuous. "Hence the riddle presented by money is but the riddle presented by commodities; only

---

[1] Karl Marx, *Capital*, vol. 1 (Moscow, Foreign Languages Publishing House, 1959), p. 71.

[2] Karl Marx, *Capital*, vol. 1 (Moscow, Foreign Languages Publishing House, 1959), p. 72.

it now strikes us in its most glaring form." [①] In the eyes of Marx, the fetishism of money is the completed form of the fetishism of commodities, for it tightly covers with the form of natural objects the social properties of individual labor and the social relations of individual laborers.

Needless to say, from the perspective of economic and practical philosophy, and contrary to what is said in traditional philosophy textbooks, Marx did not rest content with grandiose talk about the proposition that "the universe is unified in matter," but tried to reveal the real social relations among individuals in modern society through his analyses of the commodity (the concrete form of matter in this society) and the phenomena of fetishism of the commodity (including the fetishism of money). This incisive critical consciousness heralded an essential and correct approach to the interpretation of modernity. Just as the contemporary scholar David Frisby pointed out in his *Fragments of Modernity* (1985), Marx's analysis of commodities directly involved a methodological approach of starting with fragments of social reality in the study of modernity. [②] It must, of course, be noted that what Marx was concerned about was not the "fragments" of modern society, but its general characteristics and developmental trend.

Georg Simmel, the German sociologist, in his book *The Philosophy of Money* (1900) continued Marx's analysis of the phenomena of commodities and money and further brought to light the economic origins of modernity and modern consciousness. Then, the French scholar Debord also inherited Marx's reflection on the phenomenon of modernity in his representative work *The Society of the Spectacle* (1967). He said, "The spectacle is the stage at which the commodity has succeeded in totally colonizing

---

① Karl Marx, *Capital*, vol. 1 (Moscow, Foreign Languages Publishing House, 1959), p. 93.

② David Frisby, *Fragments of Modernity* (Cambridge: Polity Press, 1985).

social life. Commodification is not only visible, we no longer see anything else; the world we see is the world of the commodity."[1] The slight difference between the two is that Marx set out to understand the ubiquity of commodities from the perspective of the material life of contemporary people while Debord used the new concept of "situation" to emphasize the fact that every inch of contemporary life, including consumption, leisure, recreation, media orientation and the mental experience of contemporaries is swayed by commodities. This omnipresent "situation" becomes the perceptual way in which modernity is manifest.

J. Baudrillard, the French philosopher who came under the heavy influence of Debord and other Situationists, wrote in his book *The Consumer Society: Myths and Structures* (1970), "Today there exists around us an astonishing phenomenon of consumption and abundance consisting of ever growing objects, service and material wealth. It constitutes a fundamental change in the natural environment. To put it rightly, wealthy people are no longer surrounded by men, they are now surrounded by objects."[2] If Baudrillard followed Marx's thinking in this book and emphasized commodities and the psychological analysis of the fetishism of commodities, he moved away from Marx in his later books *Towards a Critique of the Political Economy of the Sign* (1972) and *The Mirror of Production* (1973) and began to criticize Marx. He opined that the analyses of commodities by Marx was premised on human needs and production, i.e., Marx's diagnosis of modernity was still confined to the "mirror of production" while contemporary society has developed into a consumer society, in which

---

① G. Debord, *Society of the Spectacle*, http://www.marxists.org/reference/archive/debord/society.htm.

② J. Baudrillard, *The Consumer Society: Myths and Structures* (London: Sage, 1970), http://www.sagepub.co.uk.

commodities have changed into signs, the exchange of commodities has changed into "symbolic exchange" and the fetishism of commodities has also been replaced by the fetishism of signs. Here Baudrillard attempted to transcend Marx by borrowing the terms of semiotics, but Marx even foresaw this possibility. As every one knows, Marx wrote when he discussed money, a particular form of commodity, "Hence, in this process which continually makes money pass from hand to hand, the mere symbolic existence of money suffices."[1]

It can be seen from the above that it is Marx's commodities and the fetishism of commodities that provided a solid starting point for contemporary reflection on modernity.

The Logic of Capital: The Core of Diagnosis of Modernity

If we say that the analysis of commodities is the starting point of Marx's diagnosis of modernity, then we can say the analysis of capital is the core of his diagnosis of modernity. In the view of Marx, capital is not a stationary object to be observed, but a dynamic movement. And the logic of capital movement is to unlimitedly multiply and expand itself. Needless to say, this logic of capital movement is based on the unrestrained desire of capitalists to seek wealth. It is in this sense that Marx often called capitalists "personified capital."[2] Speaking more generally, the whole bourgeoisie

---

[1] Karl Marx, *Capital*, vol. 1 (Moscow, Foreign Languages Publishing House, 1959), p. 129.

[2] Karl Marx, *Capital*, vol. 1 (Moscow, Foreign Languages Publishing House, 1959), p. 309.

may be seen as the personification of capital. The above logic of capital movement leads to the following:

First, the everlasting movement of capital makes the modern world turbulent. "Constant revolutionizing of production, uninterrupted disturbance of social conditions, everlasting uncertainty and agitation distinguish the bourgeois epoch from all earlier ones. All fixed, fast-frozen relations, with their train of ancient and venerable prejudices and opinions are swept away, all new-formed ones become antiquated before they can ossify. All that is solid melts into air, all that is holy is profaned, and man is at last compelled to face with sober senses, his real conditions of life, and his relations with his kind."[①] According to Marx's diagnosis, the reason capital gives rise to an uncertain modern society is that it can only survive under such conditions. In fact, it could not have survived if it had not continuously revolutionized all social relations. Here Marx diagnosed in an incisive way everlasting uncertainty and agitation as one of the symptoms of modernity.

Second, wherever it has got the upper hand, capital has put an end to all feudal, patriarchal, idyllic relations. "It has left remaining no other nexus between man and man than naked self-interest, than callous 'cash payment'."[②] According to Marx's diagnosis, one of the basic symptoms of modernity is the simplification of interpersonal relationships (the relationship of the employer and the employed replaces all the complex relationships of traditional society) and their callousness ("self-interest" and "cash payment" constitute daily life).

---

① Karl Marx and Frederick Engels, *Selected Works* (in two Vol. s), vol. 1 (Moscow, Foreign Languages Publishing House, 1951), p. 35.

② Karl Marx and Frederick Engels, *Selected Works* (in two Vol. s), vol. 1 (Moscow, Foreign Languages Publishing House, 1951), p. 36.

Third, the spontaneous movement of capital will inevitably lead to a world market and the globalization of national production and consumption. "The need of a constantly expanding market for its products chases the bourgeoisie over the whole surface of the globe. It must nestle everywhere, settle everywhere, establish connections everywhere."[1] In accordance of Marx's diagnosis, globalization is the necessary logical result of the spontaneous movement of capital and one of the basic symptoms of modernity in its self-expression. The present realities have proved the indubitable foresight of Marx's diagnosis.

Then, how does capital multiply in its movement? Marx believed that in the final analysis capital fulfilled its multiplication through its absorption of living labor. "Labor is the yeast thrown into capital, which starts it fermenting."[2] Therefore, only through the analysis of the capitalist productive process could the secret of capital multiplication be truly revealed. In fact, in the capitalist productive process the capitalists as the organizers of entire productive activities extorted not only absolute surplus value through lengthening the working day but also relative surplus value through raising productivity. It is in this sense that Marx wrote indignantly, "The first birthright of capital is equal exploitation of labor-power by all capitalists."[3]

However, this secret of capital multiplication is often covered in the field of circulation, especially in the special form of existence of capital, interest-bearing capital. As Marx pointed out, "If capital originally appeared

---

① Karl Marx and Frederick Engels, *Selected Works*, vol. 1 (Moscow, Foreign Languages Publishing House, 1951).

② Karl Marx and Frederick Engels, *Collected Works*, http://www. ex. ac. uk/Projects/meia/Archive/.

③ Karl Marx, *Capital*, vol. 1 (Moscow, Foreign Languages Publishing House, 1959), p. 292.

on the surface of circulation as a fetishism of capital, as a value-creating value, so it now appears again in the form of interest-bearing capital, as in its most estranged and characteristic form."① Why does the fetishism of capital have its most glaring existence in the form of interest-bearing capital? This is because interest-bearing capital puts up a false front as if it created interest by itself. To the mind of Marx, in order to do away with interest-bearing capital we must soberly understand that capital is not an object but a social productive relation.

Marx's above ideas contain a self-evident conclusion that capital constitutes the core and soul of various phenomena of modernity as well as the basis and motive force of modern society. After Marx, Rosa Luxemburg and Rudolf Hilferding carried on consideration of this aspect in their respective works *The Accumulation of Capital* and *Financial Capital*. In analyses of modernity by contemporary scholars, their considerations are focused on the accumulation of capital and its developmental trend. The American scholar David Harvey began his reflection on capital in his works *Limit to Capital* (1982) and *The Urbanization of Capital* (1985). In Harvey's view, once Marx had seen the unlimited and excessive multiplication and accumulation of capital as an incurable disease, then the only question was how to use the various ways of expressing, curbing, absorbing or processing the trend of excessive accumulation.② Obviously, in the eyes of Harvey, Marx overlooked the potential of modernity for self-regulation. According to him, modern society is capable of checking or even eliminating the logical result of the spontaneous movement of capital by

---

① Karl Marx, *Capital*, vol. 3 (Moscow, Foreign Languages Publishing House, 1959), p. 808.

② David Harvey, *The Condition of Post Modernity* (Cambridge: Blackwell Publishers Inc., 1990).

means of macro-regulation and the flexible transfer of capital in time and space. The British scholar Istvan Meszaros said in the introduction to his book *Beyond Capital* (1995) that he named it *Beyond Capital* on the basis of the following considerations: first, the purport of Marx's *Capital* was to go beyond capitalism and the purport of his book was to go beyond capital, with more extensive implications; second, Marx died leaving *Capital* unfinished, and he aspired to continue Marx's train of thought in criticizing capitalism; third, tremendous changes had taken place since the era of Marx and he therefore hoped his work would transcend "Marx's design itself."[1] Whether or not Meszaros' work has attained its expectations, one point is certain: he takes capital as a key to the interpretation of modern society and modernity.

Unlike Harvey and Meszaros who study capital from the angle of economic life, the French scholar Pierre Bourdieu offers a supra-economic interpretation of capital in his studies of modern society and modernity. In his view, capital assumes the following three morphologies in modern society: first, economic capital, which can be immediately and directly changed into money and is institutionalized in the form of property rights; second, cultural capital, which can be changed into economic capital under certain conditions and is institutionalized in the form of educational qualifications; third, social capital, which consists in social obligations ("connections"), can also be changed into economic capital under given conditions and is institutionalized in the form of some noble titles.[2] Obviously, the appearance of the concepts "cultural capital" and "social capital" tremendously enriches the connotations of capital and provides greater and more

---

[1] Istvan Meszaros, *Beyond Capital* (New York, Monthly Review Press, 1995).

[2] Bao Yaming, *Interviews with P. Bourdieu: Cultural Capital and Social Alchemy* (Shanghai: Shanghai People's Publishing House, 1997), p. 192.

flexible space for annotation for contemporary scholars in their diagnosis of modernity.

Transcendence of Estrangement: The Way Out for the Diagnosis of Modernity

Compared with thinkers who were his contemporaries, Marx delved deeper and more profoundly in his studies, for he not only diagnosed modernity from the perspective of objects—commodity, money and capital, but also made more thorough-going reflections on modernity from the perspective of the human actions giving birth to these objects—productive labor. One concept Marx frequently used when he was engaged in these studies is "estrangement" (or "alienation"). It is an important concept Marx borrowed from Hegel and Feuerbach and to which he gave a brand-new meaning. If Hegel and Feuerbach spoke about estrangement only from the angle of pure spiritual activities, especially religious concepts, then the special angle, i. e., economic philosophy, from which Marx investigated modernity brought him into "estranged labor," the universal form of expression of productive labor in modern society. With Marx, the concept of estrangement has the following features.

First, the means by which estrangement fulfills itself is practice. "Thus through estranged labor man not only creates his relationship to the object and to the act of production as to powers that are alien and hostile to him; he also creates the relationship in which other men stand to his production and to his product, and the relationship in which he stands to these

other men. "① The reason Marx stressed the practical features of estrangement was to make people understand that estrangement is not an illusory
spiritual atmosphere in everyday life, but the practical force and relations
that control everyday life. It is through the in-depth analysis of estranged
labor that Marx discovered the four basic and practical forms of estrangement in modern society and modernity: estrangement of labor products;
estrangement of labor process; estrangement of man's nature; and estrangement of person-to-person relations.

Second, estrangement is a ubiquitous fact. Marx wrote, "Estrangement is manifested not only in the fact that my means of life belong to
someone else, that which I desire is the inaccessible possession of another,
but also in the fact that everything is itself something different from itself—that my activity is something else and that finally (this applies to the
capitalist), all is under [the sway] of inhuman power. "② Here Marx not
only explained the general meaning of estrangement, but also said the capitalists are also undergoing estrangement. Thus he held estrangement is a
universal phenomenon for all social members. Later on, he further clearly
pointed out, "The propertied class and the class of the proletariat present
the same human estrangement. "③ But there is a difference in that the latter class sees in it the powerlessness and the reality of an inhuman existence while the former class recognizes estrangement as its own power and
feels at ease. As a matter of fact, this feeling of the propertied class is to a
large degree illusory for modernity controls everything with its inhuman

---

① Karl Marx and Frederick Engels, *Collected Works*, vol. 3 (Moscow, Progress Publishers, 1975), p. 279.

② Karl Marx and Frederick Engels, *Collected Works*, vol. 3 (Moscow, Progress Publishers, 1975), p. 314.

③ Karl Marx and Frederick Engels, *Selected Works*, vol. 4 (New York: International
Publishers, 1976), p. 36.

and magical power, including, of course, the propertied class.

Third, estrangement usually goes hand in hand with objectification in modern society. Marx did not oppose objectification in general. In his view, any productive labor materializes man's energy into an object or product. What he opposed was objectification expressed through estrangement. "The monstrous objective power which social labor itself erected opposite itself as one of its moments belongs not to the worker, but to the personified conditions of production, i. e., to capital."[1]

Although Marx made full expositions of the universality and gravity of estrangement inherent in modern society and modernity, he insisted that the phenomenon of estrangement could be transcended. In the view of Marx, the estranged labor gradually taking shape on the basis of the division of labor constitutes the direct reason for private property, which, conversely, forms the basis for the continuation and enhancement of estranged labor. It is in this sense that Marx pointed out, "The positive transcendence of private property, as the appropriation of human life, is therefore the positive transcendence of all estrangement—that is to say, the return of man from religion, family, state, etc., to his human, i. e., social existence."[2] We all know that Marx in his mature years continued to use the important concept of estrangement, but the philosophical slogan of "transcendence of all estrangement" proposed in his early years was replaced by the clear-cut political revolutionary slogan of "depriving expropriators."

As Marx's theory of estrangement possesses tremendous potential and interpretative space, both macroscopically and microscopically, it has

---

[1] Karl Marx and Frederick Engels, *Collected Works*, http://www. ex. ac. uk/Projects/meia/ Archive/.

[2] Karl Marx and Frederick Engels, *Collected Works*, vol. 3 (Moscow: Progress Publishers, 1975), p. 297.

received extraordinary attention from later generations. In his *History and Class Consciousness* (1923), Georg Lukacs used the term "objectification" to make a critical investigation of modern society and modernity. He pointed out that objectification is an inevitable and direct reality for everyone living in capitalist society. [1] Although Lukacs had not yet grasped the correct relationship between objectification and estrangement, his use of the word "objectification" indicated he inherited Marx's line of thought when he diagnosed modern society and modernity.

After the publication in 1932 of Marx's *Economic and Philosophical Manuscripts of 1844*, "estrangement" almost became an everyday expression of the international philosophical community. The French philosopher Henri Lefebvre began his journey of criticism of the estrangement of everyday life and modernity with his book *Critique of Everyday Life* (1946). In fact, he broadened the meaning of estrangement: estrangement is defined not only as a man losing himself in the external material world or uncertain subjectivity; it should be defined, first of all, as the split of an individual in the process of objectification and subjectification, i. e., the destruction of the unity between the two. [2] Lefebvre is acclaimed by many post-modernist thinkers as the forerunner of criticism of modernity. In the 1960s and the 1970s the philosophers of the "School of Practice" in Yugoslavia explored a new field in the study of estrangement, i. e., reflections on the estrangement implicit in the modernization drive of Eastern socialist countries. For example, L. Tadic pointed out clearly at the beginning of his article "Bureaucratic Apparatuses: An Organization of Estrangement," "We are now living in an era dominated by the rapidly expanding forces of

---

[1] G. Lukacs, *History and Class Consciousness* (London: MIT Press, 1971), p. 197.
[2] H. Lefebvre, *The Sociology of Marx* (New York: Vintage Books, 1969), p. 10.

estrangement. "① In his argument, the bureaucratic apparatuses and the way they function are the iron-clad proof of the existence of estrangement.

Needless to say, Marx's theory of estrangement also becomes a key to the interpretation of modernity for post-modernist thinkers. As Best and Kellner have pointed out, Baudrillard and post-modernist theories have made use of Marx's expositions about the reversal of the subject and object, the control of the subject by the object and the decline of subjectivity and individuality. ② Baudrillard as an ultra-modernist in his late years was elated to think that his theory of signs surpassed Marx's theory of estrangement and the transcendence of estrangement. In fact, as Best and Kellner said in criticism of him, if objectification were to turn the world into a mysterious phantom and a sign without any social relations, this is a task Baudrillard's works can help accomplish. ③ That is, Baudrillard had returned to the incorrect standpoint he had previously criticized. In this sense, it might be said we have not gone beyond the field of vision of Marx in his diagnosis of modernity.

To sum up, Marx's diagnosis of modernity and modern society characterized by capitalism is still a very valuable intellectual legacy. David Frisby said that Marx identified in capitalism the "origins" of the experience of modernity and that his analyses show that the interested parties of capitalism themselves are not aware of these "origins. "④ Martin Albrow even regarded the theory of historical materialism Marx developed as "a

① Marcovici et al., eds., *History and Theory of the School of Practice* (Chongqing: Chongqing Publishing House, 1991), p. 331 (Chinese edition).

② G. Debord, *Society of the Spectacle*, http://www.marxists.org/reference/archive/debord/society.htm.

③ G. Debord, *Society of the Spectacle*, http://www.marxists.org/reference/archive/debord/society.htm.

④ David Frisby, *Fragments of Modernity* (Cambridge: Polity Press, 1985).

highly modern interpretation of modernity. "① All these show that Marx's diagnosis of modernity is of great contemporary importance and is worth in-depth study.

① Martin Albrow, *The Global Age: State and Society beyond Modernity* (Stanford: Stanford University Press, 1997).

1. 6   On Marx's Interpretation of the Legacy of Classical German Philosophy[①]

Definition of the Scope of Classical German Philosophy

According to the material currently available, we can say that Engels was the first to have used the concept of "classical German philosophy." In his *Dialectics of Nature* (1873-1886) he made a chance reference to this concept and in *Ludwig Feuerbach and the End of Classical German Philosophy* (1888) he made formal use of it.

Then, what was the scope of "Classical German philosophy" as Engels saw it? In his "The Three Sources and Three Component Parts of Marxism" (1913) Lenin regarded Hegel and Feuerbach as two representatives of classical German philosophy when he elaborated Marxist philosophy. This view had a profound influence. Not only

---

① Editor's note: This paper was originally published in *Social Sciences in China*, no. 4, 2006, pp. 3-15, translated by Liu Ruixiang from *Zhongguo Shehui Kexue* (《中国社会科学》), no. 2, 2006, pp. 11-22, revised by Sally Borthwick.

did Soviet and East European theoretical circles hold this view, but so did the Chinese theoretical community. For example, the *Dictionary of Foreign Philosophy* edited by Feng Qi et al. opined, "Classical German philosophy consists of German classical idealism and German classical materialism. Philosophical development from Kant to Hegel represented the trajectory of German classical idealism and Feuerbach's anthropocentric materialism gave rise to the theory of German classical materialism."

However, does this view accord with Engels' true intentions? We would say no. It is true that Engels did not make a straightforward reference to the scope of classical German philosophy, but in touching on the three forms of dialectics in Dialectics of Nature, he pointed out "The second form of dialectics, which is the one that comes closest to the German naturalists, is classical German philosophy, from Kant to Hegel." In *Ludwig Feuerbach and the End of Classical German Philosophy* he also clearly indicated, "We must here confine ourselves to Hegelian philosophy as the close of the whole movement since Kant." In his view, classical German philosophy referred to the philosophical movement from Kant to Hegel; it ended with Hegel and did not count Feuerbach as a member.

Since the full text of *Dialectics of Nature* as a manuscript was published for the first time in the Marx-Engels Archive as late as 1925, Lenin did not read the manuscript during his lifetime. Moreover, Engels' *Ludwig Feuerbach and the End of Classical German Philosophy*, which Lenin did read, did not clearly spell out the scope of classical German philosophy. Engels devoted a lot of space to Feuerbach's philosophical thought, a fact which would easily mislead readers into thinking Feuerbach was part of classical German philosophy.

One of the reasons Chinese theoretical circles still cling to this misunderstanding may be the translation of the title of *Ludwig Feuerbach and the End of Classical German Philosophy*. The original title of the book by Engels is *Ludwig Feuerbach und der Ausgang der klassischen deutschen Philosophie*. The crux of the matter is the translation of the German word *Ausgang*. The basic meaning of *Ausgang* is "outlet" or "way out." If one considers "fidelity, expressiveness and elegance" as the principles to which translation should adhere, the title should be rendered into English as *Ludwig Feuerbach and the Way Out for Classical German Philosophy*.

If we go beyond the literal meaning of the word and consider the meaning of *Ausgang* in the particular context when Engels wrote this work, it can only be translated as "the way out" rather than "the end" because the translation "Ludwig Feuerbach and the End of Classical German Philosophy" would give people a false impression that Feuerbach was the man who "ended" classical German philosophy and that he was naturally one of the German classical philosophers.

In fact, only when he was a young Hegelian could Feuerbach have been included, at a pinch, in the ranks of German classical philosophers. When he started to criticize Hegel and developed his own philosophical views, he positioned himself outside the circle of classical German philosophy. In the above book Engels criticized Feuerbach as an independent philosopher, not as a young Hegelian. So in the context of Engels' use of the word at that time, Feuerbach as an independent thinker did not have a place in classical German philosophy. We can see from this that the translation of the German word *Ausgang* involves not only its literal meaning and techniques of translation, but also the understanding of Engels' thinking, thus having substantive significance.

To sum up, in the context of Engels' work, classical German philosophy refers to the philosophies of Kant, Fichte, Schelling and Hegel. In order to express Engels' original meaning, the title *Ludwig Feuerbach und der Ausgang der klassischen deutschen Philosophie* should be retranslated as Ludwig Feuerbach and the Way Out for Classical German Philosophy (abbreviated as The Way Out below).

Now that Feuerbach's philosophy is not included in the category of classical German philosophy, how do we accurately evaluate its historical role in the formation and development of the philosophical thought of Marx and Engels? In our view, Feuerbach played a role in the history of the development of Marx' and Engels' philosophical thought, one which can be seen from the early works of Marx and Engels such as *Economic and Philosophic Manuscripts of 1844*, *Holy Family*, "Theses on Feuerbach" and *The German Ideology*. However, if we want to have a correct understanding of the relationship between Marxist philosophy and classical German philosophy and the influence of Feuerbach's philosophy on Marxist philosophical thinking, we should conscientiously read and reflect on Marx's narrative of the course of his own politico-economic studies in his work "Preface to a Contribution to the Critique of Political Economy (1859)." This very important narrative shows the following points: first, Marx did not mention Feuerbach in recalling his creation of historical materialism. Marx's exposition on the divorce of Feuerbach's materialism from history clearly made it clear that Feuerbach's materialism could not serve as a bridge to historical materialism. Second, Marx concerned himself from his youth with social and historical issues through his studies of philosophy, history and law. In the evolution of his thought there was no phase in which his interests shifted from studies of nature to social and historical studies under the influence of Feuerbach's materialism. Third, in Marx's own expositions Feuerbach's materialism did not play a fundamental and decisive role.

What the above points show us is that abstract materialism estranged from human social and historical activities could not lose its abstract character simply through the introduction of dialectical thinking, and that dialectics could not acquire new vitality simply because it took the abstract nature or matter as its own foundation or vehicle.

Marx's Interpretation of the Legacy
of Classical German Philosophy

Marx's unique views concerning the legacy of classical German philosophy were expressed mainly in his concern with the following six issues:

1. Man.

Man was always a theme that concerned classical German philosophy. The great slogan "Man is an end in himself" raised by Kant in his *Fundamental Principles of the Metaphysics of Morals* (1785) affirmed in an unprecedented way the dignity of man as a rational being (*ens rationis*) and we can hear its long echo in *Practical Anthropology* written by Kant in his later years, *The Vocation of Man* by Fichte, *On the Essence of Human Freedom* by Schelling and *Elements of Philosophy of Right* by Hegel. During the period of post-classical German philosophy, Feuerbach made his main contribution to philosophy through his thought on philosophical anthropology. All these humanistic ideas exerted a positive influence on Marx.

In *Holy Family* (1844) Marx wrote on Hegelian philosophy, "In *Hegel* there are *three* elements, *Spinoza's Substance*, *Fichte's Self-Consciousness* and Hegel's necessarily antagonistic unity of the two, the *Absolute Spirit*. The first element is metaphysically disguised *nature separated* from man; the second is metaphysically disguised *spirit separated* from nature; the third is the metaphysically disguised *unity* of both, *real man* and the real *human species*." Obviously, as Marx saw it, "real man and the real human species" was one of the basic philosophical legacies left by classical German philosophy. Since Marx remained at that time under some influence from Feuerbach, he owed his interpretation of the legacy of classical German philosophy to the inspiration the latter provided.

In "Theses on Feuerbach" (1845) Marx shifted his stand and criticized Feuerbach's philosophical thinking, especially his thinking on man: "Feuerbach does not see that 'religious sentiments' are themselves a social product, and that the abstract individual which he analyses belongs to a particular form of society." In *The German Ideology* (1845-1846), Marx made further criticisms: "he [Feuerbach] says 'Man' instead of 'real historical man'." Although Marx in his maturity criticized Feuerbach's anthropocentric thinking, he did say approvingly that Feuerbach interpreted the legacy of classical German philosophy along correct lines. It was based on this thinking that Marx pointed out, "We set out from real, active men." In the future communist society Marx yearned for, "the free development of each is the condition for the free development of all." In a sense, Marxist philosophy is, in the final analysis, a doctrine for the emancipation of all mankind. This profoundly illuminates the way in which Marx always treated the issue of man as one of the legacies of classical German philosophy.

2. Civil society.

In the field of vision of classical German philosophers, man was both a natural and a social being. This common understanding aroused their general interest in social problems with a focus on civil society. For Kant, the initiator of classical German philosophy, civil society was one of the most important topics. In "Idea for a Universal History from a Cosmopolitan

Point of View" (1784), he proposed that the establishment of civil society under the universal rule of laws was a great ideal pursued by mankind in political life. In *Elements of Philosophy of Right* (1821) by Hegel, civil society appears as an intermediary link between family and state. As a territory citizens actually live in and an embodiment of all needs, a civil society has the following features: "In a civil society, everyone takes himself as the end and everything else is in the misty void. But, if he has nothing to do with others, he will not achieve all his purpose. Others therefore become the means for a particular man to achieve his end." As Hegel drew inspiration from classical British economics in observing social problems, he actualized Kant's viewpoint about man being the end and held that in real life man was the means as well as the end.

Marx attached great importance to the theory of civil society of the German classical philosophers, especially Hegel. In the *Critique of Hegel's Philosophy of Right* (1843), Marx devoted much space to passages from Hegel's theory of civil society and comments thereon, revealing its idealist features. In "Theses on Feuerbach" Marx said, "The standpoint of the old materialism is civil society; the standpoint of the new is human society, or social humanity." In *The German Ideology*, Marx started to define the implications of the concept of civil society in his own words and treated civil society as one of the key concepts of his new historical view. He said, "This conception of history depends on our ability to expound the real process of production, starting out from the material production of life itself, and to comprehend the form of intercourse connected with and created by this mode of production (i. e. civil society in its various stages), as the basis of all history; and to show it in its action as State, to explain all the different theoretical products and forms of consciousness, religion, philosophy, ethics, etc. etc. and trace their origins and growth from that basis; by which means, of course, the whole thing can be depicted in its totality (and therefore, too, the reciprocal action of these various aspects on one another)." This also corroborates the view we mentioned above that Feuerbach's intuitive materialism could not lead to historical materialism. So it is evident that the concept of civil society is part of the basic contents of the legacy of classical German philosophy.

3. Practice.

The German classical philosophers, profoundly influenced by Greek philosophy, especially Aristotelian philosophy, all paid great attention to the issue of practice. Kant classified reason into "speculative reason" and "practical reason." In his *Critique of Judgment* (1790) Kant put forward two further concepts of practice: "practice in conformity with the concept of nature" and "practice in conformity with the concept of freedom." In Kant's critical philosophy, even though "practice in conformity with the concept of freedom," i. e., human moral activities, enjoys a higher position, empty obligations not only endow it with formalist and subjectivist characteristics, but also render it separate from the practical human activities of understanding and changing nature. If we say that Fichte, like Kant, rested content with talking about purely obligatory and formalist moral practical activities, then Hegel, through his in-depth study of British classical economics, shifted his attention to the basic practical activity, that is, labor. In his works *The System of Ethics* (1802-1803), *Real Philosophy* (1803-1806) and *The Phenomenology of Spirit* (1807), Hegel provides a profound analysis of the essence of labor and the alienation that takes place during the process of labor.

Marx set a high value on Kantian philosophy and said that "Kant's *philosophy* must be rightly regarded as the German theory of the French revolution." He stressed "The state of affairs in Germany at the end of the last century is fully reflected in Kant's *Critik der Praktischen Vernunft* [*Critique of Practical Reason*] (1788)." However, Marx did not agree with Kant in reducing practice to moral activities and empty preaching of "good will." In the eyes of Marx, although Kant stressed the importance of practical reason, his understanding of practice was still stamped with the brand of the weak German petty bourgeoisie.

Marx also spoke highly of *The Phenomenology of Spirit* by Hegel and thought that "the outstanding achievement of Hegel's *Phänomeno logie* and of its final outcome, the dialectic of negativity as the moving and generating principle, is thus first that Hegel conceives the self-creation of man as a process, conceives objectification as loss of the object, as alienation and as transcendence of this alienation; that he thus grasps the essence of *labour* and comprehends objective man—true, because real man—as the outcome of man's own labour." "Labor" was nothing but a synonym of "abstract spiritual labor" in Hegel's context, but the unique perspective from which he investigated the issue of practice exerted tremendous influence over Marx.

Marx agreed neither with Kant who isolated practical-moral activities from, and set them against, practical activities aimed at understanding and changing nature nor with Hegel who talked about labor, the basic form of practice, only on the plane of "abstract spiritual labor." In Marx's understanding, practice was the essence of all social life, the criterion to test the truth of any theory and the watershed between his philosophy and all traditional philosophies. He even called his philosophy "practical materialism."

Marx remolded and raised the concept of practice mainly in the following two directions: on the one hand, he undertook far more in-depth study than did Hegel of classical British economics, brought to light the fundamental role of productive labor, the basic form of practice, in human survival activities and the development of world history, and put forward the important concept of "alienated labor" and analyzed its various consequences. He advocated, through communist revolution, the abolition of private ownership and the transcendence of alienation in order to achieve the recovery of human nature. On the other hand, unlike Kant and Fichte, he did not rest content with abstract moral preaching and purely deontological moral practical activities, but chose the important dimension of social revolution from the unified concept of practice and maintained that "In reality and for the practical materialist, i. e. the communist, it is a question of revolutionizing the existing world, of practically attacking and changing existing things." Through these approaches Marx greatly enriched the connotations of the concept of practice defined by the German classical philosophers and extended them beyond the narrow liberalist confines of the German petty bourgeoisie.

All this points to the fact that in Marx's theoretical vision, the issue of practice was one of the most fundamental legacies of classical German philosophy. When Engels understood the purely intellectual domain, i. e., logic and dialectics, as the only legacy of classical German philosophy, he did not realize that both dialectics and logical category are, in the final analysis, products of practical activities. It is Lenin who subtly revealed the original relationship between "the scope of logic and the practice of man": "For Hegel action, practice, is a logical 'syllogism,' a figure of logic. And that is true! Not of course, in the same sense that the figure of logic has its other being in the practice of man (=absolute idealism), but vice versa: man's practice, repeating itself a thousand million times, becomes consolidated in man's consciousness by figures of logic. Precisely (and only) on account of this thousand-millionfold repetition, these figures have the stability of a prejudice, and axiomatic character."

This also proves once again that it would be futile to try to transform and raise the level of Hegel's dialectics with Feuerbach's intuitive materialism; this effort becomes feasible only when practical materialism is introduced. The epoch-making revolution of historical materialism was epitomized in the transformation of philosophical foundation and could not be accomplished merely by the grafting of dialectics on to intuitive materialism.

4. The thing-in-itself.

The interpretation of the thing-in-itself was a common task for all the German philosophers starting with Kant, and their interpretations became one of the basic legacies of classical German philosophy. Of all these interpreters, only Marx successfully revealed the secrets of the thing-in-itself.

With Kant, the concept of the thing-in-itself has three meanings: as the source of perceptual stimulus, as a boundary of intellectual knowledge and as practical reason, i. e. , the guiding principle of human will. After Kant, Fichte tried to start from self-based epistemology to eliminate Kant's concept of the thing-in-itself. Schelling and Hegel respectively used the concept of "the absolute" and the concept of "absolute spirit" to replace the thing-in-itself. For Schelling, "the absolute" may be grasped through intellectual intuition, but for Hegel, "absolute spirit" could be grasped only through dialectical thinking. The point that Fichte, Schelling and Hegel have in common is that they tried to transcend Kant from the perspective of traditional epistemology, focusing their attention on reflective reason and the first two meanings of thing-in-itself.

This interpretation also had a great influence on Engels. In *The Way out* Engels also neglects the third meaning of Kant's thing-in-itself. In fact, since Kant put practical reason in a more important position than reflective reason, as pointed out above, then the third meaning of thing-in-itself must have a particularly vital significance.

Arthur Schopenhauer was not one of the German classical philosophers, but he took an important step in understanding the essential meanings of Kant's concept of thing-in-itself. In his view, Kant's thing-in-itself was the ubiquitous will of the universe, embodied in man as the will to survive. Schopenhauer's interpretation of thing-in-itself goes beyond the perspective of pure epistemology and brings the answer back to human subsistence activities. Kant's thing-in-itself provides a guiding principle for practical reason or will; however, thing-in-itself is not the will but an existence underlying the will. As to what this existence is, Kant believed it would be impossible to know. Schopenhauer understood the will as the thing-in-itself and as the essence of the world, but he did not demonstrate, from the perspective of real human life, the basic ways in which the will functions; hence the meaning of thing-in-itself still remained unknown.

Unlike Schopenhauer who one-sidedly emphasized freedom of will, Marx believed "Neither he [Kant], nor the German middle class, whose whitewashing spokesman he was, noticed that these theoretical ideas of the bourgeoisie had as their basis material interests and a *will* that was conditioned and determined by the material relations of production. Kant, therefore, separated this theoretical expression from the interests which it expressed; he made the materially motivated determinations of the will of the French bourgeois into *pure* self-determinations of 'free will,' of the will in and for itself, of the human will, and so converted it into purely ideological conceptual determinations and moral postulates." In Marx's view, will is not entirely free and the basic way in which it is functioning is productive labor, which, in turn, is based on "the material relations of production." It is the invisible social relations of production that were mystified in Kant's philosophic language and became an occult thing-in-itself, impossible to be thoroughly understood.

Marx pointed out that in a modern society all factors in the process of production exist in the form of commodities. Commodities are the form of existence of "things" in a modern society and provide conditions for all productive labor to be carried out. According to Marx, as "things" commodities are both physical things (with use-value) and social things (with exchange-value). In modern society, people exist as producers of exchange value and will naturally develop an illusion that mistakes the social attribute of "things" for their natural attribute. "The form of wood, for instance, is altered, by making a table out of it. Yet, for all that, the table continues to be that common, every-day thing, wood. But so soon as it steps forth as a commodity, it is changed into something transcendent. It not only stands with its feet on the ground, but, in relation to all other commodities, it stands on its head, and evolves out of its wooden brain grotesque ideas, far more wonderful than 'table-turning' ever was." Marx called this phenomenon "the fetish character of commodities" and pointed out it was precisely the social relations of production hiding behind "things" with which productive labor had close connections that led to the general phenomenon of fetishism in modern society.

In this way, Marx thoroughly solved the secret of thing-in-itself, i. e., the thing-in-itself considered by Kant to be transcendent, mystical and impossible to be understood is nothing but the social relations of production that hide behind "things" with which productive labor has close connections and which act as commodities. These social relations of production are invisible and make an appearance only through criticism of "the fetish character of commodities" and after the "things" as commodities have been detranscended and de-mystified and rendered no long unknowable. Furthermore, the guiding principle of practical reason is not things-in-themselves as seen by Kant—God, liberty and the immortal soul, but the social relations of production. Just as Marx said, "In all forms of society there is one specific kind of production which predominates over the rest, whose relations thus assign rank and influence to the others. It is a general illumination which bathes all the other colors and modifies their particularity. It is a particular ether which determines the specific gravity of every being which has materialized within it."

It can be seen from the above that the thing-in-itself is a basic legacy and a key riddle of classical German philosophy. In the context of pure epistemology, it is easy to dissolve the thing-in-itself in the thing-for-itself, but the key lies in how to reveal the guiding role of the thing-in-itself in practical reason. It is Marx who solved this riddle, thus substantially transforming and raising the research achievements of classical German philosophy.

5. Historical consciousness.

We have pointed out in interpreting the secret of the thing-in-itself that this secret was brought to light in the relations of production in modern society (this specific historical period). This implies in fact the understanding that historical consciousness was also one of the basic legacies of classical German philosophy.

Kant's paper "Idea for a Universal History from a Cosmopolitan Point of View" contains his two basic views: one is that the development of human history obeys the laws of nature; the other is that as a whole human society develops along a progressive direction. Hegel went a step further and saw human history as a process of continuous conflict between reason and passion, believing that history is dominated by the "cunning of reason." The viewpoint of the "cunning of reason" affirms that history moves forward in accordance with law and purpose.

Bringing dialectics back into human history and making it historical dialectics in the context of historical materialism—this was Marx's critical inheritance and revolutionary transformation of classical German philosophy, especially the historical consciousness contained in Hegelian philosophy. The main views of Marx's historical dialectics are as follows:

First, explaining the formation of ideas from the real ground of history. Marx wrote, "It [the materialist conception of history] has not, like the idealistic view of history, in every period to look for a category, but remains constantly on the real ground of history; it does not explain practice from the idea but explains the formation of ideas from material practice." Obviously, what is involved here is historical dialectics' interpretation of the motive mechanism of real historical development.

Second, the development of socio-economic forms is a natural historical process. Marx pointed out, "No social order is ever destroyed before all the productive forces for which it is sufficient have been developed, and new superior relations of production never replace older ones before the material conditions for their existence have matured within the framework of the old society. Mankind thus inevitably sets itself only such tasks as it is able to solve, since closer examination will always show that the problem itself arises only when the material conditions for its solution are already present or at least in the course of formation." What is involved here is historical dialectics' approval of the developmental laws of real history and its limitations on the initiative of historical subjects.

Third, we will be able to correctly explain the past only when we understand the present. Marx tells us, "Human anatomy contains a key to the anatomy of the ape. The intimations of higher development among the subordinate animal species, however, can be understood only after the higher development is already known." Therefore, the capitalist economy can understand the feudal, the ancient and the eastern economies only when contemporary capitalist society begins to undertake self-criticism. Of course, the method of understanding the past from the self-conscious perspective of the essence of modern life has its own limitations, that is, it must admit the differences among different historical periods and never try to use the present to recast the past. What is involved here is precisely the core concept of historical dialectics, that is, the historical concept. According to this concept, anyone who cannot grasp the essence of life at present is unable to make a rational interpretation of the past.

Fourth, historical structure takes precedence over historical sequence. Marx pointed out, "The point is not the historic position of economic relations in the succession of different forms of society. Even less is it their sequence 'in the idea' (Proudhon) (a muddy notion of historic movement). Rather, it is their order within modern bourgeois society." What is involved here is the confirmation of the precedence of historical dialectics in modern social structure. Historical dialectics does not mean the abstract worship of historical starting points and historical process but the proactive and in-depth consideration and grasp of modern social structure.

All in all, we should not strip dialectics out of social history and then take it as the legacy of classical German philosophy. In fact, historical consciousness and the historical dialectics it contains are one of the basic legacies of classical German philosophy, one that Marx transformed with the theory of historical materialism.

6. Freedom.

It is precisely on the basis of the profound historical consciousness mentioned above that German classical philosophers, almost without exception, understood freedom as the highest goal pursued by reason and that Marx also took freedom as one of the basic legacies of classical

German philosophy.

For Kant, reflective reason involves natural law or natural necessity and falls within the sphere of phenomena while practical reason involves freedom and falls within the sphere of the thing-in-itself. Man, on the one hand, falls within the sphere of phenomena (within time and space) and, on the other, within the sphere of the thing-in-itself (beyond experience and time and space). When confronted with natural necessity, man should not talk about freedom; freedom can be talked about in the sphere of things-in-themselves, that is, when social relations and man's will are involved. Obviously, with Kant, natural necessity and freedom are separate and mutually exclusive.

For Hegel, this freedom that does not contain necessity or pure necessity that does not have freedom is nothing but an abstract and unreal view. By nature, freedom is concrete; it always determines itself and is therefore necessary. Freedom and necessity are not mutually exclusive; freedom is the recognition of necessity. It is in this sense that Hegel stressed that with the development of human history, people not only deepened their understanding of historical necessity, but also gained an increasingly keen sense of freedom.

Thus Hegel advanced Kant's concept of freedom. Although he failed to consciously deduce "natural necessity" and "historical necessity" from the concept of necessity, he inherited Kant's differentiation of natural necessity from freedom and understood freedom as the recognition of historical necessity.

In his concern with freedom Marx based himself, from the very outset, on human society and the relations between man and man. As is widely known, in his Ph. D. dissertation *The Difference between the Democritean and Epicurean Philosophy of Nature* (1840-1841) Marx espoused the great strength of self-consciousness and freedom in affirming Epicurus' theory of the declination of the atom from the straight line. In his first political paper "Comments on the Latest Prussian Censorship Instruction" (1842), Marx, while criticizing "hypocritical liberalism," pointed out sharply, *"Grey, all grey*, is the sole, the rightful color of freedom." Marx in his mature years based himself on historical materialism and, through analysis of the structural relationships between necessary labor time and surplus labor time in productive labor and between labor time and leisure time in real life, affirmed that time is the horizon by which freedom develops and that reduction of working time is the fundamental condition for mankind to acquire universal freedom. Marx' concept of freedom further deepened the views on freedom of German classical philosophers, especially of Hegel.

In short, in Marx's theoretical vision, the factors of man, civil society, practice, the thing-in-itself, historical consciousness and freedom jointly make up the legacy of classical German philosophy. It is true that Marx also attached great importance to the dialectical thinking contained in classical German philosophy, especially in Hegelian philosophy, but he always brought dialectics into the perspective of historical materialism. We do not therefore set out "dialectics" as a separate item in our exposition of Marx's understanding of the legacy of classical German philosophy, but elaborate it along with the above-mentioned elements, especially with "historical consciousness." It can thus be seen that it was Marx who restored the rich connotations of the legacy of classical German philosophy.

The Significance of Reinterpreting the Legacy of Classical German Philosophy

Needless to say, Marx's interpretation of the legacy of classical German philosophy is of extreme significance.

Firstly, it shows us that the rich connotations of the legacy of classical German philosophy must be restored. In textbooks of Marxist philosophy, this legacy is simplified and impoverished. The undue emphasis on contemporary Western philosophy to the neglect of early modern Western philosophy has in turn further aggravated the neglect of classical German philosophy. In fact, not only was traditional philosophy synthesized and brought to its highest development by the German classical philosophers from Kant to Hegel, but these philosophers also exerted tremendous influence over the formation and development of contemporary Western philosophy. Their role as a bridge between the past and the future cannot be denied. Only through conscientiously exploring classical German philosophy and digesting and assimilating its rich intellectual resources and philosophical legacy can we broaden our theoretical field of vision and offer a deeper and more rational exposition of contemporary Western philosophy.

Secondly, it shows us that the relationship between Marx and classical German philosophy, that between Feuerbach and classical German philosophy, and the relationship between Marx and Feuerbach in the post-classical German philosophy period are still important theoretical issues that need to be further studied. Traditional textbooks of Marxist philosophy are full of simplistic interpretations and even misinterpretations of these relationships and a lot of work needs to be done to overhaul these.

However, the prevailing disciplinary classification under which the history of Marxist philosophy and the history of modern Western philosophy are studied separately does not help deeper exploration of the above problem. Only cross-disciplinary research is capable of thrashing out the relationships mentioned above.

Lastly, it shows us that understanding the essence of Marxist philosophy hinges, in a sense, on our interpretation of the legacy of classical German philosophy. We can see from Marx's interpretation that what Marx was concerned about was not the pure ideological field but real social problems, so he understood man, civil society, practice, the thing-in-itself, historical consciousness and freedom as the basic legacy of classical German philosophy. It is mainly through his participation in practical struggle and his in-depth research that Marx transformed Hegel's historical idealism directly into historical materialism. Feuerbach's materialism did not play a fundamental and decisive role in Marx's founding of historical materialism; it was Feuerbach's humanistic theory that exerted a more profound influence on the young Marx. As one way out for classical German philosophy, this theory stressed that the essence of theology was anthropology. This inspired Marx, to some degree, to shift his target of criticism from religion to real life. However, Marx very soon parted company with Feuerbach. The creation of this epoch-making new concept of philosophy, historical materialism, extended Marx's theoretical horizons far beyond those of all previous materialists, including Feuerbach.

In this sense, we can say the equation that the "rational nucleus" (Hegel's dialectics) plus the "basic nucleus" (Feuerbach's materialism) equals materialistic dialectics or dialectical materialism (Marxist philosophy) is not accurate, despite the fervor with which it is upheld in traditional philosophical textbooks, because Marx never returned to the standpoint of Feuerbach's general materialism. As a matter of fact, in the first paragraph of "Theses on Feuerbach," Marx made clear the fundamental differences between his materialism and all previous materialism (that of Feuerbach included). The establishment of Marx's historical materialism is an epoch-making event in research into basic philosophical theory. In Marx's new conception of philosophy, the basis of materialism is no longer abstract matter or nature, but man's social practical activities. The epistemology implied in this new conception of philosophy no longer focuses on the intuition of objects, reality and perception, but on the observation of this presupposition—man's practical activities. In our view, the essence of Marxist philosophy is historical materialism, for Marx in his mature years did not advance any doctrines of philosophy other than historical materialism. That is to say, historical materialism is not a positive theory applicable only to the field of history, but a complete world outlook capable of covering the philosophical interpretation of all phenomena including human society, nature (matter) and man's thinking activities.

1.7 Marx's Philosophy as Hermeneutics of Praxis^①

It's well known that the adjective *hermeneutisch* ("hermeneutic") appeared only once in Marx's personal letters, and the noun *Hemeneutik* ("hermeneutics") never appeared. But it does not mean that Marx had no theory of hermeneutics. Our research will demonstrate that Marx had developed a particular theory of understanding and interpretation, which we may name as "hermeneutics of praxis" (*die Hemeneutik der Praxis*), and this theory should have an important place in the developmental history of hermeneutics.

Introduction

To expound on Marx's hermeneutics of praxis, we can't be confined to the traditional study of Marx's philosophy. Due to some misunderstand-

---

① Editor's note: This paper was originally published in *Fudan Journal of the Humanities and Social Sciences*, vol. 2, no. 2, 2009, pp. 116-133.

ings, Marx's theory of understanding and interpretation is a completely unexplored topic for previous researchers.

In *Theses on Feuerbach*, Marx remarks: "The philosophers have only interpreted (*interpretiert*) the world in various ways; the point is to change (*verönden*) it."[1] Early researchers of Marx's philosophy often misinterpreted the meaning of this statement, in the way as if Marx would argue that all previous philosophies are to "interpret the world," and only his philosophy is to "change the world." This misinterpretation has not only made Marx appear to be opposed sharply to all the philosophers that preceded him, but also made "to interpret the world" appear to be opposed sharply to "to change the world. The true meaning of this statement is: philosophers "only (*nur*)" confine themselves to interpreting the world, while Marx's philosophy is not "only" to interpret it, but pay more attention to practical activities of changing it.

This tells us that the relationship between Marx and early philosophers is, on the one hand, not entirely negative, but critical and continuous, at least with respect to "interpretation of the world"; on the other hand, the understanding and interpretation of the world is tightly interwoven with the change of the world. As a rational, sentient being, man's understanding and interpretation of the world conditions his way of activities. Conversely, in order to understand and interpret the world, man must first live in the world. That is to say, men understand and interpret the world only on the basis of existential practical activities. There is a mutual dynamic relationship: on the one hand, the understanding and interpretation determines the way of praxis; on the other hand, the understanding and

---

[1] Marx and Engels, *The Selected works of Marx and Engels*, vol. 1 (Beijing: People's Publishing House, 1972), p. 19.

interpretation unfolds only on the basis of practical activities. So, logica-lly, the practical activities are the premise of understanding and interpreta-tion. Because early researchers of Marx's philosophy dissevered the intrin-sic relationship between the activities of understanding and interpretation and the activities of praxis, they have not thought much of Marx's theory of understanding and interpretation and have not recognized that Marx had already accomplished an epoch-making revolution in hermeneutics by intro-ducing the concept of praxis.

Secondly, as for the studies of the history of western hermeneutics, how was Marx's philosophy taken then? When discussing the developmental history of hermeneutical theory, western scholars devoted almost all of their attention to Vico, Schleiermacher, Droysen, Dilthey, Heidegger, Gadamer, Habermas, and Ricoeur, and did not notice Marx's excellent contribution to this field at all. Is this because Marx had never used the term "hermeneutics"? The answer is "No." Vico is a good case in point. Many people made great contributions to the development of hermeneutics did not use the term "hermeneutics" either. Furthermore, Plato, Aristot-le, Kant, Hegel, Ranke, and Husserl, upon whom Gadamer ever touched in *Truth and Method* (1960), also did not use the concept of "hermeneu-tics." That is to say, the evaluation of a philosopher's place in the devel-opmental history of hermeneutics is not determined by his use of the con-cept of hermeneutics, but by his putting forward a few new essential ideas of the basic problem of hermeneutics—the issue of understanding and in-terpretation.

Marx's philosophy has been distorted on this issue. When talking a-bout the understanding and interpretation of religious texts, Gadamer writes: "[B]ut what will Marxists say about this? Because Marxists think that only when they regard religious doctrines as the reflection of the interests of the ruling class can they understand all religious doctrines. Undoubtedly, Marxism will not accept the premise that human Dasein is dominated by the problem of God". ① With regard to Hegel's thought of dialectic, Gadamer also points out: "the whole theory, which contains the Left's critique of pure intellectual reconciliation (it can not explain the true change of the world) and the turning philosophy into politics, is inevitably the self-cancellation of philosophy." He makes a note under this statement: "this point can still be noticed in present Marxist texts."② How do we deal with Gadamer's arguments?

1. Gadamer has not clearly distinguished Marx from the so-called Marxists. In fact, when talking about the so-called French Marxists in the 1880s, Marx says, "I only know that I myself am not a Marxist."③

2. Gadamer thinks wrongly that because Marx understands and interprets the problem of religion and philosophy from the angle of politics, he is unable to touch upon the fundamental problem of Being-in-the-world of Dasein. Actually, Marx's excellent contribution to the hermeneutical theory is that he opens a new way for the understanding and interpretation of all texts from the dimension of political-economy, which is the basic contention of Being-in-the-world of Dasein. We will discuss it when we expound the thought of Heidegger.

3. Gadamer has paid much attention to the application of hermeneutical theory, and highly values Aristotle's concept of "practical knowledge (phronesis)" in *Truth and Method*. He has also discussed the typical

① Gadamer, *Truth and Method* I (Shanghai: Shanghai Translating Publishing House, 1992), p. 426-427.
② Gadamer, *Truth and Method* I (Shanghai: Shanghai Translating Publishing House, 1992), p. 442.
③ Marx and Engels, *The Selected Works of Marx and Engels*, vol. 4 (Beijing: People's Publishing House, 1972), p. 474.

meaning of hermeneutics of law at the same time and pointed out: "we have already demonstrated that the application is not a subsequent and accidental element of phenomena of understanding, but has totally defined the activities of understanding from the very start."① Strangely, when tracing the history of hermeneutics, Gadamer puts aside Marx's treatise on the relationship between understanding and interpretation and practical activities which has influenced the development of hermeneutics more profoundly than Aristotle's concept of *phronesis*. In addition, he has also totally overlooked the great contribution to hermeneutics that Marx's *Critique of Hegel's Philosophy of Right* and other works have made. In *The Selected Essays of Philosophy* Gadamer selects three essays by Marx: *An Introduction to Critique of Hegel's Philosophy of Right, theses on Feuerbach*, and *The Fetishism of Commodities and the Secret Thereof*. Apparently, Gadamer acknowledges the general significance of Marx's works in the history of philosophy but has overlooked their important place in the developmental history of hermeneutics.

Lastly, let us take a look at how Heidegger and Habermas recognize the historical place and the role of Marx's theory of understanding and interpretation. Differing from the previous researchers of Marx's philosophy and those of hermeneutics, Heidegger recognizes subtly the importance of Marx's philosophy. He has established "hermeneutics of Dasein" (*die Hermeneutik des Daseins*) in *Being and Time*, and thereby accomplished the well-known "ontological turn" in the history of hermeneutics. According to Heidegger, understanding is the basic way of Being-in-the-world of Dasein; the task of hermeneutics of Dasein is to ask and reveal the meaning of

---

① Gadamer, *Truth and Method* I (Shanghai: Shanghai Translating Publishing House, 1992), p. 416.

Being through the existential activities of Dasein. Although Heidegger no longer used the concept of hermeneutics since then, he fully acknowledges the importance of Marx's in the history of inquiry of the meaning of Being. He remarks: "No matter how man treats the communist doctrine and its fundament, according to the history of Being, a basic experience of something which has a world-historical meaning has been disclosed in communism. "① When he touches upon Marx's theory of alienation, he further remarks: "since Marx reached an essential historical dimension through the experience of alienation, Marx's theory of history is superior to other theories of history. According to me, because neither Husserl nor Sartre has recognized the essence of the historical thing in Being, so neither phenomenology nor existentialism has reached up to the dimension of creative conversation with Marxism. "② In contrast to Gadamer's superficial attitude towards Marx, Heidegger has a deep insight into the historical depth of Marx's theory of understanding and interpretation. Although he does not expound the place and role of Marx's theory in the developmental history of hermeneutics, he inspires us to do this work.

An important contribution of Heidegger's "hermeneutics of Dasein" is that he puts forward the theory of the pre-structure of understanding from the standpoint of historicity of understanding, and justifies "the circle of hermeneutics" (*der Zirkel der Hermeneutik*). He points out: "what is decisive is not to get out of the circle, but to come into it in the right way. "③ Gadamer introduces the concept of "tradition" (*die Tradition*) in *Truth*

---

① Heidegger, *A Letter on Humanism* (Frankfurt: Frankfurt publishing company, 1975), pp. 27-28.
② Heidegger, *A Letter on Humanism* (Frankfurt: Frankfurt publishing company, 1975), p. 27.
③ Heidegger, *Sein und Zeit* (Tübingen: Max Niemeyer Verlag, 1986), S. 153.

and Method and emphasizes that any understanding unfolds in the frame of tradition, so he took Heidegger's thought to extremes. Evidently, Gadamer forgot the deep meaning of Heidegger's point "to come into it in the right way." That is to say, an interpreter is not a passive accepter of the hermeneutical situation in which he lives, but an active reflector.

Habermas has grasped this, and it has constituted the central point of his dispute with Gadamer. According to Habermas, an interpreter is not a passive carrier of tradition, but an active reflector and critic of tradition. Tradition is not unchangeable, its evolution and structural turning in some eras is always caused by the reflection and critique of its interpreters. Habermas emphasizes that the reflection and critique are not unimportant activities, but a clarification of the hermeneutical situation, which has been emphasized by Marx in his critique of ideology. If hermeneutics is not associated with the critique of ideology, its rightfulness is doubtful. Similar to Heidegger's hermeneutics of Dasein, Habermas's "critical hermeneutics" (*die kritische Hermeneutik*) also indicates the important way of returning to Marx and deepening the research of hermeneutics.

Marx's Theory of Understanding and Interpretation

The main content of the theory of understanding and interpretation in Marx's practical hermeneutics is as follows:

Practical Activities Are the Basis for All Understanding and Interpretation

For Dilthey and researchers before him, ideas and texts are always studied in a contemplative way. Although they also researched the relationship between ideas, texts, and actual human life, they did not understand actual life as practical activities. Marx's first contribution to hermeneutics is that he introduces the concept of practice into hermeneutics and regards it as the basis and the premise of all understanding and interpretation.

Firstly, Marx points out that all understanding and interpretation originate from practices. It is well known that all understanding requires at least three conditions: 1. The interpreter must live in the world; 2. The interpreter must have sound intelligence; 3. Understanding proceeds through the medium of language. Marx tells us that the three conditions are all created in the process of practical activities, especially the productive labor for the preservation of life. Hence the emergence and development of human understanding and interpretation is tightly linked to practical activities. However, with the development of human practical activities and the division of physical and mental labor, the intrinsic link between the activities of understanding and interpretation and the activities of practice became more and more blurry. So a general illusion and reversal appeared: man not only regards the ideas and texts as an independent realm, but also tries to interpret human practical activities according to it. The classical hermeneutics cannot rid itself of this illusion. It is Marx again who reverses the general illusion and reversal by clarifying the origin of understanding and interpretation, as he remarks, "Do not interpret according to ideas, but to interpret ideas according to material practice."[1]

Secondly, Marx indicates that as for their contents, all understanding and interpretation point to the activities of practice. In *Theses on Feuerbach*, Marx writes: "all social life is essentially practical, all mysteries which lead theory into mysticism find their rational solution in human

---

[1] Marx and Engels, *The Collected Works of Marx and Engels*, vol. 3 (Beijing: People's Publishing House, 1960), p. 43.

practice and in the comprehension of this practice."[①] This statement contains two meanings: 1. The contents of all ideas, theories, and texts point always to practical activities. For example, in the final analysis, the Mystic, such as natural religion, witchery, and myth which were generally believed by primitive men, originated from human practical activities. 2. The later generations must first understand practical activities in which their predecessors ever lived in order to exactly understand their predecessors, ideas, theories, and texts. Engels once talked about an anecdote in his work *The Origin of Family, Private ownership and State* that Wagner wrote in the words of the *Nibelungenlied* when concerning himself with the description of the primitive society: "who ever heard that brother regard his sister as his wife?" Obviously, Wagner understood the ideas and customs of primitive people by means of thinking of modern people. Marx criticizes this: "it is moral that sister was ever looked upon as wife in primitive times."[②] This remark indicates that any exact understanding and interpretation cannot be confined to ideas and texts themselves; rather, it requires as precondition the clarification of the intrinsic relationship between texts and the practical activities from which texts originate.

Lastly, Marx points out that as for their functions, all understanding and interpretation serve human practical activities. For example, when almost every class begins to revolt, it often explains its own interests as the general interests of the whole society. Otherwise, it would not be able to mobilize the majority of the society to join its revolutionary practice. So, Marx points out sharply: "individual class can claim the general mastery

---

① Marx and Engels, *The Collected Works of Marx and Engels*, vol. 3 (Beijing: People's Publishing House, 1960), p. 5.

② Marx and Engels, *The Selected Works of Marx and Engels*, vol. 4 (Beijing: People's Publishing House, 1972), p. 32.

only for the sake of general rights of society. "① In addition, religion is a mystic interpretation of the self and the world, and the reasons for its emergence and great development consist in its important functions, especially its consolation of human suffering. The Chinese saying "No trouble, no need to come to the temple" indicates directly the utility of religious belief. The Western religious belief is often regarded as ultra-utility, but this is not the actual state. For example, the meaning of the German adjective "fromm" is "pious," but the noun "Fromme" is interpreted as "interests," and the verb "frommen" is interpreted as "be beneficial to." We can discover from the relationship between "pious" and "be beneficial to" that Western religious belief is also conditioned by the principle of utility. ② What Marx emphasizes is to reveal the political utility for the ruling class to maintain religion. It is only in this sense that Marx says, "Religion is the opium of people. "③

To sum up, Marx clarifies the ontological premise of all understanding and interpretation by introducing the concept of practice.

Historicity is the Basic Character of All Understanding and Interpretation

According to Marx, any practical activities are the activities pursued

---

① Marx and Engels, *The Selected Works of Marx and Engels*, vol. 1 (Beijing: People's Publishing House, 1972), p. 464.

② In Western languages such as English, there are many words that disclose for us some essential relationship. For example, interest is interpreted as "interest," and its plural form is usually interpreted as "interests," which indicates that man is interested in something related to his interests. The word duty can be interpreted as "responsibility" and "obligation," and it also can be interpreted as "tax". The sum of these two meanings is that rate paying is a "responsibility" or "obligation." The word "good" as a noun can be interpreted as "good," and it also can be interpreted as "benefit" and "advantage"; its plural form "goods" is interpreted as "ware," which signifies "goods," and thus "good" is related to interests.

③ Marx and Engels, *The Selected Works of Marx and Engels*, vol. 1 (Beijing: People's Publishing House, 1972), p. 453.

by real men in the specific historical condition, and the historicity of these practices must result in the historicity of understanding and interpretation. Marx writes: "This sum of productive forces, capital funds, and social forms of intercourse, which every individual and generation finds in existence as something given, is the real basis of what the philosophers have conceived as 'substance' and 'essence of man'. "① Whether or not the interpreter is wallowing in this illusion that his understanding and interpretation is fully free, he must be factually confined to his historicity, and his understanding and interpretation always unfolds on the horizon which is set up by his historicity. From the standpoint of the historicity of understanding and interpretation, Marx has reached three conclusions:

Firstly, morality, religion, metaphysics, and other ideologies lose their own appearance of independence: "They have no history, no development; but men, developing their material production and their material intercourse, alter, along with their real existence, their thinking, and the products of their thinking. "② Here what is rejected by Marx is not the history of various forms of consciousness, but the illusion that these forms of consciousness have their own independent histories. According to Marx, the different contents of various forms of consciousness at different times are conditioned by the historicity of the practical activities at their respective times. Inspiration from this insight is that we should not confine ourselves to the surface meanings of the texts when we research them; rather, we should try to discover the imprints on the texts which were printed by the temporal practice through understanding and interpretation.

---

① Marx and Engels, *The Collected Works of Marx and Engels*, vol. 3 (Beijing: People's Publishing House, 1960), p. 43.

② Marx and Engels, *The Collected Works of Marx and Engels*, vol. 3 (Beijing: People's Publishing House, 1960), p. 30.

Secondly, the thoughts and ideas of the ruling class which dominate the material practical activities must also dominate the activities of understanding and interpretation. Marx writes: "For instance, in an age and in a country where royal power, aristocracy, and bourgeoisie are contending for mastery and where, therefore, mastery is shared, the doctrine of the separation of powers proves to be the dominant idea and is expressed as an 'eternal law'."[1] Here Marx actually puts forward the issue of "hermeneutics of power."[2] That is to say, as long as we discourse not abstractly but concretely the historicity of understanding and interpretation, we must acknowledge the basic role of power in the activities of understanding and interpretation. In other words, real hermeneutics is essentially hermeneutics of power. In fact, Marx recognized the intrinsic relation between power and understanding and interpretation earlier than Nietzsche and Foucault, which is just one of the essential historical factors hidden behind all understanding and interpretation.

Thirdly, the labor in modern society is alienated labor, which influences profoundly all our understandings and interpretations. We know that the most general and essential form of this influence is the fetishism of commodity. Marx remarks: "the fetishism of commodity regards the social economic character of things which gained in the process of social production as a natural character originated from the nature of thing."[3] Although the classical economists have true knowledge and insights on some concrete problems, when reading the capitalistic economy in totality, they

---

[1] Marx and Engels, *The Collected Works of Marx and Engels*, vol. 3 (Beijing: People's Publishing House, 1960), pp. 52-53.

[2] Yu Wujin, "Marx's Hermeneutics of Power and Its Contemporary Meaning," *Tianjin Social Science*, 5(2001).

[3] Marx, *Capital*, vol. 1 (Beijing: People's Publishing House, 1975), p. 252.

are unable to rid themselves of the influence of fetishism, and consequently consider the capitalistic way of production as natural and eternal. Marx has revealed the origin of fetishism of commodity from the standpoint of the most basic practical activities, namely, productive labor: "as long as products are produced as commodities, they must gain the character of fetishism, so fetishism is not separated from the production of commodities". ① This statement clarifies the premise of thinking for the exact understanding and interpretation. Marx's practical hermeneutics has rejected all abstract attitudes, and it aims is to reveal the insurmountable historical dimension of all understanding and interpretation.

The Critique of Ideology Is the Right Way of Coming into the Circle of Hermeneutics

Though the implications of the hermeneutical circle are fairly rich, their common core is still perceivable. It is that any text should be objectively interpreted by an interpreter, while any interpreter has his own preconceptions which are determined by the historical contexts of his understanding. It is noteworthy that these preconceptions cannot be obviated by the interpreter himself. Although Marx has not directly discussed the issue of the hermeneutical circle, he has thoroughly discussed the historicity of understanding, and this implies his affirmation of the hermeneutical circle. Marx's contribution is that he pays more attention to the problem of how to reflect exactly the historicity of understanding, and this then points to the right way of entering the hermeneutical circle.

The right way is the critique of ideology. According to Marx, the ideology of a certain era constitutes the total background for the activities of understanding and interpretation. In other words, it is the foundation and

---

① Marx, *Capital*, vol. 2 (Beijing: People's Publishing House, 1975), p. 89.

source of the preconceptions of an interpreter. Hence when the interpreter is lacking in deep reflection and critical understanding of the ideology in which he lives, he will be unable to enter the hermeneutical circle rightly. The young Hegelians such as Feuerbach and Stirner cannot put forward new insights into understanding and interpretation of the world, because they are not able to break away from the influence of Hegel's ideology. Then how can an interpreter, in Marx's words, "jump out of ideology"①? The only way is to return to the horizon of existential practical activities and establish the world view of historical materialism. Marx writes: "This conception of history depends on our ability to expound the real process of production, starting out from the material production of life itself, and to comprehend the form of intercourse connected with this and created by this mode of production (i. e. , civil society in its various stages), as the basis of all history; and to show it in its action as State, to explain all the different theoretical products and forms of consciousness, religion, philosophy, ethics, etc. and trace their origins and growth from that basis."② Conversely, if the understanding and interpretation is limited to the texts or pure thoughts and ideas, the interpreter will doubtless lose the critical reflections on his preconceptions, and thereby cannot enter the hermeneutical circle in the right way.

Deconstruction of the Independent Realm of Language

It is well known that language is the medium of all understanding and interpretation. A common mistake of classical hermeneutics and contemporary hermeneutics (the so-called " the linguistic turn ") is to regard

---

① Marx and Engels, *The Collected Works of Marx and Engels*,. vol. 3 (Beijing: People's Publishing House, 1960), p. 89.

② Marx and Engels, *The Collected Works of Marx and Engels*, vol. 3 (Beijing: People's Publishing House, 1960), pp. 42-43.

language as an independent kingdom, hence to confine all understanding and interpretation to this independent kingdom. Marx's excellent contribution to the theory of hermeneutics is to reveal the origin of language from human practical activities. In *On Wagner's Textbook of Political Economics*, Marx points out, "The linguistic name only as concept can reflect what became something experienced through repeated activities, namely, a specific external thing is the service to meet the needs of people who already lived in a certain social relationship, this assumption is necessarily deduced from being of language."① However, when language is regarded as an independent kingdom, the intrinsic relation between language and human practical activities will become blurry. As Marx has said: "as long as philosophers reduce their language into ordinary language from which philosophic language abstract, they can recognize that their language belong to the distorted world and know whether thought or language cannot consist of a special kingdom alone, which is only the expression of real life."② This point deconstructs radically the general illusion which looks upon language as an independent kingdom, and hence liberates hermeneutics from the limited mystic world of language and urges people to discover what language points to in the experiential world, namely, the practical functions of language. No matter how important language is in understanding and interpretation, it is only a bamboo kite which is sent out from the hand of human practical activities. For example, in Chinese, "man" (nan, 男) means the human who labor in the fields, "thing" (wu, 物) itself contains "bull." These hieroglyphs outline visually the picture of the

---

① Marx and Engels, *The Collected Works of Marx and Engels*, vol. 19 (Beijing: People's Publishing House, 1963), p. 405.

② Marx and Engels, *The Collected Works of Marx and Engels*, vol. 3 (Beijing: People's Publishing House, 1960), p. 525.

agricultural society of ancient Chinese. This suggests that making language, ideas, thought, and texts independent will doubtless lead all understanding and interpretation to mistakes.

An Introduction of New Methods of Hermeneutics

Marx's practical hermeneutics means not only an ontological revolution, but also a methodological renovation in the developmental history of hermeneutics. Classical hermeneutics pays methodologically more attention to research on the total structure of language, grammar, and text, whereas Marx thinks methodologically much of study on the premise of understanding and interpretation. Marx's hermeneutical method consists of two items:

The first one is the method of reduction. This method affirms factually two types of texts: one is the idealistic text which needs to be understood and interpreted; the other is the realistic text, namely, the existential practical activities per se, for which the idealistic text is intended. The latter is hidden behind the former. The method of reduction is to trace from the first type of text back to the second type, namely, from the ideal world down to the real world, and find the key to understanding the ideal world through understanding the real world. This method regards the activities of understanding and interpretation as unlimited and open from the very beginning. An inspiration we can draw from this is that only when we go out of the idealistic text can we truly understand it. Since "consciousness only is at any time the aware Being, the being of human is the actual process of life,"[1] no matter how reverse, uncanny, and absurd the idealistic text is, the method of reduction is always valid. It has very important

---

[1] Marx and Engels, *The Collected Works of Marx and Engels*, vol. 3 (Beijing: People's Publishing House, 1960), p. 29.

implications for hermeneutics of historical science, because it makes it possible for the historians, according to the handed-down texts, to reconstruct the practical ways of life for which the idealistic text is intended but which are already forgotten. For example, Morgen has reconstructed the structure of early human society according to the way of appellation of relatives, etc.

The second one is the method of archaeology. Marx has pointed out: "the dissection of human body is the key to the dissection of monkey's body. Conversely, the signs of higher animal appearing on lower animal can be understood only after recognizing the higher animal itself."[①] Unlike those classical hermeneutical researchers who believe that man must eliminate the historicity of understanding in order to understand objectively the early texts, Marx holds that only on the basis of critical understanding of the essence of his own life-world in which he lives can the interpreter understand objectively the early texts. With this interpretation, Marx tells us: "Christianity can understand objectively earlier myths only on the basis of its self-critique on certain degree. Similarly, capitalism economy can understand feudal, archaic, and oriental economy only when bourgeois society begins to go on self-critique."[②] This method is open. Its focus is not on the texts as the objects of understanding, but on the premise whole understanding activities, namely, the interpreter's critical recognition of his own historicity. It is not possible to arrive at an objective understanding and interpretation of the early texts without the resolution of the problem as a prerequisite. To sum up, Marx's hermeneutics has introduced the concept

---

① Marx and Engels, *The Collected Works of Marx and Engels*, vol. 46 I (Beijing: People's Publishing House, 1979), p. 43.

② Marx and Engels, *The Collected Works of Marx and Engels*, vol. 46 I (Beijing: People's Publishing House, 1979), p. 44.

of practice into the basic dimension of all understanding and interpretation, and thus has accomplished the "Copernican revolution" in the history of hermeneutics. In other words, we are unable to understand and interpret human existential practical activities from the perspective of idealistic texts, but understand and interpret the idealistic texts from the perspective of human existential practical activities. Marx actually clarified the ontological premise of the development of hermeneutics earlier than Heidegger did. His practical hermeneutics points to the basic direction of the development of hermeneutics.

The Historical Meaning of Marx's Hermeneutics of Praxis

We believe that the historical meaning of Marx's hermeneutics of praxis has mainly two sides:

Firstly, Marx's hermeneutics of praxis has made an epoch-making contribution to the research on hermeneutics. From the view of the developmental history of hermeneutics, Marx lived between Schleiermacher and Dilthey, and was contemporaneous with Droysen. In the 1940s, Marx established the theory of historical materialism, and determined the frame of reference for the study of all thoughts, ideas, and texts, namely, human existential practical activities. Hence he had already transcended the perspective of Schleiermacher's classical hermeneutics, and had clarified the ontological premise for further development of hermeneutics. However, one of Marx's classical texts, *Theses on Feuerbach*, in which Marx expounded his practical hermeneutics, was not published until 1888; and another classical text, *The German Ideology*, was not published until 1932, 5 years later than Heidegger's *Being and Time*! Dilthey, who died in

1911, could not thoroughly study these classical texts by Marx, and could not transcend the horizon of the classical hermeneutics. Heidegger has founded "hermeneutics of Dasein" on the basis of transcendental phenomenological method, and proclaimed definitely the ontological turning of hermeneutics. Although Heidegger's theory of hermeneutics is different from Marx's "the method of pure experience," we would find much common ground between their theories of hermeneutics if we reduced Heidegger's philosophical language to ordinary language. Generally speaking, Marx's basic contributions to the development of hermeneutical theory are as follows:

The first contribution is to reveal the practical functions of any ideas or texts, namely, the intention to practice, and affirm that the essence of understanding and interpretation is to grasp the intrinsic relationship between ideas, texts, and human existential practical activities. This point is typically expressed in his idea of hermeneutics of law: "Relations of laws, just as the forms of states, are understood according to neither themselves nor the so-called 'the general development of human mind.' Conversely, they root in the material relationships of life. The sum of these material relationships of life, according to the precedent of Frenchman and Englishman of the 18th century, is named by Hegel as 'civil society'."① Civil society is essentially practical, hence all ideas and texts will not be understood when being detached from practices.

The second one is to point out the possible method for the interpreter to critically reflect on his historicity on totality, namely, his historical situation (including the accepted tradition), that is the critique of ideology.

---

① Marx and Engels, *The Selected Works of Marx and Engels*, vol. 2 (Beijing: People's Publishing House, 1972), p. 82.

In this sense, practical hermeneutics is critical hermeneutics which regards the reflection and clarification of the interpreter on his own historical situation as the right way of entering the circle of hermeneutics, namely, as the basic premise of all objective understanding and interpretation. In this aspect, a comparison of Marx with Heidegger and Gadamer is very revealing. Heidegger argues that we could clarify the pre-structure of understanding from the principle of phenomenology, namely, "to things themselves," thereby guarantee the right way of entering the circle of hermeneutics. According to his late thought, he thinks that both phenomenology and existentialism are vastly inferior to Marxism with respect to grasping the historicity and meaning of Being. This signifies that he has acknowledged the limitation of his early thought in the aspect. Although Gadamer rightly points out that any activity of understanding is outspread in tradition, he has overlooked another side of this problem, namely, that tradition is continuously renovated through human creative understanding. At the same time, tradition always manifests itself through the ideology of a certain era. It is the critique of ideology that determines the dialectic relationship between tradition created by man and man created by tradition, and this relationship is also radically developed on the foundation of human practical activities. When criticizing the antinomy of man and environment held by the materialists of the 18th century, Marx remarks, "The coincidence of the changing of circumstances and of human activity or self-changing can be conceived and rationally understood only as *revolutionary practice*."① Thus it can be said that only Marx's practical hermeneutics delves into the issue of the circle of hermeneutics in the most profound way

---

① Marx and Engels, *The Collected Works of Marx and Engels*, vol. 3 (Beijing: People's Publishing House, 1960), p. 4.

and points the right way of entering it.

The third one is to point a new direction of "hermeneutics of power" and "hermeneutics of ideology." It is pointed out in Marx's important statement that the thoughts which are dominant in a historical period are just the thoughts of the ruling class. The hermeneutics of power pays more attention to the attachment and the intention of the power of ideas and texts, while the hermeneutics of ideology pays more attention to the role and influence of the leading frame of problems and the selection of values within the ideology in actual human activities of understanding and interpretation. This inspection can go deep into the subconscious human mind, but the importance and urgency of this inspection has not at all been noticed till this day.

Secondly, the hermeneutics of praxis is essentially Marx's philosophy. The research on Marx's philosophy will acquire a new foundation through the in-depth study of it. This turn is demonstrated in the following results:

Material hermeneutics will be replaced by practical hermeneutics. From the perspective of hermeneutic studies, early researchers of Marx's philosophy usually considered Marx's philosophy as material hermeneutics, namely, interpreting the world from the standpoint of materialism. For example, the world is unified in matter, consciousness is a product of the development of matter at a certain stage, and so on. Evidently, the way of understanding distorts totally the original meaning of Marx. In *Theses on Feuerbach*, Marx has already clearly pointed out: "the chief defect of all hitherto existing materialism (that of Feuerbach included) is that the thing, reality, sensuousness, is conceived only in the form of the object or of contemplation, but not as sensuous human activity, practice, or subjectively."① However, Marx's important point has always been over-looked.

Even the critics of Marx's philosophy have also been caught in this false understanding, so that they simply reject Marx's materialism. It is Heidegger who has the deep insight into the true meaning of Marx's materialism: "the essence of this materialism does not lie in the opinion that all is matter, but in a metaphysical regulation to which all beings appear as the material of labor."② This statement shows that the true meaning of Marx's philosophy is practical philosophy and the point of humanized nature which is necessarily contained in it, namely, all material beings are not abstract, contemplative objects, but the factors of human existential practical activities. Only from the standpoint of practical hermeneutics can we stop talking about the meaningless propositions academically, such as the proposition that the world is unified in matter. And practical hermeneutics also leads Marx's idea of matter to the critique of fetishism of commodities in a practical way, so that we can discover the essence of the relations of men from the relations of things.

The abstract epistemology will be replaced by the critique of ideology. The abstract material hermeneutics must lead to the abstract epistemology, which assumes a cognitive subject whose social-historical characters have been removed, and assumes also that the task of epistemology is to study the origin and essence of human abstract cognitive activities. Evidently, this abstract epistemology does not accord with the original meaning of Marx. When talking about his own way of cognition and observation, Marx says: "its premises are men, not in any fantastic isolation and

---

① Marx and Engels, *The Collected Works of Marx and Engels*, vol. 3 (Beijing: People's Publishing House, 1960), p. 3.

② Heidegger, *A Letter on Humanism* (Frankfurt publishing company, 1975), p. 27.

rigidity, but in their actual, empirically perceptible process of development under definite conditions."① According to Marx, the most basic activities of a real man are existential practical activities, and all his activities of cognition unfold on this basis and serve practice. Hence, a real man has already bought his historicity into any cognition of external things, and also he understands his own historicity in the frame of specific ideology in which he lives, but "almost the whole ideology either distort human history or radically put aside human history."② Hence, if we could not criticize the ideology, we could not clarify our true historicity; and if we could not clarify our historicity, all cognition, understanding, and interpretation will be totally rootless. This indicates that one of the basic tasks of epistemology is to explore the inner world. We should not ask naively, "What can I cognize?" but ask, "What do my historicity allows me to cognize?" It is the second question that leads to the replacement of the abstract epistemology by the critique of ideology.

---

① Marx and Engels, *The Collected Works of Marx and Engels*, vol. 3 (Beijing: People's Publishing House, 1960), p. 30.

② Marx and Engels, *The Collected Works of Marx and Engels*, vol. 3 (Beijing: People's Publishing House, 1960), p. 20.

1. 8   Marx's Ontology of the Praxis-based-relations of Social Production^①

Introduction

Throughout the history of Western philosophy, philosophers have proposed a variety of different types of ontology, such as the ontology of
the cosmos, the ontology of matter, the ontology
of reason, the ontology of will, theological ontolo-
gy, the ontology of emotion, the ontology of praxis, the ontology of existence, the ontology of nature, the ontology of social being, the ontology of
social relations, the ontology of humanity, and so
forth. Of all these different forms of ontology, the
ontology of matter is the most common and influential one. When it comes to interpreting Marx's
philosophy, this form of ontology affects the interpreters a lot, and as a result the interpretation,
whether it is in a direct or indirect, or obvious or

①   Editor's note: This paper was originally published in *Frontiers of Philosophy in
China*, vol. 4, no. 3, pp. 400-416, translated by Kong Hui from *Zhexue Yanjiu* (《哲学研
究》), no. 3, 2008, pp. 3-11.

covert way. In light of this, we will clarify Marx's perspective on the ontology of matter, and demonstrated that Marx actually renounced it and established his own theory of ontology, namely, the ontology of the praxis-based-relations of social production. .

The history of the ontology of matter

Although the concept of "ontology" did not occur until the 17th century in Western philosophy, the research field it indicated—being qua being—already existed for a long time. If Parmenides is supposed to first brought forward the concept of "Being, " which laid the theoretical groundwork for the subsequent rise of ontology, ① then we may argue that Aristotle made an equivalent contribution to the formation of "ontology of matter" and "ontology of form (reason). "

In his book *Metaphysics*, Aristotle cited the views of many earlier philosophers, and then concluded: "From this account it might be supposed that the only cause is of the kind called 'material'. But as men proceeded in this way, the very circumstances of the case led them on and compelled them to seek further; because if it is really true that all generation and destruction is out of some one entity or even more than one, why does this happen, and what is the cause? It is surely not the substrate itself which causes itself to change. I mean, e. g. , that neither wood nor bronze is responsible for changing itself; wood does not make a bed, nor

---

① As Nietzsche pointed out: "In the philosophy of Parmenides, the theme of ontology forms the prelude" (See Nietzsche "Philosophy during the tragic age of the Greeks, " in Maximilian A. Mugge trans. , Dr Oscar Levy ed. *The Complete Works of Friedrich Nietzsche*, vol. 2, *Early Greek Philosophy & Other Essays* (New York: Gordon Press, 1974), p. 126.

bronze a statue, but something else is the cause of the change. Now to investigate this is to investigate the second type of cause: the source of motion, as we should say."[1] As for Aristotle, although philosophers before him had already noticed that matter or material was the arche of the universe, out of which everything else had arisen from, and in practice proposed the idea of "the material cause", they did not pursue what "the motive cause" is, which drives matter or material. Aristotle also introduced the concept of "the formal cause" and "the final cause" in another part of *Metaphysics*. The so-called "formal cause" is the particular form generated by the labour process. For example, a wooden bed is a particular form made from wood by the process of human labour. The so-called "final cause" is the motivation of the person who transformed the state of matter or material by labour. For example, a person makes a bed from wood for the purpose of resting on it. Amongst "the four causes" mentioned above, Aristotle considered "the material cause" and "the formal cause" to be more important.

Needless to say, what Aristotle expressed above established a basis not only for the ontology of matter, but also for the ontology of reason, for "the form" he called was also "the idea" as a product of "reason." In fact, the concept of "materialism" we use nowadays finds its roots in the concept of "material" (synonymous with the concept matter) as its etyma, and its counterpart is "the ontology of matter." The etyma of "idealism" is idea, while its counterpart is "the ontology of reason." In other words, the "four-cause-theory," especially with "the material cause" and "the formal cause," is the origin of today's two contradictory theories—the ontology of matter (materialism) and the ontology of reason (idealism).

---

[1]　Aristotle, *Metaphysics*, Books I-IX (Cambridge, Massachusetts: Harvard University Press, 1933), p. 22.

Compared to his teacher Plato, Aristotle is more apt to stand behind "the material cause" and accept "the ontology of matter."

Although epistemology and methodology has received more attention than ontology in modern Western philosophy, the study of ontology is still a major concern of many philosophers. Considering Descartes, from whom modern Western philosophy began, he actually initiated the two contradictory forms of ontology- the ontology of reason and the ontology of matter.

On the one hand, Descartes, as a rationalist, laid an ideological foundation for modern Western philosophy. "I think, therefore I am," regarded as the first principle by Descartes, has given full expression to the fundamental position of rational thinking in the study of philosophy. He did not use the term "the ontology of reason," yet ontological thinking of such kind, based on reason, had already emerged. Hegel acknowledged the construction of a philosophical structure from a rational foundation. In *Lectures on the History of Philosophy*, Hegel wrote: "It is not until Descartes has arrived that we really enter upon a philosophy which is, properly speaking, independent, which knows that it comes forth from reason as independent, and that self-consciousness is an essential moment in the truth. Philosophy in its own proper soil separates itself entirely from the philosophizing theology, in accordance with its principle, and places it on quite another side... Descartes is a bold spirit who re-commenced the whole subject from the very beginning and constituted afresh the groundwork on which Philosophy is based, and to which, after a thousand years had passed, it once more returned."[1] In this sense, we cannot underestimate

---

[1] G. W. F. Hegel, *Lectures on the History of Philosophy*, vol. III (Bristol: Thoemmes Press, 1999), pp. 217, 220-221. Heidegger also believed: "'I think' is reason, basic action of reason. What is purely abstracted from 'I think' is what is purely abstracted from reason itself."

Descartes' role in laying a thinking foundation for the modern ontology of reason.

On the other hand, as a dualist, Descartes also attached great importance to the physical world, and thus provided a thinking premise for the rise of the ontology of matter in modern philosophy. He pointed out in his book *The Principles of Philosophy*: "From this it can also be easily inferred that the matter of the heaven does not differ from that of the earth; and that even if there were countless worlds in all, it would be impossible for them not to all be of one and the same [kind of] matter. And therefore, there cannot be several worlds, but only one: because we clearly understand that this matter (the nature of which consists solely in the fact that it is an extended substance) now occupies absolutely all the conceivable spaces in which those other worlds would have to be. Nor can we discover, in ourselves, the idea of any other [kind of] matter … Therefore, all the matter in the whole universe is of one and the same kind; since all matter is identified [as such] solely by the fact that it is extended. Moreover, all the properties which we clearly perceive in it are reducible to the sole fact that it is divisible and its parts movable; and that it is therefore capable of all the dispositions which we perceive can result from the movement of its parts. For although our minds can imagine divisions [in that matter], this [imagining] alone cannot change matter in any way; rather, all the variation of matter, or all the diversity of its forms, depends on motion. "①

Here, Descartes stated basic ideas concerning matter and motion: the world is made up of matter, matter is in a state of motion, and matter in

---

① Descartes, *Principles of Philosophy* (Dordecht: Reidel Publishing Company, 1983), pp. 49-50.

motion can be perceived by people, etc., all of which enrich the original version of the ontology of matter by Aristotle. Descartes realized the source of his thought: "However, I should also like it to be noted that I have here attempted to explain the entire nature of material things in such a way that I have used, for this purpose, absolutely no principle which was not accepted by Aristotle and by all other philosophers of all periods: so that this Philosophy is not new, but the oldest and most commonplace of all."[①] In spite of his modest words, by combining his ideas with the new discovery of modern science, he further developed the concept of the ontology of matter descended from Aristotle. Examples above illustrate his contribution to the development of the ontology of matter, including his distinction between "thinking entity" and "substantial entity," his recognition of two different kinds of properties of things, his reflection on the relationship between time and space, and so on. True, Descartes' ontology of matter bears some negative features of his time, like mechanicalness. He even thought of nature itself, animals included, as "a machine."

Marx made a positive assessment of the historical role that Descartes' theory of materialism, i.e., the ontology of matter played. In his view, French materialism consisted of two different schools: one from the British empiricist philosopher John Locke. It had a significant impact on the educated class of French philosophers, and led directly to the French utopian socialist theory. The other school came from Cartesian physics, characterized by mechanical materialism, which turned into a spiritual resource for the French natural sciences. Marx wrote: "Descartes in his physics endowed matter with self-creative power and conceived mechanical motion as

---

① Descartes, *Principles of Philosophy* (Dordecht: Reidel Publishing Company, 1983), p. 283.

the act of its life. He completely separated his physics from his metaphysics. Within his physics, matter is the only substance, the only basis of being and of knowledge. "① After Descartes, idealist philosophers, such as Kant and Hegel, did all they could to reject Descartes' ontology of matter, while endorsing his ontology of reason and exerting great effort to stimulate its theoretical development. Materialist philosophers, such as Diderot, La Mettrie, Holbach, Feuerbach, did their utmost to refute Descartes' ontology of reason, while adopting his theory on the ontology of matter.

Marx's philosophy misinterpreted
as the ontology of matter

It is still considered moderate when orthodox interpreters replace "ontology" with "world view," however, some other interpreters, without more ado, assert that the field of ontology should be entirely discarded. For instance, Mr. Gao Qinghai claimed, "In order to return to the real world, it is necessary to get rid of the ontological way of thinking. Only when we get rid of it, can we succeed in establishing a way of practical philosophical thinking, based on China's reality, facing the world and facing the future, and this is my conclusion. "② Obviously, he fell into a fallacy of generalizing about ontology, as he rapidly concluded that there was something wrong with all theories on ontology merely because there were problems in some theories on ontology. He furthermore adhered to the

① Marx, *Karl Marx*: *Selected Writings* (New York: Oxford University Press Inc, 2000), p. 164.

② Gao Qinghai, *Gao Qinghai Wencun* (*Gao Qinghai Collective Works on Philosophy*), vol. 1 (Jilin: Jilin People's Press, 1977), p. 151.

opinion that the study of ontology would result in the dehumanization of humans and the un-realizing of reality. He considered a possible consequence of the ontology of matter to be that of all types of ontology.

Here is a counter-example to such a view. Advocated by Heidegger, "fundamental ontology" clarifies the premises for the study of humans and the real-world by an existential analysis of "Dasein." At first sight, basic ontology does not appear to give a direct explanation of humans and the real world, like anthropology and sociology. Actually, it simply aims to give a fundamental explanation of humans and real-world issues. In another word, unlike positivistic sciences, fundamental ontology tries to reveal "the meaning of Being," which has been concealed by the daily state of Dasein as well as other beings. As Heidegger says: "The task of ontology is to explain Being itself and to make the Being of entities stand out in full relief."[①]

Since ontology is the basis and core of metaphysics, which lays the foundation for philosophy, it is impossible by any means to put aside ontology in philosophy. Though some ontological theories may be nonsense, it does not mean that all ontological theories are ridiculous. The child shall not be dumped out with the washing water. Even though positivists have proposed "the elimination of metaphysics," there has been a remarkable phenomenon, that is, a revival in the study of ontology in contemporary Western philosophy since the early 20th century. In *Ideas Pertaining to a Pure Phenomenology and to a Phenomenological Philosophy* Volume 1, published in 1913, Husserl used the concept of "ontology," and when mentioning the work *Logic Investigations* clarified: "On historical grounds

---

① Heidegger, *Being and Time* (Tubingen: Basil Blackwell Publisher Ltd., 1962), p. 49.

I had at that time not yet dared to make use of the alienating expression Ontology, and I described their study as a fragment of an 'a prior theory of objects as such', which A. V. Meinong has brought more compactly under the title 'Theory of the Object' (Gegenstandstheorie). In opposition to this arrangement, I now hold it to be more correct, in sympathy with the changed condition of the time, to make the old expression Ontology current once again."① Following Husserl, a large number of Western philosophers such as Heidegger, N. Hartmann, Sartre, Quine, Lukacs, Gould and others made further contributions to the study of ontology.

Thus it follows that Mr. Gao Qinghai's view of "the necessity of e-radicating the ontological way of thinking" is untenable. Unfortunately, he rejected ontology not only in his study on general philosophy, but in his interpretation of Marx's philosophy, too. He wrote in *Aspiration for Philosophy*: *A Meditation on* Metaphysics : "As a new starting point in philosophy, Marx's philosophy completely negates the theory of traditional speculative metaphysics, especially the thought of ontology as the soul of traditional philosophy; as well as places the issue of the existence of human and liberation into the center, and thus radically changes the traditional characteristics and manner of philosophy. In these two aspects, Marx's philosophy is in complete accordance with modern philosophy."② It is right for him to notice that Marx's philosophy was similar to modern philosophical trends, but he neglected that Marx never puts ontology aside. In fact, the significance of his epoch-making philosophical revolution is typified in the ontology. As Heidegger said: "No matter which of the

---

① Husserl, *Ideas*: *General Introduction to Pure Phenomenology* (London: George Allen &. Unwin Ltd. and The Macmillan Company, 1931), p. 68.

② Gao Qinghai, *Gao Qinghai Wencun* (*Gao Qinghai Collective Works on Philosophy*), vol. 1 (Jilin: Jilin People's Press, 1977), p. 250.

various positions one chooses to adopt toward the doctrines of communism and to their foundation, from the point of view of the history of Being it is certain that an elemental experience of what is world-historical speaks out in it."[①] If the theory of communism possesses a special place in "the historical significance of Being," then what other than ontology could Marx's philosophy be founded on, for "the historical significance of Being" is the focus of the study of ontology?

Although orthodox interpreters don't refuse ontological study of Marx's philosophy like Gao, they simply interpret it as the ontology of matter, which originated with Aristotle and was considerably advanced by Descartes and other modern philosophers. For example, Lenin explained Marx's philosophy in the following words: "This is materialism: matter acting upon our sense-organs produces sensation. Sensation depends on the brain, nerves, retina, etc., i.e., on matter organized in a definite way. The existence of matter does not depend on sensation. Matter is primary. Sensation, thought, consciousness are the supreme product of matter organized in a particular way. Such are the views of materialism in general, and of Marx and Engels in particular."[②]

And in Chinese academic circle, there is a chapter devoted to this kind of ontology of matter in the book *Principles of Dialectical Materialism* edited by Xiao Qian, et al. The chapter comes straight to the point in the very beginning: "Lenin said: 'The basic premise of materialism is recognition of the external world, and the acknowledgement that substance exists outside of our consciousness independently.' The ability to recognize the

---

① Heidegger, *Martin Heidegger Basic Writings, from Being and Time (1927) to The Task of Thinking (1964)* (San Francisco: Harper Collins Publishers, 1993), p. 244.

② Lenin, *Materialism and Empirio-Criticism: Critical Comment on A Reactionary Philosophy* (Moscow: Foreign Languages Publishing House, 1952), p. 48.

material unity of the world and faithfully take the world as it moves and develops in a certain time and space according to the laws within it, is the starting point for correctly dealing with basic philosophical issues and to follow monistic materialism. It is also a solid philosophical foundation from which we proceed towards reality and seek truth from facts, recognize the world as it really is, and change the world according to its laws. "[1] From the above statement, we can summarize the main points of Marx's ontology of matter: First, substance exists outside of our consciousness independently. Second, the world is unified in matter. Third, motion is the essential property of matter. Fourth, time and space are the ways in which moving matters exist. And fifth, the motion of matter follows its own laws.

The statements here on the ontology of matter are more specific than relevant statements made by Aristotle, Descartes and other traditional philosophers. However, the question remains: is there such a view of ontology of matter in Marx's philosophy, as orthodox interpreters have all voiced in unison? Or have they imposed it on Marx's philosophy? Even if Marx has his own understanding of philosophy, the question is whether it is right to interpret Marx's view of matter correctly in the traditional framework of the ontology of matter.

As we all know, the traditional ontology of matter is marked by the concept of abstract matter. By "the concept of abstract matter," we mean a concept of "matter" that is generally spoken of without taking into account the social activity of humans or historical background. The concept of "matter," if it represents all concrete things, is merely an abstract

---

[1] Xiao Qian, *Bianzheng Weiwu Zhuyi Yuanli* (Principles of Dialectical Materialism) (Beijing: People's Publishing House, 1981), p. 54.

symbol and a philosophical category. The British philosopher Berkeley noticed this, though his idea that "matter is nothing" is still denounced by many people. In *A Treatise Concerning the Principles of Human Knowledge*, Berkeley wrote: "But though it be allowed by the materialists themselves that Matter was thought of only for the sake of supporting accidents, and, the reason entirely ceasing, one might expect the mind should naturally, and without any reluctance at all, quit the belief of what was solely grounded thereon; yet the prejudice is riveted so deeply in our thoughts, that we can scarce tell how to part with it, and are therefore inclined, since the thing itself is indefensible, at least to retain the name, which we apply to I know not what abstracted and indefinite notions of being, or occasion, though without any show of reason, at least so far as I can see. For, what is there on our part, or what do we perceive, amongst all the ideas, sensations, notions which are imprinted on our minds, either by sense or reflex, from whence may be inferred the existence of an inert, thoughtless, unperceived occasion?"[1] In Berkeley's view, matter with no characteristics is merely "an abstract notion," "an empty name," and "nothingness." He even advocated expelling the concept of "matter" from people's thoughts to find real knowledge. Of course, Berkeley worried that atheism would be attached to such abstract "matter." However, apart from his somewhat cramped religious sense, there is nothing unreasonable in Berkeley's concept of matter.

In his introduction to *Lectures on the History of Philosophy*, Hegel also expressed a similar idea: "an invalid pedant was told by the doctor to eat fruit, and he had cherries, plums and grapes, before him, but he

---

[1] Berkeley, *A Treatise Concerning the Principles of Human Knowledge* (La Salle: The Open Court Publishing Company, 1963), p. 73.

pedantically refused to eat anything because no part of what was offered him was fruit, some of it being cherries, and the rest plums or grapes."① Obviously, the "fruit" that the pedant wants to eat is as empty a name as the concept of "matter." "Fruit" in itself does not exist, but is represented by the concrete form of cherries, plums, grapes, etc. In other words, there are no "fruits" without a specific form. It may be easily conceived that from Hegel's concept of "fruit," we may prove the far more universal concept of "matter" is merely an illusion. In fact, Aristotle had already taught us that matter or material was merely a thing in a potential sense, and only through its concrete form could it become a reality. There is essentially no difference between talking vaguely and generally about matter detached from any specific condition or form, and talking about "nothing."

Deeply influenced by Hegel, Engels expressed a similar idea in *Dialectics of Nature*: "N. B. Matter as such is a pure creation of thought and an abstraction. We leave out of account the quantitative differences of things in lumping them together as corporeally existing things under the concept matter. Hence matter as such, as distinct from definite existing kinds of matter, is not anything sensuously existing. When natural science directs its efforts to seeking out uniform matter as such, to reducing qualitative differences to merely quantitative differences in combining identical smallest particles, it is doing the same thing as demanding to see fruit as such instead of cherries, pears, apples, or the mammal as such instead of cats, dogs, sheep, etc., gas as such, metal, stone, chemical compound as such, motion as such."② Engels has actually proposed a similar idea to

---

① G. W. F. Hegel, *Lectures on the History of Philosophy*, vol. III (Bristol: Thoemmes Press, 1999), p. 18.

② Marx, "Marx's Critique of Hegel's Philosophy of Right," in *Karl Marx Frederick Engels Collected Works*, vol. 3 (Moscow: Progress Publishers, 1987), pp. 533-534.

Berkeley's saying of "matter is nothing", saying that matter is *a pure creation of thought and an abstraction.*" However, Engels' attempt to distinguish "matter as such" from "definite existing piece of matter" still causes theoretical confusion. In fact, it is sufficient to distinguish abstract general matter from concrete individual things.

From the above, we can see that although some interpreters advocate discarding the ontological way of thinking, orthodox interpreters still make their interpretation of Marx's philosophy by the influence of traditional Western philosophy. They secretly borrow the ontology of matte represented by the theories of Aristotle and Descartes, and try to make it a foundation of Marx's philosophy. As a result, it becomes a mainstream interpretation and the essence of Marx's philosophy is obscured.

Marx's sublimation of the ontology of matter

All those who have deeply studied Marx's thoughts have discovered that since his youth, Marx was a determined critic of "the concept of abstract matter", and thereby was also a critic of the ontology of matter. Marx had pointed out as early as 1843 in *Critique of Hegel's Philosophy of Right* : "Abstract spiritualism is abstract materialism; abstract materialism is the abstract spiritualism of matter."[①] For him, as long as concepts such as "soul," "matter," "materialism," "spiritualism," were generally discussed, there were essentially no differences between them. There was only literal difference, while as abstract concepts, they were

---

① Marx and Engels, *The Collected Works of Marx and Engels*, vol. 1 (Beijing: People's Publishing House, 1956), p. 355.

completely the same. In *Economic and Philosophical Manuscripts of 1844*, Marx made the following comment: "Industry is the actual, historical relationship of nature, and therefore of natural science, to man. If, therefore, industry is conceived as the exoteric revelation of man's essential powers, we also gain an understanding of the human essence of nature or the natural essence of man. In consequence, natural science will lose its abstractly material—or rather, its idealistic—tendency, and will become the basis of human science, as it has already become the basis of actual human life, albeit in an estranged form." [1] It is well known that in the orthodox interpretation, "material" and "natural" are interchangeable concepts, thus by "the human essence of nature" or "the natural essence of man" mentioned here, Marx advocated investigating matter or nature via the medium of human activities. Marx revealed that industry, along with its history, is "the actual, historical relationship" in which humans have contact with matter or nature.

Marx believed that if philosophers study matter or nature in isolation, while omitting human activities, especially the history of industry, such a study would run into "its abstractly material or rather, its idealistic tendency." It is in this aspect, Marx stressed: "The nature which develops in human history—the genesis of human society—is man's real nature; hence nature as it develops through industry, even though in an estranged form, is true anthropological nature." [2] Here, Marx would like to tell us that we must not leave out human activities, especially the history of industry, in the study of matter or nature; otherwise we would miss the real physical

---

① Marx, *Economic and Philosophic Manuscripts of 1844* (New York: International Publishers, 1976), pp. 142-143.

② Marx, *Economic and Philosophic Manuscripts of 1844* (New York: International Publishers, 1976), p. 143.

world or nature.

Some people might ask: Did Marx still critisize "the concept of abstract matter" in his mature time, given the *Critique of Hegel's Philosophy of Right* and *Economic and Philosophical Manuscripts of 1844* were written when he was young? After his thought matured, did he also critique "the concept of abstract matter"? Our reply is yes. In a note in Volume 1, Chapter 13, of *Das Kapital*, Marx wrote a few lines which readers pay little attention to but are of great importance: "Technology discloses man's mode of dealing with Nature, the process of production by which he sustains his life, and thereby also lays bare the mode of formation of his social relations, and of the mental conceptions that flow from them. Every history of religion even, that fails to take account of this material basis, is uncritical. It is, in reality, much easier to discover by analysis the earthly core of the misty creations of religion, than, conversely, it is, to develop from the actual relations of life the corresponding celestial forms of those relations. The latter method is the only materialistic, and therefore the only scientific one. The weak points in the abstract materialism of natural science, a materialism that excludes history and its process, are at once evident from the abstract and ideological conceptions of its spokesmen, whenever they venture beyond the bounds of their own speciality." [1]

From these words, it can be inferred that Marx was resolutely opposed to "the abstract materialism of natural science, a materialism that excludes history and its process." Actually, materialism of this kind is the traditional ontology of matter, which is satisfied with talking about the concept of "matter" or "nature" abstractly, laying aside human activities

---

[1] Marx, *Capital: A Critique of Political Economy vol.* 1: *The Process of Capitalist Production* (Chicago: Charles H. Kerr &. Company, 1915), pp. 406-407.

and historical processes. In Marx's view, it is important to uncover "man's mode of dealing with Nature" and clarifying "the history of formation of the basis of a specific social organization" through the study of the historical process of technology or technique. That is because human history is different from that of nature, for it is through practice that human beings deal with nature and the physical world, so as to create their own lives and their own history. All of these indicate that Marx kept on criticizing the ontology of matter. In particular, he was a firm critic of the concept of abstract matter, and was always opposed to discussing concepts like "matter," "nature" or "Being" in general, putting aside specific historical and social conditions.

Therefore, what Xiao Qian and others discussed is not Marx's concept of matter. Superficially, when they emphasize the independent existence of things outside of our consciousness, they refer to pure materialism, that is, talking about things while excluding the human consciousness. It is typical of the concept of abstract matter, as it means erasing all relationships with people, including people's consciousness so as to study things in isolation, but this is unrealistic. For example, when a craftsman makes a sculpture of Plato out of marble, hasn't the marble's existence been changed according to people's consciousness and will to make it change? As Marx said: "In practice I can relate myself to a thing humanly only if the thing relates itself humanly to the human being."[1] As long as they do not adhere to the concept of abstract matter, people can see that things around them, as concrete states and real forms of matter, are all marked by people's consciousness, will, and practice.

---

[1] Marx, *Economic and Philosophic Manuscripts of 1844* (New York: International Publishers, 1976), p. 139.

It is well known that according to Marx, the basic form of practice is productive labour by which people seek the material means for living. When talking about productive labour, Marx said: "So much is this activity, this unceasing sensuous labour and creation, this production, the foundation of the whole sensuous world as it now exists that, were it interrupted only for a year, Feuerbach would not only find an enormous change in the natural world, but would very soon find that the whole world of men and his own perceptive faculty, nay his own existence, were missing."[1] Orthodox interpreters always speak of such empty words as "the world's unity consists in matter", but Marx did not waste time on the abstract matter. Marx studied the various states or elements of matter such as raw materials, tools, equipment, products (goods), the waste of production, natural forces of labor, and so on, from the perspective of the history of production under capitalism.

In contrast to orthodox interpreters, Heidegger had keen insight into the essence of Marx's materialism and his concept of matter. In *Letter on Humanism*, he emphasized strengthening dialogue with Marx's materialism: "For such dialogue it is certainly also necessary to free oneself from naive notions about materialism, as well as from the cheap refutations that are supposed to counter it. The essence of materialism does not consist in the assertion that everything is simply matter but rather in a metaphysical determination according to which every being appears as material of labor."[2] In Heidegger's opinion, there is a radical difference between Marx's materialism and traditional materialism. Traditional materialism,

---

① Marx, *The German Ideology Includes: Theses on Feuerbach and the Introduction to the Critique of Political Economy* (New York: Prometheus Books, 1998), p. 46.

② Heidegger, *Martin Heidegger Basic Writings, from Being and Time (1927) to The Task of Thinking (1964)* (San Francisco: Harper Collins Publishers, 1993), p. 243.

namely, the ontology of matter, merely discusses abstract matter, but Marx's materialism studies all concrete states of matter that could be encountered in production and labour from the special perspective of productive labour. As thus, the abstract matter expressed in the ontology of matter that transcends all historical periods changes into a concrete state of matter in a specific period of time-the age of capitalism, namely, the commodity. That is what Heidegger meant when he said, "all beings appear to be material for labour."

In fact, Marx restated the above statement more clearly. In *Das Kapital* Volume 1, he came straight to the point: "The wealth of those societies in which the capitalist mode of production prevails, presents itself as 'an immense accumulation of commodities', its unit being a single commodity. Our investigation must therefore begin with the analysis of a commodity."[1] Based on this, Marx does not express any interest in the abstract matter discussed by orthodox interpreters, and his real concern lies in the concrete states of matter under capitalism, that is, how commodity comes into being, as a "social thing", through the process of productive labour, and how currency as a "general equivalent" leads to the emergence of capital and its unrestricted expansion.

Indeed, as a great successor and critic of the Western humanist tradition, the ultimate goal of Marx is not to study these things, but to change the extant world as it is and liberate all mankind, so that everyone can freely and fully develop through political revolution and social revolution. In fact, Marx not only discussed the concrete state of matter in production under capitalism—commodity, but brought to light the essence of the

---

[1] Marx, *Capital: A Critique of Political Economy: The Process of Capitalist Production* (Chicago: Charles H. Kerr & Company, 1915), p. 41.

phenomenon of "commodity fetishism": "There, the existence of the things quâ commodities, and the value relation between the products of labour which stamps them as commodities, have absolutely no connection with their physical properties and with the material relations arising therefore. There it is a definite social relation between men, that assumes, in their eyes, the fantastic form of a relation between things. In order, therefore, to find an analogy, we must have recourse to the mist-enveloped regions of the religious world. In that world the productions of the human brain appear as independent beings endowed with life, and entering into relation both with one another and the human race. So it is in the world of commodities with the products of men's hands. This I call the Fetishism which attaches itself to the products of labour, so soon as they are produced as commodities, and which is therefore inseparable from the production of commodities. This Fetishism of commodities has its origin, as the foregoing analysis has already shown, in the peculiar social character of the labour that produces them."[1]

According to Marx, the phenomenon of commodity fetishism is bound to develop with the production of commodities in a capitalist society because in the capitalist mode of production all products are produced for the market, while in traditional production products are mainly produced for the needs of producers. Patently, there is a fundamental difference between the two modes of production. That is to say, only when the product is also a commodity, can the phenomenon of commodity fetishism be widespread. For example, people generally worship goods made from gold, and are apt to believe that the price of gold products is high due to the physical

① Marx, *Capital: A Critique of Political Economy: The Process of Capitalist Production* (Chicago: Charles H. Kerr & Company, 1915), p. 83.

properties of the material itself. This kind of worship of commodities (things), according to Marx, is commodity fetishism, and commodity fetishism covers up the following truth, that is, the worship of commodities (things), especially of a commodity like gold products, is not actually caused by the natural properties of the commodity (gold), but the social properties. Gold is gold, and only in a certain historical condition and social relationship can it become a commodity with a high price. The sole purpose of Marx's devotion to critiquing commodity fetishism is to expose the real relationship between humans from the illusory relationship among things in the capitalist mode of production, and thus change this relationship through revolution. This is the revolutionary significance of Marx's concept of matter.

Therefore, it will emasculate the revolutionary significance of Marx's philosophy by interpreting his concept of matter as abstract matter in accordance with the ontology of matter. And to interpret Marx' words into something like "the world is united in matter" is definitely a distortion of his ideas. "① In a word, Marx establishes his theory of historical materialism by criticizing the concept of abstract matter contained in the traditional ontology of matter. This theory instructs us not to talk about matter in an abstract way without reference to historical conditions, as traditional materialist philosophers do. It is important to discuss matter within the context of a certain historical condition, especially under the condition of capitalism, that is, to discuss the commodity, and reveal the real relationships between people which have been concealed by the phenomenon of commodity fetishism (which only sees the relationships between things).

① Yu Wujin, "Marx Wuzhiguan Xintan, " ("A New Explore on Marx's View of Matter,"in *Fu Dan Learned Journal*, 6th issue, 1995).

Marx's philosophy as the ontology of praxis-based-relations of social production

Now that Marx has thoroughly critiqued the ontology of matter as well as its concept of abstract matter, then what is Marx's philosophy? We argue that Marx's philosophy is the philosophy of historical materialism, the essence of which is the "ontology of praxis-based-relations of social production". In fact, it is through the sublimation of the ontology of matter that this unique ontology is expressed.

As previously mentioned, Marx does not discuss matter in an abstract and static way. Matter is always in a concrete state—things. And when it comes to discussing things, he starts from human actions, especially the act of existence, namely, productive labour. To be brief, Marx's philosophy takes specific and sensual activities as the starting point, which is completely different from traditional materialism (ontology of matter) with abstract matter as its starting point. Marx pointed out: "All social life is essentially practical. All mysteries which lead theory to mysticism find their rational solution in human practice and in the comprehension of this practice."[①] Marx even claims to be a "practical materialist."[②] All this indicates that practice plays a fundamental and central part in Marx's philosophy. Because of this, Marx's philosophy has often been interpreted as the "ontology of praxis," a view held by Gramsci and the former Yugoslavian

---

① Marx, *Karl Marx*: *Selected Writings* (New York: Oxford University Press Inc, 2000), p. 173.

② Marx, *The German Ideology Includes*: *Theses on Feuerbach and the Introduction to the Critique of Political Economy* (New York: Prometheus Books, 1998), p. 44.

"school of practice."

However, it does not suffice to take Marx's philosophy as the "ontology of praxis" because it is a sensual activity that can be perceived and experienced by people. But the law of human society, especially the social movement of capitalism, cannot be grasped at a level of the sensual experience. In the introduction to the first edition of *Das Kapital*, Volume 1, Marx wrote: "In the analysis of economic forms, moreover, neither microscopes nor chemical reagents are of use. The force of abstraction must replace both."[1]"The force of abstraction" Marx mentioned here is a pretersensual faculty of reason, for objects such as "economic form" are invisible and intangible, and cannot be grasped by our sensual experience. As a matter of fact, invisible and intangible objects like economics, social being, social relations, and history cannot be explained or verified by sensual activity.

Conversely, if people try to truly understand sensual activity, in particular, productive labour, it is necessary to grasp that which is invisible and intangible. In *Wage Labour and Capital*, Marx made the point: "In order to produce, they enter into definite connections and relations with one another, and only within these social connections and relations does their action on nature, does production, take place."[2] Thus, it is the pretersensual relationship of social production that makes productive labour possible. According to Marx's point of view, of all the social relationships that connect humans, social production is the most fundamental one: "Under all forms of society there is a certain industry which predominates over all the rest and whose condition therefore determines the rank and

---

① Marx, *Capital: A Critique of Political Economy: The Process of Capitalist Production* (Chicago: Charles H. Kerr & Company, 1915), p. 12.

② Marx, *Selected Works* (New York: International Publisher, 1980), p. 81.

influence of all the rest. It is the universal light with which all the other colors are tinged and are modified through its peculiarity. It is a special e-ther which determines the specific gravity of everything that appears in it. "① In this sense, Marx's philosophy is usually regarded as the "ontolo-gy of relations of social production". Clearly, Marx's exploration into the relationship of social production is also the result of the sublimation of the abstract matter contained in the ontology of matter. For example, Marx criticized abstract matter for merely viewing capital as "a thing", when ex-amining capital as the central phenomenon of modern society, and com-mented: "Capital is conceived of as a thing, not as a relationship."② In his view, "It is thus evidently a relation, and can only be a relation of produc-tion."③ Thus, it can be seen, studying the relationship of social produc-tion goes beyond the traditional ontology of matter. It reveals the impor-tance of the social relationships between people, which is concealed by things, rather than the thing itself.

Through the above study, we can conclude: When people interpret Marx's philosophy as the "ontology of praxis", they focus on the phenom-enon of sensual experience, thus ignoring the field of essence related to pretersensual reason. This causes them to confuse Marx's philosophy with Feuerbach's. As for Marx's philosophy, although the concept of practice plays a fundamental and central role, it does not displace Marx's thinking on the field of pretersensual essence. On the contrary, when interpreting Marx's philosophy as "ontology of relations of social production," essence

---

① Marx, *The German Ideology Includes: Theses on Feuerbach and the Introduction to the Critique of Political Economy* (New York: Prometheus Books, 1998), p. 21.

② Marx and Engels, *The Collected works of Marx and Engels*, vol. 46 I (Beijing: People's Publishing House, 1979), p. 189.

③ Marx and Engels, *The Collected works of Marx and Engels*, vol. 46 I (Beijing: People's Publishing House, 1979), p. 438.

related to reason is emphasized, while neglecting Marx's examination of phenomenon related to real life and the practice of sensual activity, and confusing Marx's philosophy with Hegel's speculative philosophy. In order to fully understand and elucidate Marx's philosophy, we should combine the phenomenon related to sensual experience and the essence related to pretersensual sense, and interpret Marx's philosophy as the "ontology of praxis-based-relation of social production."

Obviously, this new view of the "ontology of praxis-based-relations of social production" has surpassed the "ontology of praxis" proposed by Gramsci and the "ontology of social being" advocated by Lukacs, as well as the "ontology of relations of social production" asserted by K Colletti. The limitations of Gramsci's theory consists in that it does not fully acknowledge the great contribution Marx's philosophy has made to the field of essence. The drawback of Lukacs' theory resides in that he merely interprets Marx's philosophy to be the ontology of social being, but does not deeply explore the foundation and core of social beings—the relationship of social production. As for Colletti, despite his understanding of the relationship of social production, his positivistic tendency prevents him from discussing ontology, and thus he does not understand the real significance of Marx's philosophical revolution. To sum up, Marx's ontology connects the field of phenomenon and the field of essence, and so only the "ontology of praxis-based-relations of social production" can fully catch the complete content and profound meaning of this ontological theory.

1.9 Creatively Advance Chinese Research on Marx's Philosophy[①]
—In Commemoration of the Thirtieth Anniversary of *Zhongguo Shehui Kexue* (《中国社会科学》)

The thirtieth anniversary of *Zhongguo Shehui Kexue* (《中国社会科学》) merits congratulations because it has substantially promoted the growth of contemporary Chinese scholarship by advocating and encouraging original thought. As a high-quality and comprehensive academic journal, its achievements in the past thirty years are unmatched in China. As a dedicated reader, contributor and scholar of philosophy, I am most impressed by the far-sighted academic vision of its editorial staff and its status as the "first violinist" in the academic development of contemporary China. Now, by drawing on my own professional background and academic experience, I want to give my own views

---

① Editor's note: This paper was originally published in *Social Sciences in China*, vol. 32, no. 3, August 2011, pp. 5-13, translated by Huang Yusheng from *Zhongguo Shehui Kexue* (《中国社会科学》), no. 6, 2010, revised by Sally Borthwick.

and reflections on the journal's important role in creatively advancing the study of Marx's philosophy in China.

A New Understanding of the Essence of Marx's Philosophy

As we all know, according to Stalin, the essence of Marx's philosophy is "dialectical materialism," and its application or extension to the field of social history gives rise to "historical materialism." Textbooks on the Marxist philosophy, whether those of the former Soviet Union, Eastern Europe, or the earlier versions produced in China, have been written with this view in mind and within a framework of dialectical and historical materialism.

Since reform and opening up, an influential view has emerged among Chinese academics that reverses this order, placing historical materialism before dialectical materialism. It claims that the foundation and core of Marx's philosophy is historical materialism, while dialectical materialism is the result of the application and extension of historical materialism to the natural world.

Comparatively speaking, this view shows a deeper understanding of the essence of Marx's philosophy, because the focus of this revolutionary and practical philosophy has always been on social history. However, it must be noted that this viewpoint has not fully thrown off the intellectual framework of the previous one. Both have their limitations. One is the dualization of the unified research object, that is, dividing the unified object into two mutually external and partial spheres, "the natural world" and "social history." The other is the dualization of Marx's philosophy, as if it contains two different philosophical systems: dialectical materialism with the natural world as its object, and historical materialism with social history as its object.

In fact, as early as his "Paris Manuscripts," Marx pointed out: "Society is the complete unity of man with nature."[1] There is no society (history) outside nature, nor any nature outside society (history). Marx also stressed that "The whole of what is called world history is nothing more than the creation of man through human labor, and the development of nature for man."[2] Marx never divided his object of study into two; on the contrary, that object always presented itself to him as a unified whole. He used "social history," "world history," "all social life" and so on to refer to it, and this totality always contained the natural world.

It was on the basis of these ideas that I wrote the article "On Two Different Concepts of Historical Materialism" and sent it to *Zhongguo Shehui Kexue*. In the article I put forward a third view different from both of two above; that is, the essence of Marx's philosophy is historical materialism, and historical materialism is not just the "base and core" of Marx's philosophy, but its complete content. In his mature period, Marx never advanced any philosophical theory other than historical materialism. Since the study of historical materialism contains the natural world, there is no need to retain the concept of dialectical materialism; if it is to be kept, it can only be as an alternative name for historical materialism. Using the concept of dialectical materialism in any other sense can only lead to the dualization of Marx's philosophy.

I distinguish two kinds of historical materialism: "the narrow concept

---

[1] Karl Marx, "Economic and Philosophical Manuscripts of 1844," in *Collected Works of Marx and Engels*, vol. 42 (Beijing: People's Publishing House, 1979), p. 122.

[2] Karl Marx, "Economic and Philosophical Manuscripts of 1844," in *Collected Works of Marx and Engels*, vol. 42 (Beijing: People's Publishing House, 1979), p. 131.

of historical materialism" upheld in the two above-mentioned positions, in which "(social) history" is a partial concept that does not include nature; the othes is "the broad concept of historical materialism" of the third view, in which (social) history is an overall concept that contains the natural world. It is only through the last view that the essence of Marx's philosophy can be made clear.

The editorial staff of *Zhongguo Shehui Kexue* was keenly aware of and fully recognized the theoretical innovation represented by my article and encouraged and supported me in further revising it. When the article was finally published in issue no. 6, 1995, it sparked off debate and discussion in academic circles, thus playing a role in promoting research on historical materialism. In recent years, *Philosophical Researches*, the *Journal of Fudan University* and many other journals have opened special columns or forums focusing on historical materialism. Some scholars argue that historical materialism can be understood as an "outlook," which is similar to the "broad concept of historical materialism" put forward in my article. The encouragement from the editorial staff further deepened my exploration of the theory of historical materialism. My research findings on this topic have been published in a series of papers, including "Changes in the Narrative of Historical Materialism from the Perspective of the Dual Functions of Science and Technology" (*Zhongguo Shehui Kexue*, 2004, no. 1, reprinted by *Chinese Social Science Digest* and *Xinhua Digest*), "Historical Facts and Objective Laws" (*Historical Research*, 2008, no. 1), "Dialectics of Nature, or Dialectics of Social History?" (*Social Science Front*, 2007, no. 4).

A New Exploration of the Development
of Marx's Philosophy

If we say that historical materialism represents the mature period of Marx's philosophy, how are we to understand the philosophy of the young Marx? The question of the relationship between the "two Marxes" is an unavoidable question for scholars of historical materialism. To explore this issue is to explore the history of Marx's philosophy. The three main points of view on the subject are given below.

The first view, represented by Herbert Marcuse and Erich Fromm, argues that the theme of Marx's philosophy in his early period was "alienation and humanism" and that of his mature period was "class struggle," with the former being more important than the latter. They advocate a return to young Marx.

The second view, represented by Louis Althusser, is that "alienation and humanism" was the theme of the young Marx's philosophy, formed under the influence of Feuerbach and subordinated to "ideology." The mature period of his philosophy was truly "scientific," and there was an "epistemological break" between the young Marx and the mature Marx.

Although these are two opposing views, their common point is that they believe in a sharp contrast between the young and the mature Marx.

The third view, upheld by most scholars, argues that there are both differences and connections between the two phases of Marx's philosophy. "Differences" refers to the fact that young Marx was influenced by Hegel and Feuerbach's historical idealism, whereas the mature Marx established the theory of historical materialism; "connections" refers to the fact that the mature Marx did not abandon the views of his youth and was still using the concept of "alienation" in his economic manuscripts of the 1850s-1860s and *Das Kapital*.

Although the third view does not oppose the mature Marx to the young Marx, it still fails to make clear why Marx continued to use the concept of "alienation" in his mature period.

In my research, I found there were two misunderstandings of Marx's concept of alienation. One is that the connotations of this concept remained the same throughout Marx's life. This misunderstanding completely fails to realize that the meaning of Marx's concept of alienation in his mature period was fundamentally different to that of his youth. Another misunderstanding is the idea that Marx never expounded the concept of alienation from an affirmative or positive angle, but always regarded it as negative. So the key to getting rid of the "two-Marx" intellectual framework and clarifying the exact relationship between the philosophy of the mature and the young Marx is to provide a rational explanation of the different meanings of the concept of alienation used by Marx in different periods from a completely new perspective, in order to correct the above misunderstandings and offer a convincing explanation for the development of Marx's philosophy.

After a period of arduous exploration, in 2002 I had a sudden flash of inspiration which led to a paper entitled "From Moral Evaluation to Historical Evaluation: A Transfer of Perspective in the Development of Marx's Theory of Alienation" which I submitted to *Zhongguo Shehui Kexue*. [1] In the paper I introduced a new approach. First of all, I used the

---

[1] The editor in charge of this article was Senior Editor Sun Hui, who gave some valuable suggestions for revision. After publication, he sought the views of academic circles, who believed that the paper had substantially advanced the study of alienation.

term "transfer of perspective" instead of Althusser's "epistemological break." "Epistemological break" implies a diametrical opposition with no theoretical connections between the philosophy of the mature and the young Marx. By contrast, the "change of perspective" viewpoint recognizes both the differences and the connections between the two periods of Marx's philosophy. Second, I found correspondences between the notion of "moral evaluation first" and the historical idealism that Marx accepted in his younger period. I also found correspondences between the notion of "historical evaluation first" and the historical materialism that Marx established in his mature philosophy. This thinking helps to clarify much ambiguity around the concept of alienation. I believe that the young Marx used the concept of "alienation" mainly to condemn all capitalist phenomena of alienation from a moral perspective, because he was then still basically a historical idealist. We can call this perspective on alienation "moral evaluation first." For example, in "Excerpts from James Mill's *Elements of Political Economy*," Marx criticized capitalist credit for regarding only a man who is "able to pay" as a morally "good" man. In the capitalist system of credit, man not only fails to gain dignity, but is degraded into the guarantee of an object of commerce, money, capital or interest; and the death of the debtor (often the poor man) is the death of the capital together with the interest of the creditor. Marx perspicaciously pointed out: "*Credit is the economic judgment on the morality of a man.*"[1] In "Economic and Philosophical Manuscripts of 1844," he further exposed the complicity between the morality advocated by political economy and alienation in capitalist society: "political economy—despite its worldly and voluptuous

---

[1]   Karl Marx, "Excerpts from James Mill's Elements of Political Economy," in *Collected Works of Marx and Engels*, vol. 42 (Beijing: People's Publishing House, 1979), p. 22.

appearance—is a true moral science, the most moral of all the sciences. Self-renunciation, the renunciation of life and of all human needs, is its principal thesis. The less you eat, drink and buy books; the less you go to the theatre, the dance hall, the public house; the less you think, love, theorise, sing, paint, fence, etc. , the more you *save*—the *greater* becomes your treasure which neither moths nor rust will devour—your capital. The less you are, the less you express your own life, the more you *have*, i. e. , the greater is your *alienated* life, the greater is the store of your estranged being. "[1] This statement shows that Marx in his youth understood alienation and its phenomena mainly from the perspective of "moral evaluation first. "

By contrast, in his mature period, Marx established historical materialism and fundamentally changed his perspective on alienation from "moral evaluation first" to "historical evaluation first. " As we all know, the most important factor that a historical materialist considers in evaluating the role of a thing or event is whether it plays a positive or negative role in the progress of history. Accordingly, in "Manifesto of the Communist Party, " Marx made an objective assessment of the positive historical role played by the early bourgeoisie: "The bourgeoisie, historically, has played a most revolutionary part. "[2] In the "Economic Manuscripts of 1857-1858, " he put forward his famous theory of the three social formations, in which he pointed out that an individual with a free personality would, in the third social formation or future communist society, gain full development. He pointed out: "The degree and the universality of the development of wealth

① Karl Marx, "Economic and Philosophical Manuscripts of 1844, " in *Collected Works of Marx and Engels*, vol. 42 (Beijing: People's Publishing House, 1979), p. 135.

② Karl Marx and Frederick Engels, "Manifesto of the Communist Party, " in *Collected Works of Marx and Engels*, vol. 4 (Beijing: People's Publishing House, 1958), p. 468.

where *this* individuality becomes possible supposes production on the basis of exchange values as a prior condition, whose universality produces not only the alienation of the individual from himself and from others, but also the universality and the comprehensiveness of his relations and capacities. "① Obviously, according to Marx, universal alienation and the full development of individuality are two facets of the same historical progress of mankind. We should not evaluate or look at alienation in capitalist society from the viewpoint of "moral evaluation first" in a sentimental way, but should adhere to "historical evaluation first" to see the positive significance of alienation in history. In Marx's view, communism and the full development of the individual would just be a beautiful myth without real and universal alienation as their medium.

But the mature Marx did not completely abandon moral evaluation in adhering to "historical evaluation first. " As theoretical perspectives, "historical evaluation first" and "moral evaluation first" are mutually exclusive, but as two dimensions of evaluation, they can be put together. For the young Marx, moral evaluation was a "strong evaluation" that was a core priority, while historical evaluation was a "weak evaluation" that was in a marginal position; whereas in his mature period, with his change of theoretical perspective, moral evaluation receded into a "weak evaluation" and historical evaluation rose to become a "strong evaluation. " Marx did not abandon moral evaluation because of his change of perspective; on the contrary, he revivified it by laying out his moral evaluation in accord with the objective requirements of historical materialism and historical evaluation, minus the petty bourgeoisie sentimentality and romanticism of his

---

① Karl Marx, "Economic Manuscripts of 1857-1858, " in *Collected Works of Marx and Engels*, vol. 46 I, (Beijing: People's Publishing House, 1979), pp. 108-109.

earlier moral evaluation.

Upon receiving the draft of my paper, the editorial staff of *Zhongguo Shehui Kexue* made some valuable suggestions and published it in *Zhongguo Shehui Kexue*, 2003, no. 2, after several revisions. Although there is still controversy about my arguments in academic circles, many scholars think that my analysis clarifies many ambiguities in previous discussions about alienation and substantially advances the study of this issue, making possible a more accurate understanding of the development of Marx's philosophy. It thus ends previous studies of alienation and raises the study of the historical development of Marx's philosophy to a new level.

With the support of the journal's editorial office, I have continued my research in this field and published a series of papers, including "Marx's Diagnosis of Modernity and the Inspiration It Gives Us" (*Zhongguo Shehui Kexue*, 2005, no. 1), "Revisiting the Position and Role of the Theory of Alienation in Marx's Philosophy" (*Philosophical Researches*, 2009, no. 12) and other articles. To some extent, these papers have taken forward the previously neglected research field of alienation and made people think again about the historical development of Marx's philosophy.

New Reflections on the Origins of Marx's Philosophy

The texts Marx left behind are the main object of our research, whether it be on a new understanding of the essence of Marx's philosophy or on a new exploration of the historical development of Marx's philosophy through the study of alienation. But Marx's philosophy is not a river without a source or a tree without roots. Only by more intensive reflection on its origins can we gain a more comprehensive and profound understanding and interpretation of Marx's philosophy.

Although, in exploring the origins of Marx's philosophy, some scholars have realized that the legacy of classical German philosophy had a significant influence on Marx, they oversimplify this legacy to a great extent. This over-simplification is reflected in two summaries. The first simplifies the legacy of classical German philosophy as the legacy of Hegel, and the second summarizes Hegel's legacy as dialectics. According to these summaries, Marx's philosophy, i.e., dialectical and historical materialism, is founded on criticizing Hegel's philosophy while inheriting its "rational core," that is, dialectics, and on criticizing Feuerbach's philosophy while inheriting its "basic core" or materialism. This interpretation is accepted by most compilers of textbooks on Marx's philosophy. For example, one textbook writes, on the origins of Marx's philosophy, Marx and Engels founded Marx's philosophy—dialectical materialism and historical materialism, on the basis of summing up the rich experience of the workers' movement and the up-to-date achievements of the natural sciences, and after discarding the idealist shell of Hegel's philosophy while critically assimilating its rational core of dialectics as well as by excluding the religious and ethical idealist impurities of Feuerbach's philosophy while critically assimilating its basic core of materialism, and at the same time integrating them into their new discovery. ① From this we can understand why dialectical and historical materialism have become a widely influential interpretive framework.

In talking about the three forms of dialectics in history, Engels pointed out: The second form of dialectics, which is the one that comes closest

---

① Xiao Qian et al. eds., *Principles of Dialectical Materialism* (Beijing: People's Publishing House, 1981), p. 30.

to the German naturalists, is classical German philosophy, from Kant to Hegel. ① Obviously, classical German philosophy here means philosophy from Kant to Hegel, and does not include Feuerbach. Thus the whole legacy of classical German philosophy was simplistically summed up as Hegel's dialectics. Such a simplistic understanding and interpretation of the origins of Marx's philosophy cannot but lead to a simplistic understanding and interpretation of the philosophy itself.

It was in this context that I wrote an article entitled "On Marx's Interpretation of the Legacy of German Philosophy" and sent it to *Zhongguo Shehui Kexue*. On the one hand, the editors affirmed the original and innovative points and academic value of my paper on the origins of Marx's philosophy but on the other, considering that it concerned the difference between Marx and Engels on the connotations of the heritage of classical German philosophy, a controversial issue in academic circles, they suggested revisions and patiently discussed it with me time and again, so that it was finally published in *Zhongguo Shehui Kexue*, 2006, no. 2.

In reflecting on German philosophy, my article put forward the question of what its legacy actually was. Based on intensive reading of classical German philosophers and Marx's writings, in addition to dialectics, I listed six other important legacies of classical German philosophy, i. e., "man," "civil society," "practice," "thing-in-itself," "historical consciousness" and freedom. In doing so I tried to restore the rich contents of classical German philosophy and the overall connotations of Marx's philosophy, issues that had traditionally been simplistically understood and interpreted.

---

① Frederick Engels, "On Dialectics," in *Collected Works of Marx and Engels*, vol. 4 (Beijing: People's Publishing House, 1958), pp. 287-288.

It may be asked: can Kant's "thing-in-itself" be considered as part of the legacy of classical German philosophy? My answer is: not only can it be so considered, but it is one of the most important legacies of that philosophy. I have written a series of papers answering this question, including "The Two Kantian Notions of Causality: An Analytic Enquiry" (published in *Zhongguo Shehui Kexue*, 2007, no. 6), "Kant is a Bridge towards Marx" (published in the *Journal of Fudan University*, 2009, no. 4) and "New Thinking on Classical German Philosophy" (published in *China Social Sciences Digest*, 2010, no. 4).

It is well known that in Kant's philosophy the thing-in-itself is transcendental and so unknowable. In a sense, the secret of Kant's philosophy is the secret of the thing-in-itself. In his book *The World as Will and Representation*, Schopenhauer reveals to us the mystery of the thing-in-itself: "What is the thing-in-itself? It is—the will."[1] Schopenhauer's important contribution was that he turned the focus of Kant's philosophy back to man. That is to say, the thing-in-itself is not on a distant further shore, but in this reachable world; it is human will. But Schopenhauer's interpretation of the will is wrong. He believed that the will was almighty, absolutely free and without restraint. Thus he made a mystery of the will despite having de-mystified Kant's thing-in-itself. It was Marx who cast the light of economics over philosophical studies and through the phenomenon of the will, completely solved the mystery of Kant's thing-in-itself. Marx wrote: "Neither he (Kant), nor the German middle class, whose whitewashing spokesman he was, noticed that these theoretical ideas of the bourgeoisie had as their basis material interests and a will that was

---

[1] Arthur Schopenhauer, *The World as Will and Representation*, trans. Shi Chongbai (Beijing: The Commercial Press, 1982), p. 177.

conditioned and determined by the material relations of production. "①
Man's will is not omnipotent. On the contrary, to live in the world, man
has to invest and consume most of his will on earning a living. Not only is
the will not absolutely free, it is determined by the "material relations of
production," relations that are as invisible and intangible as the thing-in-itself. This stimulates the idea that the true answer to the puzzle of Kant's
thing-in-itself is the material relations of production, and it is these relations that constitute the foundation and heart of Marx's philosophy. To
comprehend this, we only need to read the following words of Marx:
"There is in every social formation a particular branch of production which
determines the position and importance of all the others, and the relations
obtaining in this branch accordingly determine the relations of all other
branches as well. It is as though light of a particular hue was cast upon
everything, tingeing all other colors and modifying their specific features;
or as if a type of special ether determined the specific gravity of everything
found in it. "②

In short, in my personal experience and understanding, every important advance in the study of Marx's philosophy in China has been closely
related to the efforts of *Zhongguo Shehui Kexue*. Here I hope that the
journal, as the most creative and leading theoretical journal in Chinese social sciences, will make an even greater contribution to the development
and prosperity of scholarship in contemporary China.

---

① Karl Marx and Frederick Engels, "The German Ideology," in *Collected Works of Marx and Engels*, vol. 3 (Beijing: People's Publishing House, 1960), pp. 213-214.

② Karl Marx, "Introduction to A Contribution to the Critique of Political Economy," in *Collected Works of Marx and Engels*, vol. 8 (Beijing: People's Publishing House, 2009), p. 31.

1. 10　The Limits of Social Critique[①]
—The Revelation of Marx's Critical Theory

Since I. Kant has led critical spirit into philosophy, the influence of this spirit is incomparable. It is well known that titles or subtitles of Marx's most writings are used this term "critique," and M. Horkheimer and T. W. Adorno, as founders of Frankfort school, call their own views "a theory of social critique." Since then, this theory has been expanded from day to day by some important scholars, such as J. Habermas, L. Althusser, N. Poulantzas, A. Honneth, M. Foucault, E. laclau, S. Zizek and so on. However, those scholars who identify themselves with this theory don't pay attention to the following question: what are limits of social critique as a theoretical activity? In my opinion, Marx's critical theory just offers important resources for answering this question.

In his letter to A. Ruge in September of 1843, Marx explained the purpose of his own critical

①　Editor's note: This paper was translated from *Contemporary Marxism Review*, no. 11,2013, pp. 3-8.

theory: "The merit of new trend of thought just lies in the fact that we are not going to predict the future dogmatically, but only wish to discover a new world while we criticize the old world. "[1] Quite different from Young Hegelians who regard themselves as "critique of critique," Marx not only explains the necessity and significance of social critique, but also puts stress on its limits, refusing any attempts to deify it. According to Marx, Limits of social critique mainly embody in the following three respects.

Social Critique and Ideology

Marx told us that man is a social being. Before he becomes a social critic, it is necessary for him to receive ideological edification through family, school and society, and ideology, as a self-consciousness of the ruling class, has from beginning to end a ruling position in the social spiritual life. "The ideas of the ruling class are in every epoch the ruling ideas: i. e. the class which is the ruling material force of society is at the same time its ruling intellectual force. "[2]

Since the individual consciousness has been conformed into the frame of ideology from the beginning, then the following question appears: as he criticizes various social phenomena, whatever standpoint does he start out from? In other words, whatever does he starts out from this ideological standpoint with which has been identified by him, or does he transcend this ideology, and tries to criticize this society from another ideological

---

[1] K. Marx, F. Engels, *Complete Works*, vol. 1(Beijing: People's Publishing House, 1956), p. 416.

[2] K. Marx, F. Engels, *Complete Works*, vol. 5 (Moscow: Progress Publishers, 1976), p. 59.

position? In a word, as he criticizes this society, does he stand in this ideology or outside it? According to Althusser, "Man is an ideological animal by nature."[1]

Generally speaking, it is very difficult for an individual to cast off wholly the restriction of ideology, criticizing this society. Historically, there are fewer exceptions in all social critics, such as Marx. I think that Marx leaped out of the German ideology in his *German Ideology*.

So we find that ideology is the first limit for social critique as a theoretical activity. For example, as far as an individual's political critical consciousness is concerned, if the object of his critique is the form of government, then its starting point is still this ideology; on contrary, if his object is the state system, then it is possible for him to transcend this ideology.

Social Critique and Historical Driving Force

Marx believes that consciousness and ideology are only sublimated things from the material living process, so they have no absolute independence. "Morality, religion, metaphysics, and all the rest of ideology as well as the forms of consciousness corresponding to these, thus no longer retain the semblance of independence. They have no history, no development; but men, developing their material production and their material intercourse, alter, along with this their actual world, also their thinking and the products of their thinking. It is not consciousness that determines life, but life that determines consciousness."[2] We must pay attention to Marx's

---

[1] L. Althusser, *Essays on Ideology* (London: Verso, 1984), p. 45.
[2] K. Marx, F. Engels, *Complete Works*, vol. 5 (Moscow: Progress Publishers, 1976), pp. 36-37.

above expression "they have no history, no development." That is not to say, consciousness and ideology have no history, no development, but no independent history, no independent development, because they are restrained the material living process for ever. Although consciousness and ideology have their own dynamic role, big or small of this dynamic role is determined the material living process in the end.

Social critics often fall into the following illusion that so long as they abandon the idea about this social life in their own brains, that is to say, they abandon this social life itself. In fact, consciousness isn't equal to reality reflected by consciousness. While criticizing the above illusion of Young Hegelians, Marx wrote: "Once upon a time a valiant fellow had the idea that men were drowned in water only because they were possessed with the idea of gravity. If they were to get this notion out of their heads, say by avowing it to be a superstitious, a religious concept, they would be sublimely proof against any danger from water."[1]

Marx believes that people neither cast side irrational phenomena in actual social life, nor forsake old ideas in the field of consciousness, only through social critique theoretically. In this sense, Marx put forward: "all forms and products of consciousness cannot be dissolved by mental criticism, by revolution into 'self-consciousness' or transformation into 'apparitions', 'specters', 'whimsies' etc. , but only by the practical overthrow of the actual social relations which gave rise to this idealistic humbug; that not criticism but revolution is the driving force of history, also of religion, of philosophy and all other kinds of theory."[2] Of course, revolution, as a

---

[1] K. Marx, F. Engels, *Complete Works*, vol. 5 (Moscow: Progress Publishers, 1976), p. 24.

[2] K. Marx, F. Engels, *Complete Works*, vol. 5 (Moscow: Progress Publishers, 1976), p. 54.

practical activity, oversteps the scope of pure consciousness. That is to say, only revolution having practical force can become the real driving force of historical development and change of ideas.

So we find that the historical driving force forms the second limit of social critique. No matter social critics give enormous dynamism and independence, social critique neither becomes the driving force of history, nor the driving force of change of ideas. In *Theses on Feuerbach*, Marx comes to such a conclusion: "The philosophers have only interpreted the world in various ways, the point is to change it. "①

Social Critique and Philosophical language

Social critics don't live in a vacuum, their theories have been influenced by one or some philosophical trends of thought. Criticizing young Hegelians, Marx wrote: "German criticism has, right up to its latest efforts, never left the realm of philosophy. It by no means examines its general philosophical premises, but in fact all its problems originate in a definite philosophical system, that of Hegel. "② If Hegel's philosophy can be looked upon as "an invisible hand", then Young Hegelians' theory of social critique can be regarded as "kites" controlled by this hand.

So long as man carries out research into critics' theories seriously, he will find their critical theories have been deeply influenced by different philosophical trends of thought. Such as Hegel to Lukacs, Croce to Gramsci,

---

① K. Marx, F. Engels, *Complete Works*, vol. 5 (Moscow: Progress Publishers, 1976), p. 5.
② K. Marx, F. Engels, *Complete Works*, vol. 5 (Moscow: Progress Publishers), 1976, p. 28.

Kant to Horkheimer, the positivism to Della-Volpe, the structuralism to Althusser, Gramsci to Laclau, Lacan to Zizek, or the like. Obviously, if a critical theory looks upon a philosophical trend of thought as its own starting point, then this trend becomes a blind area of this theory necessarily. Therefore, we can say, the philosophical outlook forms the third limit of social critique as a theoretical activity.

According to Marx's point of view, the third limit has still more deep implications. It is well known that the philosophical language is quite different from the common language, however, social critics have always such an illusion that truth can only be expressed by the philosophical language, because the common language is very ambiguous. Marx finds out the fact that social critics are not only influenced by various philosophical outlooks, but also made an impact on by philosophical language. "One of the most difficult tasks confronting philosophers is to descend from the world of thought to the actual world. Language is the immediate actuality of thought. Just as philosophers have given thought an independent existence, so they were bound to make language into an independent realm. This is the secret of philosophical language, in which thought in the form of words have their own content. The problem of descending from the world of thoughts to the actual world is turned into the problem of descending from language to life. "[1]

Marx turns above view social critics insist on upside down, affirming that the philosophical language isn't reliable, but the common language is really trustworthy. "The philosophers have only to dissolve their language into the ordinary language, from which it is abstracted, in order to

---

[1] K. Marx, F. Engels, *Complete Works*, vol. 5 (Moscow: Progress Publishers), 1976, p. 446.

recognize it as the distorted language of the actual world, and to realize that neither thoughts nor language in themselves form a realm of their own, that they are only manifestation of actual life. "① Without saying, as long as social critics still use the traditional philosophical language in their theories, then it is not possible for them to criticize this society rationally.

Marx's above point of view has gotten a response from L. Wittgenstein who is one of the most important philosophers in the 20ᵗʰ century. Wittgenstein wrote in his *Philosophical Investigation*: "As a philosopher uses a word——knowledge, being, object, ego, proposition, name——in order to master the essence of things, he ought to ask himself often: how these words have been used in the daily language which is as their birthplace. He should bring their metaphysical usage back to their daily usage. "② According to Wittgenstein, because the implication of philosophical language separates severely the common language, a lot of false questions appear in philosophical research or social critique. Misled by the philosophical language, social critics, like flies, fly into the flytrap, so Wittgenstein, like Marx, believes that his task is to look for a way through which flies will escape from the flytrap.

In a word, when a man considers different theories of social critique, he ought to recognize their limits first of all, not overstating their functions irrationally.

---

① K. Marx, F. Engels, *Complete Works*, vol. 5 (Moscow: Progress Publishers), 1976, p. 447.

② L. Wittgenstein, *Complete Works*, vol. 8 (Shijiazhuang: He Bei Educational Publishing House, 2003), p. 68.

Section Two

Critical Analysis of Philosophical Topics

2.1　Three Notions of Philosophy of Economics[①]

After a long-time discussion, there is still no widely accepted view concerning the nature of philosophy of economics. The basic reason is the absence over the years of a consensus on the definition of the term "philosophy of the economics." I think that the discussion will continue to lead nowhere unless the definitions of the following three concepts and the relationships between them are properly thrashed out.

"Philosophy of economics in a broad sense." All the results achieved in the activities and attitudes surrounding a sincere search for truth with regard to the relationship between the economy, economics (a systematic, theoretical illustration of economic issues) and philosophy constitute the discipline of "philosophy of economics in a broad sense." In presenting their arguments or propositions, scholars always referred to philosophy of e-

① Editor's note: This paper was originally published in *Social Sciences in China*, no. 4, 2000, pp. 63-67, translated from *Zhongguo Shehui Kexue*(《中国社会科学》), no. 2, 1999, pp. 86-90.

conomics, but in reality, they were referring to the philosophy of the economy in a broad sense. Although this term is relatively elastic in its implications, it is merely indicate an area of study characterized by a riot of scholarly conceptualizations and carrying a world of data.

"Philosophy of economics in a narrow sense." This field of study could be rated on a par with the study of the philosophy of history, the philosophy of ethics, the philosophy of society. It is the philosophy of politics. All of these are classified as theoretical philosophy. Theoretical philosophy is not concerned with applying philosophical canons to the economy or economics, and is interested only in attempting to formulate corollaries to economic events or concepts of economics in philosophical terms. The unique methodology of philosophy of economics in a narrow sense is carrying out an overhaul of all the basic concepts of philosophy from the perspective of modern economic development and modern economics. The philosophy of economics in a narrow sense, as a branch of theoretical philosophy, sets its goal as the attainment of theoretical systematization and completeness.

Economic philosophy. Like historical philosophy, ethical philosophy, and political philosophy, "economic philosophy" is also applied philosophy. In contrast to philosophy of economics in a narrow sense, economic philosophy has little interest in formulating in philosophical terms corollaries to economic phenomena or economic concepts. It concentrates on applying philosophical theories to economic phenomena or research in the field of economics. As an integral part of applied philosophy, it attaches little importance to enriching philosophical theories or precepts, and merely contrives to interpret economic phenomena and problems posed to economics in terms of philosophical theories. Rather than construct a new theoretical fabric in the field of philosophy, economic philosophy is devoted to tackling problems related to efficiently regulating economic life, and offering valid explanations for economic phenomena and problems.

Having given clear-cut definitions of these three concepts, I will now proceed to examine how they are correlated. The definition of philosophy of economics in a broad sense is the most generic of the three concepts, since it contains the definition of philosophy of economics in a narrow sense and that of economic philosophy. In most cases, philosophy of economics is either equated with philosophy of economics in a broad sense or ranked on a par with economic philosophy as a one-dimensional philosophy. As a result, few scholars are interested in philosophy of economics in a narrow sense. It is thus time to remove some misunderstandings related to economic philosophy.

The goal of philosophy of economics in a narrow sense is an evaluation of the truth of all basic philosophical concepts in the light of modern economy and modern economics. In developing philosophy of economics in a narrow sense, the research done by Marx should be rated as epochal. His "Economic and Philosophical Manuscripts of 1844" and "Economic Manuscripts (1857-1858)" and *Capital* are exemplary works on philosophy of economics in a narrow sense. His research in the field of philosophy of economics in a narrow sense was not only pioneering in nature, but also succeeded in bringing about a radical change in our understanding of the basic concepts of traditional philosophy. This can be illustrated by the following concrete analyses.

To begin with, let us review the definitions given for the term "practice." In his *Nicomachean Ethics*, Aristotle deals with the notion that knowledge comes from practice, and refers to productive activities as a form of practice. For all the enlightenment provided by Aristotle on practice, since his time most philosophers have chosen to regard practice as an activity used as a lever to raise moral standards. It was Marx who succeeded in correctly redefining the term "practice" after he had delved deeply into the study of national economics, and it was Marx who succeeded in confirming the truth of the concept that productive labor constitutes the foundation and kernel of all forms of man's practice. It is on the basis of such concepts that Marx developed his unique philosophical theory of existence. According to this theory, man's survival depends on his productive labor. In this sense, survival presupposes production. The basis of production is the creation of the material means of life, whereas the creation of human beings, the creation of intellectual values, and the creation of social relations are various aspects of production. Therefore, it is safe for us to assert that Mark's philosophy of existence is in essence a theory of production in a broad sense. Marx succeeded in updating traditional philosophical views on the history of man, once he had made an analytical and critical study of various manifestations of "alienated labor." On the basis of his studies, he successfully developed his theory of social revolution, which was designed to eliminate a social system based on private ownership, the origin of alienated labor.

Secondly, let us examine the definitions of "matter" and "material thing." According to traditional philosophy, the world is composed of "matter." While "matter" exists specifically in the form of "material things," "material things" exist independently of man's consciousness. Man's consciousness or will alone cannot bring about any change in them. This outlook on "material things" is construed by Marx as "an abstract outlook on matter." He believed it was wrong, because in studying the material world it does not take into account man's economic life. From the perspective of economic life, especially in a commodity economy, we become instantly aware that all the metaphysical sheen has been taken from "matter" or "material things," and that both of them abruptly appear in a commodified world which is inseparable from man's survival. Commodities are unique, not so much in their use value, a natural attribute of all commodities, but in their exchange value, the social attribute of commodities. Commodities are also unique in that they camouflage the relationship between men with the relationship between things. Therefore, Marx rejected the view of "matter" and "material things" upheld by various traditional philosophical schools. The essence of his outlook on "matter" and "material thing," which was based on his standpoint with regard to philosophy of economics in a narrow sense, consisted of bringing to light the relationship between men from behind the camouflage of the relations between things by demolishing commodity fetishism.

Thirdly, let us examine the basic question of philosophy. Traditional philosophical schools hold that the basic philosophical question is the relationship between cognition and existence. Advocates of the proposition that the universe is static believe that cognition and existence are always antithetical. According to the Marxist philosophy of economics in a narrow sense, before man is able to think about the world, he first has to secure his survival through productive labor. The relationship between cognition and existence should therefore not be referred to as the basic question of philosophy, while practice should. There are two aspects of practice: one is the relationship between man and nature, which is material; the other is the relationship between men. It is only by adhering to these two aspects that philosophical researchers can save themselves from drowning in scholastic polemics.

Finally, let us review some concepts of economic philosophy. We are of the opinion that the purport of economic philosophy consists of three aspects. The first aspect refers to a re-evaluation of the premises and basic concepts of economic theories in the light of philosophical concepts. The second aspect refers to research aimed at analyzing economic phenomena and relations between economic concepts according to philosophical methods. The third aspect refers to research aimed at formulating correct interpretations of both economic activities on a social level and the norms governing economic behavior based on certain systems of values. As is well known, research related to the second aspect has produced a large number of publications, particularly those aimed at interpreting economic phenomena from a dialectical perspective, and furnishing answers to various problems confronting modern economics. It is now important for researchers looking at this aspect to make an effort to introduce into their research new methodologies, such as phenomenological, linguistic, analytical, structural, and textual methodologies, so that they can interpret economic phenomena and basic notions of economics. If researchers working on the third aspect concentrate on systems of values in general, then they are actually only engaged in tackling questions related to the relationship between economics and philosophy. If other researchers in the third group are attacking problems associated with ethical values, they are actually exploring the field of economic ethics. They must scrupulously guard against introducing value systems into their research, from subjectivist or naturalistic motives, in an attempt to synthesize new economic ethical norms, and then inviting the general public to accept such norms. They need to be aware of the intrinsic values that objectively govern economic behavior in the market economy system before they can draw inspiration from such values and formulate a system of economic ethical norms.

In order to further research in the field of economic philosophy, the most important thing to do now is to focus on encouraging the first aspect. This is because research on this aspect can be effective for re-examining the premises of economic theories and basic economic concepts. The specific analyses given below may be pertinent in this regard.

Some people believe that independent fields of study represented by such terms as "economics," and "the history of economics" actually exist. They imagine that there exists pure learning or scholarship pivoted around, say, economic issues. As a matter of fact, no such independent fields of study or pure learning ever existed. The world, including all who live in it as observers and thinkers, is merely a mobile entirety. Basing ourselves on conceived criteria for defining disciplines, we have succeeded in formulating definitions for such terms as physics, biology, chemistry, sociology, and economics. In this way, we arbitrarily split the entirety of the world into sectors. These sectors have, ever since, been enshrined as independent fields of study or systems of pure knowledge. Hence the warning: economic researchers must allow themselves to be led by philosophical concepts and strive to examine in retrospect the relations that tie economics to disciplines such as politics, ethics, and law. If they ignore this warning, researchers are bound to stray hopelessly into the expanse of "pure economic research."

Most economists believe that the whole spectrum of economic life originates with the rational individual. The fact is, however normal an individual is, he or she cannot be human and devoid of feelings or will. It is therefore incorrect to assume that all man's economic activities are strictly governed by rationality. Even if each man's economic activities are strictly governed by rationality, this does not ensure that the total effect of all economic activities is rational. The situation specified below is a case in point. Two neighboring countries can behave rationally in protecting the natural resources belonging to them, but in trying to give protection to the natural resources that cross the boundaries between them, they appeal to arms and resort to an irrational war. It is thus evident that there is no such thing as a "rational individual."

In short, to make substantial headway in furthering researches in the field of philosophy of the economics, economists should draw inspirations not only from philosophy of economics in a broad sense, but also from economic philosophy in a narrow sense.

2.2 Abschied vom Mythos der hegelischen Dialektik der „Herr-Knecht-Beziehung"[①]

Es ist bekannt, dass der deutsche Philosoph Hegel eine der umstrittensten Persönlichkeiten in der philosophischen Geschichte ist. Manche, die ihn verehren, bezeichnen ihn als einen der großartigsten Denker in der Geschichte, und sogar sehen ihn sogar „Zeus in Olympia"an; die Andere die ihn missachten, behaupten, dass seine Philosophie voll von Fehlern sei, und einige halten drei Viertel seiner Philosophie sogar für Plattheit und ein Viertel für hellen Unsinn. So verschieden sind diese Auffassungen. Wenn wir versuchen. Hegels Philosophie objektiv zu burteilen, dann werden wir wahrscheinlich das Sprichwort, das die Westen oft gebrauchen, zitieren nämlich „Großartigkeit und Schaden sind Zwillinge". Das Sprichwort ist aufschlussreich: einerseits sollen wir sehen, wie

---

① Editor's note: This paper is the German edition of the article published in *Dongnan Xueshu* (《东南学术》),no. 2,2002, pp. 66-67,55, which is found in the documents that Mr. Yu Wujin left.

großartig und tiefsinnig Hegels Denken ist; andererseits sollen wir nicht auf die von Hegel hergestellten philosophischen Mythen versessen sein. Hegels Theorie über die „Herr-Knecht-Beziehung" als ein solcher philosophischer Mythos ist heutzutage noch einflussreich. Diese Theorie scheint wie eine Insekten fressende Flasche zu sein. Viele Forscher_innen lassen sich von Hegels Magie fesseln und werden die Gefangenen derselben. Das heißt, sie werden deren Gläubige und Propagandisten der so genannten „Herr-Knecht-Beziehung" Theorie.

Alle, die mit Hegels Philosophie vertraut sind, wissen, dass diese Theorie von Hegel in seiner frühen Schrift〉Phänomenologie des Geistes〈aufgestellt wurde. Nach Hegel ist die „Herr-Knecht-Beziehung" nur ein Stadium in der Entwicklung des Selbstbewusstseins. Gegenüber dem Herrn haben die Knechte Angst um sein ganzes Dasein. Aus Angst stürzen sich die Knecht in Arbeit und ihr Bewusstsein der Abhängigkeit von ihrem Herrn entwickelt sich zu einem Bewusstsein der Selbstständigkeit, während das Selbstständigkeit-Bewusstsein des Herrn allmählich das Bewusstsein der Abhängigkeit von seinen Knechten wird weil er mit den Genüssen, die die Arbeiten der Knechte anbieten, zufrieden ist. So wird die Beziehung zwischen Herrn und Knecht umgekehrt: der Herr wird ein Knecht während der Knecht Herr werden.

Die Theorie über das Verhältnis zwischen Herrn und Knecht wurde überall von Hegels Zeitgenossen und Nachkommenden hochgeschätzt. Man kann sagen, dass jeder, solange er〉Phänomenologie des Geistes〈studiert, diese Theorie bewundern wird. Sogar hält man sie für einen der tiefsten Gedanken des jungen Hegels. Sogar versuchten die Anhänger des Existentialismus, in der Theorie der „Herr-Knecht-Beziehung" den Ursprung des Existentialismus herauszufinden. Allerdings glauben wir, dass sie einen der oberflächlichen, zweideutigen philosophischen Mythen ist, die von Hegel hergestellt wurden. Aber Warum?

Erstens: Selbstverständlich würden wir zustimmen, dass sich, wenn die Knechte unter dem Zwang ihres Herrn mit aller Kraft arbeiten, deren Körperkraft, Fähigkeiten und Charakter verändern können. Aber diese Änderung kann die Bestätigung des Selbstständigkeit-Bewusstseins der Knechte nicht spontan veranlassen. In der Tat zeigen unzählige historische Tatsachen auf, dass das Erwachen der Sklavenklasse und die Gewinnung ihres Selbstständigkeit-Bewusstseins davon abhängig sind, dass die Vorläufer ihnen bewusste Erziehung und Aufklärung geben. Die Arbeit allein kann die Entstehung und die Reife des Selbständigkeit-Bewusstseins der Sklaven gar nicht hervorbringen.

Zweitens: Hegel hat die Eigenschaft der Arbeiten der Sklaven nicht eingehend analysiert. In der Tat sind die Arbeiten, die die Sklaven wegen der Forderung ihres Herrn übernommen haben, schwerste, niedrigste leben- und gesundheitsschädlichste, wie Dienstleistungen, schwere Arbeit des Abbaus oder des Transports und Feldarbeiten usw… Zunächst sind diese Arbeiten erzwungen und Sisyphisch und können das Interesse der Knechte nicht erregen. Sie setzen sich dem Herrn oft wider, indem sie flüchten oder die Werkzeuge zerbrechen. Es ist nicht zu leugnen, dass in diesen Arbeitsformen, da die Sklaven kein Interesse daran haben, sondern sie wie die Pest meiden, die Bildung der Sachen oder des Charakters der Sklaven nur romantische Fantasie ist. Zudem drohen die schweren und schimpflichen Arbeiten der Gesundheit des Körpers und der Seele des Sklaven. Wenn die Sklaven des Hungers und der Kalte wegen in Jugend schon gestorben sind, wie können sie zum Status des Herrn werden oder das Selbstständigkeit-Bewusstsein erhalten? Als Marx in〉Ökonomisch-philosophische Manuskripte aus dem Jahre 1844〈von der〉Phänomenologie des Geistes〈sprach, obwohl er die Wörter wie „Selbstständigkeit und

Unselbstständigkeit des Selbstbewusstseins, Herr und Knecht gebrauchte, lobte und entwickelte er Hegels bekannte Theorie nicht, sondern er diskutierte das Problem „der Entfremdung der Arbeit"ausführlich und kritisierte die hegelische idealistische und romantische Arbeit-Konzeption. Marx zeigt:

„Die Arbeit, welche Hegel allein kennt und anerkennt ist die abstrakt geistige. "①

Mit anderen Worten, erkennt Hegel die Arbeit im realen Leben nicht tief. Obschon die hegelische Analyse des Problems der Beziehung des Herrn mit den Sklaven eine kritische Intention zu haben scheint, hat Marx richtig aufgezeigt:

„In der⟩Phänomenologie⟨-trotz ihres durchaus negativen und kritischen Aussehens und trotz der wirklich in ihr enthalten, oft weit der späten Entwicklung vorgreifenden Kritik-schon der unkritische Positivismus und der ebenso unkritische Idealismus der spätern Hegelschen Werke-diese philosophische Auflösung und Wiederherstellung der vorhandenen. Empirie-latent liegt, als Keim, als Potenz, als ein Geheimnis vorhanden ist. "②

Ehrlich gesagt, „ist Herr-Knecht-Beziehung"aus dem Feder Hegels keinen Beweis für seinen kritischen Geist, vielmehr, ist sie ein Zeichen für

---

① *Gesammelte Werke von Marx und Engels*, Chinesische Übersetzung, Bd. 42, Renmin Verlag, 1979, S. 162.

② *Gesammelte Werke von Marx und Engels*, Chinesische Übersetzung, Bd. 42, Renmin Verlag, 1979, S. 161-162.

seinen phantastischen Romantik! Wir können sogar in der modernen Lebensweise allerlei Bespiele gegen diese Philosophiemythos herausfinden. Warum erfinden die moderne beispielsweise Waschmaschine, Robot, Traktor, Abbaumaschine und Kranwagen, um ihre eigene Arbeit zu ersetzten. Die Idee ist einfach: Die Menschen bemühen sich, sich der schweren und trockene körperliche Arbeiten wie Wäsche, Spülen, Bewirtschaftung, Abbau zu entziehen. Sie kosten nicht nur so viele Zeit, dass die Menschen nicht in der Lage sind, ihr Interesse zu erfüllen, sondern auch schädigen ihrer körperlichen und geistlichen Gesundheit stark und setzten sie zur Erschöpfung, sogar zum frühen Tod. Deswegen dürfte keiner der gegenwärtigen Forscher, selbst wenn er die Theorie des „Verhältnisses zwischen Herrn und Knecht" Hegels unbedingt hochschätzt, freiwillig wünschen, sich mit solchen Sklavenarbeit im Kontext Hegels zu beschäftigen.

Die Darstellung des Herren in dem Verhältnis zwischen Herrn und Knecht Hegels ist auch von der romanistischen Stimmung erfüllt. Hegel schreibt so:

„der Herr aber, der den Knecht zwischen es und sich eingeschoben, schließt sich dadurch nur mit der Unselbständigkeit des Dinges zusammen und genießt es rein; die Seite der Selbständigkeit aber überläßt er dem Knechte, der es bearbeitet."[1]

Dies bedeutet nichts anderes als: der Herr beauftragt bewusst den Knechten die Aufgabe, die Dinge zu bearbeiten, nämlich die Selbständigkeit der

---

[1] Hegel, *Phänomenologie des Geistes*, chinesische Übersetzung, Bd. 1, ShangWu-Verlag, 1981, S. 128.

Dingen zu behandeln (zum Beispiel Kuchen machen), während er selbst den Dingen, die ihre Selbständigkeit schon verloren sind, gegenüber stehen lässt (zum Beispiel Kuchen essen), nämlich herzhaft genießen. Die Einseitigkeit Hegels besteht hier darin, dass er den Herrn nur als einen Genießer der Früchte der Sklavenarbeiten versteht. In der Tat ist das wirkliche Leben des Herrn bei weitem reicher als einen reinen Genießer.

Erstens, nicht alle Herren werden in das Falle des Genießens geraten. Wir könnten einmal eine Analogie einführen. Als Marx die Tätigkeiten des Kapitalisten analysierte, zeigte er: Im Brust eines Kapitalisten pulsieren zwei Herzen, die sich nach entgegen gesetzte Richtungen richten. Das eine verlangt nach Konsumieren und Genießen, während das andere die Reproduktion behalten und vergrößern will.

Zweitens wenn der Herr die Körperarbeit den Sklaven übergibt, verhält er sich nicht wie Eugen Onegin aus dem Feder Puskins, der dem „Nichts tun"als Devise folgt, sondern benutzt die Zeit, welche er von der Sklaven beraubt, eine seinem Interesse angemessene Ideologie aufzubauen, um das Protestbewusstsein und selbstständigen Bewusstsein, die unter den Sklaven allmählich entstehen und sich entwickeln, zu betäuben und aufzulösen. Mit anderem Wort, es kann unmöglich sein, dass der Herr aussetzt, sich selbst von den Sklaven stürzt zu werden.

Schließlich kann der Herr die beraubte Zeit benutzen, die Politik, die Kunst und andere Erkenntnisse zu lernen, um sich selbst zu bereichen, zu bilden und sich allseitig und frei zu entwickeln. Aber dieser Studien-und Entwicklungsweise wagt ein Sklave, der sich lebenslang in schwerer Köperarbeit verwickeln lässt, nicht sich vorzustellen. Hier könnten wir auch einmal eine Analogie zwischen dem Kapitalisten und dem Herrn machen. Als Marx von dem Reichtum des Kapitalisten sprach, weist er schafsinnig darauf hin:

Der Diebstahl an fremder Arbeitszeit, worauf der jetzige Reichtum beruht. ①

Die Ersparung von Arbeitszeit gleich Vermehren der freien Zeit, d. h. Zeit für die volle Entwicklung des Individuums. ②

Wir haben keinen Grund wie Hegel, den Herrn nur als einen reinen Genießer und Konsumer vorzustellen!

Zusammengefasst, wird in dem Mythos des Verhältnisses zwischen Herrn und Knecht der Herr zu einem echten Idioten, der außer dem Genuß Nichts zu können und sogar keine neue und wertvollere zu lernen scheint, selbst wenn er hinreichende freie Zeit hätte. Demsprechend wird der Sklave zu einer echten Weise. Sie nehmen nicht nur aufgedreht an verschiedenen schwierigen und gezwungenen Arbeiten, sondern ihr selbständiges Bewusstsein entwickelt sich auch spontan wie die Pflanzen in den Tropen. Was ist das außer einem Mythos der Philosophie? Arme chinesische Philosophen sind durch die Gedankensweise Hegels und seinen nur scheinbar richtigen Philosophiemythos zu stark inhaftiert. Wir müssen Hegels die Strahlekrone wegnehmen und müssen uns mit Entschlossenheit von allerlei Mythen, die von Hegel gestaltet wurden, abschieden. Nur dadurch können die Chinesen mit beiden Füßen fest auf der Erde stehen und mit ihrem eigenen Gehirn selbstständig denken!

---

① *Gesammelte Werke von Marx und Engels*, Chinesische Übersetzung Bd. 46-2, Renmin-Verlag, 1979, S. 218.

② *Gesammelte Werke von Marx und Engels*, Chinesische Übersetzung Bd. 46-2, Renmin-Verlag, 1979, S. 225.

2.3　Reflection on the Issue of "Man's Universal Development"[①]

The so-called "men's universal development" is a hot topic in contemporary academic studies. However, it is a pity that we talk about it so much, while in fact, we understand it so little about it. It is thus necessary and meaningful to take second thoughts about the theoretical content and essence of this issue.[②] And only then could we give a reasonable, valid elucidation of it.

Universal Development of "Men" or of "Individuals"?

As we all know, Marx and Engels wrote in *The Communist Manifesto* (1848): "die freie Entwicklung eines jeden die Bedingung für die freie Entwicklung aller ist (the free development of

---

① Editor's note: This paper was translated and revised from *Tansuo Yu Zhengming* (《探索与争鸣》), no. 8, 2002, pp. 6-8.

② Yu Wujin, "To enrich Marx's theory of 'individual universal development' in practice," in *Academics in China*, 2001, vol. 5.

each is the condition for the free development of all).	"① Here,	"jeden"
and "aller" respectively denote "each person" and "all people". Obviously,
since Marx regards each person's free development as the precondition of
all people's free development, it is thus indicated that in his mind there is
definite difference between "individuals" and "all people", and by comparison, individuals occupy the foundational position.

In *Economic Manuscripts of 1857-58*, when explaining his theory of
"three social stage," Marx points out furthermore: "Relationships of personal
dependence (which originally arise quite spontaneously) are the first form
of society, in which human productivity develops only to a limited extent
and at isolated points. Personal independence based upon dependence mediated by things is the second great form, and only in it is a system of general social exchange of matter, a system of universal relations [der univer-
salen Beziehungen], universal requirements and universal capacities [uni-
verseller Vermögen], formed. Free individuality [freie Individualität], based
on the universal development of individuals [die universelle Entwicklung
der Individuen] and the subordination of their communal, social productivity, which is their social possession [Vermögen], is the third stage. The
second stage creates the conditions for the third."② It must be emphasized
that what claimed by Marx here is the theory of "universal development of
individuals", not "men's universal development". The German noun "Individuum" (pl. Individuums or Individuen) used by Marx exclusively means
"individual", not "man" in general sense. In German, "man" is usually

---

① K. Marx and F. Engels, *Ausgewaehlte Werke*, vol. 1 (Berlin: Dietz Verlag,
1989), S. 438.

② K. Marx and F. Engels, *Collected Works*, vol. 28 (Moscow: Progress Publishers,
1986), p. 95. Also see Karl Marx, *Grundrisse Der Kritik Der Politischen Oekonomie* (Berlin: Dietz Verlag, 1974), S. 75.

meaning, expressed by another noun "Mensch" (pl. Menschen). The difference between "Individuum" and "Mensch" is obvious: the former means particular individual with independence of personality; the latter means "man" or "the whole of human being" in general. This indicates that Marx never talks about "men's universal development" in general, but what he in fact insists on is the "universal development of individuals" and the establishment of its "free individuality" in the modern society.

It is interesting that, in oriental societies especially in modern Chinese society, Marx's concept of "universal development individuals" is unconsciously transformed into the concept of "men's universal development." How does it come about? Actually, the reason is also very simple. For individuals, especially the ordinary individuals in contrast with individuals among those great people, in the modern Chinese society which is born out of a long-time natural economy, are still devoid of the independence of personality and the unattached position of spirit. Just as Marx points out, when he criticizes the view typically expressed by Adam Smith and Rousseau that there had been independent individuals in remote ancient times: "The further back we go in history, the more does the individual, and accordingly also the producing individual, appear to be dependent and belonging to a larger whole ··· It is not until the 18th century, in 'bourgeois society', that the various forms of the social nexus confront the individual as merely a means towards his private ends, as external necessity."[①] In Marx's view, there could not be genuine independent individual in the remote ancient times, for that is only the product of the modern world, especially of the civil society ("bourgeois society") since 18th century.

---

① K. Marx and F. Engels, *Collected Works*, vol. 28 (Moscow: Progress Publishers, 1986), p. 18. Also see Karl Marx, *Grundrisse Der Kritik Der Politischen Oekonomie* (Berlin: Dietz Verlag, 1974), S. 6.

It is well known that, the central notion of the Enlightenment in modern China is just the notion of releasing ordinary individual from various bondages. Lunxun's discussion about the issue of "Nora leaves her family" in *A Doll's House* by Henrik Ibsen, Ba Jin's three famous novels *The Family, The Spring* and *The Autumn*, and Qian Zhong-shu 's *Encircle a City*, are all reflections on individual freedom and the liberation of individuality. However, as Li Ze-hou ever pointed out: afterward, saving the nation from extinction (for which the collectivity is paramount) gradually overwhelmed the subject of enlightenment (for which the individual is paramount); the problem of individual's liberation and freedom was completely ignored at the end.

Textbooks of historical materialism after 1949 also discuss the relationship between "greats and the mass," however, what is emphasized is always greats, not the ordinary individual. For the ordinary individuals, they are not only still devoid of the unattached spiritual position and independence of personality, but also their basic profits and interests are simply denied, being misinterpreted as "extreme individualism." We could find here again and again, that the ordinary individual is merely like an element, subordinated to the collective concept of "mass," and that only the individual of "greats" could become the focus of people's reflection. In fact, the so-called "New Enlightenment" after the "Cultural Revolution," is just to continue the route of the ordinary individual liberation which arises near the period of "the May 4th Movement." Along with the development of market economy and the transition from the traditional social system of status to nowadays system of contract, in contemporary China, individualism, individual freedom and liberation of individuality have become the essential contents of our real, cultural life. Therefore, only by a deep understanding of the actual requests in contemporary life, could we adequately acquire the actual meaning of Marx's theory of "universal development of individuals."

Universal Development of Individuals' "Ability" or "Quality"?

Precisely speaking, Marx's "universal development of individuals" means universal development of individual's "ability." He writes: "Universally developed individuals, whose social relationships are their own communal relations and therefore subjected to their own communal control, are not products of nature but of history. The degree and the universality of development of the capacities [Vermögen] in which this kind of individuality becomes possible, presupposes precisely production on the basis of exchange value, which, along with the universality of the estrangement of individuals from themselves and from others, now also produces the universality and generality of all their relations and abilities [Fähigkeiten]."① Here, both the German words "Vermögen" and "Faehigkeiten" could be translated into "ability." For Marx, universal development of individuals is adequately embodied in that of its ability, and the latter requires certain social and historical preconditions. Marx discusses universal development of individuals from the point of ability, because he is deeply influenced by Friedrich Schiller's *Letters Upon the Aesthetic Education of Man*. Schiller incisively finds that, in modern European society,

---

① K. Marx and F. Engels, *Collected Works*, vol. 28 (Moscow: Progress Publishers, 1986), p. 99. Also see Karl Marx, *Grundrisse Der Kritik Der Politischen Oekonomie* (Berlin: Dietz Verlag, 1974), S. 79-80.

along with the narrower and narrower division of labor, the development of individual's ability has also become narrower and narrower. In this sense, Marx's theory above is just a response to Schiller's point of view. However, according to Marx, in capitalist society, it is impossible for any individual to achieve a universal development of his ability, since there are phenomena of alienation or estrangement (Entfremdung) everywhere, and this ideal could be actualized only in the communistic society in future. Of course, this actualization must be based on the highly developed material and cultural conditions of capitalist society.

The further question is: What precisely is so-called "ability"? Obviously, it means our capacity or talent. For example, one can drive a car, a plane, can manipulate a computer, can speak foreign languages, play a piano etc. All these "can" belong to the scope of ability. In daily life, when we say somebody is "versatile," that is just to say, he has various abilities. Thus obviously, if somebody is more versatile, then his ability is more universally developed; and if his ability is more universal, he then will more approach so-called "universally developed individual" claimed by Marx.

As a matter of fact, in modern society, a universal development of individual's "ability" is hard to be achieved; however, that of individual "quality" is still possible to be achieved. Perhaps with regard to this aspect, Marx's theory of the universal development of individual's ability has transformed into that of individual's quality in Chinese academic circle. Here, "quality" (Qualität) contains the meaning of "having certain ability," but it does not call for more and more abilities. Indeed we could even insist that, concerning the meaning of "quality," one's general spiritual level is essential, rather than the magnitude of his "ability." That is to say, "quality" indicates the essential characters for somebody to make his heart peaceful and his life meaningful. It is mainly composed of the following two aspects: a) the humanistic spirit, such as to cherish life, to defend human rights, to respect the others, to advocate freedom, and to insist on democracy and justice etc. ; b) the scientific spirit, such as factualism, thinking in terms of objective laws, devoting oneself to seeking truth. The "universal development of individual's quality," in accordance with its central content, thereby means a unity of scientific and humanistic spirit in individual's life. Both quality and ability arise from one's heart and are visible exteriorly, but, relatively speaking, "quality" could exhibit one's immanent world and spiritual level much more. Anyone, whose scientific spirit and humanistic spirit have got a balanced development, is able to approach a universal development of his quality; thus we insist that it is easier to be achieved. Contrary to this, for abilities as skills are limited by one's genius and physical condition, it is hard to achieve a universal development of individual's "ability." Certainly, the universal development of quality and that of ability are not incompatible. In fact, the concept of "universal development of individual's quality" is a modification and advancement of Marx's concept of "universal development of individual's ability" in a new historical context.

Universal Development in Ideal, or One-side Development in Reality?

We must clearly recognize that Marx's "universal development of individual's ability" is only an ultimate ideal. Actually, along with the rapid development of science, technology, and the evolution of the historical content of humanistic spirit, the meaning of "universal development" is also changing correspondingly; thus the understanding of "universal development" in every period only has a relative meaning. Engels, when talking about those great people in the Renaissance, writes that: "There was hardly any man of importance then living who had not traveled extensively, who did not speak four or five languages, who did not shine in a number of fields… The heroes of that time were not yet in thrall to the division of labor, the restricting effects of which, with its production of one-sideness, we so often notice in their successors. But what is especially characteristic of them is that they almost all live and pursue their activities in the midst of the contemporary movements, in the practical struggle … hence [they have] the fullness and force of character that makes them complete men [ganzen Männern]."① In a manner, we could regard the "complete men" mentioned by Engels here as the universally developed individuals in quality, in that period. And nowadays, more is required for universally developed individuals. In other words, the universal development of individuals is just an ideal state. Certainly, regarding such an ideal state as an aim will necessarily promote everyone's development.

However, as individuals in actual world, we must dialectically understand the relation between "universal development" and "one-side development." We must know exactly that today is the epoch of knowledge and information explosion, in which it is impossible for someone to acquaint himself with all kinds of knowledge and skills. Whoever wants to know everything, he could only know nothing. Consequently, concerning the topic of "universal development of individuals," we would say that it is enough to comprehend it only as a universal development of individual's

---

① K. Marx and F. Engels, *Collected Works*, vol. 25 (Moscow: Progress Publishers, 1987), pp. 319-320. Also see F. Engels, *Dialektik der Natur* (Berlin: Dietz Verlag, 1952), S. 8-9.

quality, i. e. as unison of humanistic and scientific spirit from the point of real life. Everyone, who is not immersing himself in illusions, will acknowledge that he could merely achieve one-side development in the real world. He must know himself well, must seriously consider his talent and interest, and must develop specially those elements which he is adept in and which will easily lead to success. Shakespeare's success in drama, Mozart in melodizing, Niccolo Paganini in violin and Picasso in painting, these are all results of one-side development. If one wants to universally develop his own specialties and skills, then he could accomplish nothing in actual life.

Goethe ever said: "Man says correctly that it is the best to universally develop human abilities. But it is not born with us. Everyone must bring himself up essentially as a special one, and then try to acquaint himself with what the summation of human abilities is."[①] He often advised his secretary Eckermann to concentrate on a unique learning, so that Eckermann seriously writes: "he has always, since I accompanied with him, tried to make me keep ignoring all those distractions and concentrate on a unique subject. If I show some interests in natural science, he always advised me to refrain from it and to hold myself at present only on poesy. If I want to read a book, which he knows is not helpful to my present subject, he also advised me to abandon it, by saying that it is for me no practical

---

① Johann Peter Eckermann, *Conversations with Goethe* (Beijing: The People's Literature Publishing House, 1982), p. 78. Under the tittle "Mittwoch, den 20. April 1825", Eckemanm writes, Man sagt mit Recht' fuhr Goethe fort, daß die gemeinsame Ausbildung menschlicher Kräfte zu wünschen und auch das Vorzüglichste sei. Der Mensch aber ist dazu nicht geboren, jeder muß sich eigentlich als ein besonderes Wesen bilden, aber den Begriff zu erlangen suchen, was alle zusammen sind.

usefulness. "① These words indicate not only that Goethe has strict stand-ards on studies for Eckermann, but also that Goethe insists on a one-side development of individual abilities.

What's interesting is that, it is also Hegel's experience in studies that we must promote one-side development of our abilities and strictly restrain our study area. He tells us: "The man who will do something great must learn, as Goethe says, to limit himself. The man who, on the contrary, would do everything, really would do nothing, and fails. There is a host of interesting things in the world: Spanish poetry, chemistry, politics, and music are all very interesting, and if any one takes an interest in them we need not find fault. But for a person in a given situation to accomplish anything, he must stick to one definite point, and not dissipate his forces in many directions. "② In another place, he speaks in the same strain: " 'Whoever aspires to great things', says Goethe, 'must be able to limit himself. ' Only by making resolutions can the human being enter actuality, however painful the process may be. "③ Just in this sense, Hegel tartly satirizes those, who always rest on an ideal of universal development, but are never willing to make any resolution: "The laurels of mere willing are

---

① Johann Peter Eckermann, *Conversations with Goethe* (Beijing: The People's Litera-ture Publishing House, 1982), p. 80. Under the titlle "Mittwoch, den 20. April 1825", Eckemanm writes, So hat er die ganze Zeit, die ich in seiner Nähe bin, mich stets vor allen ableitenden Richtungen zu bewahren und mich immer auf ein einziges Fach zu konzentrieren gesucht. Zeigte ich etwa Neigung, mich in Naturwissenschaften umzutun, so war immer sein Rat, es zu unterlassen und mich für jetzt bloß an die Poesie zu halten. Wollte ich ein Buch lesen, wovon er wußte, daß es mich auf meinem jetzigen Wege nicht weiter brächte, so widerrief er es mir stets, indem er sagte, es sei für mich von keinem praktischen Nutzen.

② G. W. F. Hegel, *The Logic of Hegel*, trans. William Wallace (Oxford: Oxford University Press, 1966), p. 145.

③ G. W. F. Hegel, *Elements of the Philosophy of Right*, trans. H. B. Nisbet (Cambridge: Cambridge university press, 1991), p. 47.

dry leaves which have never been green."[1] This deeply indicates that, if one wants to be successful, he can not develop his own various abilities and interests simultaneously, can not just rest on a mere ideal, but to enter reality and action, to develop those elements which he is best adept in.

In conclusion, Marx's theory of "universal development of individuals" concerns the universal development of "quality," rather than that of "ability," where the former mainly appears as a unity of the humanistic and scientific spirits. The universal development of individual's ability is only an ideal state, which is actually hard to be achieved. In actual world, what one should really pursue is: to promote universal development in his quality, and one-side development in his ability. In fact, only the whole human being could actualize a universal development in ability.

---

[1] G. W. F. Hegel, *Elements of the Philosophy of Right*, trans. H. B. Nisbet (Cambridge: Cambridge university press, 1991), p. 153.

2.4　The Two Kantian Notions of Causality[①]

—An Analytic Enquiry

It is common knowledge that the relationship between causality and freedom lies at the core of Kantian philosophy. It can even be said that all Kant's life-long explorations revolve around this central issue. At the same time, this has been the hardest problem to find a solution for in his philosophy. This is because in different writings he addressed the issue from different perspectives and in different wording, without ever giving a concentrated and systematic account of the topic. This made the problem a highly controversial one in Kantian studies.

Attempts at decoding Kant's enigmatic legacy were made after his death from different perspectives by Hegel and Schopenhauer and by neo-Kantian scholars and modern Kant researchers like Lewis White Beck, Allen W. Wood and Henry E.

① Editor's note: This paper was originally published in *Social Science in China*, vol. 29, no. 3, 2008, pp. 5-15, translated by Chen Yongyi and Zhang Zhiping from *Zhongguo Shehui Kexue* (《中国社会科学》), no. 6, 2007, pp. 29-40, revised by Sally Borthwick.

Allison. Noteworthy, likewise, are some inquires into this question undertaken in China. ①But all these attempts fell short of complete success due to a variety of causes. One of these causes was neglect of the crucial fact that there are in Kantian philosophy two different notions of causality, namely, causality of nature and causality of freedom. Some researchers, though registering the existence of these two concepts, failed to dig deep into Kant's innovative concept of "causality of freedom," but instead followed custom in researching separately his statements about "freedom" and "causality" as if dealing with two different matters. Others stuck fast to detailed analyses of Kantian texts, sentences and concepts while overlooking the differences in the context in which Kant himself addressed the problem in different writings. Most serious of all is that no researchers took seriously the critical interpretations of the Kantian notion of causality offered by Hegel and Schopenhauer and especially by Marx. This essay sets out my own view with regard to this issue, in hopes that scholars at home and abroad will assist me with their comments.

Kant's response to "Hume's hint"

In his *Prolegomena to Any Future Metaphysics*. Kant frankly admitted that it had been "Hume's hint" that many years before had aroused him from his dogmatic slumber and shown him a totally different path in speculative philosophical studies. What was Kant referring to here?

---

① Chen Jiaming, *Structuring and Guiding: Methodology in Kantian Philosophy* (Beijing: Social Sciences Academic Press, 1992), chapter 9, section 3 and 4; Deng Xiaomang, *Problems of Kantian Philosophy* (Beijing: SDX Joint Publishing Company, 2006), chapter 1, section 4, and chapter 3, section 4, to name but a few.

Kant wrote: "Hume started from a single but important concept in Metaphysics, viz., that of Cause and Effect (including its derivatives force and action, etc.). He challenges reason, which pretends to have given birth to this idea from herself, to answer him by what right she thinks anything to be so constituted, that if that thing be posited, something else also must necessarily be posited; for this is the meaning of the concept of cause. He demonstrated irrefutably that it was perfectly impossible for reason to think a priori and by means of concepts a combination involving necessity. We cannot at all see why, in consequence of the existence of one thing, another must necessarily exist, or how the concept of such a combination can arise a priori. Hence he inferred, that reason was altogether deluded with reference to this concept, which she erroneously considered as one of her children, whereas in reality it was nothing but a bastard of imagination, impregnated by experience, which subsumed certain representations under the Law of Association, and mistook the subjective necessity of habit for an objective necessity arising from insight. Hence he inferred that reason had no power to think such, combinations, even generally, because her concepts would then be purely fictitious, and all her pretended a priori cognitions nothing but common experiences marked with a false stamp. In plain language, there is not, and cannot be, any such thing as metaphysics at all."① It was Hume's subversive questioning of the traditional notion of causality. Subversive, because traditional metaphysics was based in its entirety on the notion of causality and this idea was understood as "objective necessity." If this notion was, as Hume put it, nothing more than "subjective necessity or custom," the consequences would be easy to

---

① Immanuel Kant, "Introduction" to *Prolegomena to Any Future Metaphysics*, paragraph 10.

imagine: the metaphysical edifice would then collapse in its entirety.

The seriousness of the problem was self-evident. In the context of his transcendental philosophy, built upon meticulous thinking, Kant gave a categorical answer to Hume's question, to the effect that the notion of causality came not from experience, but from reason. In other words, causality was said to be innate in reason. Thus he successfully responded in terms of transcendental philosophy to Hume's question concerning the notion of causality. However, an even more fundamental issue implicit in this difficult question remained untouched. It is common knowledge that in his book *An Enquiry Concerning Human Understanding*, chapter 8, entitled "Of Liberty and Necessity," Hume further advanced the issue of the relationship between causality and freedom, holding that since the relation between "cause" and "effect" was commonly understood as one of necessity, the relationship between freedom and causality was in essence one between freedom and necessity. But, as Hume pointed out, this turned out to be an even trickier problem, for if everything in the world happens as a relationship of necessity between "cause" and "effect," man can have no freedom whatsoever. Conversely, if man has freedom, how should the relationship of necessity between "cause" and "effect" be understood? This problem was later to become the real starting point of Kant's philosophical reflections. In his letter of September 21, 1798, to Christian Garve, he wrote: "It was not the investigation of the existence of God, immortality, and so on, but rather the antinomy of pure reason—'The world has a beginning, it has no beginning, and so on,' right up to the fourth [sic]: 'There is freedom in man, versus there is no freedom, only the necessity of nature'—that is what first aroused me from my dogmatic slumber and drove me to the critique of reason itself, in order to resolve the scandal of the ostensible contradiction of reason with itself?"① Noteworthy is the term "dogmatic slumber" Kant uses here, exactly the same one he used earlier in his *Prolegomena to Any Future Metaphysics*, a fact which seems to suggest that what is most difficult to deal with in "Hume's hint" is not so much the problem of the origin of the notion of causality as that of the relationship between causality and freedom. In fact, Kant himself points out that when reason tries to apply cognition as a category to know a transcendental thing-in-itself—the world, it inevitably falls into four antinomies, the third of which is related to reason's inappropriate (or transcendental) application of the category of causality.

Thesis: Causality based on the laws of nature is not the only causality from which all phenomena in the world can be inferred. In order to account for these phenomena, another kind of causality, stemming from freedom, needs to be supposed.

Antithesis: There is no freedom at all. On the contrary, everything in the world occurs based on the laws of nature. ②

Here, instead of paying too much attention to Kant's circular argument between thesis and antithesis, we need do no more than keep in mind

① Immanuel Kant, *Philosophical correspondence 1759-1799*, translated and edited by Arnulf Zweig (Chicago: University of Chicago Press, 1970), p. 252. What Kant refers to as "the fourth" is in fact the third Antinomy in his *Critique of pure reason*. As Henry E. Allison puts it, "[T]he third Antinomy is not only the locus of the major discussion of the problem of freedom in the *Critique of Pure Reason*, it is also the basis for Kant's subsequent treatments of the topic in his writings on moral philosophy." See Henry E. Allison, *Kant's Theory of Freedom* (Chicago: Cambridge University Press, 1990), p. 3.

② Immanuel Kant, *Critique of Pure Reason*, Trans. Deng Xiaomang (Beijing: People's Press, 2004), p. 374.

the conflict between causality (or necessity) and freedom. ① What is of cardinal importance is that Kant comes up here with two clear-cut notions of causality: "causality in accordance with the laws of nature" (*die Kausalität nach Gesetzen der Natur*, henceforth "causality of nature" for short) and "causality through freedom" (*eine Kausalität durch Freiheit*, henceforth "causality of freedom" for short). ② It is plain to see that in advancing these two notions of causality, Kant is trying to find a complete solution to Hume's tricky question of the relationship between causality and freedom. Now, can these two concepts effectively help solve the problem? We shall try to give an answer in what follows.

What Kant's concept of two kinds of causality implies

In his *Critique of Practical Reason*, Kant points out: "The notion of causality as physical necessity, in opposition to the same notion as freedom, concerns only the existence of things so far as it is determinable in time, and, consequently, as phenomena, in opposition to their causality as things in themselves. Now if we take the attributes of existence of things in time for attributes of things in themselves (which is the common view),

---

① Just as H. J. Paton points out, "the notion of freedom is one of reason without which no moral judgment can exist, any more than there can be any knowledge of nature without the cognitive category of nature's necessity or causality. These two notions, however, are obviously incompatible with each other. According to the first one, our action should be free. According to the second one, our action, as an event of the known world of nature, is bound to be constrained by causal laws." See Immanuel Kant, *Groundwork of Metaphysics of Morals*, Trans. Miao Litian (Shanghai: Shanghai People's Publishing House, 1986), pp. 156-157.

② Immanuel Kant, *Kritik der reinen Vernunft II* (Frankfurt A. M. : Suhrkamp Verlag, 1988), B472/A444.

then it is impossible to reconcile the necessity of the causal relation with freedom; they are contradictory. For from the former it follows that every event, and consequently every action that takes place at a certain point of time, is a necessary result of what existed in time preceding. Now as time past is no longer in my power, hence every action that I perform must be the necessary result of certain determining grounds which are not in my power, that is, at the moment in which I am acting I am never free."[1] In other words, in the context of speculative reason, the notion of causality of nature only applies within the boundaries of phenomena; it is only in the transcendental realm of things-in-themselves that the notion of causality of freedom makes any sense. What constitutes the antinomy with it is the causality of nature that reason brings illegitimately into the realm of things transcendental. To Kant, neither the causality of nature inherent in the realm of phenomena of speculative reason nor the causality of freedom inherent in the transcendental realm of speculative reason can in fact have anything close to genuine freedom.

Kant explains in his *Groundwork of the Metaphysics of Morals*: "As a rational being and thus as belonging to the intelligible world, man cannot think of the causality of his own will except under the idea of freedom…"[2] This means that freedom should be the cause of all human action. Such a new notion of causality of freedom is meant to suggest that all consequences of human action arise from freedom, and therefore man should be held responsible for the consequences of his actions. Such being the case,

---

① Immanuel Kant, "Critical Examination of the Analytic of the Pure Practical Reason," in *Critique of Practical Reason*, trans. Thomas Kingsmill Abbott (London: Longmans, Green and Company, 1909), paragraph 8.

② Immanuel Kant, "Third Section: Transition from the Metaphysic of Morals to the Critique of Pure Practical Reason," in *Groundwork of Metaphysics of Morals*, trans. Thomas Kingsmill Abbott and ed. Glyn Hughes, 2002, paragraph 15.

we have to redirect our inquiry toward the following question: in the context of Kant's practical reason, what does freedom mean? It is noteworthy that Kant makes a distinction between two different notions of freedom, namely, "psychological freedom" (*die psychologische Freiheit*) and "transcendental freedom" (*die transzendentale Freiheit*). The former is related to causes from the world of perception; he who perceives freedom in this way acts on account of purposes or motivations belonging in his perceptual experience. As for the latter, he who perceives freedom in this way acts solely on account of the moral laws promulgated by pure reason, while ignoring altogether causes from the perceptual world. Kant's notion of causality of freedom deals precisely with this transcendental freedom, which means that one is only entirely free when one acts entirely in accordance with the moral laws promulgated by pure reason.

It is on the basis of such reflections that Kant further points out: "The union of causality as freedom with causality as rational mechanism, the former established by the moral law, the latter by the law of nature in the same subject, namely, man, is impossible, unless we conceive him with reference to the former as a being in himself, and with reference to the latter as a phenomenon—the former in pure consciousness, the latter in empirical consciousness. Otherwise reason inevitably contradicts itself."[1] These words tell us clearly that man, as a being in existence, should appeal to the causality of nature when he deals with phenomena of nature, whereas he should appeal to the causality of freedom when he deals with other people. On the one hand, such causality of freedom resides in "pure consciousness" and can therefore only be transcendental.

---

[1]   Immanuel Kant, "Preface to *Critique of Practical Reason*," in *Critique of Pure Reason*, trans. Thomas Kingsmill Abbott (London: Longmans, Green and Company, 1909), paragraph 8.

But on the other hand, it is set up by moral law and understands freedom as unconditional compliance with moral law.

From the above it can be seen that by allocating the causality of nature and that of freedom to two separate contexts, that of speculative reason and that of practical reason, Kant's idea of two notions of causality makes it possible to delimit the spheres of application of causality of nature and causality of freedom respectively, with cognition (including the category of causality) serving to legislate for nature (or for phenomena) and reason doing so for freedom. Thus freedom means compliance with the moral law promulgated by reason, so much so that moral law may as well be essentially understood as causality of freedom. At first glance, by means of such allocation to separate spheres, Kant seems to have succeeded in solving Hume's tricky problem concerning the relationship between causality and freedom. However, the very crux of this difficult issue remains unresolved. Just as Hume pointed out long ago, "all mankind have ever agreed in the doctrine of liberty as well as in that of necessity, and that the whole dispute, in this respect also, has been hitherto merely verbal."① True, Kant made a stride forward with respect to Hume by advancing his transcendental philosophy to resolve the problem of the origin of the notion of causality. However, in the context of the transcendental things-in-themselves of speculative reason, the causality of freedom on the one hand and the causality of nature applied in an inappropriate (or transcendental) way on the other can only find themselves in a conflict of antinomy. Only in the context of practical reason can causality of freedom acquire objective reality. But even in such a context, by means of his distinction between

---

① D. Hume, *An Enquiry Concerning Human Understanding* (Oxford: Oxford University Press, 1999), p. 158.

"transcendental freedom" (consistent with the causality of freedom) and "psychological freedom" (consistent with the causality of nature in the context of speculative reason), Kant not only rules out the reconciliation of these two kinds of causality, but stresses that causality of freedom is "hard, if not impossible, to understand."

The above shows that Kant failed to successfully respond to or take forward Hume's theory on causality. At the same time, his conclusions tell us that a positive and effective response to "Hume's hint" can only be possible if one goes beyond the context of Kant's transcendental philosophy.

Hegel's and Schopenhauer's Interpretations of Kant's Two Notions of Causality

While evaluating highly Kant's notion of freedom and characterizing it as embodying the awakening of man's consciousness of himself and a step forward in the progress of the human spirit, Hegel, notwithstanding, criticizes this notion as too vague, saying, "this freedom is at first only the negative of everything else; no bond, nothing external, lays me under an obligation. It is to this extent indeterminate; it is the identity of the will with itself, it is at-homeness with itself. But what is the content of this law? Here we at once come back to the lack of content. For the sole form of this principle is nothing more or less than agreement with itself, universality; the formal principle of legislation in this internal solitude comes to no determination, or this is abstraction only. The universal, the non-contradiction of self, is without content, something which comes to be reality in the practical sphere just as little as in the theoretical. "[1] This is to say that what Kant extols as freedom is in fact something empty of content, for he starts from "pure reason" to talk about freedom in a way alien to the perceptual world, and therefore his freedom and notion of the causality of freedom remain something abstract and isolated from real life.

What, then, is to be done in order for Kant's freedom and his notion of the causality of freedom to become reality? In the "Introduction" to his *Philosophy of History*. Hegel writes, "In the process before us, the essential nature of freedom—which involves in it absolute necessity—is to be displayed as coming to a consciousness of itself (for it is in its very nature, self-consciousness) and thereby realizing its existence. Itself is its own object of attainment, and the sole aim of Spirit. This result it is, at which the process of the World's History has been continually aiming … "[2] This shows us that in order to rid Kant's notion of freedom of its emptiness and endow it with a reality of its own, "freedom" should be consciously based on a right understanding of the causality of nature, and first of all of historical causality.

To Hegel, what Kant understands as "transcendental freedom" is nowhere close to real freedom, which, instead of compliance with abstract moral laws, implies an effort to self-consciously understand and master the causality of world history and keep one's own behavior in line with such causality. It is evident that, in interpreting Kant's two notions of causality, Hegel makes a contribution in that he joins both freedom and the

---

[1] G. W. F. Hegel, *Lectures on the History of Philosophy* (London: Kegan Paul, Trench, Trubner & Co., Ltd, 1896), (London: Routlege & Kegan Paul, Ltd., 1955), p. 460.

[2] G. W. F. Hegel, *Philosophy of History*, trans. J. Sibree (New York: Willey Book Co., 1900), p. 19.

causality of nature together, separating Kant's notion of freedom from pure reason and instead basing it upon historical reason, and exploring, furthermore, in his *Philosophy of History* and other writings the dialectical relationship between freedom and historical causality. Nevertheless, Hegel's historical idealistic stance prevents him from making his notion of freedom genuinely real.

It was Schopenhauer, more or less contemporary with Hegel, who made an attempt to interpret Kant's two notions of causality from the perspective of two different contexts. In his opinion, in the context of epistemology, the world appears in man's consciousness in the form of representations, with the notion of causality being what is central to everything in man's cognition of the world, whereas in the context of ontology, will encompasses not only what Kant calls practical reason, but also things in themselves and even the world itself in its very essence. Not just free, will is all-mighty indeed, there being nothing it cannot accomplish.

What is interesting is that in his epistemological research Schopenhauer goes back from Kant to Berkeley in understanding the world as representations and the category of causality as the basic tool for grasping them. In his ontological research, he interprets in his own way practical reason and things in themselves and asserts that will is the very essence of the world. To him, will is absolutely free and in no way needs to comply with moral law. An important contribution he makes in interpreting the two Kantian notions of freedom is that he decodes the thing in itself as will and restores it to its very nature as freedom by setting it free from the fenced territory of Kant's pure reason.

It is to Schopenhauer's credit that he, on the one hand, stresses that will is not just the way man lives in the world, but also the very foundation and essence of the world, and on the other hand, asserts that, instead of remaining on the far-away and unreachable "other shore," what Kant calls the "thing-in-itself" is just on "this shore," when he says, "What is the thing-in-itself? Our answer has been the will … "① Not only did Schopenhauer transcend Kant's dualism with its distinctive separation between phenomena and the thing-in-itself, but he ushered in a totally new dimension for the understanding of Kant's transcendental philosophy, thus leaving a far-reaching legacy for later philosophers. However, in affirming the freedom of the will as something unconditional and absolute and even stressing will's omnipotence, he was in fact equating freedom of will to willfulness. Thus it was impossible for him to pay due attention, as Hegel did, to the relationship between freedom and the causality of nature and history, or to go further to explore and get at the conditions necessary for the realization of freedom. Thus a mountain gave birth to a mouse. Schopenhauer's creative research resulted in a trifling conclusion: life is pessimistic and the human soul can only attain peace by suppressing and even denying the will to survive. If, as may be remembered, Nietzsche saw in Kant a hidden Christian, we may likewise see in Schopenhauer a conscious one.

How Marx Decoded the Two Kantian Notions of Causality

Unexpectedly for Kant researchers, it was Marx who, in the post-Kantian

---

① A. Schopenhauer, *The World as Will and Representation*, trans. E. F. J. Payne (New York: Dover Publications, 1966). Dealing with Kant's notion of "thing-in-itself" Arsen Gulyga writes: "Schopenhauer also mocks it. He likens Kant to a man who at a masked ball courts a beautiful woman he barely knows. When the ball is over, the woman takes off her mask and turns out to be his own wife?" See Arsen Gulyga, *Immanuel Kant*, trans. Jia Zelin, et al (Beijing: The Commercial Press, 1981), p. 168.

evolution of philosophical research, succeeded in critically synthesizing the thought of Hegel and Schopenhauer and thus achieving a fundamental decoding of the two Kantian notions of causality.

Drawing critically, on the one hand, upon Hegel's works on phenomenology of mind, philosophy of law and philosophy of history, Marx switched his attention from Kant's stress on causality of nature to the historical causality in the process of development of human society (that is, historical necessity or historical laws). In *Capital*, the crystallization of his lifelong theoretical research, he tells us straightforwardly "it is the ultimate aim of this work, to lay bare the economic law of motion of modem society?" [①] To him, transcending the Hegelian context means, rather than talking about causality of nature and historical causality while remaining within the boundaries of purely mental movement, trying instead to incorporate these two kinds of causality into anatomizing real social history, and particularly the history of development of civil society. It is here that Marx shows us a clear path to follow in unraveling the secret of the two Kantian notions of causality, namely, the path of observing productive labor, man's basic activity for survival.

On the other hand, by means of a critical rethinking of Schopenhauer's philosophy of will, Marx managed to provide a thoroughgoing analysis of Kant's notion of freedom. "The characteristic form which French liberalism, based on real class interests, assumed in Germany we find again in Kant. Neither he, nor the German middle-class, whose whitewashing spokesman he was, noticed that these theoretical ideas of the bourgeoisie had as their basis material interests and a will that was conditioned and

---

① K. Marx, *Capital*, vol. 1, trans. S. Moore, E. B. Aveling and E. Untermann (New York: The Modem Library, 1906), p. 15.

determined by the material relations of production. Kant, therefore, separated this theoretical expression from the interests which it expressed; he made the materially motivated determinations of the will of the French bourgeois into *pure* self-determinations of '*free will*,' of the will in and for itself, of the human will, and so converted it into purely ideological conceptual determinations and moral postulates."① In this extremely insightful statement, Marx not only lays bare the origin of Kant's notion of freedom, but also tells us that this notion, like others, has "as their basis material interests and a *will* that was conditioned and determined by the material relations of production."

It is here that Marx came up with a new idea of decisive significance, in the sense that will is "determined by the material relations of production." This is, in fact, what separates Marx and Schopenhauer when it comes to will. Schopenhauer sees will as absolutely free and all mighty; will means that you can do what you see fit, without being subject to any causality. To Marx, by contrast, the answer is altogether different. Precisely by means of in-depth research into the national economy, Marx arrived at the understanding that as soon as people switch from the Kantian context of "practical reason" to the new track of researching the problem of the will with real life as the point of departure, they are sure to find that

---

① K. Marx and F. Engels, *Collected Works*, vol. 5 (Moscow: Progress Publishers, 1975), p. 195. This approach of explaining the direction of development of human history from the perspective of will found its classic expression in what Engels wrote in his old age. In his letter of September 21-22, 1890, to J. Bloch, Engels writes, "… history is made in such a way that the final result always arises from conflicts between many individual wills, of which each in turn has been made what it is by a host of particular conditions of life. Thus there are innumerable intersecting forces, an infinite series of parallelograms of forces which give rise to one resultant—the historical event. This may again itself be viewed as the product of a power which works as a whole unconsciously and without volition." See K. Marx and F. Engels, *Collected Works*, vol. 49 (Moscow: Progress Publishers), p. 35.

freedom of will is far from unconditional, but instead subject to conditions. Will comes from man, a being endowed with life. But in order to preserve life (that is, to survive), man has first of all to produce material means of sustenance for his own consumption. It takes no more than an in-depth examination of the history of human society to find that man by no means exercises his will at random. Like it or not, man in fact has to commit his will to, and have it consumed in, the productive labor that enables him to survive. The further back one goes in history and the less developed the relations of production, the greater part of man's will has to be committed to this productive labor. It was by following such a train of thought that Marx succeeded in unraveling the intrinsic and inevitable linkage between will, on the one hand, and productive labor and relations of production, on the other, a discovery that made it possible for him to reach the epoch-making conclusion that will is determined by the relations of material production.

Critical observation from the two above-mentioned perspectives made it possible for Marx to lay a foundation for solving the riddle of Kant's notion of two kinds of causality. In fact, the secret lies in productive labor. On the one hand, productive labor implicitly contains the dimension of goal and causality of freedom. Just as Marx puts it, "free and conscious activity constitutes the species-character of man."[1] In spite of the alienation of productive labor under capitalism, "free labor" is what people hope to see realized in the future ideal society.[2] On the other hand, the law of causality has to be complied with if the desired results are to be obtained in

---

[1] K. Marx and F. Engels, *Collected Works*, vol. 3 (Moscow: Progress Publishers), p. 276.

[2] K. Marx and F. Engels, *Collected Works*, vol. 3 (Moscow: Progress Publishers), p. 268.

productive labor. As Lukacs puts it, "a process of labor is nothing but the realization of an aim by acting upon a concrete causality."① Here, however, Lukács keeps in view the causality of nature only, while in fact any productive labor presupposes the simultaneous unfolding of two kinds of causality, namely, causality of nature and historical causality. The former has already been exhaustively elucidated by Kant. But the fundamental difference separating him from Marx is that he fails to observe this causality, pervasive in all phenomena of nature, from the perspective of man's productive labor. As to the latter, Marx says, "In the process of production, human beings work not only upon nature but also upon one another. They produce only by working together in a special manner and reciprocally exchanging their activities. In order to produce, they enter into definite connections and relations to one another, and only within these social connections and relations does their influence upon nature operate—i. e. , does production take place?"② In fact, historical causality is historical necessity shaped by the interweaving of the will of countless people based on relations of production yet independent of the will of any single person.

Thus it can be seen that it is amid the practical activity of material productive labor aimed at survival that Kant's two kinds of causality, that of nature and that of freedom, become merged into one. It should be pointed out, of course, that Kant overlooked what Hegel and Marx would later come up with as historical causality, which in a sense might well be understood as a derived version of causality of nature. Anyway, unraveled here is the enigma of Kant's notion of two kinds of causality; the answer is

---

① G. Lukács, *Ontology of Social Being*, vol. 2, trans. Bai Xikun et al (Chongqing: Chongqing Publishing House, 1993), p. 70.

② K. Marx and F. Engels, *Collected Works*, vol. 9, (Moscow: Progress Publishers), p. 211.

Marx's material productive labor. As he tells us in *Capital*: "In fact, the realm of freedom actually begins only where labor which is determined by necessity and mundane considerations ceases; thus in the very nature of things it lies beyond the sphere of actual material production... Beyond it begins that development of human energy which is an end in itself, the true realm of freedom which, however, can blossom forth only with this realm of necessity as its basis."[1]

As Marx saw it, productive labor constitutes the realm of necessity (causality) in human existence, and also constitutes the foundation of the realm of freedom mankind pursues. In fact, it is only when one places the narrative of the concepts of freedom and causality in the context of historical materialism that they are truly real. We have only now discovered to what a great extent Marx had already outpaced Kant. At the same time, we have also discovered what a great theoretical error it is to separate the study of classical German philosophy from study of the philosophies of Marx and Schopenhauer. This is because it is precisely Marx and Schopenhauer who throw light on the core concept of classical German philosophy: the essence of the thing in itself. In particular, Marx's introduction of the concept of material productive labor provides the most reasonable explanatory model yet for discussion of the historical question of the relationship between causality and freedom.

---

[1] K. Marx and F. Engels, *Collected Works*, vol. 37 (London: Lawrence & Wishart, 1998), p. 807.

2.5 Three Reversals in the Development of Metaphysics[①]

—Reflections on Heidegger's Theory of Metaphysics

An in-depth understanding of Heidegger's theory of metaphysics enables us to see that the history of Western metaphysics is made up of three major "reversals" (die Umkehr), with the secret of modernity lying deep within them. In fact, it is precisely the understanding and interpretation of these reversals that opens up a way out of the anxieties of modernity and enables philosophical thought to regain its dignity and retain the commanding heights, and thus avoid being buried in the petty thinking of positivism.

The First Reversal in the Development of Metaphysics

The first reversal in the development of

---

① Editor's note: This paper was originally published in *Social Sciences in China*, vol. 32 no. 2, 2011, pp. 5-18, translated by Liu Ruixiang from *Zhongguo Shehui Kexue* (《中国社会科学》), no. 6, 2009, pp. 4-19, revised by Sally Borthwick.

metaphysics is expressed in the switch from the "metaphysics of presence" represented by Platonism to the "metaphysics of subjectivity" represented by Descartes, Kant and Hegel.

It is well known that one of Aristotle's works is entitled *Metaphysics*. In Greek, "metaphysics" is written as τὰ μετὰ τὰ φυσικὰ, with μετά having the meaning of "going beyond. "[1] But Aristotle did not invent this phrase. In fact, he calls the science concerned with the study of "beings as such" (being qua being) "the first philosophy. " W. S. Sahakian points out in his *Outline History of Philosophy* that Andronicus described "first philosophy" as a set of principles coming from or going beyond physics (τὰ μετὰ τὰ φυσικὰ) and placed it after the work on physics in his edition of Aristotle's works. [2]

Although the phase τὰ μετὰ τὰ φυσικὰ was created by Andronicus to refer to those of Aristotle's writings placed after his physics, this does not mean that the history of metaphysics began with Aristotle. In his *Nietzsche*, Heidegger said, "Plato, with whose thought metaphysics begins, understood beings as such, that is, the Being of beings, as 'Idea. '"[3]

For Heidegger, Plato was not merely the founder of metaphysics; his philosophy, Platonism, was also the dominant form of metaphysics from Plato to Nietzsche. Philosophers like Nietzsche tried to overthrow Plato, but even where such efforts had an effect, the influence of Platonism was still decisive. Heidegger even believed that "The incontestable dominance

---

[1] M. Heidegger, *Die Grundbegriffe der Metaphysik*, (Frankfurt am Main: Vittorio Klosterman, 1983), S. 58; M. Heidegger, *Wegmarken*, trans. Sun Zhouxing (Beijing: The Commercial Press, 2000), p. 137.

[2] W. S. Sahakian, *Outline History of Philosophy* (New York: Barnes &. Noble, 1969), pp. 65-66. *Ta meta ta physika* is the Romanization of τα μετά τα φυσικά.

[3] M. Heidegger, *Nietzsche*, vol. 2, trans. Sun Zhouxing (Beijing: The Commercial Press, 2000), p. 904.

of Platonism in Western philosophy ultimately reveals itself in the fact that philosophy before Plato, which as our earlier discussions have shown was not yet a metaphysics—that is to say, not a developed metaphysics—is interpreted with reference to Plato and is called pre-Platonic philosophy. "[1] When Whitehead said that the European philosophical tradition consisted of "a series of footnotes to Plato, " "the European philosophical tradition" obviously refers to philosophy after Plato. Heidegger went even further in showing that Platonism had the effect of "a total eclipse;" that is, our understanding and interpretation of pre-Platonic philosophy are also permeated by Platonism.

Heidegger defined Plato's metaphysics as the metaphysics of presence (die Anwesenheit). What, then, is this "metaphysics of presence"? From the perspective of his phenomenology, Heidegger gives the name "presence" to what is revealed in man's consciousness, what already exists ("appearance"); he regards the philosophical theory that studies presence and the forms of presence as the metaphysics of presence. [2]

---

[1]　M. Heidegger, *Nietzsche*, vol. 2, trans. Sun Zhouxing (Beijing: The Commercial Press, 2000), pp. 852-853.

[2]　It must be pointed out that although Heidegger repeatedly discussed the relationship between traditional metaphysics and "presence" and although the concept of the "metaphysics of presence" was poised to come at his call, he did not directly originate this concept. It was Derrida who put it forward after a careful interpretation of Heidegger's works. Derrida believed that traditional metaphysics "might be a definition that takes 'Being' as all the meanings of the word "presence" (J. Derrida, *L'ecriture et la difference*, vol. 2, trans. Zhang Ning (Beijing: The SDX Joint Publishing Company, 2001), p. 504). In his view, Heidegger criticized the metaphysics of presence but did not break away completely from this metaphysics; "the metaphysics of presence is shaken with the help of the concept of sign. " (Ibid., p. 506) Kellner and Best have pointed out, "Derrida termed this foundationalist approach to language and knowledge a 'meta physics of presence' that supposedly guaranteed the subject an unmediated access to reality. " See Kellner Douglas and Steven Best, *Postmodern Theory*, trans. Zhang Zhibin (Beijing: Central Compilation and Translation Press, 2001), p. 27.

Heidegger believed that in Plato, "presence" takes two different forms. One is presence as "beings." "Beings" here represents concrete things, e. g., a house, a horse, a stone, a person, or a picture, the presence of which can be perceived by the senses. The other is presence as "Being," the generalization of "beings;" that is, "beings" minus all their particularities, which thus become the most universal things. People can only understand and grasp the presence of these universals, which are what Plato called the "idea" (ιδεα) through their own thinking. In Heidegger's view, Plato did not say anything substantial on "Being" itself; Platonism as the metaphysics of presence concerns itself with the difference in form of presence between "Being" and "beings."

As everybody knows, Plato saw "Being" or the idea as the most universal thing, original and eternal. It was the origin of all particular things and "beings," as individual things were but "copies" of the idea. As for works of art representing individual things, they were but "copies of a copy." As Heidegger said, "Plato defined presence as the idea."[①] That is, for Plato, only the idea, i. e., the form of presence of "Being," was original, eternal and real,[②] while the form of presence of "beings," as individual things or "copies" of the idea, were not reliable because they were changeable and therefore non-original and illusory. As for works of art, as "copies of a copy," their form of presence was subordinate to that of ordinary "beings" and was therefore even more illusory and unreliable. Thus Heidegger pointed out, "In the sequence of sundry ways taken by the presence of

---

① M. Heidegger, "The End of Philosophy and the Task of Thinking," in *Selected Works of Martin Heidegger*, vol. 2, ed. Sun Zhouxing (Shanghai: The SDX Joint Publishing Company, 1996), p. 1256.

② Heidegger says, "For Platonism, the Idea, the supersensuous, is the true, true being." M. Heidegger, *Nietzsche*, vol. 1, trans. Sun Zhouxing (Beijing: The Commercial Press, 2000), p. 169.

beings, hence by the Being of beings, art stands far below truth in Plato's metaphysics. "① Plato's *Republic* even drives out artists, especially poets.

From the above expositions of Heidegger we can deduce the following conclusions.

First, Platonism is essentially the metaphysics of presence, which is outward-oriented and concerns itself with the manifestation or presence of all things of the world in human consciousness. In this kind of metaphysics, the singularity of "man" as a being has not been subjectivized and man is treated as the same as other beings such as a house, horse, stone or work of art.

Second, at first glance, the metaphysics of presence represented by Platonism seems to be aware of the difference between "Being" and "beings" and to comprehend the original form of presence as "Being, " i. e. , "idea. " However, as it does not realize that only man, the singular "Being" in all the "beings, " is able to take on the mission of inquiring about the meaning of Being, the meaning of Being cannot be highlighted by the metaphysics of presence. So Heidegger believed that the metaphysics of presence would inevitably be replaced by a new theory of metaphysics.

The metaphysics of subjectivity was conceived and developed in the tradition of Platonism, but its mode of operational thought turned out to be a subversion of the metaphysics of presence. In contrast to the metaphysics of presence in which man, the singular being, is treated alike with all other beings, the metaphysics of subjectivity signifies the awakening of the subjective consciousness of man, who puts himself as subject in the center of the whole world of beings. As a result, the forms of manifestation

---

① M. Heidegger, *Nietzsche*, vol. 1, trans. Sun Zhouxing (Beijing: The Commercial Press, 2000), p. 207.

of all the things of the world in human consciousness are reversed. In the metaphysics of presence, man is an ordinary or even an insignificant element in the world, while in the metaphysics of subjectivity man is the foundation and center of the whole world. Just as Heidegger said, "Western history has now begun to enter into the completion of that period we call the modern, and which is defined by the fact that man becomes the measure and the center of beings. Man is what lies at the bottom of all beings; that is, in modern terms, at the bottom of all objectification and representability," i. e. , *Subjectum*(general subject). ①

Who, then, was the initiator of the metaphysics of subjectivity? In Heidegger's view, it was the French philosopher Descartes. He wrote, "At the beginning of modern philosophy stands Descartes' statement: *Cogito ergo sum*(I think, therefore I am). All consciousness of things and of beings as a whole is referred back to the self-consciousness of the human subject as the unshakable ground of all certainty. The reality of the real is defined in later times as objectivity, as something that is conceived by and for the subject as what is thrown and stands over against it. "② Clearly, Heidegger holds that the famous proposition, "I think, therefore I am"

---

① M. Heidegger, *Nietzsche*, vol. 2, trans. Sun Zhouxing (Beijing: The Commercial Press, 2000), p. 699. Elsewhere in this work, Heidegger writes, "What is new about the modern period as opposed to the Christian medieval age consists in the fact that man, independently and by his own effort, contrives to become certain and sure of his human being in the midst of beings as a whole. " M. Heidegger, *Nietzsche*, vol. 2, trans. Sun Zhouxing (Beijing: The Commercial Press, 2000), p. 765.

② M. Heidegger, *Nietzsche*, vol. 2, trans. Sun Zhouxing (Beijing: The Commercial Press, 2000), pp. 761-762. Elsewhere in this work Heidegger says more clearly, "Descartes' metaphysics is the decisive beginning of the foundation of metaphysics in the modern age. It was his task to ground the metaphysical ground of man's liberation in the new freedom of self-assured self-legislation. Descartes anticipated this ground in an authentically philosophical sense. " M. Heidegger, *Nietzsche*, vol. 2, trans. Sun Zhouxing (Beijing: The Commercial Press, 2000), p. 778.

put forward by Descartes constitutes a hallmark for the establishment of the metaphysics of subjectivity. In the post-Cartesian era, the German philosophers Kant and Hegel took this metaphysics to its highest point. Kant's metaphor of the "Copernican revolution," his concept of "transcendental apperception" and his exposition of "understanding makes laws for nature and reason makes laws for freedom" and Hegel's view that the key to all questions was that the real thing should not only be understood and expressed as an entity but should also be understood and described as a subject① are all classical expressions of the core concepts of the metaphysics of subjectivity.

The essence of the metaphysics of subjectivity is to see man, the singular being, as the determinator of all metaphysical truths. As Heidegger said, "As a metaphysics of subjectivity, modern metaphysics, under whose spell our thinking too stands, or rather inevitably seems to stand, takes it as a foregone conclusion that the essence of truth and the interpretation of Being are determined by man as the subject proper."② Put plainly, with the establishment of the metaphysics of subjectivity, metaphysics has actually been transformed into anthropology. "Thus today one thought is common to everyone, to wit, an 'anthropological' thought, which demands that the world be interpreted in accordance with the image of man and that metaphysics be replaced by 'anthropology.' In such a demand, a definite decision has already been rendered concerning the relationship of man to beings as such."③ We find that the reversal of the metaphysics of

---

① G. W. F. Hegel, *Werke* 3(Frankfurt am Main: Suhrkamp Verlag, 1986), S. 23.

② M. Heidegger, *Nietzsche*, vol. 2, trans. Sun Zhouxing (Beijing: The Commercial Press, 2000), p. 824.

③ M. Heidegger, *Nietzsche*, vol. 2, trans. Sun Zhouxing (Beijing: The Commercial Press, 2000), p. 762.

presence represented by Platonism and its replacement by modern metaphysics, i. e. , the metaphysics of subjectivity, represented by Descartes, Kant and Hegel, is expressed mainly in the following ways.

First, the metaphysics of presence adopts an outward-looking way of thought, that is, thought explores outward, serving as the form of presence of being or beings as a whole, while the metaphysics of subjectivity adopts an inward-looking way of thought, that is, thought goes inward to highlight and extract "the self" and "I think" as the object of reflection.

Second, the metaphysics of presence examines and reflects on all beings alike without any discrimination, whereas the metaphysics of subjectivity differentiates between "man," the singular being (as subjectivity) and other beings (as objectivity) and understands and interprets this subjectivity as the starting point and determinator of all metaphysical truths.

Third, the focus of exploration of the metaphysics of presence is the idea as the most universal thing, and the ultimate foundation of the idea is the "Creator," who, in the context of the Middle Ages, became God, the most fundamental form of presence; while the focus of exploration of the metaphysics of subjectivity is the foundational and key status and role of man as the subject in modern metaphysics. As Heidegger said, "Within the history of the modern age, and as the history of modern mankind, man universally and always independently attempts to establish himself as midpoint and measure in a position of dominance; that is, to pursue the securing of such dominance."[1] It is also in this sense that Heidegger understood the metaphysics of subjectivity as anthropology.

---

① M. Heidegger, *Nietzsche*, vol. 2, trans. Sun Zhouxing (Beijing: The Commercial Press, 2000), p. 777.

In short, the reversal from the outward-looking metaphysics represented by Platonism to the inward-looking metaphysics of subjectivity represented by Descartes, Kant and Hegel was the first reversal in the development of metaphysics. The decisive result of this reversal was that within the realm of beings, man was transformed into *subjectum* and the world into a picture of man. ① Only by starting from this point can we gain a real understanding of the essence of modern metaphysics and modernity.

The Second Reversal in the Development of Metaphysics

As mentioned above, for Heidegger modern metaphysics was the same as the metaphysics of subjectivity. The second reversal in the development of metaphysics took place within the wider framework of the metaphysics of subjectivity, from the "metaphysics of reason" to the "metaphysics of will."

In the metaphysics of subjectivity, "subjectivity" as a specific property of man is a very complex concept. On the one hand, philosophers in the sixteenth and seventeenth centuries usually understood man as a composite of soul and body; on the other, more modern philosophers and contemporary philosophers are inclined to understand man as a composite of reason and unreason (instincts, emotions, will and desire). This tells us that the metaphysics of subjectivity is still an abstract concept and we cannot rely

---

① Heidegger says "The interweaving of these two events, which for the modern age is decisive—that the world is transformed into picture and man into subjectum—throws light at the same time on the grounding event of modern history, an event that at first glance seems almost absurd." See M. Heidegger, "The Question Concerning Technology and Other Essays," in *Selected Works of Martin Heidegger*, vol. 2, ed. Sun Zhouxing (Shanghai: The SDX Joint Publishing Company, 1996), p. 902.

on this concept alone to judge which factor or factors in subjectivity should be given prominence.

Heidegger pointed out, "Western metaphysics does not define man simply and homologously in every epoch as a creature of reason. The metaphysical inception of the modern age first manifests the historic unfolding of that role in which reason attains its full metaphysical rank."① In other words, in the early period of the establishment and development of modern metaphysics, the dominant form of expression of the metaphysics of subjectivity was the metaphysics of reason, while "The metaphysical essence of reason consists in the fact that being as a whole is projected as a guideline for representational thought and is interpreted as such."② In Heidegger's view, the metaphysics of reason as "representational thought" first appeared in the context of epistemology.

Let us first look at Descartes, the initiator of modern metaphysics, that is, the metaphysics of subjectivity. Although Descartes himself did not use the concept of the "metaphysics of reason," reason always occupied the fundamental and core position in his entire theory of philosophy.

Despite this, the inherent problems of reason and its limits did not attract his attention. After Descartes, Kant's explorations of metaphysics made an impressive volte-face: instead of thinking of everything on the basis of reason, he took reason as the object of his investigation. "It is obviously the effect not of levity but of the matured judgment of the age, which refuses to be any longer put off with illusory knowledge. It is a call to reason to undertake anew the most difficult of all its tasks, namely, that of

---

① M. Heidegger, *Nietzsche*, vol. 2, trans. Sun Zhouxing (Beijing: The Commercial Press, 2000), p. 925.

② M. Heidegger, *Nietzsche*, vol. 2, trans. Sun Zhouxing (Beijing: The Commercial Press, 2000), p. 924.

self-knowledge, and to institute a tribunal… This tribunal is no other than the critique of pure reason."① Kant provided a critical summary of the philosophical thought of rationalism and empiricism and substantially advanced the metaphysics of reason initiated by Descartes in the following three areas.

Firstly, metaphysics itself is a product of reason. Driven by its nature, human reason has created one metaphysical system after another, but there are numerous contradictions and controversies between these systems; "the battle-field of these endless controversies is called metaphysics."② In order to change this situation in metaphysical studies, we must make a critical investigation of their origin—"reason."

Secondly, there are two different forms of the metaphysics of reason: one is "metaphysics as natural endowment" and the other "metaphysics as science." In Kant's view, traditional metaphysical theories are subordinate, almost without exception, to "metaphysics as a natural endowment." The essential feature of this metaphysics is that, driven by its nature, reason applies the category of understanding that is applicable only to the scope of experience to the super-experiential object, i.e., the thing-in-itself, thus falling into fallacious inference, antinomies or ideals.

Thirdly, metaphysics as science is further divided into two different forms of expression: "the metaphysics of nature" and "the metaphysics of morals."③ The former, Kant believed, lays the foundation for the natural sciences while the latter, that is, the metaphysics of morals, holds an even

---

① I. Kant, *Critique of Pure Reason*, trans. Li Qiuling (Beijing: Renmin University of China Press, 2004).

② I. Kant, *Critique of Pure Reason*, trans. Li Qiuling (Beijing: Renmin University of China Press, 2004).

③ I. Kant, *Foundations of the Metaphysics of Morals*, trans. Miao Litian (Shanghai: Shanghai People's Publishing House, 1986), p. 36.

higher position. In Kant's metaphysics of morals, the will is absolutely subservient to reason: "We stand under a discipline of reason, and in all our maxims we must not forget our subjection to it, or withdraw anything from it, or by an egotistical illusion detract from the authority of the law (even though it is one given by our own reason), so that we could place the motive of our will (even though it is in accordance with the law) elsewhere than in the law itself and in respect for it."[①] Kant even called will "practical reason" and repeatedly stressed that it is higher than "speculative reason." But, in fact, his metaphysics of morals is a more important form that he created for the metaphysics of reason.

After Kant, Hegel further developed the metaphysics of reason. However, in spite of the fact that reason is an important symbol of man as subject, it does not represent the whole man, just as a head cannot be counted as the whole body. In short, the metaphysics of reason represented by Descartes, Kant and Hegel was destined to be subverted and reversed.

There are hints of interest in the human body and in desire in ancient philosophy, and modern philosophers like Leibniz and Hegel also discussed these problems; however, the true subversion and reversal of the metaphysics of reason was primarily undertaken by Schopenhauer and Nietzsche. Of course, this reversal took place within the framework of the metaphysics of subjectivity; as Schopenhauer pointed out, "It [the subject] is accordingly the supporter of the world, the universal condition of all that appears, of all objects, and it is always presupposed; for whatever

---

① I. Kant, *Critique of Practical Reason*, trans. Han Shuifa (Beijing: The Commercial Press, 1999), p. 89.

exists, exists for the subject."① However, with Schopenhauer, both the concept of "the world" corresponding to the subject and the concept of "man" as synonymous with the subject acquire completely new meanings that never existed in the discourse of Descartes, Kant and Hegel.

For Schopenhauer, the thing-in-itself of which Kant wrote is none other than will, which consists in the essence of the world, while the human body is objectified will that has become a representation. "First I put *the will, as things-in-itself*, as something wholly original; secondly, its mere visibility, its objectification, namely the body; and thirdly, knowledge as a mere function of a part of this body." ② Hence, Schopenhauer subverted the dominant idea put forward by Platonism that knowledge (reason) is primary while will (desire) is secondary, and made a subversive explanation of "man," the subject. "With me the eternal and indestructible in man, which forms his very principle of life, is not the soul, but, if I may be permitted to use a chemical expression, the radical of the soul, and this is the will. The so-called soul is already a compound word, namely the union of the will with the intellect. This intellect is the secondary element, the posterius of the organism, and, as a mere function of the brain, is conditioned by the organism. The will, on the other hand, is primary, is the prius of the organism, which is conditioned by it."③ Here, Schopenhauer not only differentiated man's activities in knowledge from his activities in will, but also said categorically that in the compound organism will is always primary while intellect (whose function is to be engaged in

① A. Schopenhauer, *The World as Will and Representation*, trans. Shi Chongbai (Beijing: The Commercial Press, 1982), p. 28.

② A. Schopenhauer, *On the Will in Nature*, trans. Ren Li et al (Beijing: The Commercial Press, 1997), p. 35.

③ A. Schopenhauer, *On the Will in Nature*, trans. Ren Li et al (Beijing: The Commercial Press, 1997), p. 34.

activities in knowledge) is always secondary. "Will is not conditioned by knowledge, as was hitherto assumed without exception, although knowledge is conditioned by will."① With the transposition of the relationship between will and knowledge (involving intellect or reason), the metaphysics of reason met its fated reversal.

However, Schopenhauer's reversal was not complete, because the starting point of his philosophy affirmed the will to live though its conclusion denied it. In his youth, Nietzsche was strongly influenced by Schopenhauer; it was not until around 1876 that he began to realize the fundamental difference between Schopenhauer and himself. If we say that Schopenhauer indulged in the ideals of moralistic Christianity and therefore denied the will to live, then Nietzsche pleaded for life.② What is life? Nietzsche replied: "Life is will to power."③ For Schopenhauer, life could only maintain itself passively and "Ultimately death must triumph, for by birth it has already become our lot." Hence "life swings like a pendulum to and fro between pain and boredom."④ For Nietzsche, however, the essence of life was to preserve and improve itself and to win the power to dominate other wills.

It was through starting with the basic theory of the will to power that Nietzsche surpassed Schopenhauer and completely reversed the metaphysics of reason represented by Schopenhauer, Kant and Hegel.

---

① A. Schopenhauer, *On the Will in Nature*, trans. Ren Li et al (Beijing: The Commercial Press, 1997), p. 20.

② F. Nietzsche, *Will to Power*, trans. Sun Zhouxing (Beijing: The Commercial Press, 2007), pp. 405, 434.

③ F. Nietzsche, *Will to Power*, trans. Sun Zhouxing (Beijing: The Commercial Press, 2007), pp. 405, 190.

④ A. Schopenhauer, *The World as Will and Representation*, trans. Shi Chongbai (Beijing: The Commercial Press, 1982), p. 427.

Nietzsche reversed not only the relationship between the will (desire) and reason (knowledge), but also that between mind (soul) and body (soma); as Heidegger put it: "Body is the name for that configuration of will to power in which the latter is always immediately accessible, because it is always within the province of man identified as 'subject.' Nietzsche therefore said: 'Essential: to start from the body and employ it as the guideline.'"①

It can thus be seen from the foregoing that through the transposition of the will (desire) and reason (knowledge) Schopenhauer reversed the metaphysics of reason represented by Descartes, Kant and Hegel and made it the metaphysics of the will, while Nietzsche, starting from the theory of the will to power, went further and overturned the relationship between the mind (soul) and body (soma) and thus reversed the metaphysics of reason and made it the metaphysics of will to power.②

Within the wider framework of the metaphysics of subjectivity, Nietzsche subverted the metaphysics of reason represented by Descartes, Kant and Hegel and replaced it with the metaphysics of will to power, thus completing the second reversal in the development of metaphysics. Through the important concept of the will to power, Nietzsche developed all the implications of the metaphysics of subjectivity to the fullest possible extent.

---

① M. Heidegger, *Nietzsche*, vol. 2, trans. Sun Zhouxing (Beijing: The Commercial Press, 2000), p. 931.

② M. Heidegger, *Nietzsche*, vol. 2, trans. Sun Zhouxing (Beijing: The Commercial Press, 2000), p. 906.

The Third Reversal in the Development of Metaphysics

The third reversal in the development of metaphysics appears in the process of the development of Heidegger's philosophy. We might call it the reversal from the "metaphysics of being-there (Dasein)" to the "metaphysics of the world-fourfold."

As is well known, Heidegger's metaphysical thinking developed around the "metaphysics of being-there." In his *Kant and the Problem of Metaphysics*, he wrote, "The metaphysics of Dasein as a laying of the foundation of metaphysics has its own truth, which in its essence is as yet all too obscure."[①] In the metaphysics of being-there, being-there is a fundamental core concept.

For Heidegger, the form of being of Dasein as the being of man can be nothing but existence, and existence inherently means "being-in-this-world." In other words, existence involves "being with (Mitsein)" others and the world. Therefore, being-there as "being-in- this-world" is the true and original starting point for exploring all questions of metaphysics: "The constitution of the Dasein's existence as being-in-the-world emerged as a peculiar transposition of the subject which makes up the phenomenon which we shall yet more particularly define as the Dasein's transcendence."[②] In other words, the subjectivity that modern metaphysics takes as

---

① M. Heidegger, "Kant and the Problem of Metaphysics." in *Selected Works of Martin Heidegger*, vol. 1, ed. Sun Zhouxing (Shanghai: The SDX Joint Publishing Company, 1996), p. 125.

② M. Heidegger, *The Basic Problems of Phenomenology*, trans. Ding Yun (Shanghai: Shanghai Translation Publishing House, 2008), p. 232.

its starting point is grounded in the existential structure of being-there and it is precisely the transcendence of being-there in this existential structure that throws light on the concept of subjectivity. Thus we find that, through its exposition of the inherent existential structure of being-there, Heidegger's metaphysics of being-there far exceeds the superficial forms of the metaphysics of subjectivity of philosophers from Descartes to Nietzsche.

Starting from the analysis of the existential structure of being-there, Heidegger distinguishes between authentic and inauthentic states in the existence of being-there and elucidates the issues of "care," "dread," "death," "conscience," "decision," "temporality" and "historicity," thus constructing the system of the metaphysics of being-there. However, Heidegger's metaphysical thinking in his later period indicates that he not only transcended the metaphysics of being-there of his early period but also undertook an outward reversal of it, making it the "metaphysics of the world-fourfold." Why did this reversal in Heidegger's thinking on metaphysics take place? We believe it was due to the following causes.

On the one hand, both in his *Being and Time* and in "The Self-affirmation of the German University," his inaugural speech as the Rector of Freiburg University, the early Heidegger placed his hopes on what he called "authentic being-there" (that is, the German elites as he saw them, such as Hitler, Heidegger himself, and so on) to change Germany's post-World War I image of pettiness and inferiority. However, with his resignation from this position in April 1934, his plan for the reform of German universities was thwarted and his relations with the Nazi authorities became tense. In his later period, Heidegger had a deep understanding of the limited use of "authentic being-there" and realized that only by complying with the truth revealed by being itself would it play its due role.

On the other hand, although in his early period Heidegger substituted the existential structure of being-there for subjectivity, the metaphysics of being-there does, after all, take being-there as its basis and starting point. Heidegger himself said in "On the Essence of Ground" that some people criticized his *Being and Time* for its anthropocentric position. ① Despite his rejection of this criticism, his discussions on "care," "dread," "death" and "mortal being," on "utensils," "indication" and "integrated involvement" and on "idle talk," "curiosity," "ambiguity" and "falling" all revolve around the being-there of man. So the early Heidegger's metaphysics of being-there can also be understood, in a sense, as a "fine edition of the metaphysics of will to power." But insofar as its essence is concerned, this metaphysical theory is still not completely free of the shadow of modern metaphysics, i. e., the metaphysics of subjectivity.

For these reasons, Heidegger came to realize that the metaphysics of being-there of his early period must make a fresh start, that is, the limitations to the role of being-there should be elevated to the theme of the new era. As a result, in his later period, Heidegger changed his earlier approach to metaphysical thinking and proposed the metaphysical theory of the "world-fourfold." In his view, the "world-fourfold" refers to "the earth and the sky, the divine and the mortal." In "The Thing," he gave a brief explanation of these four concepts: "Earth is the serving bearer, blossoming and framing, spreading out in rock and water, rising up into plant and animal... The sky is the vaulting path of the sun, the course of the changing moon, the wandering glitter of the stars, the year's seasons and their changes, the light and dusk of day, the gloom and glow of night,

① M. Heidegger, "On the Essence of Ground," in *Selected Works of Martin Heidegger*, vol. 1, ed. Sun Zhouxing (Shanghai: The SDX Joint Publishing Company, 1996), p. 196.

the clemency and inclemency of the weather, the drifting clouds and blue depth of the ether. The divinities are the beckoning messengers of the godhead. Out of the sway of the godhead, the god appears in his presence or withdraws into his concealment … mortals are … human beings. They are called mortals because they can die… Each of the fourfold—the earth, the sky, the divinities and the mortals—belong together by way of a simple unified fourfold. Each of the four mirrors in its own way the presence of the others. At the same time, each of the fourfold mirrors itself in its own way and enters into its own within the simple onefold of the fourfold."[1] From the above and other relevant expositions, we can infer the following conclusions: firstly, in the early metaphysics of being-there, being-there was the foundation and core of the world, but in the later metaphysics of the world-fourfold, mortals were relegated to one element of the world-fourfold. Heidegger says: "This enowning mirror-play of the simple onefold of the earth and sky, divinities and mortals, we call the world."[2] This reveals to us that in the overall structure of the world, the subjectivity of man is strictly limited. Man must never destroy the fourfold; only thus will this "enowning mirror-play" be sustained forever.

Secondly, in the early metaphysics of being-there, being-there had an important historic mission: arousing its own "conscience," making "decisions" and changing and creating history in its own way. By contrast, in the metaphysics of the world-fourfold of the later period, the mission of mortals was only dwelling in a simple way. In Heidegger's view, dwelling was the form of being for mortals. Saving the earth, receiving the sky,

---

① M. Heidegger, "The Thing," in *Selected Works of Martin Heidegger*, vol. 1, ed. Sun Zhouxing (Shanghai: The SDX Joint Publishing Company, 1996), p. 196.

② M. Heidegger, "The Thing," in *Selected Works of Martin Heidegger*, vol. 1, ed. Sun Zhouxing (Shanghai: The SDX Joint Publishing Company, 1996), p. 1180.

awaiting the divinities and initiating mortals: this fourfold preservation constituted the simple essence of dwelling. ①

Thirdly, in his early metaphysics of being-there, Heidegger attached importance to starting from the discourse of being-there in his understanding of language phenomena. He said, "it [discourse] is language. In language, as a way things have been expressed or spoken out, there is hidden a way in which the understanding of Dasein has been interpreted."② However, in the metaphysics of world-fourfold in the later period, Heidegger maintains that in inquiring into language we should not pull language to the side of being-there; on the contrary, we should bring the mortals to the essence of language. "Language, then, is not a mere human faculty. Its character belongs to the very character of the movement of the face-to-face encounter of the world's four regions."③ That is to say, the essence of language is to guard the earth, the sky, divinities and mortals so that they will live forever face to face and on intimate terms, while any mortal discourse must always comply with the essence of language.

Brief Conclusions

Summing up these three reversals we can come to the following four

① M. Heidegger, "Building, Dwelling, Thinking," in *Selected Works of Martin Heidegger*, vol. 2, ed. Sun Zhouxing (Shanghai: The SDX Joint Publishing Company, 1996), p. 1201.

② M. Heidegger, *Being and Time*, trans. Chen Jiaying et al, (Beijing: The SDX Joint Publishing Company, 1987), pp. 203-204.

③ M. Heidegger, "On the Way to Language," in *Selected Works of Martin Heidegger*, vol. 2. ed. Sun Zhouxing (Shanghai: The SDX Joint Publishing Company, 1996), p. 1119.

conclusions: first, in spite of the fact that the second reversal takes place in the wider framework of the metaphysics of subjectivity, it is no less significant than the first reversal. This is because the first reversal still occurred in the rationalist tradition, while the second expounds, through subversion of the traditional relationship between reason and will, the primordial nature of will that exists in an irrational way, thus inspiring us to solve the mystery of modernity.

Second, Heidegger repeatedly stated that the metaphysics of being-there he advanced in his early period and modern metaphysics (the metaphysics of subjectivity) came from completely different starting points; however, in a sense, it was the metaphysics of being-there that provided the metaphysics of subjectivity with a solid intellectual foundation through the clarification of the existential structure of being-there, i. e. , being-in-the-world. In this sense, Heidegger's metaphysics of being-there as a "fine edition of the metaphysics of the will to power" does not ultimately emerge from the shadow of the metaphysics of subjectivity.

Third, the metaphysics of world-fourfold advanced by Heidegger in his later period seems to transcend metaphysics through poetical "thinking." In fact, what he transcends is traditional metaphysics from Plato to Nietzsche and the metaphysics of being-there he advocated in his early period. In brief, Heidegger's "thinking" in his later period still falls within the scope of metaphysics, but it reflects a new form of metaphysical thinking that differs from traditional metaphysics. At first glance, the metaphysics of world-fourfold seems to be regression to the metaphysics of presence of Platonism, but in fact it is not. The fundamental difference between the two is that according to Platonism, all things of presence, including humans, are ready-to-hand beings. Since the difference between man and other beings has not been subjectivized and since only man is able to inquire about the meaning of being, the metaphysics of presence is confined to "beings" to the neglect of "being" itself. For the later Heidegger, mortals, as close neighbors of being in the world-fourfold, are already aware of their limited capabilities and consciously shoulder the task of complying with the doctrine of being and guarding the fourfold in their dwelling.

Fourth, our using the "three reversals" to sum up the history of metaphysics to the present day does not mean we agree with what is known as the "theory of the end of metaphysics" or with Habermas' and Rorty's ill-considered use of the concept "post-metaphysics." In reality, people can neither free themselves from metaphysics nor put an end to metaphysical thinking. Our studies of the development of metaphysics are aimed at gaining a more in-depth understanding of the essence of metaphysics and trends in its future development, with a view to ensuring that our reflections on man's destiny and, in particular, our explorations of modernity will always be at the high level that is philosophy's due.

2.6　The Persistence of Modernity

—Value Options Amid Massive Historical Dislocation

The point of view in this paper is: contemporary Chinese must start from the concrete situation of China, and persist on basic standpoint for seeking modernity, meanwhile he should absorb rational elements from the fact that modernism and post-modernism have criticized and reflected modernity, in order to revise and re-write modernity in the background amid massive historical dislocation.

How Should We Research Contemporary Chinese Culture?

Concepts of value always play a key role in culture. If we want to deeply understand a culture, and not be content with intuiting its various phenomena, such as tools, technical abilities,

---

① Editor's note: This paper was originally published in G. F. McLean ed. , *Cultural Tradition and Social Progress, series III. Asia*, vol. 28, 2011, pp 157-167.

customs and institutions, then we must inspect its values. In contemporary Chinese culture there are different trends of thought behind which hide various ideas of value, and even value systems. If we try to analyze all cultural trends one by one, we will be bound to lose ourselves in the minute differences between them. And in fact, many scholars have lost themselves in this way in studying contemporary Chinese culture. They have been researching the so-called "culture of tea," "culture of wine," "culture of games," "culture of prostitution," and so on, so that the whole culture has been broken to pieces. In other words, real contemporary Chinese culture as a unified whole has disappeared from their field of vision. So we must turn our attention back to important cultural problems, especially grand ideas of value, and away from these marginal cultural phenomena. Which problems are important for us to consider in order to understand contemporary Chinese culture? To answer this question, we must reflect seriously on the historical situation of contemporary China.

Another difficulty in the study of culture lies in the fact that a scholar always has his own prejudices, which affect his research into anything, based on his own conceptions of value. In fact, scholars always put their own conceptions of value onto all objects they study, consciously or unconsciously. If the scholar fails to reflect critically on his own conceptions of value, but simply brings his own subjective ideas of value into his field of study, then his study will necessarily give rise to the wrong results. Hence a scholar must inspect his own conceptions of value before studying anything. And to make this critical self-inspection effective, he must have objective and reasonable value coordinates in advance, in order to inspect or reflect on his own conceptions of value. So how does one obtain objective value coordinates? In my opinion, these coordinates depend on understanding the historicity that hides in all basic trends of contemporary Chinese society. In order to firmly grasp this historicity, we must also seriously observe contemporary Chinese society.

What's the Meaning of "Massive Historical Dislocation"?

By "massive historical dislocation" we mean the great time lag between contemporary Chinese society and contemporary Western society, as seen through the theory of morphology. This dislocation can be recognized in the following two historical stages of modern and contemporary China's development.

The first stage lasted from the late 1800s to the 1940s. Intellectuals of the late Qing Dynasty and the Republican period opposed invasions from and oppression by Western capitalist nations. They insisted on developing China's domestic capitalist industry and commerce, in order to pursue wealth and power, and resist this foreign pressure. However, coincidentally an influential socialist movement appeared in Western societies, exposing and criticizing the overall essence of Western capitalism. Consequently, intellectuals were in a puzzle. Just as they sought Western capitalism as a great ideal, capable of solving China's ills, the Western socialist movement was ripping capitalism into pieces in the lands of its birth. So, the question arose, should China develop Capitalism or not? In this massive historical dislocation, most intellectuals lost their way, and began to naively accept socialist ideals. For example, Mr. Sun Yatsen (孙逸仙), who was a political representative of the national bourgeoisie, not only put forward such slogans as "equalizing land rights and controlling capital," but also expressed explicitly his desire "to unite Russia, to unite the Communist Party and to help peasants and workers." He thus became quasi-communist.

During this period in China a dual socialist influence came externally from the Soviet Union, and internally from the newly revived traditional ideal of Datong (大同, meaning Great Harmony, an ideal and perfect society), which was seen as a primitive form of communism. Under this dual influence, many intellectuals accepted Marxism, under the name of Socialism. For instance, *Shen Bao Monthly* (《申报月刊》) published an influential special issue on "the modernization of China" in Shanghai in July of 1933, which discussed the problem of modernization in explicitly socialist terms. [①] The majority of scholars who took part in this discussion maintained that the realization of China's modernization couldn't and shouldn't rely on the sort of individualism which had been prevalent in Western countries for so long.

The second stage of this dislocation started in the 1950s, and continues till today. The government began to put Soviet-style socialism into practice in China in 1949, particularly after the remoulding of capitalist industry and commerce in 1956. However, due to fear of the restoration of capitalism, [②] this model of socialism regarded markets and the commercial economy with hostility, and tried to set up an ideal society using supra-economic forces. The failure of "the Great Leap Forward" in 1958 gave rise to the so-called "natural calamities" which lasted three years, and still the

---

① It is said that Westerners first put forward the concept of "modernization" in the 1950s or 1960s. If so, Chinese intellectuals raised it earlier than Westerners. However, the modernization consciousness of Chinese wasn't of a rational type, but rather an emotional one, which was actually a protest against repression by Western capitalism.

② Lenin put forward an influential point of view, claiming that even small-scale commercial production tends to bring capitalism into being night and day. Under the influence of this point of view, Mao Zedong was on careful guard over commodities, the commercial economy and capitalism. In my opinion, China never had powerful large-scale capitalism, so why discuss "the restoration of capitalism"?!

Chinese government wasn't able to rid itself fully of this model of Social-ism, even though a great controversy between China and Soviet Union a-rose in the 1960s. Indeed, the government didn't fully recognize the harm coming from this model of Socialism until the end of the Cultural Revolu-tion. At that time they raised the slogan of "Four-Modernizations". These included the modernization of industry, agriculture, national defense, and science and technology; but all this was only an empty talk in the disorder of the period.

Since 1978, China's modernization has truly become goal and common understanding for all China's people. However, at the beginning of this transformation, Chinese who were only just rid of the Soviet-style Social-ism could only imitate other models of socialism, such as Hungary's, Yugoslavia's, Northern European socialism, and so forth. Finally, "so-cialist modernization with Chinese characteristics" became the new flag and rallying cry for reformers. ①

Meanwhile, however, the new movement of post-modernism was ap-pearing in the West, starting in the sixties and seventies, and becoming significant in the eighties and nineties. This movement inspected the over-all historical process of Western modernization, and acutely criticized the whole value system which guides modernity. As a result, another massive historical dislocation appeared. Westerners began the historical process of modernization several centuries ago, even as Chinese fell into the deep sleep which Napoleon described, frozen in a traditional society based on an agricultural economy. Then, just as Chinese made the historic decision to pursue modernization in the seventies and eighties, Westerners began to

---

① This is, in fact, also idle talk, because any country's modernization necessarily has its own features.

question the results of their own modernization. As a result, contemporary Chinese lost their way again. They asked whether China needs to seek modernization or not.

By reflecting on this massive historical dislocation, we can recognize at last the real historicity of contemporary Chinese society, which is still engaged in the painful process of transition from a traditional to a modern society. The most essential events in contemporary China's life-world lie in the development of her market economy and modernization, and in her transformation from a primitive ethical spirit centered on the family, to a spirit of modern law and morality centered on the individual and society. ①
After understanding this real historicity of modern and contemporary Chinese society, we can see that trends of cultural thought in contemporary Chinese society can be divided into three main periods of value systems— pre-modern or traditional, modern and post-modern. So long as we firmly grasp these three value systems, it is impossible to lose our way in minute cultural problems. At the same time, as critics of Chinese culture, we can get clues as to an objective and rational value coordinate, based on real historicity.

We might as well call these three value systems "pre-modernity", "modernity" and "post-modernity" for short.

---

① Many people fail to understand this social phenomenon. The moral quality of Lei Feng had a great impact on Chinese in the sixties, but this was lost in nineties in the background of the market economy. Why? In my opinion, his moral quality belonged to the primitive ethical spirit emphasizing simple obligation, however, the spirit of times has greatly changed. Now people place more stress on the spirit of modern law and morality, and on emphasizing individual rights.

What's the Meaning of Pre-Modernity, Modernity and Post-Modernity?

We find that these three concepts are often used ambiguously in different discussions. For example, in his noted book, *The Postmodern Condition: A Report on Knowledge*, J. F. Lyotard writes: "I will use the term modern to designate any science that legitimates itself with reference to a meta-discourse of this kind making explicit appeal to some grand narrative, such as the dialectics of Spirit, the hermeneutics of meaning, the emancipation of the rational or working subject, or the creation of wealth." Elsewhere, he writes "Simplifying to the extreme I define postmodern as incredulity toward meta-narrative. This incredulity is undoubtedly a product of progress in the sciences; but that progress in turn presupposes it." [1] Although these two passages give some indication on the concepts of "modern" and "postmodern", their meanings are still not clear, at least not complete. In my thinking, it is better and clearer for us to regard these three concepts as three different leading value systems.

With the concept "pre-modernity" we mean the leading value system of a traditional society, in which a universal consciousness of modernization hasn't appeared, and a rigorous approach to the natural sciences also hasn't arisen. As a result, people maintain a special psychology of fearful admiration of nature. So ancient scholars, in general, insisted on concepts of harmony between nature and man. For instance, Lao Tzu says: "Tao

---

[1] Jean-Francois Lyotard, *The Postmodern Condition: A report on Knowledge* (Minneapolis: University of Minnesota Press, 1984), pp. xxiii-xxiv.

obeys nature."

Meanwhile, in such traditional societies, people lived in communities based on blood lineage and hierarchical institutions. Everyone had a fixed status. Maybe he was a grandfather, a father, a brother, a son in certain family, or a subject in some dynasty. But he wasn't absolutely a real individual, or an independent personality. Such social structures were also mutually supported by official belief systems. Why was Confucianism given such weight by the ruling classes of so many dynasties in Chinese history, for instance? Because it is based on xiao (孝, a son's filial obedience to his father) and ti (悌, a man's love and respect for his elder brother). Both these beliefs were well-suited to the existence and development of all those communities and hierarchical relationships which depend upon blood lineage. Another related concept, so-called zhong (忠, the relation of subjects to an emperor) was in turn based on xiao. This created a system which attempted to ensure that every family was stable, that is to say, all sons obedient to their fathers. And in turn, the whole country would be stable, because every subject was loyal to the emperor. As compared with men, women had no position in traditional Chinese society. They submitted themselves to their husbands, or to their sons after their husbands died.

By contrast, why weren't the theories of Mohism and Legalism given enough emphasis by the ruling classes? Precisely because the Mohist concept of jian ai (兼爱, equal love, non-hierarchical love), and the legalist concept of fa(法, law), especially the consciousness of rights championed by Legalism, were in basic conflict with the fundamental values of traditional society. It became a truism among Chinese historians that the Qin Dynasty only lasted 15 years because its ruling thought stemmed mainly from Legalism. As a result, egalitarian Legalism was seen as a threat, and hierarchical Confucianism became the leading school of thought for the ruling classes of most historical periods in ancient Chinese society. In a sense, it can be said that the value system of Chinese pre-modernity was mainly embodied in ideas of Confucianism.

So we can say that the leading value ideas implicated in "pre-modernity" are as follows: harmony between nature and man, blood lineage, human feeling, hierarchical relationships, status institutions, worship of administrative power and ancestors, attaching importance to men and looking down on women, stressing agriculture and despising commerce, and so forth.

Now, what is the meaning of the concept "modernity"? This means the leading value system of a society that is seeking modernization, or has basically realized modernization. To my thinking, modern Europe (from the 16th century to the 1940s) represents such a society. Such a society has the following features:

First, the link between nature and man has undergone a decisive change. Together with the rise of the natural sciences in the 17th century and the invention of technology, a new set of ideas became popular: that natural resources are limitless, that man can completely conquer nature and ask for everything from nature infinitely. "Knowledge is power," in the exciting phrase of F. Bacon, and this embodied in full the heartfelt wish of human beings as conquerors. It reminds us of Caesar, the great commander of Rome, saying: "I came, I saw, I conquered."

Second, along with the development of industrialization and commercialization comes a reform or revolution of traditional political institutions. Independent individuals or personalities, and contractual relationships among persons become the basis of the new society. If Liebniz's 'monad' was a philosophical symbol of such individuality, then Defoe's Robinson was its literary symbol. In such societies, blood lineage and hierarchical relationships declined in importance, and the legal state becomes uniquely essential in daily life. The state and legal relationships affect family life; the poetic dignity of king and father in traditional society gives way to the popular point of view "everyone is equal before the law". In some sense, Montesquieu's *The Spirit of Law* describes the fundamental spirit of modern society and modernity.

Third, individuals in turn become under the protection of a new 'civil society,' which forms the basis of this state. Under the guidance of rationality, a complete set of political and social institutions suited to modernity were set up.

So we may say that the leading value ideas of modernity are as follows: admiration of science and technology, the belief that man can and should conquer nature, a worship of rationality, and of contractual relationships, human rights, individualism, freedom, equality, democracy, justice and so on.

By the concept of "post-modernity" we mean the leading value system which has been put forward by some Western intellectuals living in highly developed modern societies such as Western European countries, the United States, and so forth. Post-modernity comes from a comprehensive criticism of the leading value systems of modernity. The idea of modernization and its historical background has the following negative features, according to these critics:

First, modern technology has controlled the whole life of human beings. In his well-known book, *The Question Concerning Technology*, M. Heidegger points out that modern technology isn't a neutral element in social life, and its essence is Gestell (which means "enframing" in English):

"where enframing reigns, there is danger in the highest sense."[1] because the consciousness of enframing compels people to conquer nature unceasingly. Meanwhile, however, people are under the rule of modern technology. In his later works Heidegger believed man should limit the infinite extension of his own subjectivity, and be peacefully coexistent with nature.

Second, National Socialism, especially the phenomenon of genocide, has become a touchstone for reflection on and criticism of modernity. How, critics ask, could the totalitarianism of National Socialists and their extermination camps have appeared in modern Europe, with all its long traditions of civilization, the spirit of freedom, justice, equality and universal love? In their writing *Dialectic of Enlightenment*, Horkheimer and Adorno see the Enlightenment as the origin of modernity, and show us how the spirit of the Enlightenment degenerated from reason, freedom and democracy into barbarity, totalitarianism and extermination. As is well known, in later years Heidegger was criticized severely by his students because he not only took part in the National Socialist movement, but also kept silent on its crimes.

Third, seen from a philosophical standpoint, Derrida's theory of deconstruction, Wittgenstein's anti-essentialism, Adorno's negative dialectic, Foucault's doctrine of knowledge and power, Levinas' idea of the absolute other and Rorty's negation of capital philosophy form a strong backlash against the leading value systems of modernity.

With the help of this critique, the leading value system of post-modernity comes into being. Its main content is: to cancel grand narratives, attack rationality, suspend universality, shake up certainty, negate essentialism

---

① Martin Heidegger, *The Question Concerning Technology* (New York: Harper & Row Publishers, 1977), p. 28.

and fundamentalism, deconstruct logo-centralism, eliminate the privileging of Western culture, and so forth.

How to Understand the Relations among Pre-modernity, Modernity and Post-modernity?

First of all, we give our attention to the phenomenon that westerners are more interested in the relations between modernity and post-modernity, and are almost unconcerned about pre-modernity. [①] By contrast, contemporary Chinese are more interested in the link between pre-modernity and modernity, and less interested in post-modernity. The discussion on the connection between modernity and post-modernity in Western countries has two antagonistic views. On the one hand, J. Habermas' standpoint is to insist on modernity, and he put forward the theory of communicative action in order to overcome and transcend passive aspects of modernity. On the other hand, Derrida and Rorty try to antagonize post-modernity with modernity. The former pays more attention to the continuity between these two concepts, but the latter notices more discontinuity. As the other discussion, on the relations between pre-modernity and modernity in developing countries such as China, there are also two antagonistic views. Some scholars persist in believing that if Chinese try to realize modernization in China in the future, then they will have to fundamentally discard traditional culture, especially the Confucianism which was so consistent with the

---

① R. J. Bernstein writes, "During the past decade—in virtually every area of cultural life—there has been an explosion of discourse about 'modernity' and 'post-modernity'." See R. J. Bernstein, *The New Constellation* (Massachusetts: The MIT Press, 1993), p. 199.

basic ideas of pre-modernity. Other scholars believe that, supposing Chinese want to promote the development of modernization, they must draw all invaluable elements from traditional culture, particularly from Confucianism. The former group only sees the gap between pre-modernity and modernity. However, the latter only take note of the union.

According to my point of view, the above phenomenon is natural, because people always consider any problems from their own actual need and standpoint. As contemporary Chinese, we ought to put more weight on the relations between pre-modernity and modernity, but not to rule out post-modernity. In effect, only if we observe the overall connection among these three concepts, will it be possible for us to understand deeply the relationships between pre-modernity and modernity.

Then, we also pay attention to the phenomenon that the common enemy of pre-modernity and post-modernity is modernity. On the one hand, scholars who insist on pre-modernity often look for new ideas from post-modernity; on the other hand, scholars who insist on post-modernity always gain various inspirations from the literatures of pre-modern societies. In this situation, modernity has to struggle at the same time against pre-modernity and post-modernity. As far as modernity itself is concerned, certainly, there is an essential difference between the standpoint of pre-modernity and post-modernity. Pre-modernity criticizes modernity from the right, and hopes that Chinese society will stay in traditional form forever. Post-modernity criticizes from the left, and it tries to correct the errors of modernity.

The Persistence of Modernity: Our Choice

How to choose our own standpoint in conflicts among pre-modernity, modernity and post-modernity? This is the problem we can't avoid.

First, it is difficult for us to choose. If we regard traditional society-concerned with pre-modernity-as a mother, we can see contemporary Chinese society-concerned with modernity-as a 'son' seeking modernization. Modernization is like a beautiful but flawed woman. contemporary Western society concerned with post-modernity is like that son's friend who is divorced from that woman modernity. The son's difficult position is: on the one hand, he loves this woman, modernity, very deeply. On the other hand, his mother and his friend try to persuade him not to love her, because she has many shortcomings. How does the son rid himself of this difficult situation? As Hamlet says: "to be or not to be".

Second, in our choice, we must try to avoid the wrong attitude we can call "standpoint drift." By this we mean that the majority of contemporary Chinese scholars don't take their own standpoint seriously enough, or recognize the value of their deep understanding of the real historicity of contemporary Chinese society. As a result, their standpoints are floating everywhere like drifting duckweed on a river. Some of them substitute contemporary Western standpoint for their own. They worship post-modernism and deny completely the leading value of modernity and the idea of modernization. However, the others put themselves into the standpoint of the ancient Chinese, whose conceptions were based on pre-modernity. When they do so, it is necessary for them to deny the leading value system of modernity and safeguard the main value ideas of pre-modernity.

Obviously these two attitudes, or two different "standpoint drifts," are both wrong, and these scholars ought to go back to their own standpoints, based on real historicity, in order not to lose their way in the massive historical dislocation of contemporary Chinese society.

Third, we should persist in modernity and modernization as goals despite this great historical dislocation. It should be recognized that contemporary Chinese society is quite different from contemporary Western society, which has basically realized modernization. After realizing modernization, it goes without saying that contemporary Westerners want to reflect on and criticize negative elements of modernization and modernity. This is the current Western imperative in finding a better way of life and thinking, suited to this new world, so greatly changed in science and technology, as well as in the political, social and cultural environment. However, for contemporary Chinese, the process of modernization has just begun. They must persist in modernity. If they allow their own standpoint to be shaken under the influence of post-modernity or pre-modernity, China's modernization will be in danger of abortion.

History and practice have indicated that the value systems of modernity have some weaknesses by nature, and we will revise modernity in the process of China's modernization through absorbing rational elements from the critical inspection of pre-modernity and post-modernity.

In a word, as contemporary Chinese, we shall adhere to seeking modernity and modernization over time, not allowing ourselves to be shaken. Meanwhile, we shall not refuse to study and understand both pre-modernity and post-modernity. Here we ought to bear in mind the saying of Dante, the great Italian poet:

Segui il tuo corso, e lascia dir le gentil! (Go along your own road, let others laugh.)

2.7 Important and Thoughtful Ferments in the Reflection on Modernity[①]
—Seen from Young Hegel's Perspective

J. Habermas told us that although Hegel isn't the first philosopher of modern times, but the first philosopher looking up modernity as a problem.[②] In fact, there are important thoughtful ferments of his reflection on modernity in young Hegel's manuscripts. Together with the deepening of criticism of modernity, young Hegel's manuscripts become a focus to which people pay attention again. According to my opinion, young Hegel's reflection on modernity can be summarized the following three main aspects:

Reflection on "Positive Religion"

While analyzing young Hegel's thought, G.

---

① Editor's note: This paper was translated from *Shijie Zhexue* (《世界哲学》), no. 6, 2012, pp. 6-12.

② J. Habermas, *The Philosophical Discourse of Modernity* (London: Polity Press, 1987), p. 43.

Lukacs said, "We have observed that the philosophically and historically crucial concept of Hegel's thought in this period is that of positivity."① As T. M. Knox pointed out that the two parts of *The Positivity of the Christian Religion* were written in 1795-1796, when Hegel was twenty-five and living in Bern. ② In this manuscript, young Hegel put forward a surprising idea that the modern Christianity had become a positive religion, after investigating the history of Christianity. In other words, positivity has become the fundamental feature of modern Christianity. Then, what's the meaning of a positive religion or positivity of Christianity? Young Hegel wrote: "A positive religion, i. e. , a religion which is grounded in authority and puts man's worth not at all, or at least not wholly, in morals."③ According to Hegel, so-called positive religion is essentially outside authority sitting loose to human reason, dignity and freedom. However, when Christianity was just founded, it had not only this feature of the outside authority, but also put stress upon human reason, dignity and freedom by nature as a natural religion or a virtue-religion, because Jesus "urged not a virtue grounded on authority (which is either meaningless or a direct contradiction in terms), but a free virtue springing from man's own being."④ Young Hegel believed that Jesus is only a teacher of a moral religion in the original Christianity.

The next question we are going to ask is: How to be formed this positivity or outside authority in the history of Christianity? Young Hegel

---

① G. Lukacs, *Young Hegel* (Boston: The MIT Press, 1976), p. 74.

② G. W. F. Hegel, *Early Theological Writings*, trans. T. M. Knox (Chicago: The University of Chicago Press, 1948), p. vii.

③ G. W. F. Hegel, *Early Theological Writings*, trans. T. M. Knox (Chicago: The University of Chicago Press, 1948), p. 71.

④ G. W. F. Hegel, *Early Theological Writings*, trans. T. M. Knox (Chicago: The University of Chicago Press, 1948), p. 71.

argued that miracles appeared in the Christian doctrine played an important role: "Nothing has contributed so much as these miracles to making the religion of Jesus positive, to basing the whole of it, even its teaching about virtue, on authority."[1] After his resurrection, Jesus fixed the number of his disciples at twelve as his messengers and successors he gave a wide authority and these disciples made it authorization to the best of their power, while disseminating Jesus' doctrine. "The result of this was to make reason a purely receptive faculty, instead of a legislative one."[2] Meanwhile, "the religion of Jesus became a positive doctrine about virtue."[3] Two important elements——sects and states which promoted the original Christianity to develop towards to a positive religion, also appeared. If sects of Christianity have had a great zeal for their own expansion, then states have thought Christianity as the best means which controls people.

Obviously, young Hegel has reflected the positivity of Christianity, starting from modern reason, especially from I. Kant's practical reason. However, Young Hegel has had transcended the region of religion when he reflected the issue of positivity in the third part of *The Positivity of the Christian Religion* written in 1800. He said, "Any doctrine, any precept, is capable of becoming positive, since anything can be proclaimed in a forcible way with a suppression of freedom."[4] That is to say, positivity is not only the fundamental characteristic of modern Christianity, also modernity.

---

① G. W. F. Hegel, *Early Theological Writings*, trans. T. M. Knox (Chicago: The University of Chicago Press, 1948), p. 78.

② G. W. F. Hegel, *Early Theological Writings*, trans. T. M. Knox (Chicago: The University of Chicago Press, 1948), p. 85.

③ G. W. F. Hegel, *Early Theological Writings*, trans. T. M. Knox (Chicago: The University of Chicago Press, 1948), p. 86.

④ G. W. F. Hegel, *Early Theological Writings*, trans. T. M. Knox (Chicago: The University of Chicago Press, 1948), pp. 171-172.

Reflection on "Mechanicalness of Labor"

What is more, young Hegel deepened the criticism of modernity through considering on the issue of labor in *System of Ethical Life* (1802/03) and *The real Philosophy* (1803/06), as Lukacs pointed out: "In our discussion of the Frankfurt period we pointed out in a rather different context that Hegel was decisively influenced by Adam Smith's conception of labor as the central category of political economy."[1]

Young Hegel told us that human lift is formed by following three parts, i. e., need, labor and enjoyment in which labor is a medium between need and enjoyment. In order to raise the efficiency of labor, various instruments had been used in the process of labor on one side, a division of labor had been developed greatly on the other side, so following results have been brought naturally:

The first of all, each laborer doesn't produce what he needs by himself, at the same time, he doesn't need what he had produced. In a word, his labor separates itself from his need.

Secondly, together with the transition from the hand labor to machine labor, more mechanical is labor itself, and more duller is each laborer, as young Hegel wrote, "By the same token the abstraction of labor makes man more mechanical and dulls his mind and his senses. Mental vitality, a fully aware, fulfilled life degenerates

---

① G. Lukacs, *Young Hegel* (Boston: The MIT Press, 1976), p. 321.

into empty activity. " ①

Thirdly, modern labor, especially the capitalist labor expands the difference between rich and poor, in order to have modern society come back to its barbarian state: "Great wealth, which is similarly bound up with the deepest poverty (for in the separation [between rich and poor] labor on both sides is universal and objective), produces on the one side in ideal universality, on the other side in real universality, mechanically. This purely quantitative element, the inorganic aspect of labor, which is parceled out even in its concept, is the unmitigated extreme of barbarism." ②

Although Marx did not read Hegel's *System of Ethical Life* and *Real Philosophy*, he put forward the concept of the alienated labor in "Economic and Philosophical manuscripts (1844)" and conception of the fetishism of commodities in *Capital* (vol. 1, 1867) through reading Hegel's *Phenomenology of Spirit* (1807) and *The Philosophy of Right* (1821), hence a leading clue for the criticism of modernity has been formed from Hegel to Marx. As H. S. Harris pointed out in his *Hegel's System of Ethical Life: An Interpretation*: "These analyses anticipate Marx in a quite starling way." ③

---

① G. W. F. Hegel, *Jenenser Realphilosophie* 2 (1805-1806)(Leipzig: Felix Meiner, 1931), p. 232.

② G. W. F. Hegel, *System of Ethical Life and First philosophy of Spirit*, ed. and trans. H. S. Harris and T. M. Knox (New York: State university of New York Press, 1979), p. 171.

③ G. W. F. Hegel, *System of Ethical Life and First philosophy of Spirit*, ed. and trans. H. S. Harris and T. M. Knox (New York: State university of New York Press, 1979), p. 75.

Reflection on "the Other Side of the Enlightenment"

To be sure, the basic position resisted on by young Hegel is one of the Enlightenment, but he found out some weakness of it by nature, so we may say that his reflection on the other side of the Enlightenment also includes an acute criticism of modernity based on the main spirit of the Enlightenment. In his *Phenomenology of Spirit*, young Hegel told us: the Enlightenment as pure insight is "the self-consciousness of Spirit as essence; it therefore knows essence, not as essence, but as absolute self. It therefore seeks to abolish every kind of independence other than that of self-consciousness, whether it be the independence of what is actual, or of what possesses intrinsic being, and to give it the form of Notion. Pure insight is not only the certainty of self-conscious reason that it is all truth: it knows that it is."[1] Go without saying, as pure insight the Enlightenment stays, all the time, in the region of the self-conscious reason, regarding itself as the absolute certainty and the highest court all the time:

On one side, as was said before, because the Enlightenment set out from the self-conscious reason, it looked upon utility as its own real object, as young Hegel wrote, "Pure insight is simple, pure self-consciousness which is for itself as well as in itself in an immediate utility."[2] According to Hegel, the Enlightenment not only observes the whole world

---

[1] G. W. F. Hegel, *Phenomenology of Spirit*, trans. A. V. Miller (Oxford: Oxford University Press, 1977), p. 326.

[2] G. W. F. Hegel, *Phenomenology of Spirit*, trans. A. V. Miller (Oxford: Oxford University Press, 1977), p. 353.

from utility, also reason itself and believes that reason is a useful instrument.① Of course, the conception of utility in the Enlightenment offers a thoughtful basis for the core idea of modernity—instrumental reason.

On the other side, when the Enlightenment as the absolute self expands itself infinitely, it begins to believe that it is not only a pure insight or a reason court, also a universal will seeking an absolute freedom, so, "This undivided Substance of absolute freedom ascends the throne of the world without any power being able to resist it."② Certainly, the absolute freedom can only result in an absolute terror and a severe damage of social life, as young Hegel said, "The sole work and deed of universal freedom is therefore death, a death too which has no inner significance of feeling, for what is negated is the empty point of the absolute free self. It is thus the coldest and meanest of all deaths, with no more significance than cutting off a head of cabbage or swallowing a mouthful of water."③ It is easy to say, this absolute freedom put forward by young Hegel in his *Phenomenology of Spirit* is just the state of anarchy in the French Revolution. Young Hegel's reflection on the other side of the Enlightenment reveals us that as pure insight the Enlightenment is essentially a bridge to the universal will and the absolute freedom, in some sense, the phenomenon of fascism in 20 Century is a result coming from the universal will and the absolute freedom.

In a word, young Hegel's reflection on modernity remains one-sided

---

① G. W. F. Hegel, *Phenomenology of Spirit*, trans. A. V. Miller (Oxford: Oxford University Press, 1977), p. 342.

② G. W. F. Hegel, *Phenomenology of Spirit*, trans. A. V. Miller (Oxford: Oxford University Press, 1977), p. 357.

③ G. W. F. Hegel, *Phenomenology of Spirit*, trans. A. V. Miller (Oxford: Oxford University Press, 1977), p. 360.

and unsystematic. In fact, he only opposes some expressive forms of modernity in the total formation of modernity. However, his reflection provides still remarkable reveals for us to deepen the understanding of modernity.

2. 8　The Limits of Critical Theory[①②]

—A Reflection on the Central Idea
of the Frankfurt School

Having many important members, such as
M. Horkheimer, T. W. Adorno, W. Benjamin,
H. Marcuse, J. Habermas, A. Honneth, Based
on the Institute for Social Research in Frankfurt,
the Frankfurt School has become one of the most
influential schools in the international academic
kingdom in a long process of development. It is
well known that the central idea of the Frankfurt
School is the critical theory put forward by
Horkheimer in his *Traditional and Critical Theory* published in 1937, and carried forward by his
younger colleagues. Not intending to repeat those
conclusions about the historical position and role of
critical theory of the Frankfurt School debated by
many scholars in various countries, my presentation

---

①　*Editor's note:* This article is based on Professor Yu Wu-jin's manuscript prepared
for the international academic conference "Frankfurt School: Criticism of Capitalist Culture"
in Canada in July 2014.

②　Mr. Ouyang Guangwei, Vice President of Douglas University in Canada, Mr.
Wang Xingfu and Mrs. Zhang Shuangli from Fudan University have made great contributu-
ion for it. Thanks for their hard work!

will investigate the limit of this theory through asking the following question: which issues do members of the Frankfurt School always try to avoid? And my purpose is to make a rational and objective evaluation on the developing potentialities and the critical validities of the critical theory of the Frankfurt School looking upon capitalism as its own main reflective object.

Praxis as A Limit of the Critical Theory

There is no denying, "theory" is an indefinite concept, so it will be defined as a group of systematic and conformable statements round the same subject in this presentation. According to my point of view, theory should be further divided into the following two different types: one of them is "theories must be appealed to praxis" which can be put forward, only because praxis needs its conduct; the other is "theories separated completely from praxis" which can be advanced, only owing to the advisor's simple theoretical interest. It goes without saying that it is possible for "theories separated completely from praxis" that praxis is only their limit.

It is well known that in his sixth volume of *Nicomachean Ethics*, Aristotle put forward a new concept of "practical wisdom" (phronesis) which is different from other four different abilities by which a soul tries to master truth. ① According to Aristotle's view, practical wisdom is only concerned how people deal with various daily affairs, especially political and

---

① *The Basic Works of Aristotle*, ed. R. Mckeon (New York: Random House, 1941), Bk. Ⅵ: Ch. 5, p. 1026.

moral affairs. Kant differentiated further "practical reason" from "theoretical or speculative reason" and stressed the former's always having priority to the latter in his *Critique of Practical Reason*. ① Hegel looked upon praxis as a will be led by goodness, in his *Logic*② which had a powerful impact on K. Marx's thought.

It is not difficult for us to find out the fact that the concept of praxis played a fundamental, central role in Marx's writings. In his *Theses on Feuerbach*, Marx told us: "The philosophers have only interpreted the world, in various ways; the point is to change it. "③ If Marx affirmed the fact that changing the world is always more important than interpreting it in the above eleventh item of *Theses*, then he didn't forget to express the following meaning in the eighth item: "All social life essentially is practical. All mysteries which lead theory to mysticism find their rational solution in human practice and in the comprehension of this practice. "④Obviously, Marx believed that praxis plays from time to time a basic role even in various activities of interpreting the world. Therefore, it is not irrational for

---

① Kant says: "Nor could we reverse the order and require pure practical reason to be subordinate to the speculative, since all interest is ultimately practical, and even that of speculative reason is conditional, and it is only in the practical employment of reason that it is complete. " See *Kant (The Great Books)*, published by W. Benton (Chicago: Encyclopedia Britannica, Inc.) p. 343.

② As Hegel mentions Gute (Goodness), he writes: Diese Idee ist höher als die Idee des betrachteten Erkennens, denn sie hat nicht nur die Würde des Allgemeinen, sondern auch des schlechthin Wirklichen. Sehn G. W. F. Hegel, *Wissenschaft der Logik* Ⅱ (Frankfurt A. M. : Suhrkamp Verlag, 1986), S. 542. Lenin gives a following opinion to Hegel above statement: Die Praxis ist höhe als die (theoretische) Erkenntnis, denn sie hat nicht nur die Würde des Allgemeinen, sondern auch der unmittelbaren Wirklichkeit. See Lenin, *Über Hegelsche Dialektik* (Leipzig: Reclam Verlag, 1986), S. 151.

③ K. Marx, *Selected Writings* (Second Edition), ed. David Mclellan (Oxford: Oxford University Press, 2000), p. 173.

④ K. Marx, *Selected Writings* (Second Edition), ed. David Mclellan (Oxford: Oxford University Press, 2000), p. 173.

Marx to call his own doctrine "Practical Materialism." ①

As important representatives in the early period of western Marxism's development, G. Lukacs, K. Korsch, A. Gramsci revived Marx's theory of practical materialism to a certain extent, while criticizing the so-called "Scientific Marxism" put forward by the Right theoreticians of the Second International. Like Marx, they actively participated in contemporary revolutionary practical activities by themselves. Thus, we may say that Marx's, Lukacs', Korsch's and Gramsci's theories without doubt belong to "theories must be appealed to praxis." However, we have to point out that the critical theory of Frankfort School, actually belongs to "theories separated completely from praxis," quite different from Marx's, Lukacs', Korsch's and Gramsci's theories.

To put it fairly, members of the Frankfurt School also care about the relationship between theory and praxis. In his paper *Traditional And Critical Theory*, Horkheimer divorced the critical theory from the traditional theory and stressed: "The thinker must relate all the theories which are proposed to the practical attitudes and social strata which they reflect."② In a similar manner, in his *Theorie Und Praxis*, Habermas also pointed out: "der Historische Materialismus als eine in praktischer Absicht entworfene Theorie der Gesellschaft begriffen werden,"③ and deeply considered the relationship between theory and praxis from three different

---

① Although Marx never used the term of "practical materialism" immediately, he did mention another term "practical materialists" in the first chapter of *German Ideology*. In my opinion, there are no "practical materialists" without "practical materialism."

② M. Horkheimer, *Critical Theory* (Selected Essays), trans. M. J. Connnell and Others (New York: The Continuum Publishing Company, 1972), p. 232.

③ J. Habermas, *Theorie Und Praxis*(Frankfurt A. M.: Suhrkamp Verlag, 1978), S. 10.

directions, even advancing a new interesting concept "Praxeologie."①

However, Horkheimer, Adorno and Habermas shrank back from the Left practical activities, particularly from the Left students' movements which had been just encouraged by their own critical writings. They not only broken away from any political organization and practical activities, but also involved themselves in radical conflicts with the Left students' movements. According to Martin Jay's record, in January 1969 at a party in New York, where he was introduced to Mark Rudd, the fiery leader of the Columbia Student Democratic Society. When he told Rudd he was going to write a dissertation about the Frankfurt School, Rudd "contemptuously responded that Adorno and Horkheimer were craven sell-outs, who had betrayed the revolutionary cause; Adorno's very change of name from the Jewish-Sounding Wiesengrund, Rudd snarled, betokened his cowardice."②In early February 1969, when Martin Jay arrived at Frankfurt, he surprisingly discovered that the Sociology Department had been rebaptized "the Spartacus Department" and "Institut für Sozialforsung itself had been taken over by radical students, Adorno and Ludwig von Friedeburg, who had called the police to clear the building."③ Similarly, after Habermas called the Left students as "Left-Fascism,"④ he had to leave Frankfurt in 1971.

All of these show that the critical theory of the Frankfurt School not

---

① J. Habermas, *Theorie Und Praxis*(Frankfurt A. M. : Suhrkamp Verlag, 1978), S. 13.

② Martin Jay, *The Dialectical Imagination*(Berkeley: University of California Press, 1996), p. xii.

③ Martin Jay, *The Dialectical Imagination*(Berkeley: University of California Press, 1996), p. xii.

④ Martin Jay, *The Dialectical Imagination*(Berkeley: University of California Press, 1996), p. xiii.

only separated itself from any practical activities revolting the rule of capitalism, including the Left student movements, but also kept a radical antagonism. In this sense, we can say that praxis is a limit of the critical theory of Frankfurt School.

Revolution as A limit of Simple Thoughtful Criticism

Members of the Frankfurt School believed that they had inherited Kant's and Marx's critical tradition without exception, however, they weren't aware of the fact that Marx's critical theory included also an important reflective consciousness on the limit and validity of pure thoughtful criticism which had been formed and pushed in the process of Marx's struggle with Young Hegelians. In the first chapter of *German Ideology*, Marx wrote: "all forms and products of consciousness cannot be dissolved by mental criticism, by resolution into 'self-consciousness' or transformation into 'apparitions,' 'specters,' 'whimsies,' etc., but only by the practical overthrow of the actual social relations which gave rise to this idealistic humbug; that not criticism but revolution is the driving force of history, also of religion, of philosophy and all other kinds of theory."[1]

In terms of Marx's view, thoughtful criticism is only a pure spiritual or conscious action that can awaken people to recognize the essence of capitalism in a definite range, but people's awakening remains an affair which happens in simple spiritual field. In a word, recognizing the essence of capitalism from idea isn't equal to overthrowing it in revolutionary mode,

---

[1] K. Marx and F. Engels, *Collected Works* (vol. 5) (New York: International Publishers, 1976), p. 54.

as Marx pointed out: "Once upon a time a valiant fellow had the idea that men were drowned in water only because they were possessed with the idea of gravity. If they were to get this notion out of their heads, say by avowing it to be a superstitious, a religious concept, they would be sublimely proof against any danger from water."①

Evidently, Marx believed that it is impossible for people to try to eliminate those idealistic ideas through critical activities in a pure thoughtful domain, because they would be reproduced unceasingly by capitalist relations of production. That is to say, only if people overthrow the existing capitalist relations of production in revolutionary mode, it is really possible for them to eliminate those wrong ideas based on the above relations, so Marx announced: "…in reality and for the practical materialist, i. e., the communist, it is a question of revolutionizing the existing world of practically coming to grips with and changing the things found in existence."② According to Marx's critical theory, criticism is only to do preparation for revolution in the future. In other words, criticism is only the means, yet revolution is the real goal.

However, it's really a pity that as for members of the Frankfurt School, the criticism of capitalism itself becomes a goal, what had been emphasized by them is such as a fact that they are criticizing capitalism, but they don't care about these following issues: whether or not their criticism is related to actuality? Whether or not their criticism will bring about the overturn of existing society? Whether or not their criticism will give rise to a series of revolutionary activities against capitalism? Even trying to

---

① K. Marx and F. Engels, *Collected Works* (vol. 5) (New York: International Publishers, 1976), p. 24.

② K. Marx and F. Engels, *Collected Works* (vol. 5) (New York: International Publishers, 1976), pp. 38-39.

avoid responses to the above issues by every possible means.

While talking about the economic field related closely to the critical theory of the Frankfurt School, Horkheimer expressed: "The economy is the first cause of wretchedness, and critique, theoretical and practical, must address itself primarily to it."① Worthy of note, Horkheimer subdivided "practical critique" and "theoretical critique" here. Evidently the former means revolution which abolishes capitalistic relations of production, but it's a pity for Horkheimer and his colleagues that "practical critique" is always an empty talk. If Horkheimer didn't dare to publish his own early writings after his coming back to Frankfort from the United States since 1949, then Adorno took up the so-called "strategy of hibernation"②, refusing to take part in any active revolutionary movements. All these show that the criticism of capitalism is only revolutionary activities in pure thoughtful field. In this sense, revolution becomes an impassable limit of Frankfort School's all critical activities.

Affirmation as A Limit of Negative Dialectics

The dialectical thought of the Frankfurt School mainly incarnated *Dialectic of Enlightenment* (1947) and *Negative Dialectics* (1966), carrying and developing Hegel's and Marx's tradition of dialectics.

What should be pointed out is an important fact that Hegel's

---

① M. Horkheimer, *Critical Theory* (Selected Essays), trans. M. J. Connnell and Others (New York: The Continuum Publishing Company, 1972), p. 249.

② Martin Jay says: "What Habermas once called Adorno, 'strategy of Hibernation' now looks less like the cowardice the Mark Rudds of a generation ago so scornfully dismissed than a model of radical intellectual survival during and less political winter." See Martin Jay, *The Dialectical Imagination* (Berkeley: University of California Press, 1996), p. xx.

methodology is not equal to Hegel's dialectics. In His *Logic*, Hegel wrote: "In point of form Logical doctrine has three sides: (α) the Abstract side, or that of understanding; (β) the Dialectical, or that of negative reason; (γ) the Speculative, or that of positive reason."① That is to say, Hegel's methodology consists of the above three moments in which the second moment is briefly called as "dialectic" by Hegel in other places in his *Logic*. Worthy of attention, the first and the third moments play a commonly affirmative role with the exception of the second moment serving as a negative role in his entire methodology. If the third speculative moment is often condemned as "eclecticism" by critics, then, in my opinion, the affirmative aspect included in the first moment is absolutely necessary for Hegel's methodology to prevent dialectic from sliding to nihilism.

As a revolutionist, Marx was mainly interested in the second moment (dialectic) in Hegel's entire methodology, because dialectic "lets nothing impose it, and is in its essence critical and revolutionary."② It goes without saying that it's not possible for Marx's dialectic to slide to nihilism, because he from time to time insists on an affirmative objective——the communism as alternative project of capitalism. In Germany Ideology, Marx pointed out: "Communism is for us not a state of affairs which is to be established, an ideal to which reality [will] have to adjust itself. We call communism the real movement which abolishes the present state of things."③

However, the negation which is insisted on by Adorno's dialectics, is

---

① G. W. F. Hegel, *The Logic of Hegel*, trans. W. Wallace (Oxford: Oxford University Press, 1999), p. 143.

② K. Marx, *Selected Writings* (Second Edition), ed. David Mclellan (Oxford: Oxford University Press, 2000), pp. 173, 458.

③ K. Marx and F. Engels, *Collected Works*, vol. 5 (New York: International Publishers, 1976), pp. 54, 49.

such a negation refusing any affirmation absolutely, as he announced in the preface of *Negative Dialectic*: "Negative Dialectics is a phrase that flouts tradition. As early as Plato, dialectics meant to achieve something positive by means of negation; the thought figure of a "negation of negation" later became the succinct term. This book seeks to free dialectics from such affirmative traits without reducing its determinacy. The unfoldment of the paradoxical title is one of its aims."[①] In my opinion, Adorno called his own dialectics as negative dialectics refusing any affirmative elements, mainly because of the following two different reasons:

One of them is a hostility to positivism. It is well known that the central idea of positivism mainly embodies the adjective "positive" which has also affirmative meaning. In this sense, refusing the affirmative aspect means refusing positivism. Actually, the key difference between positivism and dialectics lies in the fact that the former has only an affirmative aspect, but the latter has two opposite aspects, affirmative and negative, so the latter has colorful resources denying capitalism, but the former can only identify itself with capitalism. As far as I can see, although Adorno actively made a clear distinction between his own thought and positivism, his dialectics refusing any affirmative aspect was obviously wrong.

The other is a complex of Auschwitz which had Adorno abandon the affirmative aspect of all thing based on identity. In his *Negative Dialectics*, Adorno wrote: "Auschwitz confirmed the philosopheme of pure identity as death."[②] As I see it, Adorno confused the following two different

---

① T. W. Adorno, *Negative Dialectics*, trans. E. B. Ashton (London: Routledge & Kegan Paul Ltd., 1973), p. xix.

② T. W. Adorno, *Negative Dialectics*, trans. E. B. Ashton (London: Routledge & Kegan Paul Ltd., 1973), p. 362. Cf. Adorno's original sentence in German: "Auschwitz bestätigt das Philosophem von der reinen Identität als dem Tod." Sehn T. W. Adorno, *Negative Dialektik* (Frankfurt A. M.: Suhrkamp Verlag, 1966), S. 353.

concepts: identity and homogeneity. According to my point of view, what Adorno should be against isn't the identity, but the homogeneity between conception and actuality. Supposing that there is not any identity between conception and actuality, then it's impossible for Adorno and his colleagues to try to give an impact to actuality through their own writings and conceptions. In fact, what we should cast aside is "the identity based on the homogeneity between conception and actuality" insisted on by Hegel, but should keep to "the identity based on the heterogeneity between conception and actuality" defended by Kant and Marx.

If skepticism can be understood as a dogmatism in negative meaning by Hegel, then Adorno's negative dialectics also as a positivism in negative meaning by us. ①At first sight, Adorno insisted on absolute negation which refuses any affirmative aspect, but in their "Zur Neuausgabe" (1969) of *Die Dialectik der Aufklärung*, Adorno and Horkheimer pointed out: "Kritisches Denken, das auch vor dem Fortschritt nicht innehält, verlangt heute Pateinahme für die Residuen von Freiheit, für Tendenzen zur realen, Humanität, selbst wenn sie angesichts des grossen historischen Zuges ohnmächtig scheinen."② I dare say, freedom (Freiheit) and humanistic tendency (die Tendenz zur Humanität) remain a minimal affirmative aspect that Horkheimer and Adorno sought as best as they might.

Actually, whether Adorno's negative dialectics and Marcuse's great refusal③ in the negative meaning or Habermas' theory of communicative action, A. Wellmer's persistence of modernity and A. Honneth's theory

---

① See Yvonne Sherratt, *Adorno's Positive Dialectic* (Cambridge: Cambridge University Press, 2004). In my opinion, the term "positive dialectic" itself a paradox!

② M. Horkheimer, *Gesammelte Schriften* vol. 5 (Frankfurt A. M.: Fischer Taschenbuch Verlag, 1987), S. 13.

③ H. Marcuse, *One Dimensional Man* (Boston: Beacon Press, 1966), p. 257.

of recognition in the affirmative meaning, their common purpose is to rationalize capitalism further, but not replacing it with communism as an alternative project through Marx's revolutionary mode.

According to Marx's view, the essence of dialectics based on human praxis is critical and revolutionary. However, Horkheimer's and Adorno's dialectics lacking a definite revolutionary alternative project for capitalism is necessarily pale and weak. In the end, it is a more concealed positivism.

In a word, what members of the Frankfurt School have till now done is to criticize, to revolt, to deny certain phenomena of capitalistic society but in a great institutional formation of capitalism. Although the critical theory of the Frankfurt School remains to have its thoughtful potentialities and remarkable influences, its revolting against capitalism looks like wheat against sickle or fetus against his mother's belly which can only result in the perfecting of capitalism.

Critical Analysis of Contemporary Chinese Culture

3.1 The Loss of Subject and the Disorder of Value[①]
—A Critical Reflection on the Present Cultural Research

Under the circumstances that most people are talking about culture and all kinds of viewpoints on culture are disorderly on display, what is the historic mission of philosophy at present and in the future? I think, the urgent task of philosophy is not to follow the fashion in the way of drifting with the tide, for example, to build a new system of cultural philosophy, or to translate and introduce all sorts of new trends of cultural thought, etc., but is to aim at critically reflecting on and clearing up the essential viewpoints which exist generally in the present cultural research. Otherwise, the more we talk about in cultural research, the further we are from the truth probably.

In the present cultural research, coexistence and conflict of different viewpoints are obvious, so

---

① Editor's note: This paper was translated from *Shehui Kexue Zhanxian* (《社会科学战线》), no. 2, 1995, pp. 37-42.

some people call the state "the plural cultural state." Of course, this is beyond reproach. Moving from the past "unitary cultural state" to the present "plural cultural state," in a sense, is a kind of historical progress. However, it is inappropriate to stop on this point. Admitting the existence of "the plural cultural state," and treading different ideas on culture in the manner of lenience and opening, although it is necessary, is not the same as the view that the existence of each viewpoint on culture is reasonable, or each viewpoint on culture has no right to critically think about the other viewpoints on culture. In fact, without critical thinking, not only "the plural cultural state" will degenerate into a kind of simple shape, but all the cultural research will also lose its vitality.

I

Provided that we inspect in earnest all sorts of different viewpoints and thoughts of culture, we will find that a general and non-negligible phenomenon is the loss of subject and disorder of value.

The "subject" we here talk about refers to the Chinese in 1990s, and so-called "loss of subject" refers to subject's misunderstanding and losing the objective position which he ought to stand on. Not to speak, this kind of loss of subject necessarily causes disorder, even reverse, of the view of value of subject, thus, make subject float like duckweed on all kind of different ideas.

Loss of subject appears roughly three sorts of circumstances below:

The first is the misplacement of subject, namely, subject don't regard itself as Chinese in 1990s, but replace his own position by other people's position when he researches all sorts of cultural phenomena and problems.

Of course, the "other people" here talked about have varied possibility, but the most typical and the commonest is two kinds below: one is the ancients, especially Confucianist represented by Confucius. Although such research position and manner as "approve the past, not the present," "stress the past, not the present" don't flagrantly manifest itself like the school of the quintessence of Chinese culture whom Mr. Lu Xun had bitterly attacked, it's latent appearance in the present cultural research can be found everywhere. For example, unanalytically praising Chinese cultural; tradition, unconditionally worshipping ancient text such as *The Confucian Analects, The Works of Mencius, The Book of Change*, etc., avoiding and concealing the historic limitations of representative of Confucianism, etc. All these indicate subject misplacing his position on the ancient. Another is the contemporary western, especially the representative of west modernism and post-modernism cultural thoughts. In recent years, internal scholars scramble for new thoughts coming from the western like nonrationalism, existentialism, the Absurd, deconstructuralism, post-colonialism, etc., and uncritically employ the position, attitude, method of these new thoughts to describe and even to comment on Chinese modernization, social problem and cultural problem. They neglect the point below to great extent, that is, contemporary Chinese society pursuing modernization have completely different living interest and value-orientation from contemporary western society. Therefore, when subject uncritically misplaces his own position on the position of such representative of the western modernist school post-modernism cultural thoughts as Lyotard, Derrida, etc., he not only can't correctly solve sorts of problem which contemporary Chinese society is faced up with, but also mislead the discussion in this respect.

The second is subject's prejudice, that is, subject is not able to master the objective value-orientation which Chinese in 1990s should master, but replace the objective value leading by pure subjectivity prejudice, i. e. subjectivity value-orientation. Subject's prejudice mainly takes the form of two tendencies below: one is that subject treats and evaluates sorts of cultural problems and phenomena completely depending on his own liking, for example, the man who worships Lao Zi lifts him up to heaven; those who worship Confucius and Mencius boast them as perfect sage, forgetting Confucius himself has even said: "I am fortunate! If I have any errors, people are sure to know them." (*The Confucian Analects · Shu Er*). Another is that when subject investigate sorts of cultural problems and social problems, he often misses the essence of these problems, and only grasps some partial, accidental, temporary or detail elements to weave text. This just echoes what people often say "prejudice is further off the truth than innocence." In a word, setting out from pure subjectivity value-orientation, and writing the articles as "six scriptures interpret me", which seem to raise highly activity of subject, in fact, is still metamorphosis appearance of subject's ignorant, homeless and embarrassed state.

The third is subject's absence, namely, when subject researches any cultural phenomenon (for example, culture character, culture event, text, etc.), he attempts to clear up any elements and any feeling elements which he might take in. This is so-called "purely objectively" investigating all object, or in other words, is not to make value judgment but factual judgment. It seems that this research attitude is extremely fair, even can be honored by the good name of "scientific research". In fact, it is a kind of timid behavior that subject avoids difficultly researching the living-world which he lives in, and avoid making certain the value-orientation which he should possess. Actually, the factual judgment completely parting from value judgment never exists. Even if in the research of nature science, our choosing the research theme and our interpreting its meaning also reflect our value system.

It can be made out from the analysis above that loss of subject is a prerequisite problem in cultural research. If we leave it aside, blindly expand the range of cultural research (for instance, prostitute culture, tea culture, dietary culture, etc.), or endlessly argue on some side issues, we can't lead general cultural research to healthy trajectory. Loss of subject also won't be avoided only by using continually such sentence as " I think…""I find…" "I believe…" in the text of cultural research. On the contrary, the more these sentences are used, the more rootless, homeless, embarrassed states of subject are revealed. Besides, it can also be made out from the analysis above that loss of subject necessarily causes confusion, even disorder, of his value systems, as well as absense of cultural critic, thus, deforming "plural cultural state" into pure exterior and pseudomorph.

II

Now, we'll go further into what reasons actually cause the universal existence of the phenomena of loss of subject and disorder of value. I think the primary reasons are the following two:

One reason is in the objective respect. With the development of market economy and the speeding of society transition in our country, sorts of problems have been springing up. To solve these problems, people resort to various thoughts and viewpoints of culture. When all forms of cultural views are chaotically on display, however, contemporary Chinese scholars, who have just freed themselves from the pure ideological cultivation of "the Great Cultural Revolution style", are at a loss what to do just as Grandma Liu visits the Grand View (a Chinese idiom, which means that a simple person is overwhelmed by new experiences and luxurious surroundings). Under the clash of thoughts of culture pouring in, their standpoint, as well as the monistic axiological idea, is oscillated. By keeping on translating and introducing new thoughts and in a semi-skilled manner, they try to indicate that they are unceasingly thinking in earnest. To pursue unceasingly new thoughts and terms and to transform unceasingly subject's position (some people believe in one's thought after reading his works, as if believing at will equals to thinking in earnest), however, just means loss of subject. Of course, in all fairness, whenever the development of society is in the period of great transition, the phenomena mentioned above are almost inevitable, but it should not go on existing in a long time, for going with the stream without thinking and criticizing is contrary to the mission of contemporary scholars.

The other reason is in the subjectivity respect. I name it "peeling of historicity." It is shown in the two respects below:

The first is peeling of subjectivity historicity. What is the exact meaning of it? As what is mentioned above, the "subject" used in this article refers to the Chinese living in 1990s, and it is just contemporary Chinese if I use an inexact concept. Then, what is the historicity of contemporary Chinese? How can it be peeled off? Generally speaking, I think the historicity of contemporary Chinese means the historical circumstances which they have placed themselves on. No need for reticence, the historical circumstances is complicated. The historicity said here doesn't refer to the whole scopes and details of the historical circumstances, but to the essential things which are necessarily shown as developing trend in it. As to contemporary Chinese, this kind of historical circumstances unfold as an extremely rich and concrete living-world, the essential things which are in the inner of the world and compel it to reveal the nature of itself is the Chinese style market economy of Chinese style in the ascendant—this is exactly where the so-called "historicity of contemporary Chinese" lies in. Chinese market economy possesses both general character of common market economy and the particularity which has formed under Chinese cultural background. With regard to its general character, the rising and developing of market economy is bound to lead to the disintegration of primitive ethical spirit based on blood relationship and local connections, and to the rise of new thought based on independent personality and centrally characterized by the spirit of democracy, freedom, equality and science. With regard to its particularity, Chinese market economy emerged and developed under the conditions of planned economy radically characterized by administrative decree. Therefore, the existence of such phenomena as administrative power's interference of economic life in an unreasonable, or even illegal manner, and using one's power for his own profit, corrupting, degenerating, is a fact beyond arguing against. Under the circumstances, it is extremely important to advocate equal opportunity and social fairness and to set up and perfect various laws and regulations.

In a word, as for contemporary Chinese, especially those living in 1990s, their inescapable historicity is just embodied in the Chinese style market economy. To develop the market economy more healthily, namely, to develop it towards a state of being more reasonable, it is necessary to establish a new value system, the core idea of which is just the spirit of freedom, equality, democracy, science and social fairness, and all these values presuppose the establishment of independent personalities which we have mentioned above. It is just the objective value-orientation that we are stressing and that contemporary Chinese, especially those living in 1990s, should possess. In my opinion, those who can consciously apply this value-orientation for analyzing and researching different cultural phenomena are the people who really understand their own historicity. Otherwise, subject's historicity is in the state of being peeled off. Not to speak of this state's being naturally leading to loss of subject and disorder of value. For example, the basic theme of western modernism and post-modernism is to reflect the social problems caused by the highly developed science and technology. Obviously, this kind of reflection is just that contemporary Westerners profoundly apprehend and grasp their own historicity. But, can we simply move the theme of contemporary western into contemporary Chinese society? The answer is negative. For being different from contemporary western countries, Chinese are heading for modernization. That is to say, in contemporary Chinese society, it is still very important to devote effort to developing science and technology and to expand scientific spirit. If only one gives a glance at various chaotic state in administration (such as many times repeated and destroyed construction of roads and houses), and think of the superstitious thought congested in popular culture, especially in rural culture, we have cause to repeat the discourse which Hu Shi gave seventy years ago in the well-known "debate between science and metaphysics":

> *Let's try to open our eyes and have a look: everywhere the altar for diving and the house for Taoist and Buddhist, everywhere the divine prescriptions and the ghost photos, so underdeveloped traffic, so underdeveloped industry—where do we acquire qualifications to exclude science?*

Certainly, compared with the time when Hu Shi lived, contemporary

Chinese science and technology are already developed in some degree, but, who will suspect that China still needs to develop scientific technology and scientific spirit for realizing modernization? In recent years, some mainland scholars continuously advocated objecting to scientism and expanding the spirit of humanism. Outwardly, it seems that they try to let contemporary Chinese society absorb in advance the experience and lessons which western society have undergone in the procession of modernization. However, it is actually the complicated response of a conservative psyche contending with the historical process of Chinese modernization. Indeed, to watch out for and contain the extension of scientism in some degree is significant. We should also realize, however, in contemporary Chinese society, the urgent matter is not to prevent popularization and the development of science and technology in China under the excuse of anti-scientism, but to develop scientific technology and to cultivate the scientific spirit which is beyond utility and brave in devoting oneself to the truth (such as Copernicus, Galilei, Bruno, Darwin, Auxley, etc. In western history). To advocate ill-timed and excessively containing scientism, to disregard the scientific spirit and expand lopsidedly the spirit of humanism is just typical appearance of the peeling of historicity of subject. This state of peeling will naturally lead to loss of subject and disorder of value. Maybe we can call this state "the conflict between the life situation of pre-industrial society and the cultural state of mind of post-industrial society."

The second is peeling of objective historicity, that is to say, when subject researches cultural object (such as cultural character, cultural ideas and cultural affairs, etc.), he doesn't organically associate theoretical side of object with social and historical side of object, thus, it causes peeling of historicity of object. For example, when some scholars conceal large difference between Chinese ancient society and contemporary society in his historical circumstance, and discuss abstractly the successive relation in theory, the historicity of object which they talk about is peeled off. Equally, when scholars conceal the historicity circumstances of Chinese society and western society and abstractly compare similarities and differences of eastern and western culture, they make the same mistake.

For instance, some contemporary Chinese scholars stand for expanding the humanistic spirit of Confucian school, and it is beyond reproach on the side of abstracted theory. How can we say that humanistic ideas such as "father kind, son filial", advocated by Confucian scholars, are wrong? The problem is that we can't stay remain in the domain of abstract theory, but should present the concrete, social and historical connotation which the Confucian humanistic spirit possessed in the historical circumstances at that time, namely, historicity. Only in this manner can we clarify the correct attitude to treat the spirit. *The Confucian Analects · Xue Er* have such a maxim: "the superior man bends his attention to what is radical. That being established, all practical courses naturally grow up. Filial piety and fraternal submission—are they not the root of all benevolent actions? That is to say, in the time of Confucius, what he hoped to found was a humanistic spirit basing on "filial piety and fraternal submission." In this spirit man was first taken for son and brother, in other words, was regarded as an element of patriarchal clan system which regarded blood relationship as ties and regarded patriarchy as center. In Confucius' opinion, not only man and woman are not equal, but father and son are also not. Thus, there is such a wording "son conceal something for his father" in *The Confucian Analects*. It is well known that the humanistic spirit in the sense of modern civilized society is based on independent personality, that is to say, man is not first regarded as son and brother but as independent personality. In family life, modern people still advocate "father kind, son filial", but this cultural idea has been given a new social and historical connotation, i. e. the "kind" and the "filial" are discussed on the basis of independent personality and equal relation of people. To disregard concrete aspects of society and history, and to discuss abstractly humanistic spirit of Confucian school, necessarily obliterate the essential difference between modern and ancient humanistic spirit, and thereby leads to chaos and even crises, of cultural construction.

For another example about western culture. When philosophy circles of our country inquire into the thoughts of "identity philosophy" represented by Fichte, Schelling and Hegel, they often analyzed it restricting in the pure theoretical respect, namely, it maintains that thinking and being have identity, thereby denies agnosticism in epistemology, etc. They completely neglected its social and historical characteristics. In fact, identity philosophy was put forward under the effect of the French Enlightenment and the French Great Revolution. Its social and historical connotation, in accordance with Hegel's view, is "according to thought, constructing reality." In other words, it means using the general principles of the Enlightenment's thoughts to remodel German social reality. Therefore, "identity philosophy" is not an abstract and tasteless philosophy doctrine, but a kind of revolutionary theory expressed by German philosophers by obscure language. At the time of studying "identity philosophy," if we disregard this kind of concrete historical intentionality, it equals to peeling off the historicity of this research object, and also leads to loss of subject and disorder of value.

By summing up the analysis above, it isn't difficult to find that the subjectivity reason of phenomena of loss of subject and disorder of value is mainly caused by peeling of historicity. This tells us, in any cultural research, it is significant that subject clarifies in advance historicity so as to identify consciously with the objective value-orientation which subject should establish.

III

As for the main point of what we investigated above, it still stays in the shadow of negation and critic. Now, we must answer such question from positive side, namely, how to avoid loss of subject and disorder of value in cultural research? In other words, that is how to clarify beforehand his historicity before cultural research, thus, to establish the objective value coordinate which subject should have.

Before solving these problems, I think, we still need do some clarification in advance to clear up those preconceived ideas that most easily lead subject to wrong path. Perhaps man can say the "Axial Age" theory put forward by German philosopher Jaspers is just such preconceived idea. It seems to him that the era of 8th century B. C. -2nd century A. D. is the time when Confucius, Sakyamuni, Socrates, etc. founded respectively different cultural normal form. The reason why this age is called the "Axial Age" is that the development of culture in later time are all in the direction of the cultural normal forms of this era. If one understands Jaspers only according to the transference and development of sorts of cultural normal forms, one can say he is not wrong. His error lies in regarding that era as "Axial Age," which implicate such a conclusion: namely, the development of culture of later times revolve around "Axial Age." This theory is an example of the subjectivity's misplacement. In fact, "center axis era" never lies in the past, but in the present. Of course, the present is only a relative concept. Whenever history of human being reaches, the livings is only those who are called contemporaries at that time. Only contemporaries, life interest is genuine center axis, just starting from which, one interprets ancient culture and ancient characters. Therefore, Croce said:

> *Roman and Greek lay in tombs, wasn't aroused until the Renaissance European spirit acquire newly-come maturity ... ... thereby, long periods of history which we now regard annals and many documents which is still silent now will be shone orderly by the light of new life, and will speak once again.*

Just in view of these, Croce puts forward that well- known proposition "all genuine history are contemporary history", affirmed center function of contemporaries and contemporary culture. In fact, if we go on according to Croce's logic, even such a wording as "the Renaissance" is not exact, because it easily causes such misunderstanding: modern European suddenly comes back ancient civilization. What really happens, however, is just on the contrary. Modern European only employs the slogans and costumes of ancient characters to perform new life program. Here, Croce actually put forward a kind of "New Axial Age" theory radically opposed to Jaspers', which tells us that to avoid the misplacement of subject's position on ancient position (namely, replace contemporaries' position by ancient position), the most important is to realize that centre axis lies in contemporary from beginning to end. Therefore, only to apprehend the essential significance of contemporary living-world where subject lives is authentic prerequisite preparation for keeping subject independent and free. We shouldn't rest on such a shallow common knowledge as "not to know the past not to understand the present." But should apprehend this much more profound truth below: "not to understand the present, not to interpret the past. "

Another preconceived idea which greatly affects us, and whose affection even reach the side of our unconscious psyche, is "worship of chronicle time." So-called "chronicle time" refers to international current concept of time at present. "1990s" which we mentioned above just belongs to chronicle time. In any case, this kind of time is indispensible for contemporaries' life, just because of which, people take invisibly this idea of time into cultural research, especially comparative cultural research, and thereby, extend the faulty idea of "isochronal." Such is just one of deep reasons that cause peeling of subject's historicity and loss of subject.

For example, Chinese people usually think that they are at the same time as the western 1990s is. In fact, the concept "isochronal" here have only formal meaning in the sense of chronicle time. If we extend this meaning to that they are isochronal at their cultural state of mind, that is greatly and especially mistaken. In fact, contemporary Chinese live in two different kinds of time: one is chronicle time that we have mentioned above, according to which, people arrange their life and sorts of communication activities (especially international communication activities). Another is what I call the time of form of society, which is decided by economic relation that occupy dominant statues in social life, and this kind of relation restricts cultural state of people's mind. For cultural research, especially comparative cultural research, only the time of form of society is radical premise. In accordance with such time idea, we can say, Chinese in1990s is not at the same time at the cultural state of mind as the western in 1990s. In other words, western culture in 1990s and Chinese culture in 1990s are not isochronal. In this research of this respect, we can't be puzzled by such exterior: namely, there are also color televisions, compact discs, break-dance and rock in china in 1990s just like the west in 1990s.

Thus, we affirm that contemporary Chinese culture is at the same time as western culture. We admit that chronicles time idea may also intrude into the cultural state of mind to certain extent in a stage of development of society, but the effect produced by it is next to nothing as compared with the time of form of society. That is to say, the grounds on which if two kinds of culture is isochronal is fundamentally determined by the time of form of society. Up to now, what man have undergone and are undergoing is ante-commodity-economy-social-form and commodity-economy-social-form. As for the circumstance of contemporary china, it is just on the primary stage of commodity economy. Even if it is reluctantly put into commodity - economy - social - form, it still lies in different stage of development from contemporary western society whose commodity economy has been highly developed, thus, their cultural state of mind is not isochronal, let alone cultural state of mind of contemporary Chinese society is still deeply marked with natural economy and planned economy. People often say, Chinese are either sluggish or unpunctural, while westerners are swift and punctual. It is just because contemporary Chinese society lies in different state of time from contemporary western society. Therefore, investigated from the view of the time of form of society, the cultural state of mind of contemporary Chinese society is rather more resemblance to, or to be more exact, is at the same time as the cultural state of mind western society in 16-18th century. Contemporary Chinese society's stress on the use of transport and technology, it's appeal to the conscious of morality and right, it's attention on the civil society and social fairness, etc., are just the past events which western society have undergone in 16-18th century.

The cultural research, especially comparative cultural research, only stays in the chronological time, and this state inevitably leads itself to a dead lane, where the loss of subjectivity is also inevitable. Just as what has been mentioned above, subject's misplacing his standpoint on that of western modernism school and representative character of post - modernism, abstracting respective historical background, generally comparing Chinese culture state of mind with the western, researching similarities and differences of thoughts of eastern and western cultural character (such as Lao Zi and Heidegger, Zhuang Zi and Derrida, Zhu Xi and Hegel) by shallow sight pursuing superficial resemblance, etc. All these are closely relative to error of time theory. In fact, comparative cultural research should be based on the foundation of the time of form of society. Provided that people are blind to this foundation, such a research has no scientific nature.

After being demasked, we need to directly probe into philosophical premise of cultural research. Such premise, I think, should be Ontologic Hermeneutics. And the Ontology talked about here is that in the existent sense. This kind of Hermeneutics ask for cultural researchers to apprehend advancedly their historicity, and grasp essence of living world where they place themselves, and therefore, set up a kind of objective value coordinate which they should possess. When doing so, researchers should have courage to clear up their own subjectivity value-orientation and step out from the misplacement of loss of subject and disorder of value.

3. 2 The Relationship Between the Human Spirit and the Scientific Spirit in Contemporary China[①]

Introduction

As a man observes seriously the spiritual life of contemporary Chinese, he will find out the fact that there is a sharp antagonism between the human spirit and the scientific spirit. On the one hand, authoritative scholars stress on that China ought to develop energetically science and technology, popularize rapidly scientific knowledge and carry forward scientific spirit. They even believe that China will realize the modernization if only science and technology can arrive at the level which western countries have reached. On the other hand, however, nongovernmental scholars claim that China should develop the human science, raise the human quality and promote human spirit.

---

① Editor's note: This paper was translated and revised from *Tansuo Yu Zhengming* (《探索与争鸣》), no. 1, 1996, pp. 4-7.

According to their point of view, it won't be possible for contemporary Chinese to realize the modernization with lack of the human spirit. This phenomenon is analogous to "the split consciousness" in the French Enlightenment put forward by Hegel in his *Phenomenology of Spirit*.

In my opinion, this antagonism is dangerous for healthy development of the whole contemporary Chinese cultural thought in the process of modernization, especially as scholars haven't paid full attention to this phenomenon and its danger yet. And I believe there should be a necessary tension between the human spirit and the scientific spirit in order that the entire Chinese cultural spirit will keep its vital energies in every part.

Three Concepts of Science

Let's analyze, first of all, the following three concepts:

The first concept is that of "science and technology". What is science and technology? It is well known that science mainly refers to natural sciences, such as physics, chemistry, biology and so on. If science is still in the theoretical domain, then technology by which people remake and control the nature is, in some sense, in the practical domain, so we can say science is technology in the theoretical domain and technology is science in the practical domain. Or to say it in other words, technology is employment of scientific theories in the practical life; however, it has more and more enormous force when it was born in the historical development of human being.

Generally speaking, people regard science and technology as something neutral which have different meanings under the guide of various value systems. Under the guidance of the value system of modernization people easily see positive elements of science and technology, because they have become the first productive forces promoting the economic development in any contemporary societies and they play an important role in the physical life and the spiritual life of human being. It goes without saying that it is more necessary and imminent for developing countries like China to develop science and technology rapidly.

On the contrary, under the guide of the contemporary western value system, especially of the value system of post-modernism people easily find out negative elements of science and technology. H. Marcuse criticizes the phenomenon of "technological fetishism"[1] in the contemporary capitalist societies, as J. Habermas points out:

Marcuses Kritik an Max Weber kommt zu dem Schluss: Der Begriff der technischen Vernunft ist vielleicht selbst Ideologie. Nicht erst ihre Verwendung, sondern schon die Technik ist Herrschaft (über die Natur und über den Menschen), methodische, wissenschaftliche, berechnete und berechnende Herrschaft. Bestimmte Zwecke und Interessen der Herrschaft sind nicht erst 'nachträglich' und von außen der Technik oktroyiert-sie gehen schon in die Konstruktion des technischen Apparats selbst ein; die Technik ist jeweils ein geschichtlich-gesellschaftliches Projekt; in ihr ist projektiert, was eine Gesellschaft und die sie beherrschenden Interessen mit den Menschen und mit den Dingen zu machen gedenken. Ein solcher Zweck der Herrschaft ist 'material' und gehört insofern zur Form selbst der technischen Vernunft.[2]

---

[1] Herbert Marcuse, *One Dimensional Man*(Boston: Beason Press, 1966), p. 235.

[2] Jürgen Habermas, *Technik und Wissenschaft als Ideologie*(Frankfurt A. M. : Suhrkamp, 1970), p. 49.

Martin Heidegger is in a strong way against this point of view that science and technology is neutral in value: "We are delivered over to it in the worst possible way when we regard it as something neutral; for this conception of it, to which today we particularly like to do homage, makes us utterly blind to the essence of technology. "[1]

According to Heidegger's doctrine, the essence of the modern technology is "Gestell" (enframing in English): "Where Enframing reigns, there is danger in the highest sense. "[2]

Because the modern technology has controlled the whole life of the human being and made man a simple thing which K. Marx calls "alienation".

The second concept is that of "scientific spirit." What is the scientific spirit? By "scientific" we mean, of course, something concerning natural sciences, and the scientific spirit has been put forward by people who always try violently to recognize and remake the nature in their daily life. It is well known that the scientific spirit includes mainly two sides: one is to respect facts and objective laws, the other are to investigate bravely and to seek and persist in truths. As a general thing, the scientific spirit has a positive meaning, particularly under the guide of the value system of modernization it is emphasised on by people who promote actively the popularity of scientific and technological knowledge. But contemporary western philosophers have criticized the tendencies that the scientific spirit only cares about facts, not values, and that there is a will to power through

---

① Martin Heidegger, *The Question Concerning Technology* (New York: Harper & Row, 1977), p. 4.

② Martin Heidegger, *The Question Concerning Technology* (New York: Harper & Row, 1977), p. 28.

which the human being has been trying to conquer and control the nature forever. This limitless inflation of the subjectivity has formed the leading characteristic of the modern western philosophy and science since F. Bacon, and also formed the subjective cause of today's worldwide ecological crisis.

The third concept is "scientism". By "scientism," we mean people directly employ conceptions, methods and results of natural sciences to human disciplines. Generally speaking, philosophers refuse to support the scientism, because they believe that it brings about necessarily a serious result, i. e. the dictatorship of technological bureaucrats. However, it isn't easy for people who are living in developing countries to recognize this danger implicit in the scientism. For example, in daily life people often say: "Teacher is an engineer for human soul"; "Education is an engine of hope"; "Everybody is a screw on the huge machine of social life" and so forth. It goes without saying that these words-engineer, engine, screw, machine-usually used in mechanics, are now simply used in the social life. Of course, the overflowing of terminology, methods and mode of thinking of the natural sciences in the social life brings about necessarily the loss of the human spirit, so the scientism is a doctrine which people must refuse in their life and their researches into social sciences.

After analyzing the above three concepts, we can say that the scientific spirit comes from the development of science and technology, and the former exerts a great influence on the latter; the scientism is an overflowing of ideas of science and technology in social sciences and life world, and people ought to reflect consciously the scientism, and limit rigorously the domain for the thinking mode of the natural sciences, in order to leave space for social sciences and human spirit in the contemporary Chinese society.

Science and the Human

Now we will turn to another three concepts.

The first concept is "human discipline" which includes language, literature, history, philosophy, art, religion and so on. And why do we use the word "human discipline", not "human science"? And what's the difference between discipline and science? Because the term "science" is only used for calling the natural sciences. If people employ this term "human science," that is to say, they don't refuse the scientism, i. e., overflowing of the thinking mode of the natural sciences in the human disciplines; discipline is only a neutral concept which is concerned with the domain scholars are carrying out a research for, hence they will refuse the scientism when people use the term "human discipline," not "human science," especially in terms of the studies of arts or religion.

The second concept is "human spirit." By the human spirit we mean a common spiritual tendency which is concerned with meaning and value of the human being in existence. This kind of concern is a special one, which may be called as "the ultimate concern"(a term coined by Tillich, appearing in philosophy, religion and arts. The human spirit has different contents in different cultural backgrounds and in different historical periods.

The third concept is "humanism" through which people, in general, reflect and investigate the nature, essence, meaning and origin of the human being. If people employ this word "humanism" in the strictly historical sense, it ought to be concerned with the special movement in Europe from 14th to 16th century which was against the feudalism, the religious power, and for the human rights and human nature. The concept "humanism" we discuss about here doesn't relate to this special movement, but only involves general meaning.

We ought to distinguish, by any means, the ancient human spirit which is consistent with the hierarchical system from the modern human spirit which is consistent with ideas of independent personality, freedom, equality, charity and justice etc. On this basis we ought to distinguish further the modern, contemporary Chinese human spirit which has been placing emphasis on reason, individuality, freedom, democracy and legality since the May 4th Movement of 1919 from the Chinese classical human spirit which put stress upon family ethics, blood relationship, human feelings and hierarchical system etc., represented by the Confucian doctrine. If so, we may understand exactly the link between human spirit and scientific spirit in the contemporary Chinese society.

Relationship Between Human and Scientific Spirit

After investigating some basic concepts with regard to our subject, we can consider further the relationship between the human spirit and scientific spirit.

At first, we try to ask: why is there an acute antagonism between the human spirit and the scientific spirit in the cultural, spiritual scope of the contemporary Chinese society? Because Chinese authoritative scholars have been under the influence of the scientism for a long time which has come from western countries since 17th century. According to the doctrine of scientism, a country can smoothly realize its modernization if only its science and technology arrive at, first of all, modern level. Although science and technology play an important role in the entire process of modernization, human element is the key in any process of modernization. In other words, the modernization of the human being is crucial in the contemporary Chinese society. History and experience of western countries have told us that a healthy modernization is always based on the consistence between the human spirit and the scientific spirit.

Is it possible for the cultural life of the contemporary Chinese society to realize the coordination between the human spirit and the scientific spirit? According to K. Marx's point of view, it is possible and he criticizes acutely this abstract manner of separating itself from the human spirit in study of the natural sciences.

> *Die Naturwissenschaft ihre abstrakt materielle oder vielmehr idealistische Richtung verlieren und die Basis der menschlichen Wissenschaft werden, wie sie jetzt schon-obgleich in entfremdeter Gestalt-zur Basis des wirklich menschlichen Lebens geworden ist, und eine andre Basis für das Leben, eine andre für die Wissenschaft ist von vornherein eine Lüge. ⟨Die in der menschlichen Geschichte-dem Entstehungsakt der menschlichen Gesellschaft-werdende Natur ist die wirkliche Natur des Menschen, darum die Natur, wie sie durch die Industrie, wenn auch in entfremdeter Gestalt wird, die wahre anthropologische Natur ist. ⟩*[1]

Marx says further: "Die Naturwissenschaft wird später ebensowohl die Wissenschaft von dem Menschen wie die Wissenschaft von dem Menschen die Naturwissenschaft unter sich subsumieren: es wird eine Wissenschaft sein. "[2]

---

[1] Karl Marx, *Pariser Manuskripte* (Berlin: Dietz Verlag, 1989), p. 89.
[2] Karl Marx, *Pariser Manuskripte* (Berlin: Dietz Verlag, 1989), p. 90.

Although there is an important difference between the natural sciences and the human discipline, i. e. , the former refers to facts, but the latter to value, they are based on the common life world. In other words, the human spirit and the scientific spirit should be consistent. Viewed from the cultural ecology, the contemporary Chinese society can smoothly march only if the scientific spirit and the human spirit are consistently based on the modernization-value-system.

3. 3　Internal Conflicts and Outlets
of Contemporary Chinese Culture^①

Since 1978, under the guidance of the spirit of
the reform and opening-up, the cultural life of Chinese society seems to have become extraordinarily
prosperous. Traditional operas, such as Beijing
opera, Kunqu opera, Shaoxing opera and so on
have been put on a show, on the same stage as
with modern dance troupes, fashionable songs,
and pop music. The writings of Chinese traditional
scholars are displayed on the same shelf with
books written by contemporary Western thinkers,
even post-modern thinkers. Various trends of
thought and cultural crazes have appeared and
change unceasingly. Since the beginning of the
1980s, intellectual circles have debated many issues. Some recent book titles include: "Practice
As the Unique Criterion Testing All Theories,"
"Humanism and Alienation," "J. P. Sartre and

①　Editor's note: This paper was originally published in *Proceedings of the International Symposium on Tendency of Philosophy——Dialogue between Chinese and American
Scholars*, Oct. 2002, pp. 39-50, translated from *Zhejiang Daxue Xuebao (Renwen Sheke)*
(《浙江大学学报》〈人文社科版〉), vol. 37, no. 4, 2007, pp. 6-13.

His Existentialism," "The Crazes of S. Freud," "New Novels, Pop Music and New Confucianism from Hong Kong and Taiwan," "Craze of Studies of Ancient Chinese Civilization," "Mania for Traditional Culture," "Mania for Comparative Studies between Eastern and Western Culture," "Fortune-telling with the Book of Changes," "Climax of Heidegger's Philosophy," "S. Huntington and His Neo-Authoritarianism," "F. Fukuyama and His Theory of the End of History," "Rise of Nationalism," "Rise of Neo-conservatism," "Climax of Post-modernism," "E. Said and His Theory of Orientalism," "S. Huntington and His Theory of Clash of Civilization," "Reflections on Humanism," "Climax of Studies of Religion," "Debate about Theory of Civil Society," "Craze of Liberalism and Constitutionalism," "Popularity of Palace Drama." And on and on.

In fact, this co-existence of different trends of thought, and shifting sand of cultural crazes does not signify any truly flourishing cultural life, or even of cultural studies. Instead, these trends reveal inner conflicts in contemporary Chinese culture. So, how can we promote real prosperity in contemporary Chinese culture while also joining in globalization? This is the problem Chinese have to answer.

The Survey of Contemporary Chinese Culture

For the sake of comprehending contemporary Chinese culture, we ought to recognize first of all the following three concepts.

First "China" as a word is often used in two different senses. One is geographic; the other is cultural. This latter sense has been called "Cultural China" by professor Tu Weiming, of Harvard, representing the totality of worldwide Chinese culture. In this paper I refer to "China" in a geographic sense, and especially China's Mainland.

The second concept is "contemporary" which covers here the period from 1949 to now. This can be further divided into two stages. The first lasted from 1949 to 1977, and was marked by a closing of the country to international intercourse. The second stage, from 1978 to now, is characterized by the reform and opening-up. The crazes of culture discussed above are a phenomenon of the latter stage.

The third concept is "culture." We might simply differentiate two concepts. The first is "culture in a broad sense" which includes all products human beings have created in their long existence. This consists of three levels: tools, institutions and ideas in which value systems play an important role. The other concept is "culture in a narrow sense." This refers to the formal or ideal level of culture. That is the concept of culture we are going to inspect today. Seen from the structure of ideal culture, contemporary Chinese culture can be divided into three parts.

The first part is Chinese local culture, which is a fusion of Confucianism, Taoism and Buddhism coming from India since the Han Dynasty. This culture has a remarkable influence still among China's people, especially in the countryside. For example, peasants usually hold Taoist and Buddhist ceremonies as part of funeral arrangements and happy events. For instance, the peasants of Hua Xi production brigade (华西大队) in Jiangsu province, having grown weathy in the new economy, set up statues of 24 Xiao(孝, son's filial obedience to his father). Thus do moribund ancient traditions continue into modern life. ①

The second part is based on Marxism, influenced by Lenin and Stalin. In other words, this is "Soviet-style Marxism", philosophically called "Dialectical Materialism and Historical Materialism". We might as well regard this kind of Marxism, based on the ontology of matter, as "Marxism I". Since 1978 Chinese theorists have step by step recognized that there are differences between Marx and Engels, Lenin and Stalin, and also between the young and mature Marx. Dialogues with Western theorists, studies of Marx's manuscripts (made available in the 20th century) and of the Western Marxism founded by G. Lukacs have all influenced Chinese thinkers. For the more open-minded Chinese theorists, the theoretical image of Marx has been renewed, and Marxism re-founded based on the ontology of praxis, which we might as well call "Marxism II." Today, administrative officers of the government and a few theoreticians still believe in "Marxism I," but, the majority of theoreticians insist on "Marxism II."

The third part is affected by Western non-Marxist cultural trends, especially Liberalism and Constitutionalism. Seen from the development of classical Liberalism, J. Locke's *Two Treatises of Government* and his theory of separation of powers, and J. Rousseau's *The Social Contract* and his theory of general will, represent two key trends. After World War

---

① With some scholars, the pattern of Chinese belief in religions is utilitarian. For example, one common popular saying advises: "Don't go to the temple without trouble (无事不登三宝殿)." However, the religious attitude of Westerners is both pious and non-utilitarian. As I see it, this opinion isn't fixed. In fact, the religious belief of Westerners also has its utilitarian side. In Germany the meaning of adjective "fromm" is pious, but the meaning of verb "frommen" is "profitable," and the meaning of the noun "Fromme" is profit. This may indicate a deep utilitarian motive behind the pious religious attitude. Similarly, in English the noun "interest" has two different meanings: one of them means personal taste; but the other profit. As a matter of a fact, people are always interested in what influences their own profit.

Two, a new trend of Liberalism, represented by I. Berlin, J. Rawls, F. Hayek, K. Popper, R. Nozick, M. Sandel, C. Taylor and so forth, appeared in the West. This group has a certain unity. The controversy, for instance, between J. Rawls, R. Nozick and C. Taylor is really only a family spat. Generally speaking, J. Rawls belongs to Kant's tradition, in which freedom is transcendent. But C. Taylor belongs to Hegel's tradition, in which freedom ought to be observed in historically evolutionary communities. Certainly, this third part of contemporary Chinese culture has had a great impact on Chinese intellectuals, particularly young intellectuals. Certain fields of study, such as Philosophy of Law, Constitutionalism, and Studies of Comparative Constitutions, have become key centers of study in the new culture.

It's not accidental for China to be influenced by these three cultures. As a developing country, China has faced compelling objective situations (such as poverty and helplessness), which have influenced the conscious choices of Chinese intellectuals. And the historical invasions by Western capitalist countries influenced the dissemination in China of universal cultural values perceived as "Western." At the same time, Chinese intellectuals' reception of Soviet-style Marxism after May 4th, 1919 was also a key influence on the formation of contemporary Chinese culture. [1]

The interactions among these three parts, these three influences, forms the locus of evolution for contemporary Chinese culture. From the perspective of mass media, Soviet-style Marxism would be the key factor

---

[1] We don't approve of Hegel's centralizing of Western culture, and also refuse P. A. Cohen's centralizing of China. We believe the invasions of Western capitalism are basic elements in the history of modern China. However, we disagree with the analysis represented by the so-called "impact-response model," which is too simple to be used in the complicated situation of modern China.

shaping contemporary Chinese culture. However, the actual situation isn't so. If Soviet-style Marxism gained advantage over other cultural influences between 1949-1977, then it has declined to a large extent since 1978, especially since 1989. Today, we may say that traditional culture and religious ideas function as the most important elements among people, particularly in the countryside. At the same time universal values-especially such ideas as Liberalism and Constitutionalism-implicated in Western culture have made a notable impact on intellectuals, particularly those in China's coastal cities. Religion, and especially Christianity, has begun to play a major role as well. ① We view this situation as "the heterogeneous relationship between language and actual life."

In a word, after recognizing the basic structure of contemporary Chinese culture and the interactive relationship among its three parts, we have found a key to understanding cultural phenomena in contemporary Chinese society.

Internal Conflicts of Contemporary Chinese Culture

To my thinking, the most profound issue in contemporary Chinese

---

① In recent years, the influence of Christianity has expanded in contemporary society. On the one hand, institutes studying Christianity have increased on a big scale in the academic world; on the other hand, individual Christian followers have also increased to some extent. Christmas has become a popular festival. As I stayed in the U.S. and Canada and visited some Chinese churches during 1997-1998, I found that many Chinese students and scholars studying abroad, especially intellectuals studying science and technology, now believe piously in Christianity. The motives of these believers may range from learning about Westerners and Western life, to removing spiritual loneliness. But the motives of at least a few are superficial and selfish. One story goes that the Chinese Christian prayer is: "Thank God, my daughter has obtained her visa at last."

culture is the internal conflicts or paradoxes formed in the historical encounters of modern and contemporary China. These conflicts are as follows:

First, the conflict between Universalism and Ethnocentrism.

On the one hand, contemporary Chinese recognize that Chinese must seriously study the science and technology, knowledge of management and humanist spirit developed in Western countries. Only thus can China realize modernization and grow wealthy and powerful. In Western culture, we can find universal values, such as constitutional government, human rights, freedom, equality, democracy, justice, respect for facts, pursuit of truth, market economy, international trade, civil society, separation of powers and so forth. These form the main spiritual content of modernization and it is, in fact, impossible for developing countries, including China, to avoid these universal values. Of course, it is very painful for eastern governments with a long totalitarian tradition to choose these universal values and institutions as their own political home. This is like Hamlet's difficult position in which he sighs: "To be or not to be." The fact is that any culture is an organism, a whole. So there are really only two polar choices, as Westerners often say: "all or nothing." That is to say, either Eastern governments receive all universal values, or they refuse everything. There is no intermediate road.

Most Chinese intellectuals believe China's government must accept these universal values sooner or later. However, we must note that, despite their vaunted universal values, Western countries once acted as invaders in the history of modern China. This stamped deep scars on Chinese emotions and recollections. And today, even after the recovery of diplomatic relationships starting in the 1970s, the Taiwan problem keeps these scars aching. As a result, contemporary China always hesitates between two poles. Some would stress universal values and learning from Western culture, even equating these universal values with Westernization. Others stress the particularity of China and supremacy of her Nationalism, denying the existence of universal values in their blind anti-foreign extremism. This closed, anti-foreign Ethnocentrism held the lead in China from 1949 to 1977. Cultural Universalism has held the lead since 1978. But the dangers of sliding back to Ethnocentrism increase with every frustration of diplomatic relationships with the West. In some sense, so long as the union of Mainland and Taiwan doesn't come into being, the problem of Taiwan will always threaten to blast the development of healthier relationships. [1]

Second, the conflict between Totalitarianism and Individualism.

As an eastern totalitarian society, China neither underwent the historical stage of slave society, nor had a feudalistic society in the European sense. China is, in effect, a society based on natural blood lineage and on family institutions that hold totalitarianism in esteem, both in the family and at the national level. In Chinese traditional society, "family" and "country" were inseparable. In Chinese "国家" indicates the close connection between country and family. According to Confucianism, a stable society ought to be built on the basis of xiao (孝), filiality. If every family is stable, the thinking went, the country will be also stable. In such a family or country, there is no true individuality. Personhood consists of blood lineage and status. In the family a man may be father, brother or son, but not an independent personality. In his country a man is only a subject, not

---

① J. K. Fairbank recognizes the seriousness of this problem, so he writes: "Both American expansion (or imperialism) and China's modern nationalism have their origins deep in the past but continue to shape current policy." See J. K. Fairbank, *The United States and China* (Fourth Edition) (Cambridge: Harvard University Press 1983), p. xvii.

a free individuality. According to Hegel, only the emperor had freedom in traditional Chinese society. In fact, I believe not even the emperor was free, because his freedom was always limited by the whole royal family. If he acted against the royal family, his freedom and even his existence could be abolished.

However, driven by the market economy, individuality has grown as a basic trend in contemporary Chinese society, because the contractual relationships required by a market economy are based in turn on free and equal individuals able to sign them. In a sense, there is no real market economy without independent individuality. So the contradiction between Totalitarianism and Individuality has become more and more incisive. ①

Coming from a traditional society based on agriculture, contemporary Chinese society also went through the planned economy of Marxism, and now is totalitarian in many economic activities. That is to say, it still safeguards totalitarianism, mainly in the form of state-owned enterprises. In this mixed economy, the contradiction between totalitarianism and individuality showed in the following ways:

Conflicts in the idea of reform. The reform and opening-up asks the central government to delegate important powers to local governments and enterprises. However, the central government always tries to re-concentrate these powers through so-called 'macroscopic controls.' As a result, mixed economic phenomena appear. We call this "putting powers down in disorder; taking powers up in times of calm."

---

① In the process of the reform and opening-up, many young peasants have flowed into coastal cities seeking jobs. Some scholars have called this "the blind flow." To my thinking, it is wrong for us to call this phenomenon "the blind flow," because such a flow is based on the value laws of a market economy, and are part of the great historical change from traditional to modern society.

Conflicts in political ideas. Totalitarianism always stresses the "great unity" of the country as the highest form of political thought. This makes it difficult for varying political standpoints to co-exist with the central government's point of view. This gives hegemony to official discourse, making the leadership the unique judge of everything. However, individualism emphasizes difference, and tolerance of political standpoints. In Western language, we can say: "Although I disagree with your standpoint, I will defend your right to speak." As a matter of fact, no contemporary society can effectively integrate all political standpoints into one.

Contradictions in ethical ideas. Generally speaking, collectivism conforms with totalitarianism and individualism with individuality. Chinese often equate individualism with selfishness, and criticize it. However, individual rights need to be affirmed and individualism needs to be carried forward for the market economy and contractual institutions to flourish. By contrast, the ethical ideas of collectivism are a challenge in the modern world. Suppose that a collective, as carrier collective ethical ideas, went bankrupt in commercial competition. Should we safeguard the continuing existence of this collective using a supra-economic force such as government intervention? Even such phenomena as collective crime have started to appear often. It is obviously meaningless for us to speak of collectivism abstractly.

As contemporary Chinese culture developed, the contradiction between totalitarianism and individuality will become more penetrating, and individuality will necessarily lead. Of course, this will be a long historical process in which the universal establishment of practical morality and legal systems be core problems.

Third, the conflict between unbalance of development of market economy and maintaining the commonwealth.

Chinese traditional cultures, in the old saying, "Stressed Agriculture,

Despised commerce" (重本抑末). Ruling classes always emphasized "Eating is the Most Important Problem for the People" (民以食为天) and privileged the development of agriculture. Even intellectuals have felt honored when they could claim "A Family of Plowing and Reading with a Longstanding History" (耕读世家). As a result, commerce lost many opportunities to develop, and the ruling classes maintained control over those commercial activities with the highest profits, exploiting and repressing producers of commodities and handicrafts and other small-scale commercial activities. Traditional Chinese society regarded the egalitarian commonwealth as the highest cultural ideal. The commercial economy was gravely repressed and no true trading class emerged.

Starting in the 1990s, as part of the painful transformation from a planned to a market economy, society slipped to another extreme. The new slogan became "All People Engage in Trade" (全民经商). Long-repressed desires for wealth suddenly awoke, and the search for wealth became almost everyone's aspiration[①]. Some people made false commodities, violated contracts, cheated others out of money or belongings and so on, using every possible trick. Actually, only some have become wealthy. The majority will continue to remain poor. Polarization has emerged.

How to solve this contradiction? The official ideology puts forward the new concept of "Socialist Market Economy," claiming that a "market economy" should create the conditions for everyone to become wealthy, while "socialism" still guarantees the commonwealth, and safeguards against polarization. According to Deng Xiaoping's theory, the Socialist

---

① The fifth day of each year is the festival of the god of wealth. Every household, from cities to the countryside, sets off fireworks in order to welcome the god of wealth home. Many city streets in cities become "red carpets" and many grassplots are burned down. This shows the universally impetuous mentality in search of wealth.

Market Economy ought to make some individuals wealthy as early as possible. These individuals will then create opportunities for the commonwealth as a whole. However, the following questions must be raised: which people ought to become wealthy earlier? How can we ensure they use their wealth to focus on the commonwealth? These are not easy questions.

In fact, market economy usually expands differences between the wealthy and the poor. But the egalitarian ideas of traditional Chinese society and the idea of "Shrinking the Difference between Wealth and Poverty" coming from the socialist ideology of contemporary China, put an anti-capitalistic spin on contemporary Chinese culture. Western capitalism seems to equal polarization. Hence Chinese seek "Democratic Socialism" or "Market Socialism".

Fourth, the conflict between the development of science and technology and the overflow of scientism.

We must clarify basic concepts before inspecting this contradiction. First of all, science and technology". Of course, "science" means the natural sciences which seek to discover the laws of experiential phenomena, and "technology" is a practical form of sciences by which people make tools to improve human life, using applied science. Technology is generally viewed as neutral in value judgements. However, scholars such as M. Heidegger disagree. He emphasizes that modern technology not only controls nature, but also man, and keeps man in a state of serious alienation. Next, the concept "scientific spirit" means the respect for facts, esteem for reason, pursuit of truth, emphasis on cooperation and so on. People, in general, regard this as positive. By contrast, the concept of "scientism" refers to a belief that science is omnipotent, that science can solve all problems, and that the concepts and methods of the natural sciences should be applied to the humanities and even to actual life unconditionally. Undoubtedly, scientism is negative in normal value judgements, and must be restrained. Finally, the concept "humanist spirit" means affirmation of human dignity, carrying forward human values. This is the antidote to scientism.

In the special environment of contemporary Chinese culture, the development of science and technology has conflicted sharply with the restraint of scientism. On the one hand, China is a developing country and its science and technology are backward. In order to catch up with the advanced level of Western countries, China must popularize scientific knowledge and promote the expansion of science and technology. On the other hand, restricting the extension of scientism is also critical. First of all, the majority of today's top administrative cadres come from the fields of science and technology. They bring the mode of thought of the natural sciences into their work, applying instrumental reason and calculations to various complex problems. They also apply technical terms, such as pressure, engineering, engineer, machine, screw, design and so forth, to daily work and life.

Some examples of this creeping use of technical jargon in modern Chinese life: "Teachers are engineers for the human soul", "Education is an engineering of hope,"①"We are all screws in the social machine" etc. The government emphasizes science and technology as solutions to all problems, almost ignoring the humanities, especially the study of religion and mysticism, overlooking the significance of humanist spirit and concerns. For this reason, a great split has appeared in contemporary Chinese Society. On the one hand, official theoreticians hold meetings about science and technology, stressing the importance of popularizing scientific knowledge.

---

① In contemporary Chinese society, the concept of "engineering" has been used so extensively that the majority of social activities have been called "engineering".

On the other hand, folk scholars appeal to the decline of humanism, seeking to revive it. Obviously, this contradiction will become more and more sharp.

Fifth, the conflict between Radicalism and Conservatism.

China has a longstanding traditional culture in which cultural Conservatism has usually held the lead, forming an inert cultural mentality and a closed-door policy. After 1840, attacked by Western countries, China was compelled to open the door. At that time, advanced intellectuals, especially in the May 4th period, were fond of comparing Chinese and Western cultures and decrying China's backward scientific knowledge and political institutions. This cultural backdrop fostered radical thoughts, and a complete negation of the Chinese cultural tradition. In the May 4th movement, scholars threw ancient books into toilets, proposed to romanize the written Chinese, and even suggested abolishing Chinese. A half century later, the "Great Leap Forward" fostered a similarly radical climate, with slogans such as "Nothing can't be done, unless you are unable to think", and "The output of the land depends on your courage." Some maintained that China entered a true communist society in 1958, and should put into practice the slogan "To each according to his need." In the Cultural Revolution, more radical ideas appeared, such as "liberate all human beings," "Only public without private," "break with all traditional ideas" and so on.

Since 1978, together with continued reform and opening-up, a new self-consciousness has arisen among intellectuals. Shifts from relative wealth to relative poverty, and societal worship of money, have created new impetus for the culture of radicalism. However, radicalism met with frustration in the political wave of 1989. As a result, in the 1990s, conservatism has been on the rise in cultural fields. In the past, the common understanding was that the French Revolution was radical, therefore good, but the British Revolution was conservative, therefore bad. However, today's scholars have turned this understanding upside down. Now the British Revolution becomes the best form of all revolutions, but French Revolution, including its thoughtful founder J. Rousseau, is criticized firmly. Meanwhile a Neo-conservative trend has appeared, with Edmund Burke's *Reflections on the Revolution in France* as its bible.

In a word, political and cultural conservatism has flourished in the 1990s, acting against various forms of Radicalism. At the same time, much popular literature and art has turned to historical themes, such as emperors' private lives and palace coups. Traditional folks practices such as "fortune telling," "landscape geomancy," "practice of physiognomy," "traditional customs of marriages and funerals" and so on, have also been revived.

If the longstanding tradition of Chinese culture offers a hotbed of Conservatism, then the great drop between West and East also provides Radicalism with fertile soil. This contradiction will be always part of Chinese culture.

Outlets of Contemporary Chinese Culture

Before discussing this question, let's inspect the following three standpoints:

First of all, "Naturalist Cultural-Pluralism." This recent slogan refers to the cultural multiformity which has become common currency among intellectuals in today's China. The idea is that people can intentionally advocate certain cultural ideas, which will then achieve a sort of hegemony in discourse, and thus bring about the appearance of cultural-totalitarianism. So, according to this view, people should take a naturalistic attitude towards this multiformity.

In my thinking, this naturalistic attitude is definitely wrong, because it rejects any critical mechanism regarding the development of culture. There is no cultural development without real criticism, so maybe the correct concept should be "Critical Cultural-Pluralism." Of course, we need rules for critical engagement which will help avoid creating a discourse hegemony of ideology.

Next, "the Determinism of Cultural Ideas." This means that cultural ideas always play a determinative role in the development of society. Provided that a few intellectuals abandon certain old ideas, the old world will collapse. Similarly so long as a few intellectuals put forward new ideas, a new world will come into being. There is some truth to this, but it is naive to regard cultural ideas as determinative of all elements. In effect, when cultural ideas haven't been universally accepted, they are only nothing. Even if there is extensive popular identification with an idea, it takes on actual strength only through practical implementation. At first sight, simple cultural ideas are everything; in fact, nothing. ①

Thanks to the extensive influence of Determinism of Cultural Ideas on contemporary Chinese intellectuals, they long hankered after receiving and imitating Max Weber's thinking in *The Protestant Ethic and the Spirit of Capitalism*. Weber insisted that the most important thing is to set up a new ethical spirit in the construction of contemporary Chinese culture, in

---

① According to my point of view, the term "culture" is only "a spiritual refuge" in contemporary Chinese society. When people can't directly discuss political problems, they have to talk about so-called "political culture", similarly, when people can't directly discuss the problem of corruption and honest government, they have to talk about so-called "the culture of honest government". If all problems can be openly discussed, maybe this word "culture" will disappear from the contemporary Chinese discourse.

order to modernize. He suggested that even as the protestant ethic promoted Western capitalism, so the Confucian ethic could guide Asian capitalism. And so it was with the economic revival of Southeast Asia. However, the crash in Southeast Asia following the 1999 financial crisis led people to suspect Weber's thinking. In retrospect, the Confucian Ethic is too lacking in spiritual force to fully achieve the ends of modernization. In the end, the actual strength of politics, economics, technology and military affairs determines the development of any contemporary society, including China. In a sense, cultural ideas are only paper money. Their value depends on the actual gold stock.

Finally, "the Pursuit of Perfection." Many scholars have sought to combine the best of Chinese and Western cultures into a new "perfect culture." In my opinion, this is also an ignorant idea. Culture is organic, and has structures, not mechanical accumulations of different elements. When people try to accept Western culture, the valuable and the valueless come together. Similarly, it is difficult to pull out only the good in ancient Chinese culture. There are neither perfect things nor perfect cultures in the world. Hegel writes in *Enzyklopaedie der philosophischen Wissenschaften*: "people can't see anything in pure light, any more than in pure darkness." In *Grundlinien der Philosophie des Rechts,* he also says: "The biggest enemy of the good is the best." We can only pursue better things, not perfect or best things. We must have the ability to work in the real world, resisting the siren-call of nonexistent "perfect cultural Utopias."

So, after all that, how are we to construct contemporary Chinese culture? As to the concept of culture in a broad sense, the importance of institutional culture appears more and more in the reform of political institutions, the establishment of constitutional government, the formulation of civil law and federalism, and so on. These will become the core of constructing a new institutional culture.

As to culture in the narrow sense, we ought to recognize that contemporary Chinese culture is in the transformation from "the Primitive Ethical Spirit" of the traditional society to "the Modern Spirit of Law and Morality". "The Primitive Ethical Spirit" is based on blood lineage, and is family-centric, focused on Xiao and Ti (孝悌) as fundamental ethical principles, and on hierarchical systems, status relationships, human feelings and so on. "The Modern Spirit of Law and Morality" is based on the social relations of modern society, such as individuality, personal conscience, contracts and law, independence and freedom, equality and universal love, human feelings etc. It will be a long historical process to transform from "Primitive Ethical Spirit" to "Modern Spirit of Law and Morality." In this process we must coordinate the following four relations from the standpoint of cultural ecology so as to promote the healthy development of Chinese culture:

We should not only accept the most universal of values from foreign cultures in order to guide China's modernization, but also inherit the rich resources implicit in Traditional Chinese culture, so as to constantly revise the idea of modernization. In a word, we should combine the particularity of Chinese culture with the universality of globalization.

We should not only regard the economic construction as the core of all works, but also emphasize the urgency of political reform, because it is not possible for China's reform to keep the development of politics and the economy separate forever. Only if we harmonize political and economic reform can Chinese culture develop smoothly.

We must not only stress on the establishment of legal systems so as to foster independent personalities, but also emphasize moral construction and recommend moral consciousness. Lao Tsu says: "The more laws are promulgated, the more thieves and bandits there will be." For example, the Qin dynasty emphasized severe laws, so it only lasted 15 years. As a result, we must not only foster legal personalities, but also moral individuals, so as to keep the ecological balance of Chinese cultural spirit.

We must not only develop science and technology, popularize scientific knowledge, and carry forward the scientific spirit, but also emphasize the humanities, advocate humanist concerns, and deal correctly with religious problems. As I. Kant says: "We must restrict knowledge in order to open up the space for belief."

3. 4　A False but Meaningful Issue[①]

—A Reading of the "Legitimacy Issue in Chinese Philosophy"

Philosophical circles have conducted in-depth discussions on the issue of whether the discipline of Chinese philosophy possesses "legitimacy." Whether or not these discussions lead to a commonly acknowledged understanding, at least one thing is clear: scholars are universally dissatisfied with the current state of research in Chinese philosophy, and such dissatisfaction is so strong that queries are being raised about its legitimacy. Such sentiments are understandable, but from the perspective of linguistic analysis, the problem of the legitimacy of the discipline of Chinese philosophy is a false one.

The issue becomes meaningful, however, if the essence of the problem becomes one of how to standardize the discipline of Chinese philosophy in terms of form. What we refer to here as the

①　Editor's note: This paper was originally published in *Contemporary Chinese Thought*, vol. 37, no. 3, Spring 2006, pp. 20-33, translated by Ted Wang from *Fudan Xuebao (Shehui Kexue)* March 2004, pp. 27-34.

"standardization in terms of form" of the discipline of Chinese philosophy includes not only the latter's identification with and adherence to internationally acknowledged academic standards, but also its reflections on its own traditional ways of thinking and its drawing on the methods of research and narration contained in contemporary philosophy. In sum, the essence of the issue does not rest in Chinese philosophy's differences from Western philosophy, which is often used as a frame to understand the legitimacy of the Chinese philosophy; on the contrary, such differences are precisely the reason for the legitimacy of the existence of Chinese philosophy. The nature of the legitimacy issue is that Chinese philosophy must be changed and improved, otherwise it will lose its right to occupy a niche in today's world.

The Theoretical Premise Contained in the Legitimacy Issue

Whether people admit it or not, when they doubt whether the discipline of Chinese philosophy possesses legitimacy, they always consciously or unconsciously presuppose two premises: (1) an expectation that Western philosophy will be used as the frame of reference, and (2) affirmation that the mode of existence of the discipline of philosophy should be unitary rather than pluralist.

Let us look at the first premise. As we all know, the term "legitimacy" comes from the West. As a word, it has more or less two meanings. The first and basic meaning is generally used in law and the philosophy of law to indicate whether an existing matter or activity is permissible under the law. The second is the extended meaning, and is generally used in the linguistic contexts of other disciplines to denote whether an existing matter or activity is right and proper (*zheng dang*). What the "right and proper" referred to does not involve the "law," it merely denotes that an existing matter or activity is consistent with its concept or with the concept to which it pertains per se. If it does, then it is "legitimate," or "right and proper"; if it does not, it is not legitimate and not right and proper.

There is no denying that the discussion on whether the discipline of Chinese philosophy is legitimate involves only the extended meaning of "legitimacy," or, in other words, the question people in fact raise about whether the content of "Chinese philosophy" is consistent with the content of the higher concept of "philosophy" to which it pertains. The answer to this question will decide whether Chinese philosophy is legitimate or otherwise. The crux of the matter lies in what concept of philosophy people use as their criterion of judgment when they determine whether Chinese philosophy possesses legitimacy. People of discernment know at first sight that the concept of philosophy that people use as their criterion of judgment comes—just like the "legitimacy" concept mentioned above—from the West.

Here there is a common "game of signifiers," that is, proceeding from whether "Chinese philosophy" is consistent with the "philosophy" to which it pertains in order to prove whether it is legitimate or right and proper. However, the true subject signified by "philosophy"—the signifier used—is Western philosophy. Situations like this, in which the "signifier" is larger than the "signified," are ubiquitous. ① That is to say, it would look as though people are exploring the legitimacy and propriety of "Chinese philosophy" from the latter's consistency or otherwise with the concept of "philosophy" to which it pertains, whereas, in fact, they are often judging whether it possesses legitimacy based on whether it is consistent with the content of Western philosophy. This is because the term *zhexue* (philosophy), as translated by the Japanese scholar Nishi Amane, comes from the Western term "philosophy," ② and people were also deeply influenced by Western scholars, especially Georg W. F. Hegel, who maintained that China had no philosophy.

Hegel maintained, "We have conversations between Confucius and his followers in which there is nothing definite further than commonplace moral[s] put in the form of good, sound moral doctrine, which may be found as well expressed, and better, in every place and amongst every people." That is to say that Confucius's teachings were merely ethical sermons about the relationships between rulers and subjects, between fathers and

---

① For example, the term "antiglobalization," which emerged after the Seattle demonstrations [of 1999], is also a game of the "signifier" being larger than the "signified." The fact is that no person could truly oppose globalization. For example, the Internet, international communications, international tourism, and international sports competitions are all forms of globalization, and who could oppose them? In this sense, one might say that the concept of "antiglobalization" is one in which "the concept exists but not its object," or, in other words, the concept is there, but there is no suitable subject for it to qualify. In fact, the subjects that the signifier "antiglobalization" actually signifies are the measures, situations, and results that are harmful to the interests of the opponents of globalization, which emerge in the course of globalization. Another example is when a certain student at a certain university becomes a criminal and the media reports the matter under the sensationalist headline "University Student Commits Crimes," as though university students the world over have become criminals, whereas in fact the subject signified by the signifier "university student" in the headline is an individual—"a certain student at a certain university."

② Li Bo, *The origins and Effects of Marxist Terminology in the Chinese Language* (Beijing: Chinese Social Sciences Publishing House, 2003), p. 47.

sons, and among brothers, and were not philosophy in the true sense of the term. As for the Daoist teachings, in Hegel's view, these did not constitute philosophy either, since they mixed abstract reasoning together with perceptual materials. Hegel went further to negate the real meaning of Eastern philosophy in the history of philosophy, stating: "That which we call Eastern Philosophy is more properly the religious mode of thought and the conception of the world belonging generally to the Orientals." In that case, what is true philosophy? Hegel's answer is quite clear: "True philosophy started in the West."[1] It is obvious that in the minds of Western discursive ethnocentrists like Hegel, "Western philosophy," which originated in Greece, is the other name for "philosophy."

It is evident from the above discussion that people doubt the legitimacy of Chinese philosophy because they have consciously or unconsciously taken to the perspective of Western philosophy. In other words, they generally use Western philosophy as their frame of reference when doubting the legitimacy of the discipline of Chinese philosophy.

Let us now look at the second premise. Just as the concept "fruit" contains apples, oranges, bananas, pineapples, and other fruits, the concept "philosophy" may also contain such different categories as Western philosophy, Chinese philosophy, Indian philosophy, Japanese philosophy, Arab philosophy, and Jewish philosophy. If people believe that the mode of existence of philosophy is the same as that of fruit, in that it should be pluralist, they would not be entertaining doubts about the legitimacy of the discipline of Chinese philosophy. Conversely, if they believe that philosophy's mode of existence should be unitary, or, in other words, that

---

[1] G. W. F. Hegel, *Lectures on the History of Philosophy* (Beijing: Commercial Press, 1981; first published in German, 1805-1806), vol. 1, pp. 98, 115, 121.

Western philosophy is philosophy's sole legitimate mode of existence, they will inevitably come to the conclusion that Chinese philosophy does not possess legitimacy, and, by extension, they may go along with Hegel's line of thinking and dismiss as illegitimate all other modes of philosophical existence, such as Indian philosophy, Japanese philosophy, Arab philosophy, or Jewish philosophy.

Whether or not people who doubt the legitimacy of the discipline of Chinese philosophy are aware of it or not, they generally put forward questions and ponder issues from a unitary standpoint, that is, the standpoint that Western philosophy is the sole legitimate mode of existence of the discipline of philosophy. However, they overlook the important fact that Western philosophy, in which they place so much trust, is itself an indeterminate reality.

As everyone knows, Western philosophy is manifested in the course of its development as the history of Western philosophy, but this history is comprised of many philosophers or schools of philosophy that are different, or even fundamentally opposed to one another, in terms of their philosophical viewpoints. All philosophers, or all schools of philosophy, answer the same question—"What is philosophy?"—in their own manner. In the history of Western philosophy, there are rationalists as well as irrationalists, empiricists as well as non-empiricists, realists as well as terminists, idealists as well as materialists, structuralists as well as antistructuralists, and so forth. This naturally gives rise to the question of which philosophical viewpoint is, in the final analysis, legitimately qualified to represent Western philosophy throughout the history of that philosophy. Clearly, the answers to this question by different researchers will be widely divergent. In this situation, where everyone has his or her own views, the abstract concept of "Western philosophy" loses all determinacy and becomes a hazy and indistinct conglomeration of viewpoints.

In sum, when we reflect deeply on the two theoretical premises on which people rely to query the legitimacy of the discipline of Chinese philosophy, we find that both of them lack theoretical grounds.

Answering the Question "What Is Philosophy?" from a Different Angle

As related above, people furnish entirely different answers to the question "What is philosophy?" and this is what turns Western philosophy, which contains innumerable disparities, and even contradictions, into a reality that lacks clear content and determinacy. It is inadvisable to use an indeterminate reality as a frame of reference in attempts to produce determinate conclusions on the question of the legitimacy of the discipline of Chinese philosophy. However, the perplexing issue of the legitimacy of the discipline of Chinese philosophy is very easily resolved when we try to understand the question "What is philosophy?" from a different angle.

To explain what is meant, in the final analysis, by using a different angle to understand "What is philosophy?" one might as well start by discussing an interesting proposition in ancient Greek philosophy. As we all know, the following proposition is found in Heraclitus's fragmented sayings (D91): "One cannot step into the same river twice."[1] According to

---

[1] Foreign Philosophy Teaching and Research Section of the Department of Philosophy at Beijing University, *Ancient Greek and Roman Philosophy* (Beijing: Beijing Sanlian Bookstore, 1957), p. 27.

Aristotle's records, Heraclitus's student, Cratylus, took his teacher's view to a further extreme. He criticized Heraclitus's "statement about a person not being able to step into the same river twice, and maintained that a person cannot step into the same river even once."[①] Obviously, if we wish to judge whether Heraclitus's view or his student's view is correct, we must first ascertain the question "What is a river?" Needless to say, both Heraclitus and his student understood and answered the question "What is a river?" from the angle of the water flowing in the river. Since the water flowing in a river is constantly renewed, the river, too, is constantly renewed. In line with this understanding and this answer, we are fully justified in saying that Cratylus's view is more thoroughgoing than his teacher's, and more rational. Since the water flowing in a river is constantly being renewed, and people judge the changes in a river from the water flowing in it, "a person cannot step into the same river even once."

Actually, if we take our considerations still further, we will find that even Cratylus's view is not thoroughgoing. If using the constantly renewed water to answer the question "What is a river?" is legitimate, then we are entirely justified in making an even more radical statement, that is, that before the person steps into a certain river, that river is no longer the river in its original sense. We could even say that the designation "the same river" is also impossible. If we use the same method to understand "man", whose cells are constantly being renewed, there is absolutely no way we could find "the same person" in this world, nor could we find Heraclitus and his student. Since the cells in their bodies were constantly being renewed, there is no way the same Heraclitus or the same Cratylus could

① Richard McKeon ed. , *The Basic Works of Aristotle* (New York: Random House, 1941), pp. 1010-1014.

exist. That is also to say, the same person cannot exist for stepping into the river, nor can the same river exist for people to step into.

If we try to change the perspective for understanding and replying to the question "What is a river?" the spuriousness of the above propositions by Heraclitus and his student become evident immediately. The truth is that in everyday life, people never understand and answer the question "What is a river?" from the perspective of the water flowing in it; they do so from the perspective of the banks on both sides of the river. That is to say, so long as the banks on both sides of the river remain unchanged, ① the river is still the same river. In other words, a river only means the domain of a stretch of flowing water fixed in place by the relatively definite riverbanks on either side. If this perspective of understanding and answering the question holds up, then we may put forward a view that is completely different from those of Heraclitus and his student, that is, that a person or persons can step countless times into the same river. ②

Needless to say, the reason we have devoted so much space to discussing an interesting proposition from the history of philosophy is to derive inspiration from it, so that we may understand and answer the question

---

① Of course, the term "unchanged" is used here only in the comparative sense. In reality, the banks of the same river may undergo changes corresponding to dry and flood seasons or to the effects of other incidental factors, and a river may even change its course. However, when we refer to a river, such as the Yellow River or the Yangzi River, these factors are generally disregarded. Also, people may use different names to designate the same river in different historical periods, but these different names do not change the essence of the issue, that is, that this river is always this river, just as a person may change his or her name but cannot completely change his or her own body.

② If the "persons" referred to here are in the plural form, the supposition that they may step into the same river countless times is self-evident; if "person" is in the singular form, then that person may step into the same river within the time prescribed by the length of his or her life, in which case the term "countless" is used only in an exaggerated, rhetorical sense.

"What is philosophy?" from a new perspective. Just as for the question "What is a river?", there may be two different perspectives for understanding the question "What is philosophy?"

People generally proceed from the perspective of their own understanding of what content philosophy should include in order to answer the question "What is philosophy?" For example, Hegel believed that "philosophy may be defined in brief as a ratiocinative examination of matters."[①] [Ludwig] Wittgenstein, on the other hand, was convinced that "the entirety of philosophy is *Sprachkritik*" [critique of language].[②] Obviously, as long as one understands and answers the question "What is philosophy?" from the angle of what content philosophy should include, there will be countless answers. These answers, like constantly renewed flowing water, will immerse our thinking in endless retrospection. In other words, there is no way the question "What is philosophy?" will elicit a unified answer. There is no denying the fact that if people link this usual perspective of understanding philosophy with the question of whether Chinese philosophy possesses legitimacy, we will never obtain a definitive conclusion.

We must strike out a new course and ponder the question "What is philosophy?" from a new perspective. What, in the final analysis, is this new perspective? Actually, the answer is quite simple. We should no longer understand philosophy from the perspective of what content philosophy should have, but rather from the perspective of which domains philosophy should be concerned with. Just as we may understand a river as "the

---

① G. W. F. Hegel, *Small Logic* (Beijing: Commercial Press, 1980; first published in German, 1830), p. 38.

② Ludwig (Josef Johann) Wittgenstein, *Tractatus Logico-Philosophicus* (Beijing: Commercial Press, 1986; first published in German, 1921), p. 38.

domains of a stretch of flowing water fixed by relatively definite riverbanks on both sides," we may also understand philosophy as a domain situated between science, ① religion, and the arts.

In this respect, the following conclusion by Bertrand Russell provides us with useful inspiration: "Philosophy, as I shall understand the word, is something intermediate between theology and science. Like theology, it consists of speculations on matters as to which definite knowledge has, so far, been unascertainable; but like science, it appeals to human reason rather than to authority, whether that of tradition or of revelation. All *definitive* knowledge—so I should contend—belongs to science; all *dogma* as to what surpasses definite knowledge belongs to theology."② We could perhaps criticize Russell's exposition as having overlooked the existence of the arts, which are neither religion, nor science, nor yet philosophy. Nevertheless, Russell expressed an important thought, that is, that a domain that is situated between science and religion, and that neither science nor religion can replace, exists in humankind's spiritual world; this "no-man's-land" is the domain of philosophy. If I were to draw a not very precise a-nalogy, science and religion are akin to the "riverbanks" on either side, and philosophy is the "domain of the stretch of flowing water" fixed in place between the two riverbanks.

Clearly, if we are to understand and answer the question "What is

---

① There are two concepts of "science"—the broad and the narrow. When used in the broad way, Germans are even wont to call philosophy "science" (*Wissenschaft*), but here we still use the concept in the narrow sense, to mean all of the empirical sciences.

② Bertrand Russell, *A History of Western Philosophy* (London: Unwin, 1985; first published in 1945), p. 13. It is written in *Yijing*, "Xi ci shang": "Hence that which is antecedent to the material form exists, we say, as an ideal method, and that which is subsequent to the material form exists, we say, as a definite thing." This formulation displays a similar tendency to define different domains. Although their definition is quite inadequate, the ancients deserve credit for having such a perception.

philosophy?" from the perspective of the domain that philosophy is concerned about, then the legitimacy issue of the discipline of Chinese philosophy becomes a false issue—a "big to-do" about nothing. Why? Because in different civilizations there exists, without exception, a domain that neither science, nor religion, nor art is able to replace, and it is unimportant whether people wish to call the discipline that studies this domain "philosophy," as do Westerners, or *zhexue*, as do the Japanese, or *yuanxue*, *lixue*, *daoxue*, or *zhexue* in the manner of the Chinese. The crux of the matter is whether this domain situated between science, religion, and art exists. And as long as it does exist, what people of different civilizations call it is merely a matter of signifiers and has nothing to do with the "legitimacy" issue. If people insist on using such a big word as "legitimacy," then we are fully justified in stating that in different civilizations (including, of course, Chinese civilization) it is legitimate for people to use different signifiers as their name for this domain. This is like the word *shui* (water) in Chinese. The German term is *Wasser*, the English term is "water," and the French term is *eau*, but does that mean there is a need for us to discuss the legitimacy of *shui*—the Chinese form of expression? If we regard this issue—which really does not constitute a real issue—as an issue, are we not being modest to a fault? This may indicate that the criticism of Western discursive ethnocentrism by China's philosophical circles remains to this day at the conscious level, and that at the level of the unconscious, a good many scholars are devout worshippers of such ethnocentrism.

A Substantive Change in the "Legitimacy Issue"

As related above, when people answer the question "What is philosophy?" based on their understanding of what content philosophy should have, and understand Western philosophy as a synonym for philosophy, the issue thereby elicited regarding the legitimacy of the discipline of Chinese philosophy is an entirely false issue. Does this false issue then possess any meaning? Our answer: it acquires real meaning only when people explore the issue from another dimension.

What, after all, do we mean when we say "another dimension?" In ordinary circumstances, people query the legitimacy of Chinese philosophy from the dimension of what sort of content it should have, and such queries generally occur against the backdrop of identifying with Western philosophy. The "other dimension" emphasized here refers to queries about the legitimacy of Chinese philosophy, as a discipline, from the dimension of what form it should have. "Form" here implies, in the main, three meanings:

The first meaning has to do with whether research in the discipline of Chinese philosophy has attained the level of universal and conscious abidance by the academic standards generally acknowledged in international philosophical circles, or whether it continues to operate in an environment of unsound and incomplete academic norms.

As we all know, any genuine philosophical work should conscientiously study and actively respond to the relevant research achievements of one's predecessors and one's contemporaries. However, there are works appearing in Chinese philosophical studies that pay no attention to the relevant research achievements of our predecessors or our contemporaries and content themselves with low-level repetition. Are such works, in the final analysis, philosophical "trash," or are they philosophical achievements? We also know that no system of anonymous evaluation has yet been universally adopted for the publication of China's philosophical works, and even in places where the system has been adopted, there is little conscientious implementation of it. So how can academic impartiality be ensured? Furthermore, a strange phenomenon is universally found among contemporary scholars of Chinese philosophy: those who research ancient Chinese philosophy are not conversant with ancient Chinese, those who research Marxist philosophy do not understand German, those who research contemporary analytical philosophy do not understand mathematical logic, those who research the philosophy of science and technology do not understand the natural sciences, and so forth. Clearly, this universal flaw in the knowledge structure of researchers makes it impossible for research in contemporary Chinese philosophy to go any deeper, or to form schools and attain corresponding academic results that would have a lasting influence on international academic circles.

Even if we set aside the hardly ideal implementation of academic norms as described above, today's Chinese philosophical circles also abound with the copying and plagiarizing of other people's works, glaring absences of common knowledge, indiscriminate fabrications and concoctions, and other such low-level faults and errors. If the discipline of Chinese philosophy is to secure legitimacy in terms of form in a society where rashness and impetuosity run rampant, it must, place a minimum demand on itself, that is, all academic behavior and all products of academic research that occur in Chinese philosophical circles must unconditionally adhere to academic standards generally acknowledged in the international academic world.

The second meaning has to do with whether the discipline of Chinese philosophy has already rid itself of the negative factors in traditional ways of thinking, or whether it still revels in these negative factors, and even refuses to change its ways where research on modern Chinese philosophy is concerned. These negative factors in traditional ways of thinking refer, in the main, to the following four factors:

The empiricism factor. It is general knowledge that Hume divided knowledge into two types. One type consists of the "relations of ideas," and involves knowledge of mathematics. The other type consists of "matters of fact," or, in other words, knowledge that one obtains in empirical life and that is based on the concept of cause and effect. ① The first type of knowledge is unrelated to sensory experience, and is therefore innate and universally necessary. The second type of knowledge is related to sensory experience, and is therefore merely fortuitous by nature. Immanuel Kant criticized [David] Hume as having ignored the first type of knowledge, while he himself derived inspiration from this type of knowledge. He put forward the question "Why is an a priori synthetic judgment possible?" and thereby established transcendental idealist philosophy. The research orientation of the discipline of Chinese philosophy bears some similarities to Hume's empiricism in that it places emphasis on researching the second type of knowledge while ignoring research on the first type of knowledge—knowledge that is related to mathematics and logic②—and is therefore

---

① David Hume, *An Inquiry Concerning Human Understanding* (Beijing: Commercial Press, 1981; first published in 1748), p. 26.

② Wittgenstein placed even more emphasis on the innateness and inevitability of logic. He wrote: "Logical research means the investigation of all *regularity*. And outside logic, all is accident." (see *Tractatus Logico-Philosophicus* 6. 3)

lacking not only in profound thinkers of the caliber of Kant and Edmund Husserl, but to this day remains content with floundering about in propositions of a fortuitous nature and unblushingly extols such propositions as truths that possess universal inevitability.

The psychologizing factor. This factor finds concentrated expression in the frequent "put-oneself-in-the-place-of-the-other" way of thinking in Chinese philosophical research. Confucius's proposition "Do not impose on others what you do not desire others to impose on you" (the *Analects: Yan Yuan*) is a typical example of this way of thinking, and is called by many the "golden rule" of ethical teaching. However, people have not noticed that this proposition merely stresses that one should not force on others things that one does not wish for oneself, and it may very well contain another, complementary proposition, that is, "do unto others what you yourself wish to be done to you." In fact, Confucius once said: "A good person installs others if he himself wishes to be installed, and has others reach something if he himself wishes to reach it" (the *Analects: Yong Ye*). Yet the "himself" of *renzhe*(the good person) is something indefinite that tends toward psychologizing. For example, Confucius believed that *renzhe* or *junzi* (gentleman) could sometimes commit errors, for which reason he should "not hesitate to correct an error when it is found" (the *Analects: Xue Er*). Let us suppose that a certain *renzhe* or *junzi* is "putting himself in the place of the other" precisely when he is in the state of committing an error; would he then be able to draw accurate and correct conclusions? Needless to say, this psychologizing factor, which is rife in Chinese philosophical research, virtually causes all research conclusions to lack definite and universal meaning.

The cavemanship factor. Here we borrow Plato's "cave metaphor" and Francis Bacon's "idols of the cave" to put forward the new concept "cavemanship" for the purpose of indicating that some philosophers habitually ponder philosophical issues from the standpoint of their cave-dwelling forebears. This "cavemanship" way of thinking is ubiquitous in Chinese philosophical research. For example, Chinese philosopher A, like housewife A, presents the argument: "The sky is always clear when I hang my laundry out to dry." But Chinese philosopher B may, like housewife B, similarly present the argument: "The sky is always overcast when I hang my laundry out to dry." The arguments presented by both A and B proceed from their own point of view, and both smack of talking from the top of one's head. Actually, any discerning person can see that the following kinds of weather may occur when a housewife hangs her laundry out to dry: sunny skies, cloudy skies, rain, clear to cloudy skies, cloudy to clear skies, rain to cloudy skies, cloudy skies to rain, rain to clear skies, clear skies to rain, or rain while the sun shines, and so forth; there may even be fog, snow, hail, tornadoes, solar eclipses, and other possible celestial phenomena. Hence, these rampant "cavemanship" sorts of philosophical arguments are absolutely meaningless. Yet to this day, not a few Chinese assemble only those materials that are consistent with their own points of view when they research philosophy, turning a blind eye to materials that are not in accord with their point of view. Is "doing philosophy" with such a crude way of thinking not a profanation of the discipline of philosophy?

The pragmatism factor. As everyone knows, the Chinese have a very strong pragmatic sense, one that permeates research in Chinese philosophy and is manifested as (a) a lack of interest in abstract concepts and categories, (b) marginalization of the issue of truth and spuriousness, and (c) raising usefulness or otherwise to the position of a core concern of philosophy. Hence, research in Chinese philosophy is constantly answering the question "Of what use is philosophy?" Much more attention is paid to this question than to the question "What is philosophy?" This is not to say that the question "Of what use is philosophy?" is of no significance; the point is that dwelling merely on such questions is far from sufficient. In fact, because the researcher lacks interest in abstract concepts and categories that are separated from practical uses, it is very difficult to develop research in such directions as modern logic, analytical philosophy, and the philosophy of language, and this has the reverse effect of causing the discipline of Chinese philosophy always to remain at the level of crude empiricism, psychologizing, and cavemanship.

The foregoing arguments tell us that if the discipline of Chinese philosophy is to achieve legitimacy of form, it must conscientiously examine its traditional ways of thinking, rid itself of the effects of their negative factors, and raise itself to the level of modern philosophy. Of course, traditional Chinese methods of thinking also contain some very valuable elements, and such things as reflections on sociohistorical dialectics, explorations into the relationships of social exchanges, the use of conceptual antiessentialism, ① and so forth have yet to be tapped in greater depth.

The third meaning has to do with whether the discipline of Chinese philosophy has conscientiously absorbed and critically drawn on the newest research achievements of the international philosophical world in terms of its own research and narrative methods, or whether it contents itself

---

① Of course, this is not to say that explicit "antiessentialist" slogans had emerged among China's ancient philosophers, but that the tendency toward "antiessentialist" thought had already found expression among certain ancient philosophers. For example, when Confucius's students asked him the meaning of "benevolence" (*ren*), he gave each student a different answer. This shows that he tried hard to prevent the important "benevolence" concept from becoming essentialized or from being restricted to some rigid state of thinking. Regrettably, philosophical circles have not devoted due research to Confucius's important contributions in this respect.

with merely copying some half-understood new terms while in fact continuing to hold onto obsolete philosophical views in an insular, go-it-alone manner.

No one doubts that logic plays a most important part in philosophical research as a whole and in modern philosophical research in particular. However, the discipline of Chinese philosophy lags far behind international philosophical circles in terms of logical studies, and especially in terms of research in modern logic, and even evidences a dearth of successors in this respect. In fact, the grave dislocation in studies on logic already raises a serious challenge to the legitimacy of the discipline of Chinese philosophy. For example, we often see documents from research on Chinese philosophy that only quote concepts as evidence but lack argumentation in terms of logic, as though all argumentation completes itself if one cites a few excerpts from certain great philosophers or presents one of their viewpoints. Even worse, the viewpoints expressed in one and the same paper may even be logically incompatible. Indeed, how can a philosophical dissertation or a philosophical opinion be convincing if its proponent even violates the basic rules of formal logic?[1]

---

[1] Among China's contemporary philosophers, Feng Youlan, influenced by logical positivism, attached a fair amount of importance to logic, but even his narrations of his own philosophical views did not conform to the rules of logic in all respects. In his book *Xin yuan ren*(A new treatise on the nature of man), he wrote: "As far as the world at large is concerned, men may attain four realms: the natural realm, the realm of fame and wealth, the ethical realm, and the realm of heaven and earth. " Clearly, the definition of these four realms is problematic in terms of logic. Are the natural realm and the realm of fame and wealth not at the same time a realm of ethics? Does the realm of heaven and earth not contain dimensions of the realm of ethics? Contemporary Chinese frequently contend that certain phenomena in everyday life are "unethical. " Actually, the habitual term "unethical" is in no way consistent with logic. One should say that all phenomena conform to ethics, and the problem rests entirely in the sort of ethics they conform to—the ethics of egoism, the ethics of altruism, or some other sort of ethics.

Also, the maturation of methods of "language shifts" and language analysis that emerged during the course of twentieth-century evolution in philosophy are the newest achievements of contemporary research in philosophy. Yet the language analysis method is still universally excluded from the research and narrative methods of contemporary Chinese philosophy. In my opinion, without any background or training in this respect, researchers in Chinese philosophy can hardly achieve any accurate studies or presentations of philosophical issues. In academic research, people often make indiscriminate use of such concepts as "philosophy," "world," "existence," and "practice," or of such propositions as "philosophy is the essence of the spirit of the times" and "science and technology are the first forces of production," but lack the necessary language analysis of these concepts and propositions. Let us analyze these two propositions.

As I recall, Karl Marx put it this way: "Any true philosophy is the essence of the spirit of that era."[①] That Marx places the attribute "any true" before the term "philosophy" amply proves that he tried to narrate his thought in a rigorous manner. If one were to make indiscriminate use of such a careless statement as "philosophy is the essence of the spirit of the times," how is one to confront queries as to whether dogmatist and obsolete philosophical thought is also the essence of the spirit of the times? Similarly, from the perspective of language analysis, the formulation "science and technology are the first forces of production" is also careless and inaccurate. Before a scientific viewpoint is transformed into technology, and before a piece of technology enters the production process, how can they become the first forces of production? The accurate statement of this

---

① *The Complete Works of Marx and Engels* (Beijing: People's Publishing House, 1956), vol. 1, p. 121.

proposition should be: "Science and technology that have already entered the production process are the first forces of production."

We have full reason to say that a serious defect of research in Chinese philosophy is the universal neglect of the achievements gained in contemporary philosophical logic and in research on the philosophy of language. Indeed, when people use a lot of concepts and propositions they themselves do not clearly understand to compose a philosophical text, is it possible for them to make substantive advances in research on a given aspect or given issues of philosophy? In my opinion, even to create such an illusion is shameful. ①

In this sense, if the discipline of Chinese philosophy is to secure legitimacy in terms of form, and if it is to conduct equal and creative dialogues with international philosophical circles, it should assimilate as much as possible from contemporary philosophy in terms of research and narrative methods, and especially from the groundbreaking achievements already obtained in the philosophies of logic and language, thereby elevating itself to a level truly commensurate with that of present-day philosophy.

To sum up the above, when Western philosophy is used as the frame of reference and the legitimacy of the discipline of Chinese philosophy is explored from the perspective of what content philosophy ought to have,

---

① As is generally known, many philosophers advance the development of philosophical thought by means of in-depth analysis of conceptual disparities. For example, Kant differentiated between "empirical judgments" and "judgments of experiences"; Marx differentiated between "the value of labor" and "the value of the forces of labor"; Martin Heidegger differentiated between *Sein* and *Seinde*, and so forth. In a certain sense, one could say that new philosophical viewpoints are very difficult to express if there is no in-depth reflection and differentiation of the basic concepts and propositions of philosophy. Of course, philosophy cannot be summed up as simple language analysis. Fundamentally speaking, research in philosophy must draw its inspiration from real life, and this is precisely where one finds the differences between the thought of Chinese and Western philosophy.

this issue is in fact a false problem. Since a domain exists in various civilizations that cannot be replaced by religion, art, or the sciences, the discipline that studies this domain also acquires corresponding legitimacy. The particular name used to designate this discipline is not essential and has nothing to do with the legitimacy issue. Although the issue of the legitimacy of the discipline of Chinese philosophy is a false one, it acquires true meaning when we understand the issue not in terms of what content the discipline of Chinese philosophy ought to have, but in terms of the form it should have as a discipline.

3.5 Contemporary Chinese Marxist Philosophy^①
—Viewed from an Ontological Perspective

Since the 1990s, studies of Marxist philosophy in contemporary Chinese society have begun to transform from the dimension of epistemology and methodology to the one of ontology under the influence of different ontological theories established by Husserl, Heidegger, N. Hartmann, Quine, Lukacs, Sartre, and C. C. Gould. It is well known that Marx never treats ontology as a special philosophical problem, though he uses the adjective "ontological" in his early manuscripts. Quine's theory of ontological commitments inspires us that Marxist philosophy can be considered and explained from the angle of ontology.

Three Current Ontological View

There are mainly three different doctrines of ontology in contemporary

---

① Editor's note: This paper was translated from *Fudan Xuebao (Shehui Kexue)* no. 5, 2006, pp. 6-11.

Chinese Marxist philosophy.

The first doctrine understands Marxist philosophy as "ontology of matter" which is a leading idea in textbooks of contemporary Chinese Marxist philosophy under influence of Engels, Lenin and Marxist philosophical textbooks of Soviet Union. According to this doctrine, the key task of philosophy is to investigate the nature of the physical world which is separated from human teleological activities. In fact, Engels just insists on the same standpoint and he believes that the difference between nature and society lies in: society is formed by human teleological activities, however, when people consider nature, they can eliminate human teleological activities completely. ① Based on the above point of view, Engels calls his own dialectic as "dialectic of nature." That is to say, like Spinoza and French materialists of 18 century, Engels tries to explain the physical world removing any human teleological activities. It goes without saying, Engels' opinion is reasonable when he refuses to the fact that traditional theological teleology interferes nature or the physical world. However, as Engels does so, he has abandoned washing water and boy together, because he should not deny another fact that it is necessary to human teleological activities take part in the change of nature or the physical world. Obviously, there are great differences between Marx and Engels as for the concept of nature or matter. Marx believes that nature or the physical world which is separated from human teleological activities equals nothingness

---

① Engels says: Nun aber erweist sich die Entwicklungsgeschichte der gesellschaft in einen Punkt als wesentlichverschiedenartig von der der Natur. In der Natur sind es—soweit wir die Rueckwirkung der Menschen auf die Natur ausser acht lassen—lauter bewusstlose-blinde Agenzien, die aufeinander einwirken und in deren Wechselspiel das allgemeine Gesetz zur Geltung kommt. See Marx and Engels, *Ausgewaehlte Werke*, vol. 6 (Berlin: Dietz Verlag, 1990), S. 301.

and only humanized nature is actual nature. ① Under the influence of Engels, Lenin also put forward the following point of view:

Matter is a philosophical category denoting the objective reality which is given to man by his sensations, and which is copied, photographed and reflected by our sensations, which existing independently of them. ②

It is well known that Lenin is always satisfied with talking about abstract matter, often putting forward the following question: Is matter first, or spirit first? And he overlooks fundamental differences between Marx's materialism and the traditional materialism. No doubt, Marx's materialism is a materialism of praxis according to which praxis, human teleological activity, is first and it is a starting point of investigating all other philosophical questions. Under the influence of Engels and Lenin, Marxist philosophical textbooks of Soviet Union also insist on this doctrine of ontology of matter, often talking about the following views: the world is formed by matter which is for ever moving. Time and space are existing forms of moving matter and movements of matter have their own laws, separated from human teleological activities. It goes without saying that this doctrine of the ontology of matter, which is based on the traditional materialist standpoint, doesn't identify with Marx's view of materialism of praxis.

The second doctrine understands Marxist philosophy as "ontology of

---

① Marx says: Aber auch die Natur, abstract genommen, fuer sich, in der Trennung vom Menschen fixiert, ist fuer den Menschen nichts. See Marx, *Pariser manuskripte* (West Berlin: das europaeische buch, 1987), S. 133. Marx also says: Die in der menschlichen Geschichte—dem Entstehungsakt der menschlichen Gesellschaft—werdende Natur ist die wirkliche Natur des Menschen, darum die Natur, wie sie durch die Industrie, wenn auch in entfremdeter wird, die wahre anthropologische Natur ist. See Marx, *Pariser manuskripte* (West Berlin: das europaeische buch, 1987), S. 89.

② See Lenin, *Materialism and Empirio-Criticism* (Moscow: Foreign Languages Publishing House, 1952), p. 127.

praxis", which comes mainly from Gramsci's philosophy of praxis. According to this doctrine, praxis is not only the basic concept of Marxist epistemology and methodology, also, first of all, the one of Marxist ontology. Practical activities, especially productive labor, form the starting point and the core of all other social phenomena. That is to say, all other social phenomena ought to be rationally explained only by praxis. ① Obviously, in comparison with the ontology of matter, the ontology of praxis touches on the essential feature of Marx's materialism of praxis, but it doesn't express this essential feature completely. Because ontology is a learning about Being, and the difference between Being and beings just lies in that beings are visible, touchable, sensible, but Being isn't visible, touchable, sensible. That is to say, the ontology of praxis is only concerned in a level of Marx's ontology, i. e., the level of sensible practical activities, not in the other more important, beyond sensible level. Only if the tatter level becomes our reflective object, it is possible for us to grasp completely the essence of Marx's ontology.

The third doctrine understands Marxist philosophy as "ontology of social being" which comes from late Lukacs' writing *Ontology of Social Being*. In Lukacs' context, social being is different from natural being and the latter is just the basis of the former. Similarly, the ontology of social being is based on the one of natural being. In other words, the ontology of social being isn't original. Because late Lukacs came back Engels' ontology of matter, hence he understood ontology of natural being as the basis of ontology of social being in order to weaken the important meaning of

---

① Marx says: Alles gesellschaftliche Leben ist wesentlich praktisch. Alle mysterien, welche die Theorie zum Mystizismus veranlasen, finden ihre rationelle Loesung in der menschlichen Praxis und in dem Begreifen dieser, praxis. See Marx and Engels, *Ausgewaehlte Werke*, vol. 1 (Berlin: Dietz Verlag, 1989), S. 200.

Marx's ontology of social being. In effect, the concept of social being, like concept of Being, isn't also sensible and it is only grasped by reason. According to Marx's theory, man is a social being, thus when man looks upon Being as his own thinking object, Being is, in effect, social being, even though natural being is also concerned in man and society, so it is essentially humanized natural being or socialized natural being. Speaking generally, contemporary Chinese Marxist scholars don't agree with late Lukacs' view, insisting upon the fact that the ontology of social being should be original and there isn't any natural being can be separated from social being. That is to say, it isn't possible for us to know natural being directly, but possible for us to know them only through the media of social practical activities. We find out the fact that Lukacs' great achievement looks upon Marxist philosophy as an ontology of social being, because the concept of social being relates to the other more important level in Marx's ontology. Although Lukacs has paid attention to this fundamental function of praxis in Marx's philosophy, he doesn't synthesize these two concepts of praxis and social being into Marx's ontology. Meanwhile, he doesn't also bring the concrete implication of the concept of social being in Marx's philosophy to light.

In a word, the above three doctrines have their typicality in contemporary Chinese Marxist philosophy and they don't explain Marxist theory of ontology rationally.

Re-understanding Marx's Theory of Ontology

Before putting forward my new ontological view about Marxist philosophy different from the above three standpoints, I have to clarify the following three theoretical premises:

What should become the exact object as a man begins his own study here? A general answer is "Marxist philosophy." However, the meaning of the concept "Marxist philosophy" isn't clear, because it is possible for any scholars who come from Soviet Union, East Europe, China or western countries, to call their own philosophical theory as "Marxist Philosophy," so I believe that we should withdraw from the ambiguous concept "Marxist philosophy" back to another clearer concept "the philosophy of Marx and Engels as founders of Marxism." However, the exact object hasn't be determined, because there are definite differences between Marx's philosophy and Engels' philosophy. Hence we have to withdraw further from the concept "the philosophy of Marx and Engels as founders of Marxism" back to the more rigorous concept "Marx's philosophy." Of course, when we analyze deeply the concept of "Marx's philosophy," we find out that its meaning isn't clear yet, because it is able to include not only "young Marx's philosophy", but also "mature Marx's philosophy." Obviously, "young Marx's philosophy" is quite different from "mature Marx's philosophy." So I believe that the exact object of our study here isn't "Marxist philosophy," but "mature Marx's philosophy."[1]

What is his special thinking way as Marx does philosophy? Man would like to substitute the thinking way of traditional philosophy for Marx's special thinking way. However, Marx's thinking way is the one of the economic philosophy quite different from the traditional philosophy. In fact, philosophical visions link closely economic questions in Marx's writings and manuscripts. For example, the traditional philosophy often talks about abstract matter, while Marx's philosophy talks about concrete existing forms

---

[1]   Yu Wujin, "A Consideration of Marx's Thought Using the Method of Analysis of Difference," see *Philosophical Trends (Monthly)*, no. 12, 2004.

of matter, i. e. , things which are commodities having using value and exchange value in the modern bourgeois society. Similarly, the traditional philosophy talks about praxis or action, while Marx's philosophy talks about the fundamental form of praxis or action, i. e. , productive labor as one of human economic activities. Additionally, the traditional philosophy talks about the general relationship among entities, while Marx's philosophy talks about the basic form of all relationship, i. e. the social productive relationship in human economic activities. So we may say that the thinking way of Marx's philosophy, particularly mature Marx's philosophy, is completely an economic philosophy. Only after understanding this situation, we can exactly recognize the essence of mature Marx's philosophy from ontological vision. ①

What type of ontology should be chosen as man narrates mature Marx's philosophy? It is well known that ontology has various types, such as ontology of cosmogony、ontology of reason、ontology of matter、ontology of emotion、existentialistic ontology and so on. I believe that mature Marx's philosophy ought to be narrated as an existentialistic ontology, because Marx is always concerned about existence, development and freedom of the whole human being, particularly of proletariat life in the lowest level of modern bourgeois society. In this sense, only if man reads Marx's writings from the standpoint of existentialistic ontology, he can understand and explain mature Marx's philosophy rationally. ②

Based on the above three premises, I put forward the following new

---

① Yu Wujin, "Thing, Value, Time and Freedom: A Consideration of Some Key Concepts in Marx's Philosophical System, " see *Frontiers of Philosophy in China*, vol. 1, 2006, pp. 114-123.

② Yu Wujin, "From the traditional Theory of knowledge to Existential Theory of Praxis, " see *Journal of Literature*, no. 2, 2004, pp. 12-14.

idea that mature Marx's philosophy is an ontology of praxis-social relations of production. In my opinion, this theory of ontology has two different dimensions. Seeing from the field of sensitive phenomenon, mature Marx's philosophy is an ontology of praxis and praxis forms the starting point and the core of all other phenomena when mature Marx makes researches on any philosophical questions. Because mature Marx introduces the concept "praxis" as basis of all other sensitive observations into his philosophy, thus his ontological theory is quite different from traditional ones. However, the philosophical investigation of mature Marx should not stop on the level of praxis, putting forward further from the perspective of economic philosophy that the most fundamental form of praxis is productive labor which comes into being only in definite social relations of production. So seeing from the field of essence, the mature Marx's philosophy is also "an ontology of social relations of production." If praxis and productive labor belong to the field of sensitive phenomenon, hence they are visible, then social relations of production belong to the field of essence, hence it is invisible and it can be recognized only through thinking. In this sense, we can say that only if man understands the mature Marx's philosophy as the ontology of praxis-social relations of production, it is possible for Marx's whole theoretical figure to be not damaged.

First of all, the term "praxis-social relations of production" has its own theoretical rationality. Because not only productive labor is a basic form of human practical activities, but also other forms always have to appear in a definite social relation of production and have to be controlled by the latter. Of course, no social relations of production is unchangeable. Rather, these relations are changeable either slowly or radically. Without doubt, the changes of quality always appear together with great historical events. However, each generation deals with, in general, theoretical and practical activities in a background formed by definite social relations of production which isn't able to be chosen by anybody. That is to say, only if man grasps social relations of production deeply, it is possible for him to interpret cause, result and limit of praxis rationally.

Second, "the ontology of praxis-social relations of production" shows this process human consciousness develops from phenomenon (sensible field of praxis) to essence (beyond sensible field) in order to offer us a whole theoretical figure of Marx's epistemology.

Third, "the ontology of praxis-social relations of production" also includes the fact that Marx's philosophy has an integrated methodology which relates to a special dialectic from abstract to concrete. According to Marx's point of view, if man investigates human society only on the level of praxis, then it is difficult for him to grasp its essential field, whether or no, he can only describe various sensational phenomena he has observed.

Contemporary Meaning of the ontology of Praxis
—Social Relations of Production

In the first place, the concept of the ontology of praxis-social relations of production shows exactly position, function and limit of praxis in Marx's philosophy, transcending the traditional ontology of matter. On one side, the concept of praxis plays a fundamental role in Marx's theory of ontology and it has not only the meaning of epistemology and methodology, also the meaning of ontology. In effect, the latter meaning is more important than the former, because it relates to the basis of Marx's philosophy. On the other side, we have to pay attention to the fact that the concept of praxis has its own limit, because it is only concerned in sensational experience and it can't replace Marx's thinking in the beyond sensible, essential field. ① In fact, it is very difficult for man to separate his own thought from positivists and pragmatists when he tries to understand Marx's philosophy rationally, only stopping on the level of praxis. Obviously, only if man isn't satisfied with explaining Marx's philosophy only using the concept of praxis, but is going to spread his own thinking to the essential level of social relations of production, it is possible for Marx's whole theoretical figure to be grasped completely.

In the next place, the concept of the ontology of praxis-social relations of production transcends either Lukacs' theory of ontology of social being or Colletti's Theory of social relations of production. If Lukacs is only satisfied with understanding Marx's philosophy as an ontology of social being, not arriving at the following conclusion that the central content of social being should be social relations of production, then Colletti recognizes the important meaning of social relations of production in Marx's philosophy. He writes:

Marxism is not epistemology, at least in any fundamental sense in Marx's work *Widerspiegelungstheorie* as such has little importance. Nonetheless, it is important to take epistemology as one's point of departure, in order to understand how a concept like the "social relations of production", so original and also so foreign to the entire speculative tradition, could be born out of the development and transformation of the very problems of classical philosophy. ②

---

① Mrax says: bei der Analyse der oekonomischen Formen kann ausserdem weder das Mikroskop dienen noch chemische Reagentien. Die Abstrakttionskraft muss beide ersetzen. See Marx and Engels, *Werke*, vol. 23 (Berlin: Dietz Verlag, 1973), S. 12.

② Lucio Colletti, *Marxism and Hegel* (London: NLB, 1973), p. 199.

He also points out: "Historical materialism reaches its point of culmination in the concept of "social relations of production". This concept, in turn, had its first and decisive elaboration in the 1844 *Manuscripts*, in the form of the concept of man as a "generic natural being". What remains is the task of attempting the analysis of this concept. ①

Although Colletti makes comments on Marx's theory of social relations of production highly, as a positivist, he refuses to talk about any theory of ontology, hence he never expresses the real meaning of Marx's philosophical revolution.

In the last place, with the help of the concept of social relations of production, we arrive at a new integrated understanding of the essence of Marx's philosophy. On one side, the concept of praxis forms the starting point of Marx's philosophy, but Marx's philosophy shouldn't be reduced to practical philosophy or philosophy of praxis, because it isn't a theory of phenomenalism or positivism, but it has more important content. On the other side, although the great achievement of Marx's philosophy lies in the fact that he has found out social relations of production as the core of social being, but Marx's philosophy can't also be reduced to a theory of metaphysics or transcendentalism. Only if the concept of praxis is understood as a fundamental concept in Marx's philosophy, Marx's ontology may be understood wholly.

In a word, mature Marx's philosophy is the ontology of praxis—relations of production and it transcends either abstract "ontology of matter" and "ontology of praxis" which stops on the level of sensitive phenomenon, or so called "ontology of social being" which doesn't clarify what is social being and what is the basis and core of social being. In fact, Marx's phi-

---

① Lucio Colletti, *Marxism and Hegel* (London: NLB, 1973), pp. 233-234.

losophy synthesizes two fields of phenomenon and essence, thus it is reasonable for Marx's philosophy to be called the ontology of praxis——relations of production.

3.6 A Declaration of the Aesthetics of Comedy[①]

Problem-oriented studies are of extreme importance in philosophical studies. There would be no philosophical explorations in the real sense of the term without them. However, more important than problem-oriented studies are the credos those who ask questions already have in their minds. People's credos shape their mode of thinking and this in turn frames the field where they find problems, and determines the mode and direction of the questions they ask. In this sense, people who have never carefully reflected on their own credos and mode of thinking would be the last to find new problems and ask new questions. It is, therefore, important to make careful examinations of the mode of thinking where problems arise, as well as the credos that provide the foundation for these modes of thinking, rather discussing problems and problem-oriented studies in general

---

① Editor's note: This paper was originally published in *Social Sciences in China*, no. 1, 2007, pp. 119-125, translated by Huang Jue from *Zhongguo Shehui Kexue* (《中国社会科学》), no. 5, 2006, pp. 23-27, revised by Sally Borthwick.

terms. As Wittgenstein pointed out, "if we clothe ourselves in a new form of expression, the old problems are discarded with the old garment."① This may be the best starting point for us to analyze the fields of aesthetics as a branch of philosophy.

Studies of aesthetics appear lively in current China, with contending ideas and prolonged debates. Researchers seem tireless in exploring important aesthetic questions. However, a careful look may reveal that there is no substantial progress in discussions that consist of nothing more than old ideas and new jargon. It is also interesting to note that theatre, particularly comedy, remains marginal in the aesthetic field of vision of contemporary Chinese. Starting from the conscious sense of existence of people today, this article is meant to raise questions about aesthetics from a new perspective, and particularly to show the new direction of aesthetic studies by revealing universal and substantial elements that stimulate and intrigue thinking in the art of comedy. These elements are, we believe, antidotes to the emptiness and hollowness in current aesthetic studies in China, and catalysts for originality and creativity in the aesthetic process. In a word, aesthetic questions are raised in a new way, and the aesthetics of comedy is taken as a new direction that will guide the development of aesthetics.

1

An undeniable fact about aesthetic studies in China today is that no matter what school or "-logy" researchers consider their views belong to,

---

① Ludwig Wittgenstein, *Culture and Value* (Chicago: University of Chicago Press, 1984), p. 48.

and no matter how they exaggerate the differences or conflicts among them, there are actually no different schools or theories in the field. All discourse comes from the same source of epistemological philosophy.

Epistemological philosophy, with the essence of things as its focal concern, generalizes from daily life the following way of asking questions: What is this? In introspective mode, the question turns to "What is philosophy?" and in aesthetic studies to "What is beauty?" In fact, when Chinese researchers into aesthetics unanimously take "What is beauty?" as the ultimate question aesthetics is supposed to answer, they have chosen, consciously or unconsciously, the same stance of epistemological philosophy. As it gradually departs from examining the existence of those who ask questions, such an epistemological philosophical way of asking questions is finally reduced to a baseless questioning for the mere purpose of knowledge. Even though such a way of asking questions remains meaningful after the raison d'être of aesthetics has been reasonably acknowledged, aesthetic research will definitely lose its existential foundation and historical context, and be degraded into a pale appeal to the vulgar, if it limits itself to such a baseless and empty way of raising questions. Anyone with insight will not deny that aesthetics has developed into a branch of science on its own because it has irreplaceable significance in man's activities for survival. Therefore, a more fundamental question in aesthetic studies is "Why do human beings need beauty?" rather than "What is beauty?" Answers to the latter can gain an existential foundation and find their way into historical context only when the former has been thoroughly understood. ①

The perspective of existentialism has drawn some attention from aesthetic researchers in recent years. However, still blindly stressing tragedy as the only worthy art form, they have not yet to go beyond the limits of epistemological philosophy in the recesses of their minds. As the ideals of tragic heroes are usually the highest values in epistemological philosophy, a departure from epistemological philosophical conventions will be impossible as long as such ideals are affirmed, pursued and magnified as abstract goals separated from man's survival activities and historicality. ②

Ideals are the soul of tragedy: the tragic hero endeavors to realize a certain ideal out of his strong sense of mission, but fails because of personality flaws or contingency. As Aristotle stresses in *Poetics*, tragedy aims to inspire pity in the audience through fear, in order to purge their hearts and lift them to a higher spiritual sphere. However, research shows two types of tragedy. One may be called "healthy tragedy," where the goal of the hero is realistic, such as that of Hamlet. Hamlet's goal is to avenge

---

① The Chinese character indicating "beauty" (美) consists of two parts, one part is the character for sheep" (羊), the other the character for "large" (大). Sheep were a major source of food in ancient China, so a large sheep meant beauty. The composition of the character for "beauty" reflects a close inter-relationship between man's conditions of existence and his aesthetic ideas. Kantian aesthetics fails to study how aesthetic subjects perceive their conditions of existence and bring their conscious sense of existence into their aesthetic activities. As a result, it reveals neither the life energy and value orientation of aesthetic subjects, nor the stamp of different historical periods on man's aesthetic activities.

② A common phenomenon in China's philosophical and aesthetics community is that researchers indulge in studies of Western existentialism, particularly Heidegger's. They talk passionately about the "value of life" and the "meaning of existence." At the same time, they show great indifference to various real-life phenomena that disregard life, such as the unending coalmining accidents, serious traffic accidents, trafficking of women and children, loss of life and physical trauma caused by poor-quality products, cruel killing of animals and so forth. They seem to indulge in the metaphysical concepts of "life," "existence" and "value" solely for the purpose of averting their eyes from this type of phenomenon in real life.

and kill his uncle who usurped the throne from his father. However, his indecisiveness prevents him from reaching his goal, and hence comes the tragedy. The other type may be labeled "unhealthy tragedy," as the goal of the hero is impossible to realize no matter what he/she does, such as in some "model dramas" (*Yangbanxi*) during China's Cultural Revolution. In those dramas, the heroes cherish an unrealistic goal of being completely altruistic. Instead of portraying the hero as real and close to life, such an ideal makes the hero unnatural and lifeless. Despite its apparent seriousness, such unhealthy comedy is ridiculous in nature, and is nothing more than a farce.

As is widely understood, man is a being with purpose, for whom reasonable ideals are indispensable. In this sense, tragedy as an art form will exist for a long time. However, the current priority is to shift the dominant aesthetic perspective from tragedy to comedy. This provides an important opportunity for the renaissance of human life and the art of aesthetics. ① A fundamental transcendence over the tradition of epistemological philosophy will be possible only when such a shift toward the aesthetics of comedy is realized and aesthetics is established on the basis of existentialist philosophy, as it is the goal of comedy to deconstruct the ideals that are excessively magnified in unhealthy tragedy. Once such anti-life, anti-passion and illusory ideals are deconstructed, ease, humor and laughter will return to human life and aesthetic activities, and the most natural possibilities of contemporary existence may be reasonably presented.

---

① Nietzsche rediscovered the art of tragedy. However, when he related this art form to his "superman" and overstressed the importance of this form of art, he actually fell into the trap of epistemological philosophy that he had always criticized. Indeed, innumerable events in his time showed that unhealthy tragedy should be rejected and the art of comedy should be encouraged.

2

The first question we need to answer is: Why is a conscious shift to the aesthetics of comedy necessary from the perspective of contemporary existentialism? The answer is simple: because comedy as a special form of art cherishes a spirit that provides significant inspiration for people today to improve their conditions of existence. As Hegel argued longtime ago, "comedy has for its basis and starting-pointing what tragedy may end with, namely an absolutely reconciled and cheerful heart. Even if its possessor destroys by the means he uses whatever he wills and so comes to grief in himself because by his own efforts he has accomplished the very opposite of what he aimed at, he still has not lost his peace of mind on that account."[1] Hegel sees comedy, an art form that took shape at a later date than tragedy, as transcendence over tragedy. It is in this sense that he affirms that "comedy has for its basis and starting-point what tragedy may end with."

How does comedy attain the "absolutely reconciled and cheerful heart" in its transcendence over tragedy? According to Hegel, "this subjective self-assurance is only possible if the aims, and so with them the characters in question, either have no real substance in themselves or, if they have, then their essentiality has been made an aim and been pursued in a shape really opposed to it fundamentally and therefore in a shape without substance; and the result is that it is always only what is inherently

---

[1] G. W. F. Hegel, *Asthetic*, vol. 3-2, trans. Zhuang Guanqian (Beijing: The Commercial Press, 1981), p. 315.

null and in different that comes to grief, and the individual remains firm on his feet and undisturbed. "① As discussed above, while tragedy starts from an ideal of the hero that is to be realized, comedy starts from deconstruction of such ideals, seeing them as insubstantial and unimportant. When the ideal that guides the actions of the hero ceases to be substantial, the hero's state of mind changes from seriousness to relaxation. It is in this regard that Hegel states, "this seriousness always carries with it, in the eyes of the individual himself, its own destruction. "② Cheerfulness comes once tension and conflicts arising from tension disappear.

It must be pointed out that there are two types of comedy, too. One type may be labeled "healthy comedy"; it contains profound and thought-provoking elements, rather than lingering over trivial details of daily life. *Le Tartuffe ou L'Imposteur* by Molière is a good example of this type, offering a profound criticism of religiosity and the entire church. The other type, with vulgar themes, poorly written lines, forced artifice and obtrusive jokes, but with no real significance, may be labeled "unhealthy comedy." Some low-grade, vulgar farces, local folklore and folksongs, *xiang sheng*-talk shows and *er ren zhuan* (a traditional performance popular mainly in the Northeast China) performances often provide misleading and crude interpretations of the comic. Obviously, healthy comedy and percep-

---

① G. W. F. Hegel, *Asthetic*, vol. 3-2, trans. Zhuang Guanqian (Beijing: The Commercial Press, 1981), pp. 315-316.

② G. W. F. Hegel, *Asthetic*, vol. 3-2, trans. Zhuang Guanqian (Beijing: The Commercial Press, 1981), p. 316. in "Comments on the Latest Prussian Censorship Instruction," Marx also quoted Tristram Shandy's definition of seriousness as "hypocritical behavior of the body in order to conceal defects of the soul." Cf. *Collected Works of Marx and Engels*, vol. 1 (Beijing: People's Publishing House, 1956), p. 8.

tions of healthy comedy are the prerequisite of this discussion. ①

One may ask: How can recognition and advocacy of the aesthetics of comedy enable people today to improve their conditions of existence? This is because people today are living in a world of rapid global expansion of capital and technological development, where the relationship between human beings and between man and things, as well as man and his environment, is becoming ever more alienated. Man has produced things and relationships that have become obstacles on his path to full development. People today live with ever more pressure, tension and conflicts, both physically and psychologically. In such severe conditions of existence they will only fall deeper into alienation, tension and conflict if they continue to follow the Nietzschean superman and the spirit of tragedy that sings the praises of heroes' will to power, ideals and values.

The ease, jocularity, humor and cheerfulness in comedy, on the contrary, provide an effective cure for our age. After the end of the Cold War in the 1980s, the West raised the cry of "the end of ideology." With it have come other declarations such as "the end of philosophy," "the end of art," "the end of science," "the end of history," "the end of grand narrative" and so forth. The US philosopher of science Paul Karl Feyerabend's famous line, "Anything goes," reveals the truth of the philosophy of science as well as the entire intellectual culture of human beings. It reveals the meaninglessness of opposition or confrontation with regard to ideology and other conceptual aspects that have been taken so seriously and been so

---

① It is interesting to note that Rousseau, rather than categorizing comedy, provided a general negation of this art form (including the comedies of Molière): since the entertainments that comedy offers take man's moral defects as their foundation, the more successful and fascinating they are, the more they corrupt our morality. Cf. Jean-Jacques Rousseau, *Letter to M. D'Alembert on Spectacles*, trans. Wang Ziye (Shanghai: SDX Joint Publishing Company, 1991), p. 43.

exaggerated. In China, the "hooligan literature" led by Wang Shuo, *Fortress Besieged* by Qian Zhongshu, the soap opera *Stories in the Editorial Office*, and various parodies of history have gained great popularity, which also implies the de facto deconstruction of the grand narratives of impractical ideals that provide the foundation for the aesthetics of tragedy. Since impractical ideals have ceased to have substantive meanings, tragedy as an art has been marginalized. In other words, there comes a time when the aesthetics of comedy takes the lead, an era that may be labeled "post-aesthetics" or "aesthetics of comedy." In a sense, only those who have a profound understanding of this turn in the development of the spirit of the times can gain a real understanding of the historicity of aesthetic consciousness.

3

Discussions of the historical context of the rising aesthetics of comedy must be followed by further exploration of this new concept.

In the first place, as was mentioned above, comedy is transcendence over tragedy, according to Hegel. It must be noted, however, that by transcendence is meant sublimation of one art form over another. This does not in the least mean that man no longer needs the tragic and the art of tragedy. As a matter of fact, the tragic and tragedy as an art form will live on as long as human beings exist, since human beings must have ideals. However, such ideals should not be blown up excessively to the extent that they grow into a force lethal to life. Milan Kundera sees the worship of tragedy as more dangerous than childish nonsense. The eternal prerequisite of tragedy, he points out, lies in the existence of ideals that are more precious than human life. That is also the cause of wars. It forces you to die, because there is something more important than life itself. War only exists in the world of tragedy, and man has known only this world of tragedy for as long as anyone can remember. He can't move even one step out of this world. The only way to end this era of tragedy is to make a frivolous break from it. There will be a day when tragedy will be seen off from the world stage like a hoarse and tremulous old actor. Cheerfulness and relaxation are the best diet for losing weight. Things will lose ninety percent of their weight and become ethereal. There will be no war in this burdenless world as blind obedience and fanaticism will disappear.① We may disagree with Kundera on his total negation of the art of tragedy, or his simplistic views on war, but he did offer, from a certain perspective, a profound insight into the negative elements in tragedy. Should such negative elements be blown up and disseminated in daily life, they would be likely to cause a series of real life tragic events. Human history is to a large extent one that displays this possibility.

Secondly, in our term "aesthetics of comedy," comedy refers to healthy comedy in particular, and in general, to all works of art and literature that take the comic as their main principle. We advocate an aesthetics of comedy that focuses on art and literary works and aesthetic theories that take the comic as their core. Unfortunately, the comic, in either the narrow or the broad sense of the word, has not received adequate attention. Serious research should be made of this precious and rich intellectual resource by means of in-depth studies of artistic and literary works home and abroad, taking our own historicity as a starting point. We believe that

---

① Milan Kundera, *L'immortalité*, trans. Ning Min (Beijing: Writers' Publishing House, 1993), p. 119.

research that takes the comic and the aesthetics of comedy as its core will, once established, change the path that has been adopted by all aesthetic studies till now.

Finally, the core content of the aesthetics of comedy is to relieve the tension between subject and object, ideal and reality, self and others, as well as the individual and society, by means of the comic. The alienation prevailing in our current societies intensifies tension and causes various conflicts. It is the objective of the aesthetics of comedy, through parody and deconstruction of the "great ideals" and "grand narratives," to restore human beings, things and ideals back in their original state, and let them be what they are. What then is the comic? According to Hegel, "what is comical… is a personality or subject who makes his own actions contradictory and so brings them to nothing, while remaining tranquil and self-assured in the process."[①] To put Hegel's words in plain and simple language, the comic is nothing more than the thought-provoking element shared by contending phenomena such as ugliness, absurdity, jocularity, exaggeration, the unnatural, wit, humor and ridicule. By the sudden deconstruction and loss of the expected goals and meanings, and the contradictory actions of fictional characters, this element reveals to the audience the truth of human beings, things and ideals, eliciting understanding smiles. As they smile, the audience feels an easiness and pleasure they did not have before. If tragedy points to depression, frustration and the force of death, comedy points to easiness, cheerfulness and indomitable life, as it breaks the barriers of illusory ideals and notions, and restores the original, daily meanings of human beings, things and ideals, bringing them

---

① G. W. F. Hegel, *Asthetic*, vol. 3-2, trans. Zhuang Guanqian (Beijing: The Commercial Press, 1981), p. 315.

back to their multiplicity and diversity. If tragedy seeks to elevate the ideas of ordinary people to "a noble spirit," comedy eases the fever and brings them back to the ideas of ordinary people. No one doubts that a cup of water is worth nothing more than a cup of water, and grass is worth nothing more than grass. Why do we have to over-value them? When the light is magnified into the weighty, the only result is that the weighty becomes light. Everything will lose its weight as if in outer space, or in a bubble. Comedy will sooner or later take the place of tragedy as the dominating form of contemporary aesthetics. That is a logical result of the development of tragedy. The overly serious becomes funny; universal weightiness leads to light-heartedness; bigoted seriousness becomes wit; and inappropriate exaggeration results in humor. Aren't these truths that the world of life shows us daily?

Having considered all the above, we believe that the aesthetics of comedy is an important direction for the future development of aesthetic studies. Therefore, in-depth studies are needed of all artistic and literary works that take the comic as their keynote. We should draw from the repertoire of comic art from Aristophanes in the West and the Tang and Song Dynasties in China, to open up new directions for development and new questions for aesthetic studies.

3.7 The Absence and Reconstruction of Enlightenment[①]

—Thinking on the Construction of Chinese Culture Today

The psychological endurance for cultures bears essential significance to contemporary Chinese people. On the one hand, they have to take in a variety of new phenomena and new ideas springing up from their rapidly changing surroundings, and adapt to them. On the other hand, they must reflect seriously upon the momentous ideological and cultural events that the western society, especially the European society, has experienced, and summarize them. The concept "Enlightenment" we are discussing today is such a crucial topic that it cannot be evaded, when it comes to the construction of the present-day Chinese culture.

---

① Editor's note: This paper was translated by Kong Hui, Master student in School of Philosophy, Fudan University, from *Shanghai Shifan Daxue Xuebao (Zhexue Shehui Kexue)*, vol. 39, no. 4, 2010, pp. 5-13.

The Comparative Study and Enlightenment as the Theme

It is well-known that the Enlightenment arose in Europe during the 18th century. Needless to say, the topic Enlightenment, when spoken of by the contemporary Chinese people, implies a comparison to be made between Chinese and Western cultures. The comparative study has been in anarchy ever since a long time ago, so much so that any researcher could make a comparison between two minds merely by arbitrarily selecting one from the Chinese culture, say Chuang-tzu, and the other from the West, like Heidegger. In fact, comparisons of this kind just pay attention to the surface to the similarities that objects share "in appearance", without any regard to whether they have something in common "in spirit" by the essence of their thoughts. From my point of view, an approach to breaking this "state of anarchism", so that the comparative study could develop into a science, is to introduce a new type of concept of time.

In my opinion, there are two distinct types of concept of time operating in the comparative study of Chinese and Western cultures: one is the type of "chronological time". According to this concept of time, what goes on in China on April the 29th, 2009 should be "contemporary" with that of in Europe; the other is "morphological time". As we all know, morphology is a branch of biology, specializing in the shape and structure of animals and plants, as well as their components. Morphological time can be further subdivided into two types as the following:

One is morphological time in the sense of biology, initiated by Spengler the German philosopher of history. In his book *The Decline of the West*, he illustrated in the tables of "parallel columns of culture" the four cultural patterns as Egyptian, Classical, Western, and Arabic, each of which went through the phases of evolution as pre-culture, culture and civilization. In his view, only by the same phase, could different cultural patterns be compared. This kind of morphological time was inherited by the British philosopher of history Toynbee.

The other is morphological time in the sense of sociology, which was originated by Karl Marx. He brought forward the famous theory of "three general social forms". The first form of society lay in the dependence of human upon nature; the second, the dependence of human upon things, and a development of a free personality, as the third. With regard to this concept, China today is of the second form. In this sense, China at present can be said as "contemporary" in the cultural mentality with European society from the 16th to 19th century. ①

From my viewpoint, to develop the comparative study of cultures into a science requires it to be carried out on the basis of the concept "contemporary" implied in "morphological time in the sense of sociology", which was advocated by Karl Marx. As spoken previously, since the Enlightenment of Europe took place in the 18th century, while China today, on the part of "morphological time in the sense of sociology", is "contemporary" with the European society of 16th to 19th, it follows that, Enlightenment is exactly a theme of the Chinese society nowadays. When introducing the concept of morphological time, of course, we do not mean to deny the concept of chronological time, as after all, we physically, as well as some certain ideas, belong to the 21st century. In other words, the concept of chronological time also has an effect on our cultural mentality. However,

----

① Refer to another paper of mine: "The Comparative Study on Cultures and the Morphological Time in the sense of Sociology," in Yu Wujin, *The Pursuit of a New Coordinate of Value* (Shanghai: Fudan University Press, 1995), pp. 382-389.

we have to appeal to the concept of morphological time, when trying to thoroughly grasp the cultural mentality of the contemporary Chinese people, especially their deeper cultural mentality.

Next, we turn to the meaning of the concept "Enlightenment" and its leading spiritual elements implied in that movement. Etymologically, the verb "enlighten" has its original meaning of "to light", with a derivative meaning of the inspiration and illumination to the spirit. The Allegory of the Cave by Plato, the Idol of the Cave by Francis Bacon, the metaphor of the Dark Room by Lu Xun all imply that one should break away from darkness, and embrace the illumination and guidance of brightness. The German philosopher Immanuel Kant proposed in *What is Enlightenment?* (1784) that

> *Enlightenment is man's emergence from his self-imposed immaturity. Immaturity is the inability to use one's understanding without guidance from another. This immaturity is self-imposed when its cause lies not in lack of understanding, but in lack of resolve and courage to use it without guidance from another. Sapere Aude! 'Have courage to use your own understanding!'——that is the motto of enlightenment.* ①

Enlightenment is often explained with these words put down by Kant, while the fact is that as it was said by the contemporary French philosopher Michel Foucault, when he mentioned that essay of Kant's in his article "What is Enlightenment?" (1984) that,

---

① Immanuel Kant, *Perpetual Peace, and Other Essays on Politics, History, and Moral Practice*, trans. Ted Humphrey (Indianapolis and Cambridge: Hackett Publishing Company, 1983), p. 41.

I do not by any means propose to consider it as capable of consti-tuting an adequate description of Enlightenment; and no historian, I think, could be satisfied with it for an analysis of the social, politi-cal, and cultural transformations that occurred at the end of the eighteenth century. ①

Howsoever, being concerned on the theme of his time, Kant interpreted Enlightenment as a spiritual movement of man's emergence from his self-imposed immaturity, which also expressed the core of it.

As a noun, "the Enlightenment" basically refers to an intellectual movement that happened in Europe, particularly in France during the 18th century, while as a derivative meaning, it denotes all the liberation of spir-it and thought.

Taking the ideas of Kant's and other enlightenment scholars' togeth-er, we could find that there are mainly four idealized leading principles of Enlightenment:

First, reason as the court. During the long night of the Middle Ages, the Europeans had been lulled to sleep by the Christian faith. With the rise and development of modern science, the reason for sleeping within men was awaked little by little. Consciously taking reason as its supreme prin-ciple, Enlightenment not only encouraged individuals to think independent-ly, but also claimed that the whole society should take the reason, rather

---

① Du Xiaozhen edit, *Foucault's Works*, (Shanghai: Shanghai Far East Press, 1998), p. 532. Translation referred to: Michel Foucault, "What is Enlightenment?" in P. Rabinow ed., *The Foucault Reader* (New York: Pantheon Books, 1984), pp. 32-50.
(Source: http://foucault. info/documents/whatIsEnlightenment/foucault. whatIsEnlighten-ment. en. html)

than the faith, as the standard of a judgment from right to wrong. Thus, "the court of reason" came into being, and the authority of reason was set up at least in people's minds. Galileo the Italian scientist was allegedly imprisoned by the Inquisition, because of his advocacy of Copernicus' "heliocentric theory." He was compelled to swear by the *Holy Bible* to renounce heliocentricism, but with his mind occupied by reason, he still muttered: "And yet it (the earth) moves." By the same token, the Italian scientist Bruno was burned alive at the stake in the Campo de' Fiori, a central square in Rome, because he defended, on the basis of reason, Copernicus' and Galileo's heliocentricism, and thus firmly rejected bending to the Church's doctrines of faith. Likewise, the Spanish scientist Servetus' defense for the truth about blood circulation which was found by his reason, led to his sentence to being burned at stake in Geneva, by order of Calvin, a leader of Reformation.

Great minds of Enlightenment in France were devoted to an intense critique on the Church's faith during the 18th century. When talking of the stake executed upon heretic or heresy by the Inquisition in *Théologie Portative*, Holbach wrote down these lines in a mocking tone:

> *(The Inquisition's sentence, the stake) is a delicacy occasionally served to God. It is roasted* ceremoniously *with the flesh of the heretic and the Jews, with a purpose of securing a salvation of their souls, while teaching the onlookers a lesson as well. Needless to say,*

merciful Father always has a partiality for this dish. ①

Holbach then exposed the nature of religion—the elimination of reason:

> *For a rational being, there is nothing ever more harmful than*
> *reason. God gives reason to whom he is destined to suffer an after-*
> *life punishment; to whom God will save or whom God will allow to*
> *be in favor of the Church, God kindly deprives his reason. Beat rea-*
> *son down! This is the foundation of religion.* ②

Another Enlightenment French scholar Diderot said:

> *If reason is a gift from heaven, and the same thing can be said*
> *of faith, then heaven has given us two* incompatible *and contradicto-*
> *ry presents.* ③

---

① Holbach: *Théologie Portative*, trans. Shan Zhicheng (Beijing: The Commercial Press, 1996), p. 20. The British scholar Gibbon mentioned in Chapter 47 in his book *The History of the Decline and Fall of the Roman Empire*, a lady who "adhered to the Neoplatonic philosophy and devoted her talents to mathematics. She was 'torn form her chariot, stripped naked, dragged to the church, and inhumanly butchered by the hands of Peter the Reader and a troop of savage and merciless fanatics: her flesh was scraped from her bones with sharp oyster-shells ad her quivering limbs were delivered to the flames. The just progress of inquiry and punishment was stopped by seasonable gifts'." Referred to Bertrand Russell, *A History of Western Philosophy* (New York: Simon and Schuster, 1945), p. 368. And in his book *The Right to Heresy: Castellio against Calvin*, Zweig made a description on how Servetus the Spanish scientist was burned at stake in Geneva by order of Calvin. Referred to: Zweig, *The Right to Heresy*, trans. Zhao Tai'an (Beijing: Sanlian Bookstore, 1986), p. 143.

② Holbach, *Théologie Portative*, trans. Shan Zhicheng (Beijing: The Commercial Press, 1996), p. 58.

③ Diderot, *Diderot Selected Works*, trans. Chen Xiuzhai (Beijing: Sanlian Bookstore, 1956), p. 36. Translation referred to: Diderot, *Thoughts on Religion* (Addition to the "*Philosophical Thoughts*"), Source: Oeuvres Complètes, vol. 1 (Paris: Garnier Fréres, 1875), trans. Mitchell Abidor, Creative Commons (Attribute & ShareAlike) marxists. org 2005, revised 2008.

(Source: http://www. marxists. org/reference/archive/diderot/1770/religion. htm)

And he continued with these words:

> *Lost in an immense forest during the night I only have a small*
> *light to guide me. An unknown man appears and* says *to me: "My*
> *friend, blow out your candle so you can better find your way." This*
> *unknown man is a theologian.* ①

Critiques on religious superstition from Enlightenment scholars freed Europeans' minds immensely. After the publication of *The System of the World* in 1796, Laplace the French scientist was questioned by Napoleon why his work on the universe did not have any mention of the world's Creator, and he replied:

> *I had no* need *of this hypothesis, Your Majesty.* ②

All of these suffice to show that, by the end of the 18th century, the authority of reason as the court had been fully acknowledged.

Second, the disenchantment of the world. The concept "disenchantment" (Entzauberung), initiated by Max Weber the German sociologist, indicates an emergence from ideas of mysticism, especially from "the city of God" which was built and sanctified by the religion (it is also the title of a work by Augustine, a philosopher known as "Father of the Church"), and as well as a review on everything from man's perspective instead of

---

① Diderot, *Diderot Selected Works*, trans. Chen Xiuzhai (Beijing: Sanlian Bookstore, 1956), p. 36.

② W. C. Dampier, *A History of Science*, trans. Li Heng (Beijing: The Commercial Press, 1979), p. 259.

God's, that is, to return to a secularized real life which is based on human nature. As is known to everyone, as early as in the Renaissance, the Italian scholar Boccaccio wrote in *Decameron* many readable and popular tales about disenchantment. For example, a pious Christian gave away all his possessions to the church after the death of his wife, and took his son with him to the top of a mountain for a devoted service of God, while breaking off his boy's connection with any other people. One day when the son reached manhood, his father took him down the mountain into the city for alms. He got excited when seeing young women, while his father explained to him: these young women were young geese, a kind of wicked thing. Back to the mountain, the son still could not get these young geese out of his mind. This suggests that not only could human nature and native desires be changed by the asceticism sanctified by Christianity, but also the more oppressed they get, the stronger they become.

In the Enlightenment, "disenchantment", to a broader extent, became the theme of the spiritual movement. This significant theme ran through the book *The Persian Letters* by the French scholar Montesquieu: a Persian nobleman named Roxana, as paying a visit to Europe, left his harem at home in the charge of eunuchs. Under the torture of desires, wives tried all means to keep a tryst with their lovers. When Roxana, Usbsk's favorite wife was having a tryst, her lover was caught and killed by the eunuchs, so she poisoned all the eunuchs to get even. Before she killed herself with poison, she wrote a letter to Usbek saying:

I have lived *in slavery, but I have always been free. I reformed your laws by those of nature, and my spirit has always held to its* independence. ①

The Persian Letters manifests that no mystic or sanctified constraint could ever restrain the natural and worldly human desires. Taine conceived the idea in *A Philosophy of Art* that the Olympian gods was no more than the sanctification of a secular family. This was a profound revelation to us that all the sanctified things were the products of the alienation of secular things. By the 19th century, there had been two products resulted from the disenchantment in Enlightenment: for one thing, the French novelist Balzac fully showed, through his book *The Human Comedy*, a panorama of the secular capitalist society; for another, all the secrets of God and Christian Theology were brought to light by the German philosopher Feuerbach in *The essence of Christianity* (1841). He told us that God was the product of the alienation of human nature, thus the essence of theology was an anthropological one.

Third, the pursuit of equality. The political dimension of the Enlightenment showed itself in its rejection to hierarchy and privilege institutions, and also in its dream and pursuit of a Democratic Republic of the bourgeois on the basis of equality. As early as the Italian scholar Machiavelli, the Dutch scholar Grotius, and the British scholar Hobbes, they began to look upon the worldly political arrangements from the perspective of man's instead of God's, while the European social-political institutions and state system had thrown off the mysterious veil. In the 18th century, the Enlightenment French thinker Rousseau, in *The Origin of Human Inequality* (1755), made an analysis on two kinds of inequality existing in the

---

① Montesquieu, *The Persian Letters*, trans. George R. Healy (Indianapolis and Cambridge: Hackett Publishing Company, 1964), p. 272.

human society: one is natural or physical inequality; the other is mental or political. He attacked the latter, directly pointing the finger at monarchy and hierarchy in France, thereby having the French Revolution armed with spiritual forces. It just went like what the German poet Heine said in his long article "On the History of Religion and Philosophy in Germany":

> *Mark this, ye proud men of action: ye are nothing but uncon-*
> *scious hodmen of the men of thought who, often in humblest still-*
> *ness, have appointed you your inevitable task. Maximilian Robespi-*
> *erre was* merely *the hand of Jean Jacques Rousseau, the bloody hand*
> *that drew from the womb of time the body whose soul Rousseau had*
> *created. May not the restless anxiety that troubled the life of Jean*
> *Jacques have caused such stirrings within him that he already fore-*
> *boded the kind of accoucheur that was needed to bring his thought*
> *living into the world?* [①]

After the current of Enlightenment, not until the 19th century did people generally come to realize that it was the market economy in capitalism that was the most forceful terminator to the traditional rank and privilege, and it was the currency as a universal equivalent that was the most powerful e-galitarian. As what was said in *The Communist Manifesto* by Marx and Engels when referring to the historical part the bourgeoisie played:

> *All fixed, fast frozen relations, with their train of ancient*

---

① Heinrich Heine, *Heine Selected Works*, ed. Zhang Yushu (Beijing: People Litera-ture Press, 1983), p. 291. Translation referred to: Heinrich Heine, *Religion and Philoso-phy in Germany A Fragment*, trans. John Snodgrass, Beacon Press, 1959). (Source: ht-tp://www. archive. org/details/religionandphilo011616mbp) *and venerable prejudices and opinions, are swept away, all new-formed ones become antiquated before they can ossify. All that is solid melts into air, all that is holy is profaned, and man is at last compelled to face with sober senses his real conditions of life and his relations with his kind.* ①

Fourth, freedom of personality. Rousseau said his famous words in *The Social Contract* (1762): "Man was born free, and everywhere he is in chains."② Seeking the freedom of personality, as the main melody of the Enlightenment, was embodied fully in both *Declaration of Independence* of the United States and *Declaration of the Rights of Man and of the Citizen* of France. In *The Phenomenology of Spirit* (1807), Hegel described how the European society turned from an original ethical substance into a legal status based on the individual, and during this transforming, *The Spirit of the Laws* (1748) by Montesquieu was regarded as a marked intellectual being. We would find in the pre-enlightened society, if having the narrative perspective modified in a way, individuals, as restricted to a vertical system of identity, had no actual freedom, while in the enlightened society, as a contract system based on equality took the lead, the freedom of personality was universally recognized and manifested. The Danish philosopher and theologist Kierkegaard, therefore, even had his own epitaph signed with "the individual."

These leading principles of Enlightenment listed above had been represented over and over again in the Enlightenment movements of different

---

① Karl Marx and Friedrich Engels, *The Communist Manifesto* (New York: New American Library, 1998), p. 54.

② Jean-Jacques Rousseau, *The Social Contract*, trans. Christopher Betts (New York: Oxford University Press Inc., 1994), p. 45.

nations.

The Absence of Enlightenment: History and Status quo

The Enlightenment of the modern Chinese society, under the background of saving the nation from extinction, had been carried out in terms of "trilogy" since 1841. The first stage may be called "Westernization Movement," with its representative figures as Zeng Guofan, Li Hongzhang and so on. Drawing lessons from the two defeats in both the first and the second Opium War, they decided to embark on the way of "learning from the westerners' fortes to compete with the westerners," which was proposed by Wei Yuan. In their view, once they acquired the foreign technologies, especially the military technology, they would be able to keep the foreign invaders out. However, the fact that the Sino-Japanese War of 1894-1895 ended up with the Chinese North Marine Navy's defeat, brought Westernization Movement to naught. It came to light that only through the reform of political system, could China be saved. The second stage can be called as "Political Reform," with Kang Youwei, Liang Qichao, Tan Sitong, and so forth as its exponents. Yet the failure of Wu Hsu Reform Movement of 1898 led to the end of this way. In practice, the history of modern Europe had already revealed to us that, neither political reform nor revolution could succeed, without the Enlightenment in thought and culture as the guide (fighting in the van). At that time, the Chinese intellectuals learned the lesson from the painful experience, and believed that to eliminate China's crisis should by the root start with a reform of the national characteristic of Chinese people. The third stage may be called "the New Culture Movement," with its representative Chen

Duxiu, Li Dazhao, Lu Xun, etc, and it had the May Fourth Movement of 1919 as its paradigm.

It is well-known that traditional Chinese society used to be a patriarchal clan and hierarchal society, which was based on blood lineage. In such a society, nation and family took the sovereign authority, so much so that there was no place for individual and personality. For that reason, during the New Culture Movement, the theme of Enlightenment was rather expressed in individuals' dream and pursuit of freedom. As it was, the theme of *A Dream of Red Mansions* is mainly focused on both Jia Baoyu's seeking for the freedom of personality (including free love) and his departure from Grand View Garden. Although he could but go to Buddhist imagery to grasp the spiritual freedom, he rebelled against conventional Confucian and feudal ethical code after all. The topic of "Nora's leaving" in Ibsen's play *A Doll's House*, discussed by Lu Xun and his like, also had a universal significance to the Chinese society at that time. In fact, either Ba Jin's novel series *Family, Spring, Autumn*, or Qian Zhongshu's *Fortress Besieged*, contained a subject of main characters' departure. The former expressed this topic in the leaving of Jueming and Juehui, and as for the latter, expressed in that of Fang Hongjian. The enlightening meaning of all these works was conveyed through the individual's pursuit of personality.

However, in contrast to the European society of the 18th century, the Chinese society has so far never had the theme Enlightenment thematized throughout its development. On the contrary, this important theme has been pushed aside constantly, and remains in marginalization. Then we would investigate the phenomena of lacking Enlightenment in real life of present Chinese society:

First, the spread of religious ideas and the overflow of superstitious thinking. No one will deny that there are still quite a few thoughts and behaviors at the mercy of superstition. Palm reading, face reading, fortu-netelling, belief in and fear of supernatural beings, fondness for talismans and mascots, have been the unfading topics in everyday conversations; e-ven numbers are divided into two camps: on one side, it would be better to have a connection with the number "8", regardless of the license plate number, street number, mobile number, or landline number, and even a good sum of money may be invested to get a bunch of 8. Actually, almost all of the festival activities are held on the 8th, 18th, 28th of a month, or other auspicious days; on the other side, people evade the numbers like 4, 14, 24, exactly the same way as they evade a plague. Even in many build-ings, the 4th, 14th floor are not marked. In the rural area, especially where lacks of culture, different kinds of superstition revive, so much so that witch-doctors, witches, fortune-tellers even domineer there illegally. We need to point out particularly that superstitious thoughts are completely re-flected in funeral and interment. Things often go in this way: the deceased has not got proper care and medical treatment during his lifetime, while receives a great postmortal honor after death. He is buried with full hono-rs by his family, even furnished with some exquisite villa made by crafts-man, ladyloves, mistresses, housemaids, motor vehicles, TVs, hell bank notes and things like this, so that he could lead a luxury life in the after-world.

Different from superstition, the religious belief is protected by law. However, equally recognized by law, the atheism exercises little active or leading effect on social life. As known to all, in recent years, at home there has been a sharp increase in the number of people with religious be-liefs, especially belief in Buddhism, while in addition, as to people going a-broad, particularly the scientific and technical personnel who lack classical humanistic nurture, most of them convert to Christianity. Interiorly, quite a few government officials have a fancy for burning the first stick of incense, striking the first ring of the bell in the temple, wearing a mascot, and even donating money to "coat the Buddha statue with gold." The custom of the whole society sinks into a smoky religious atmosphere. This is a negative proof of the fact that how feeble and pallid the Enlightenment sense is in social consciousness of contemporary China.

Second, the revival of hierarchy idea and the rage of privilege sense. In so far as proposed by Marx, socialism aims at the elimination of classes and the realization of political equality among people. Yet we find in the real life of present Chinese society, both hierarchy idea and privilege sense are untimely reinforced. As known to all, under the background of a planned economy, resources are to be distributed in accordance with the level of a unit or a person. For example, it makes a great difference in the distribution of resources to a unit whether it is on the bureau level or vice-ministerial level. Hence, to rival for the level is one of the commonest phenomena in administration career in China; as for individuals, especially for cadres, to rival for the level, such as section level, department level, bureau level, ministerial level, actually becomes the covert motive of his entire life and behaviors. It results from the fact that his pay, housing, medical care and other resources vary completely with his level. This kind of hierarchy idea is rooted so deep in people's minds, that there is a monk who has his name card printed as "provincial department level monk," and the name card of an old retired cadre has the impressive words "equal to a bureau level inspector" on it.

Say as it is known to everyone, under the condition of an ideal market economy, resources distribution is supposed to be determined by the market, while in the Chinese mode of market economy, the fact that the administrative power highly engages in it leads to not only the solidification of the established hierarchy idea, but also the further reinforcement of privilege sense. Administrative power, if applied improperly, or even misused, would collude with lawless businessmen or even gangdom during the rent-seeking. On the other hand, in order to expand their interests and domains, those lawless businessmen and gangdom try all kinds of ways to collude with administrative power, resulting in the distorted distribution of resources, great losses of national assets and the rapid widening of the gap between rich and poor. Obviously, both hierarchy idea and privilege sense are solidified and reinforced in the present Chinese society, which also means that the Enlightenment atmosphere is thin in contemporary Chinese society.

Third, the prevalence of nostalgia and the re-enchantment of traditional ideas. Compared with the United States as a burgeoning nation, the renewal of thought and culture in China today is bound to confront much more resistance, for China bears a traditional culture of thousands of years, and during the culture development, the Chinese get used to "looking back nine times every ten steps," and even constantly regress to "chasing fleshpots of Egypt." Previous to Culture Revolution, Mao Zedong once criticized the Central Propaganda Department and the Ministry of Culture for their performance as ministry for emperors and generals, ministry for the talent and the beauty, and ministry for the dead, while this is just the exact situation that we are now falling back on. Once we turn on the TV—the barometer of contemporary culture, we see immediately all kinds of historical drama, nostalgic drama and chivalrous drama overwhelmingly pouring in. Although the historical period that characters live in, and the masks they wear vary with different dramas, the structures and the themes of these dramas completely conform to a conventional pattern, no more than the pattern of regalism, hierarchy, male chauvinism (the orientation as man is superior and woman inferior), Code of Brotherhood, romance of the hero saving the beauty, and fondness of bravery and fighting, while the moral teaching—"Bad deeds, as well as good, may redound on the doer," implied in these dramas is lean and pale, without any truly profound critical sense. As to Chen Kaige, Zhang Yimou and their alike, who has been placed infinite hope on, not only do they inevitably fail to make any extra contribution to the development of the contemporary Chinese film, but instead, they have gone sour, fermented, and rotten as well.

As the development rush overspreads across the country, various of traditional ideas are ready to re-enchant. In the intellectual and cultural circles, we do not see any truly weighty critical works, but merely see so-called "the merits singing" or "the praises chanting" everywhere. Traditional culture is extolled indiscriminately, while the contemporary sense is denounced as ignorant or naive at a promiscuous manner. There is an odd phenomenon emerging in contemporary Chinese thought and culture: on one hand, people are talking about "originality and innovation" all the time; on the other, they fall on their knees before the idol of traditional culture at every turn. It seems like they are Faust with two hearts in the chest beating in opposite ways.

Fourth, the ruling of collectivism and the submergence of free personality. As for contemporary Chinese thought and culture, collectivism is often taken as the acute antithesis of free personality. For instance, "the spirit of devotion," as people promote, means interminably evacuating the personality and the individual's life, so as to devote them to some abstract collective. People seldom go deep into this issue, that is, what if a collective does not aim at protecting all its individuals' lives and values, but in reverse, it rests itself on individuals' lives for nourishment, is it legitimate for such a collective to exist? Is it true that the existence of an abstract collective counts for more than that of a specific life does? As a little more moderate than "the spirit of devotion," the so-called "the spirit of the screw" regards individuals as purely passive beings with no rights but merely obligations. This kind of spirit quite as much has individual's independence and integrality emasculated. In contemporary Chinese cultural views, "individualism" is still often confused indiscriminately with "ultra-individualism." In fact, the former confirms the legitimate rights and obligations of an individual, while the latter has an anti-social tendency, which people should be against.

Besides, collectivism is not as praiseworthy in all cases as people have supposed it to be. For instance, "regional protectionism" is an expression of collectivism; Xiamen Smuggling Scandal has also taken the form of collectivism; an enterprise producing fake and shoddy commodities, a fraud clan, or a corporation engaging in financial legerdemain, often appears in manner of collectivism as well. Anyhow, such equations should be set in no event: collective=good; individual=wicked. In actual fact, what Enlightenment tries to arouse is none other than everyone's independent personality and individual freedom.

In contemporary Chinese culture, the common individual and personality are left marginalized all the time. To our knowledge, the common individual is often attributed to the collective noun "people," a term that does not suggest any proper respect for every common individual's legal rights. In daily life, everyone could possibly encounter such a situation: when someone is doing the shopping in a store, but treated badly by a shop assistant, he points at the board with the words "serve the people" on it, hung above the shop assistant, and criticizes the shop assistant for not having taken him seriously. The shop assistant answers back sarcastically at once: "does that serve the people mean to serve for you?" Suppose that if the shop assistant cannot do a good job in serving for others in every single case, then "serve the people" is merely an empty talk all along in his mind. For this reason, from my point of view, what is required in real life is not such kind of empty slogans as "serve the people, " but the respect for the rights of every common people, while these rights are inviolable. Usually, people are used to interpreting human rights as right to life and right to development. This interpretation is problematic. In my opinion, the human rights mean that one lives in the world with dignity, and develops himself. If to admit one's human rights merely meant to let him survive, then slave society would have justified itself by this reason. In a word, both the history and the practice tell us that as for a kind of culture, the more deficient it is in the notions like the individual, personality, the more obviously it suggests that this culture has not been baptized by Enlightenment.

The Absence of Enlightenment: An Exploration to its Causes

The Absence of Enlightenment in modern and contemporary Chinese society is mainly due to all sorts of different reasons as following:

The first is that Enlightenment was extruded by the national salvation. As stated previously, since the First Opium War in 1841, subjected to repeated foreign aggression, the Chinese society had been at stake all the time. In other words, the political attention was always given to the theme of salvation, while Enlightenment was automatically left expelled and marginalized. Furthermore, the values that Enlightenment advocated were at least superficially contrary to those of the salvation. The salvation laid emphasis on collective strength and iron discipline, while Enlightenment supported for personal independence and individual freedom. In the national salvation, an individual was often taken as a segment, a section, ready to sacrifice for the collective. However, in Enlightenment, personal independence and individual freedom were the supreme goals, and in order to securely achieve these values, individuals had to fight against the collective, or even break away from it, so as to get themselves a free space. Before 1949, when the national salvation was the overwhelming goal, the topic of Enlightenment was always a marginalized one. After 1949, when Enlightenment could have had a chance to become the first topic, people followed the train of thought during the salvation period, and insisted on the abstract antagonism between the collectivism, as the positive value and the individualism, as the negative. Up to now, in so far as the thought and culture, the leading values implied in Enlightenment, especially that of personal freedom, still have been left in the state of being pressed.

The second is the lag of the development of the commodity economy. The traditional Chinese society adhered to the political line that "lay stress on the root (the agriculture) and restrain the branch (the trade)" all the while, accompanied with the social structure of "scholars, farmers, artisans, and merchants" and the cultural idea that "He who is a merchant must be wily while he who is not wily cannot be a merchant." In the light of this cultural idea, the commerce was almost the equivalent of fraudulence. In such a cultural atmosphere, it would certainly have difficulty in taking a step to develop the commodity economy. While the bourgeoisie, with Sun Zhongshan as its representative intended to make a great effort to develop national industry and commodity economy, the utopian socialism, rising among major European countries, gradually infiltrated to the

Chinese culture through the spread of Marxism. Therefore, after Lenin founded the first socialist state in the world through the October Revolution, the Chinese intellectuals, including the bourgeois intellectuals took Soviet Union as their ideal to strive for. Meanwhile, Lenin's idea that the small producers were producing capitalism daily and hourly had a great influence on contemporary Chinese society. After 1949, "cutting the tail of capitalism" became the supreme goal in real life, and it was impossible for the commodity economy to play a dominant role. Under the background of the Reform and Opening-up since 1978, with the social life transforming, the commodity economy has just been promoted at full blast. Synchronous with the development of commodity economy, legitimate individual interests are also fully identified in addition to the national interests and collective interests. This provides the conditions for the reconstruction of the broken Enlightenment spirit in the realm of thought and culture. However, due to the particularity of the Chinese modes of commodity economy, that is, the administrative power's high degree of participation, the task of Enlightenment is twofold: on the one hand, Enlightenment is supposed to arouse the individual's rights and obligations, and on the other, Enlightenment has to struggle with the privilege stemmed from the power, the hierarchy idea, and the rent-seeking phenomenon. So far since the commodity economy has still been in the initial stage, the Enlightenment still lacks the corresponding economic foundation.

The third is the shrink of natural science in contemporary Chinese society. As there was not enough room for the commodity economy to develop in the modern Chinese society, the study and development of natural science also lost the relevant driving force, and the imperial examination system implemented ever since Sui and Tang Dynasty made the most talented intellectuals taken up with the official career. Just as what Hu Shi had pointed out in his book *The Development of the Logical Method in Ancient China*: as for the saying that "investigate things is to attain knowledge" which was brought forward by the Chinese intellectuals, with its original meaning, the word "things" referred to the physical objects, and "knowledge" referred to the knowledge of natural science, but this meaning got distorted gradually. The meaning of "things" changed into the social relationship, and "knowledge" turned into the knowledge of how to keep the official position and get a promotion in the official career. That is to say, the Chinese intellectuals were worldly-wise, while to a large extent they looked down upon the study of natural science. Because of the lag of the study in this field, the religious ideas and superstitious thoughts overflowed everywhere, and the reason could not get proclaimed, hence it was difficult for Enlightenment to get a permanent and powerful driving force.

The fourth is an acute opposition set up between the socialist value system and the universal values implied in the Enlightenment sense, such as to cherish life, to respect personality and human rights, to value freedom and democracy, to promote equality and justice, to pursue the truth, to advocate science and so on. People strive to set an opposition between Marxism and humanitarianism, socialism and capitalism, and accuse the Enlightenment sense, along with its universal values, of "starting with an abstract human nature," even of being false, so much so that they totally overlook the internal relation between the socialist value system and the universal values implied in the Enlightenment sense, and it seems to them that only when all the fruits derived from the Enlightenment are abandoned, can the socialist value system get established. It is this antagonism that has all the Enlightenment ideas in the social life suppressed. Actually, this kind of antagonism goes exactly contrary to Marx's theory on historical materialism.

Anyone who shows respect to history could find that, it is, historically, the universal values implied in the Enlightenment sense that provides the historical foundation for the construction of the socialist value system. Lenin had already told us in his writing *The Tasks of the Youth Leagues* (1920):

> *A proletarian culture ··· is not clutched out of thin air; it is not an invention of those who call themselves experts in proletarian culture. That is all nonsense. Proletarian culture must be the logical development of the store of knowledge mankind has accumulated under the yoke of capitalist, landowner and bureaucratic society.* ①

According to Lenin, the socialist value system would just be formed and developed on the basis of the universal values implied in the Enlightenment sense. Without this foundation, the socialist values system would possibly have degenerated into a value system of the traditional society, for only when the collectivism, as the core value of socialism, receives the baptism of Enlightenment, can the abstract antagonism between the collective and the individual be averted and can every common individual's personality and human rights get identified and respected universally.

The fifth is that the western scholars' reflection and critique on the Enlightenment movement sways the contemporary Chinese from their acceptance of Enlightenment. As is well known, in his work *The Phenomenology of Spirit*, Hegel had already reflected comprehensively on the Enlightenment movement. In his view, the Enlightenment movement, along with its spirit mainly had the following problems: firstly, Enlightenment

---

① Lenin, *Lenin Selected Works* vol. IV, People's Press, 1995, p. 285. Translation referred to: Vladimir Lenin, "The Tasks of the Youth Leagues, " in *Collected Works*, vol. 31, 1920.

just simply renounced the tradition, especially the religion, while in practice, religion was still indispensable for human survival and development; secondly, Enlightenment one-sidedly advocated the scientific thinking, which was easily diverted to utilitarianism, and also neglected the important part the value rationality played in people's effort to have both body and soul settled down; thirdly, Enlightenment went after the freedom free from any constraint, i. e. , absolute freedom, which led to the terror in the French Revolution.

After Hegel, there were quite a few thinkers reflecting Enlightenment, reviewing the experience, and drawing the lessons from it. *Dialect of Enlightenment* is a representative work of this type, written by Horkheimer and Adorno. They called Fascism as a "myth", and sought its origin in Enlightenment: for one thing, in ancient mythology, like Homer's *Odysseus*, there were myths; for another, Enlightenment was also a myth, as the mythic factors of Enlightenment were exactly those negative values implied in it, such as the deification of reason, and things like that. Afterwards, the post-modernists roundly attacked the tradition of Enlightenment and modernity. Impacted by such a depression, the contemporary Chinese are much more vigilant against Enlightenment.

For these reasons explored above, we come to realize why there is a great deficiency of Enlightenment in the present Chinese society. In fact, the situation of thought and culture for the contemporary Chinese can be truly said as "poor, " since before the Chinese could ever taste the fruits of Enlightenment, they have already shared in the misfortune brought by it.

The Enlightenment Spirit:
The Reconstruction and the Revise

The reconstruction of Enlightenment in the title of my lecture does not mean a reconstruction of the Enlightenment movement. As being a historical movement, the Enlightenment happened and developed due to a series of both subjective and objective conditions, while by the reconstruction of Enlightenment I mean the reconstruction of the Enlightenment spirit, which always keeps company with the revise. As stated previously, with reference to the concept of morphological time, the contemporary Chinese society is "coetaneous" with the European society from the 16th to 19th century, and for this reason, it calls for a reconstruction of the Enlightenment; however, with regard to the concept of chronological time, the contemporary Chinese society is "coetaneous" with the contemporary European society, and hence it needs to take in the estimable ideas put forward by the contemporary European intellectuals as they reflect the Enlightenment movement, so as to "revise" the Enlightenment spirit if necessary.

As for the reconstruction of the Enlightenment spirit, the following measures could be constructive:

Firstly, work hard on the works by the French materialists of the 18th century, criticize thoroughly on the religious sense and superstitious idea, and establish the authority of reason and science (not only the natural science, but humanistic study and social science included as well).

Secondly, inhibit the hierarchy idea, privilege sense and the rent-seeking by power, expand the middle class to form a civil society so as to counterbalance the state power, and compose and publish Civil Code as soon as possible so that to settle the individual's rights and obligations in the legal form.

Thirdly, promote the leading spirit and universal values of Enlightenment, and establish the socialist value system on the basis of these universal values.

Fourthly, refer to the Enlightenment elements contained in the traditional culture. Review the traditional culture from the contemporary height, select from it those elements which contain the Enlightenment spirit and values, and creatively transform them.

Fifthly, develop the education, promote the humanism, and set up universally the personality with rights and the subject of moral practice.

As for the revise of Enlightenment, these following steps could also count for much:

Firstly, be acutely conscious of the "time difference (historic dislocation)" between the contemporary Chinese society and the contemporary European society. On the one hand, we should start with the specific conditions of China, while stick to the basic position of Enlightenment and modernity, and thus develop the market economy and advance the modernization; on the other, we must refer to the post-modern vision, so that we can adjust the way of modernization from time to time, and direct it to fit into the reality in China.

Secondly, go deep into the history of critiques on Enlightenment by the western modern and post-modern scholars, and reflect the experience of the Enlightenment movement, along with the contribution and limitation of the Enlightenment spirit, meanwhile draw the lesson from the Enlightenment movement as well, in order to strive to suppress the influence exercised by the negative factors in the reconstruction of the Enlightenment spirit and avoid following the old way of the spiritual development in European society.

3.8　The Teaching of Philosophy in Today's China[①]

Whether a country has great philosophers will determine if she can stand up on high in the field of thought and guide its own spiritual life to develop healthily. With a long philosophical tradition, today's Chinese Government puts weight on the philosophy education and take it as one part of the liberal education. However, there are some problems in the teaching of philosophy in today's China. We wish we would like to learn advanced experiences from other countries taking part in this conference, in order to make the future teaching of philosophy in China better. My presentation mainly includes the following four sections.

The Scope of Teaching and Studying of Philosophy

According to relative announcements of the

---

① Editor's note: This paper is found in the documents left by Prof. Yu Wujin.

Ministry of National Education, philosophy as a discipline includes the following eight branches: Chinese philosophy, philosophy of foreign countries, Marxist philosophy, science of religion, ethics, logic and Aesthetics in which the first three are more important.

Chinese philosophy is essentially the history of Chinese Philosophy, main consideration of the formation and development of Confucianism, Taoism and their fusion with Buddhism coming from India.

Philosophy of foreign countries is western philosophy, investigating the ancient Greek-Roman philosophy, philosophy of the Middle Ages, metaphysics of 17th century, philosophy of the Enlightenment in 18th century and German-French-British-American philosophy since 19 Century. Of Course, some institutes for philosophy and philosophy departments at different universities are interested in making researches on Indian, Arabian, Judaic, Japanese and Russian philosophy.

Marxist philosophy is majorly concerned with basic theories of Marx's philosophy, history of Marxist philosophy and contemporary Marxism abroad, including East-European Marxism on which has been put stress, because the Chinese Communist Party looks upon Marxism as its own leading thought.

The Teaching of Philosophy as Quality Education

Due to the guidance made by the Ministry of National Education, the quality of the teaching of philosophy is improved by two different ways:

One is the teaching of philosophy in society, which is put into practice through various public philosophical lectures set up by local governments, universities or institutes and so on. All these public philosophical lectures are arranged, focusing on remarkable problems coming from actual life and theoretical debates. Their content has been known by TVs, Transmitter-receivers, or newspapers, magazines and books. Everybody is interested in these lectures has an opportunity to learn in some way or other.

The other is the teaching of philosophy at high schools and universities which is chiefly formed by the following three stages:

The first stage is at high schools. At this time, philosophy is not an independent course and it is taught only as a part of the course of political thought in which also includes political situation, moral education and knowledge of law, and so forth. And the content is limited to the basic principles of Marxist philosophy and some Chinese traditional culture, which does not suffice for a systematically elaborated philosophical theory.

The second stage is for students at universities. Generally speaking, universities have a course of Introduction to Philosophy as a public elective course. Students either form science department or from liberal arts can go to this lecture if they like philosophy. At synthetic universities, there are usually core curricula of general education which contains some philosophical courses, like Lao Tzu's *Tao Te Ching*, Confucius' *Analects*, Plato's *Republic*, Wittgenstein's *Tractatus Logico- Philosophicus*.

The third stage is for post-graduates at universities. Post-graduates need guides in thinking way and method of study for their researches into academic problems. So there are courses on critical thinking in some universities containing courses both of liberal arts and natural science, such as *Yi Ching* (Book of Change), *Chang Tzu*, Descartes' *Meditation of The First Philosophy*, Kant's *Critique of Pure Reason*, Heidegger's *Being and Time*, Dewey's *How We Think*, to encourage post-graduates to think critically and creatively like those great philosophers in the history.

The Teaching of Philosophy as Major Education

Philosophy becomes a major only at universities in today's China. The training goal for Bachelors in philosophy is to grasp philosophy from the whole discipline. Courses for students are usually formed by following four parts:

The first part can be called courses of background knowledge, such as history of world, history of religion, history of science, history of psychology, political economics, logic, Aesthetics, rhetoric.

The second part can be called courses of basic theories of philosophy, for example, introduction to philosophy, metaphysics (including ontology), epistemology, methodology, philosophy of mind, and so on.

The third part can be called courses of philosophical history, just like history of Chinese philosophy, philosophical history of foreign countries, History of Marxist philosophy, and such like.

The fourth part can be called courses of special philosophical topics, including the reading of some classical texts like Wang Shou-jen's *Ch'uan Hsi Lu* (Record of Instruction), and some particular subjects, like the conceptual history of ideology.

The training goal for Masters in philosophy is to know well one of eight branches, such as philosophy of foreign countries, based on the philosophical knowledge grasped during their undergraduate education.

The training goal for doctors in philosophy is to master deeply certain research-direction of certain branch in philosophy as a discipline, for example, Kant's theory of epistemology is only a research-direction in philosophy of foreign countries.

Problems and Counter-Measures
in the Teaching of Philosophy

According to our opinion, there are following problems in the teaching of philosophy in today's China:

The first problem is related to the teaching of philosophy at high schools. Because features of schoolchildrens' age and mentality have been not considered seriously in the process of teaching, it is difficult for schoolchildren to understand politicized ideas of philosophy. So they are very easy to lose interest in philosophy.

The second problem has reference to the teaching of philosophy as quality education at universities. Without saying, this kind of teaching isn't systematic and ideal, because its courses are always designed by which professors have actual ability to instruct philosophical knowledge.

The third problem is concerned in the role of ideology in all teaching activities of philosophy. It is well known that ideology has an outstanding position in teaching materials and teaching activities of philosophy, even Marxist philosophy is, on some occasions, understood as philosophy.

Our counter-measures against above problems in the process of teaching of philosophy are as follows:

Firstly, the Ministry of National Education ought to emphasize highly on the teaching of philosophy at high schools which should have such a goal that schoolchildrens' interest in philosophy could be stimulated, not declined. So we should write and edit independent high-level teaching materials of philosophy for school children.

Secondly, the teaching of philosophy as quality education for students at universities should set up an ideal teaching pattern plate, formed by systematical teaching materials and high-qualitative teaching activities.

Thirdly, except for keeping some philosophical courses with Chinese characters, we should strive to learn advanced experiences of other countries in order to have the future teaching of philosophy in China internationalized rapidly.

Section Four

Short Essays

4.1 The World Expo and the City's Humanistic Spirit[①]

The World Expo of 2010 is not only an important power to lift Shanghai residents' standard of life to a new level but also a significant opportunity to promote our city's humanistic spirit. Shanghai is a city full of fine and age-old traditions with humanistic spirit. It has been famous throughout the world for its acute political awareness, ardent national feelings, diversified ideological ferment and advanced cultural consciousness, especially in the modern Chinese history. Nowadays, the world's political landscape has been significantly changed. China has been making much headway in the road of reform and opening-up. And Shanghai has interacted more and more with the outside world, carrying on its aim to be an international metropolis. With the coming of Expo, it's time to discuss such questions like how to enhance our humanistic spirit and how to leave a good impression with the

---

① Editor's note: This paper is the English translation of the speech in World Expo Forum. The original Chinese version of which could be found in the following link: http://news.sina.com.cn/c/2003-10-31/11381029057s.shtml.

world.

The humanistic spirit of a city, especially. a city like Shanghai, should not result from some intellectuals' subjective determination or free stipulation, but be lively unfolded in the following varied aspects and levels of the city's daily life.

Firstly, it's the level of implements which mainly refers to a city's fundamental facilities, the overall pattern, important architectures, symbolic sculptures, unpolluted rivers, tidy streets, wide-ranged green area, prosperous supermarkets and the bright showcases, etc. We may say this level is the most outer expression of a city's humanistic spirit. And it is in charge of giving the first impressions to a new visitor.

Secondly, it's the level of behavior which contains not only individual behavior but also collective or social activities. In fact, every city's humanistic spirit is bound to be expressed through such actions of single resident, collective or social groups, as the following examples: A city government advocates residents to obey different conduct norms, and to follow the 'civilized ideas' and the 'volunteer consciousness' in collective and social actions. What's more, there are all kinds of large-scale activities and celebrations, such as donations to the Hoping Project, culture symposiums, sports meets, academic conferences, International Culture Festivals. It's exactly through these kinds of behaviors that the residents' humanistic qualities and the city's culture are demonstrated. Obviously, the connotation of a city's humanistic spirit is still far beyond the behaviors of its residents.

Thirdly, it's the level of systems which contains the policies, regulations, laws, rules, etc, laid down by local cities for routine. When one who lives in a city temporarily or for a long time, dealing with either public business or private affairs, he or she will inevitably experience all kinds of systems. And it's the quantities of the humanistic spirit contained in these systems that determine whether every citizen's personality, character and basic human rights are respected, whether every citizen feels comfortable, convenient or even cozy under the current systems.

Fourthly, it's the level of psychology which means residents' universal feelings, intentions and character traits. These expressions which are always turned up in pop songs, grapevines, hearsay and proverbs can universally reflect the residents' psychological state and the humanistic quality to large extent. Undoubtedly, the psychological level is the more intrinsic one of the humanistic spirit.

Finally, it's the level of value ideas which means the residents' common understanding in culture, esp. in moral norms. Such ideas are generally demonstrated through media, public opinions, best sellers, experts' speech, the youth's ideality and the elders' experience. Actually, the core of a city's humanistic spirit is composed of ideas of value.

Thus, we can draw the conclusion that a city's humanistic spirit is an organism formed by the five different levels we just talked about. If we consider levels of implements and behavior as the organism's appearance, then levels of systems and psychology can be regarded as its connotation, and the level of value ideas will play the core role. Undoubtedly, as an organism, each level of the city's humanistic spirit should be improved coordinately.

Shanghai should take the opportunity of the World Expo of 2010 to promote its humanistic spirit all-around. And the following suggestions would be considerable:

First of all, to form a complete city humanistic spirit, both its appearance and connotation are indispensable, especially the latter. In other words, Shanghai ought to pay more attention to levels of systems, psychology and value ideas. To enhance the level of systems, a revolution in management is required. So we should make reasonable policies and regulations that respect everyone's personality and basic human rights, and always obey rules strictly. To promote the level of psychology, we should try to form the universal, healthy feeling, consciousness and character. And in order to uplift the level of value ideas, we must get rid of fetters in our thoughts and universally establish the consciousness of legal personality and subject of moral practice.

Next, in the long way of improving the connotation of the city's humanistic spirit, we should especially emphasize the following two aspects: One is to encourage the emergence, growing and discussion among different academic schools. As a metropolis, Shanghai ought to give birth to not only academic schools of different styles, and masters in theoretic researches, but also great achievements in academic works. In fact, a city lacking creations in thought and theory can not take a broad and long-term view. The other aspect is to supply enough chances to develop public culture and to push on the free competition among culture saloons and art schools. As a metropolis, Shanghai should not only have country-wide and world-wide famous literary and artistic works, book review periodicals and media, but also foster great artists, critics, poets, novelists and athletic and film stars.

Last but not least, education, esp. humanistic education plays a significant role in the whole development of the city's humanistic spirit and the universal rise of the residents' humanistic quality. To put the humanistic education into effect, we must stop attaching importance to natural sciences and looking down on liberal arts excessively. Instead, we should realize the significant position of the humanities in modernization to rebuild social order and to shape human soul. What's more, necessary tension is needed between the scientific spirit and the humanistic spirit.

In conclusion, the coming Expo is an important opportunity for Shanghai's developing, so we should make full use of the chance to show Shanghai in front of the world and to have it become an economic, financial and cultural center of Southeast Asia, even the whole world. And we should do all we can to lift our city's humanistic spirit and the quality of residents' culture to a new level, making Shanghai a brilliant star on the international stage!

4.2 Today's China and the Revised Enlightenment①

Why is the topic of the Enlightenment often put forward, but isn't discussed deeply in the contemporary Chinese society? According to my opinion, this situation shows the following fact: on one side, the Enlightenment is still an important subject for contemporary Chinese; on the other side, there are tensions between the leading principles of the Enlightenment and the contemporary Chinese society. How can Chinese go away from this dilemma? Obviously, they should divide following two pairs of conceptions.

The first pair is related to ideas of chronological time and morphological time. As for the chronological time, the Enlightenment happened in the 18th century, but contemporary Chinese are living in the 21th century. There are definite time difference for over two centuries, so we can understand why contemporary Chinese society had a certain

① Editor's note: This paper was originally published in Center for Contemporary Marxism in Foreign Countries of Fudan University (ed.), *Proceedings of the International Conference for Enlightenment and Its Contemporary Reevaluation*, Jun. 2009, pp. 74-75.

intense relationship with the leading principles of the Enlightenment. As to the morphological time, contemporary Chinese society and the European society from the 16th to the 19th century are in the same historical stage. So the Enlightenment of the 18th century is, of course, in the same historical stage with the contemporary Chinese society. This is just the main reason the Enlightenment has been put forward in the contemporary Chinese society from time to time.

The second pair is related to the original enlightenment and the revised enlightenment. The former is concerned with the European Enlightenment of the 18th century, the latter in the enlightenment of the contemporary Chinese society in the 21th century which is good for both ideas of chronological and morphological time. Contemporary Chinese society should initiate the revised enlightenment to avoid intense relationships of leading principles between the original enlightenment and contemporary Chinese society. In my opinion, main principles of the revised enlightenment are as follows:

Firstly, setting up a necessary tension between the positive function of reason and the negative function of reason. It is well known that the original enlightenment tried to set up a court of reason which would determine all things. However, people have begun to recognize it is possible for reason to become an instrumental reason in the age of post-Enlightenment, so Max Weber and Frankfort School insist that people should separate the reason of value from the general conception of reason, controlling the negative elements from the instrumental reason. In a word, the revised enlightenment understands reason in a more rational way.

Secondly, setting up a necessary tension between individuality and totality. The original enlightenment looks upon the independence of individuality and liberalism of individual character as its own main goal. However, people have begun to find out that the absolute independence of individuality and absolute liberty of individual character would result in tragedies of social life necessarily. Hegel has reflected on the historical tragedy from absolute freedom in the French Revolution since 1789. Now contemporary Westerners also criticize liberalism and neo-liberalism as results of the original enlightenment through the financial crisis. On the contrary, Eastern countries, including China, still keep to the absolute position of totality, ignoring the position of individuality and its rights. Therefore, the revised enlightenment will remember this lesson of the age of post-original enlightenment, not only identifying with individuality and universal values, but also with recognizing the government and social institutions as a representative of the totality

Thirdly, setting up a necessary tension between the theoretical critical reflection on religions and promotion of their practical function. The original enlightenment had simple attitude towards religions, thinking of reason as the pure light and religions as the pure darkness. In effect, as Hegel says that man doesn't see anything in the pure light like in the pure darkness. People should come back to Kant's attitude towards religions. That is to say, we should construe the religious thought in the context of theoretical reason and comprehend their social function in the context of practical reason based on the separation of religions from politics.

In the end, I concede that the contemporary Chinese society does need enlightenment. However, it does not mean that we need to go back to the original form of enlightenment; instead, a pursuit of the revised form of enlightenment is needed here.

4.3 Cultural Concepts to be Examined^①

China will have to choose between three schools of cultural concepts influencing the country: the traditional, the postmodern and the pro-modernization.

China should choose modernization, though the other two schools of thought might have some strong points.

And to realize modernization, China must thoroughly examine all its cultural connotations.

People might have different interpretations of the concept of culture, but according to common understanding, it includes three levels: the material, system, and conception.

Chinese people have been promoting modernization for generations, but few have come to the complete grasp of its cultural connotations. Mostly they have only stressed one aspect and hence have failed.

In the later half of the 19th century, a group of people headed by Li Hongzhang (1823-1901) launched China's Westernization Movement. They

---

① Editor's note: This paper was originally published in *China Daily*, May 15, 1996.

focused mainly on the material level of modernization: equipment.

The rout of the Chinese navy in the 1894-95 Sino-Japanese War demonstrated the shallowness of the society's understanding of modernization.

The modernization efforts later launched by Kang Youwei (1858-1924), Liang Qichao (1873-1929), and Sun Yat-sen (1866-1925) focused on institutional reform. They did not succeed either.

The corruption-riddled election for parliament members and the gruelling wars launched by the warlords demonstrated the inadequacy of focusing mainly on system reform.

The New Culture Movement around 1919 gave special attention to the reform of conceptions.

Apparently, the Chinese people had been deepening their understanding of cultural connotations of modernization. However, due to outside interference, they did not have the chance to analyze and reflect on this process thoroughly. And again since the 1970s, the Chinese people's perceptions of the cultural connotations of modernization have undergone a similar process.

Modernization at first stayed on the material level. It meant modernization of industry, agriculture, national defence, science and technology.

With the establishment of the reform and opening-up policy, more people came to realize that to modernize China, reform of systems, particularly the economic system, was inevitable. Also, with the introduction of market mechanisms, more people came to recognize the importance of legislation and the legislature.

At this stage, their understanding of modernization reached the level of the system.

Concepts of value

More recently, they have come to the conclusion that the modernization of human concepts, especially concepts of value, is the most important feature of modernization.

Besides fully understanding the cultural connotations of modernization, Chinese people must acknowledge and dispel four complexes that have been troubling them.

First, they agree that to modernize China, they have to learn from industrialized countries in the West-to borrow and digest their cultural heritage, advanced technologies and management.

But at the same time, they remember that it is these countries that plundered China and stalled its development since the Opium War (1840-1842). To pursue modernization, they had to fight these intruders for independence.

Contradiction

For more than a century, the Chinese people have been perplexed by this contradiction. As a result, their opinion towards the West has vibrated between two extremes: the isolationist, who wanted to exclude everything Western, and the "xenophile," who wanted to copy everything Western.

In 1949, China drove out aggressors and gained independence. But the ghost of this contradiction still haunts many, as is clear from recent history, starting in the late 1970s.

Second, they know that China must introduce a market economy so as to modernize itself; but on the other hand, under the influence of traditional egalitarianism, they fear that the development of a market economy could lead to the polarization of property.

This situation came to an end with the start of the reform and opening-up policy, when the government decided to uphold social justice on the basis of a market economy.

Third, modernization must include the enlightenment of cultural concepts. One of the key tasks of the enlightenment is to clarify the rights and responsibilities of individuals; however, the nation's early modernization efforts were made against the backdrop of the struggle for national salvation, which stressed discipline and respect for the collective.

This theme was reiterated for a long time since the founding of the People's Republic of China, when a planned economy prevailed.

The importance of elucidating the significance of individual rights and responsibilities has become more acutely felt in the transition from a planned economy to a market economy.

The relationship between individuals and the institution should be handled with full respect for individuals' legitimate rights.

Fourth, after numerous setbacks, the idea of pursuing modernization became a mainstream thought in the late 1970s; meanwhile in the West there has evolved a school of post-modernization thought, which is critical of the modernization-oriented value system.

Under the impact of these theorists, some Chinese intellectuals doubt the value orientation of modernization.

Complexes

These four complexes have been playing a negative role in the country's modernization drive. Even the reform and opening-up policy has not fully enabled the Chinese people to resolve and get past these complexes. Many people are still baffled, not knowing whether to conduct modernization and what kind of modernization they should choose.

With an overall review of the history of this country in the past century, it should be clear that only when we firmly stick to modernization-in its full sense-can we proceed with confidence in a time replete with confusing cultural conflicts and phenomena.

编者说明

　　(一)本卷收录了俞吾金先生生前发表和未发表的外文文章，包括从中文论文转译为外文的文章和直接以外文发表的文章，共计29篇。其中1篇为日文，1篇为德文，其余27篇为英文。编者将这些文章分为"对于马克思主义哲学的诠释(Interpretations of Marxist Philosophy)""对一些哲学话题的批判性分析(Critical Analysis of Philosophical Topics)""对当代中国文化的批判性分析(Critical Analysis of Contemporary Chinese Culture)"及"短论"(Short Essays)四个部分。

　　(二)编者对原文文字进行了校订，并对原文中出现的马克思恩格斯经典文献的英文译文进行了核对。

　　(三)各篇文章的来源等信息都以编者注的形式予以标注。

　　(四)本卷由张双利、徐英瑾编校。

《俞吾金全集》编委会

2022 年 2 月

图书在版编目（CIP）数据

外文文集/俞吾金著 . —北京：北京师范大学出版社，2024.9
（俞吾金全集）
ISBN 978-7-303-28354-5

Ⅰ.①外…　Ⅱ.①俞…　Ⅲ.①外文—文集　Ⅳ.①H3-53

中国版本图书馆 CIP 数据核字（2022）第 242669 号

营　销　中　心　电　话　010-58805385
北 京 师 范 大 学 出 版 社
主题出版与重大项目策划部

WAIWEN WENJI

出版发行：北京师范大学出版社　www.bnupg.com
　　　　　北京市西城区新街口外大街 12-3 号
　　　　　邮政编码：100088
印　　刷：北京盛通印刷股份有限公司
经　　销：全国新华书店
开　　本：730 mm×980 mm　1/16
印　　张：28.25
字　　数：400 千字
版　　次：2024 年 9 月第 1 版
印　　次：2024 年 9 月第 1 次印刷
定　　价：118.00 元

策划编辑：祁传华　　　　　　责任编辑：赵雯婧
美术编辑：王齐云　　　　　　装帧设计：王齐云
责任校对：段立超　陶　涛　　责任印制：马　洁　赵　龙